Art after Philosophy

Art after Philosophy

Boris Pasternak's Early Prose

Elena Glazov-Corrigan

PG3476.P27 Z654 2013
Corrigan, Elena, author.
Art after philosophy : Boris
Pasternak's early prose
Columbus : Ohio State
University Press, c2013.

 The Ohio State University Press | *Columbus*

Copyright © 2013 by The Ohio State University.
All rights reserved.
Library of Congress Cataloging-in-Publication Data
Corrigan, Elena.
  Art after philosophy : Boris Pasternak's early prose / Elena Glazov-Corrigan.
    p. cm.
  Includes bibliographical references and index.
  ISBN 978-0-8142-1206-6 (cloth : alk. paper) — ISBN 0-8142-1206-9 (cloth : alk. paper) — ISBN
978-0-8142-9308-9 (cd)
  1. Pasternak, Boris Leonidovich, 1890–1960—Criticism and interpretation. I. Title.
  PG3476.P27Z654 2013
  891.78'4208—dc23

                                    2012025253

Cover design by Jennifer Shoffey Forsythe
Type set in Adobe Minion Pro and New Caledonia
Text design by Juliet Williams
Printed by Thomson-Shore, Inc.

∞ The paper used in this publication meets the minimum requirements of the American National
Standard for Information Sciences—Permanence of Paper for Printed Library Materials. ANSI
Z39.48–1992.

9 8 7 6 5 4 3 2 1

To my daughters, Maria and Sarah

Contents

Abbreviations

PSS   Boris Pasternak, *Polnoe sobranie sochinenij s prilozheniiami, v odinnadtsati tomakh* [Complete Collected Works with appendices, in Eleven Volumes], ed. D. V. Tevekelian, compiled and provided with commentaries by E. B. Pasternak and E. V. Pasternak, introd. Lazar Fleishman (Moscow: Slovo, 2003–05). References to particular pages are done in the following manner: *PSS* 3:25 for *Polnoe sobranie sochinenij,* volume 3, page 25.

PSSCom   Commentaries by E. B. Pasternak and E. V. Pasternak to *Polnoe Sobranie sochinenij,* 2003–05. References are given to the volume and the page in the following manner: *PSSCom* 3:641.

CSP   Boris Pasternak, *Collected Short Prose,* ed. Christopher Barnes (New York: Praeger, 1977). References indicate the page: *CSP* 35.

Lehrjahre   *Boris Pasternak's Lehrjahre: Neopublikovannye Filosofskie Konspekty i Zametki Borisa Pasternaka.* [Unpublished Philosophical Notes, Abstracts, and Synopses, in Two Volumes], ed. Lazar Fleishman, Hans-Bernd Harder, and Sergei Dorzweiler (Stanford, CA: Stanford University Press, 1996). References to particular pages are given in the following manner: *Lehrjahre* II: 35 indicates volume 2, page 35. References to the Introduction to the Philosophical Notes are given in the following manner: Fleishman *Lehrjahre* 10 indicates the introduction in Volume 1 and page 10.

Zhivago   Boris Pasternak, *Doctor Zhivago,* trans. Max Hayward and Manya Harari, introd. John Bayley. "The Poems of Yurii Zhivago" trans. Bernard Guilbert Guerney (New York: Pantheon. 1997).

MG   Angela Livingstone, ed., *The Marsh of Gold: Pasternak's Writings on Inspiration and Creation* (Boston: Academic Studies Press, 2008). References indicate the page: *MG* 35.

Poma-Denton   Andrea Poma, *The Critical Philosophy of Hermann Cohen,* trans. John Denton (Albany: State University of New York Press. 1997). When the translations of Cohen are given from this edition, the references are indicated in the following manner: Poma-Denton 55, which refers to page 55. This notation is also followed in references to the other writings of Cohen (see below).

The following abbreviations have been used for the works of Hermann Cohen:

KTE   *Kants Theorie der Erfahrung* (Berlin: Dümmler, 1877; Bruno Cassirer, 1918).

KBE   *Kants Begründung der Ethik* (Berlin: Dümmler, 1877; Bruno Cassirer, 1910).

KBA   *Kants Begründung der Ästhetik* (Berlin: Dümmler, 1877).

PIM   *Das Prinzip der Infinitesimal-Methode und seine Geschichte. Ein Kapitel zur Grundlegung der Erkenntniskritik* (repr. Frankfurt: Suhrkamp, 1968).

E   *Einleitung mit kritischem Nachtrag zu F. A. Langes Geschichte des Materialismus* (Leipzig: Baedeker, 1896, 1905; Leipzig: Brandstetter, 1914).

LRE   *System der Philosophie. Erster Teil: Logic der reinem Erkenntnis* (Berlin: Bruno Cassirer, 1902, 1914).

ERW   *System der Philosophie. Zweiter Teil: Ethic des reinem Willens* (Berlin: Bruno Cassirer, 1904, 1907).

ARG   *System der Philosophie. Dritter Teil: Ästhetik des reinem Gefühls,* 2 Bde. (Berlin: Bruno Cassirer, 1912).

Logic   *Logik der reinem Erkenntnis. System der Philosophie. Erster Teil* (Berlin, 1902, 1914).

Ethik   *Ethik des reinem Willens. System der Philosophie. Zweiter Teil* (Berlin, 1904, 1907).

Ästhetik   *Ästhetik des reinem Gefühls. System der Philosophie* (Gieben, 1915).

BR   *Der Begriff der Religion im System der Philosophie* (Giessen: Töpelmann, 1915).

RoR   *Religion of Reason: Out of the Sources of Judaism.* Trans. Simon Kaplan (1919; Oxford University Press, 1995).

Note on translations from the Russian:
Unless otherwise referenced, all translations from Russian are the author's.

Acknowledgments

It is said that it takes a village to bring up a child. This particular book has had so many aunts and uncles that to count would not be simple. I'll start from my adolescence—Moscow of the late 1960s, a decade after Pasternak's death.

In my parents' three-room apartment I was introduced to *Doctor Zhivago*. The novel came to us in the form of a thick carbon copy, typed from a text that had been published in the West and distributed in Russia by samizdat. I cannot remember the name of the young gentleman who typed the novel, but I can see him distinctly. Of a Dostoevskian rather than Pasternakian appearance, in his small room he typed while lying down on a sofa; he made a special wooden contraption that permitted him to place the typewriter on his stomach; an ashtray resided on an adjacent chair. As he typed three or even four copies at once, he registered in brackets his own, always quite eccentric, views of particular scenes. This manuscript stayed in our family for a whole week (we were to pass it on to Valentin Turchin, one of Moscow's leading physicists, and to his wife Tatiana). In our apartment the individual chapters travelled from my father to my step-mother Marina, and then to me.

Our friends discussed the merits of the novel for hours around our dinner table. Most said that Pasternak was unquestionably a great poet, but a weak prose-writer. Some loved the novel, and some, Valentin Turchin among them, argued that this text was a key to all that was happening to us—we, the dissident circles of the sixties, were not meant to win, but to perish fighting. Among these ideas and conversations—and pondering the typist's cryptic insertions— I was introduced to the extraordinary life that surrounds an extraordinary text. As we like to say today, this book definitely came surrounded by meta-texts, full of ruptures and contradictions.

Within the next few years most of the people gathered around my father's table left Russia and emigrated to the West. It seemed to me then that the decisions stirred by the text of *Doctor Zhivago* were not only about how to read, but how to live. And yet for me caught in the middle of these cataclysms, it remained very much a question of reading. I grappled with the text's transparent simplicity; I felt that I had come upon a complexity that had been carefully erased, and I stumbled every time I tried to identify it. And, thus, my first deep gratitude is to the faces of my childhood and early youth—to their passionate approach to the written word, to the excitement of their vision, and to the integrity of their lives—to my beloved parents, my father Yuri Glazov and my step-mother Marina, and to their friends. It was among them that I first understood what I wanted to be.

Then there were our years in Canada—my parents' new home, my university training, and our first academic jobs. I want to acknowledge the influence of Hilary Armstrong who taught me Greek philosophy and Plato, and Lubomir Doležel who accepted the fact that after two years of working with Pasternak I was simply unable to write a Ph.D. dissertation elucidating his prose. I also want to mention the kindness and support of the then-Chair of the Comparative Literature Department at the University of Toronto, Peter Nesselroth. My friendship with Victor Yampolsky, enriched by his clear-sighted understanding about the connection between Alexander Scriabin and Pasternak, also started then. And I cannot pass over that time in Canada without recollecting the generous hospitality of Margot King and her children Sarah, Bernard, and David, Ernie McCullough and his wife Sue, and the welcome of my family by our very close friends Roswitha and John Hardenne.

I returned to Pasternak after I came to Emory University, to teach Russian Literature and Culture. Maria Lunk, a much loved instructor of Russian language and culture, died unexpectedly in January of 2010. I remember her with particular gratitude. I also want to thank my colleagues, Juliette Stapanian Apkarian, Mikhail Epstein, Vera and Oleg Proskurin, for their intellectual energy, friendship, advice and support. Melissa Miller and Tony Brinkley, who so quickly became my friend, were the first editors of this work. Thank you.

No book on Pasternak could be written in these last many decades without the help and advice of Lazar Fleishman, Angela Livingstone, Konstantin Polivanov, Yevgeny Borisovich and Yelena Vasilievna Pasternak. Whether or not these scholars agreed with my conclusions, I am deeply grateful for their help. The death of Yevgeny Pasternak is the end of an era, but it is also a personal loss for so many of us, Pasternak scholars, whom Yevgeny

Borisovich and Yelena Vasilievna invited to their apartment and met with hospitality, kindness, thoughtful advice—presenting throughout the spirit of Russia's world that has been under such vicious attack. The studies of Pasternak by Alexander Zholkovsky and Natalya Fateeva have been living on my desk and have become my daily interlocutors; and ever since my Toronto days I have deeply valued the work and priceless words of encouragement of Christopher Barnes. As this book was written, in the middle of uncertainty and self-doubt, I was helped and supported by the advice of Olga Hasty and Sibelan Forrester, who read the manuscript at several stages and carefully considered its structure and argument.

When the manuscript was finished, Sandy Crooms, Senior Editor at The Ohio State University Press, permitted no delay in ensuring the work's progress to the publication stage. Sandy's magic includes an unusual mixture of hard work, precision, humor, and a lightness of touch. I cannot begin to articulate my gratitude to you, Sandy. I also want to thank the two readers of the book for the Press, Karen Evans-Romaine and the other reader who remains anonymous. And I wish to acknowledge the excellent editing work of Martin Boyne which included help with the index and, of course, the editorial help of Eugene O'Connor.

And then there is my family—all the Glazovs and Corrigans, so very generous in their support. I want to thank my mother, Asya Glazova. A most devoted lover of Russian film and theater, she took up the uneasy path of immigration, so she could be near her daughter. Some of the chapters of this book were written as she was recuperating after several surgeries. My mother died in the summer of 2011. Thank you, mama, for what you taught me about strength, love, and forgiveness.

More than a decade has passed since the unexpected sickness and death of my father, Yuri Glazov. This book could not have been written without his presence in my life. After his death, my step-mother Marina took upon her shoulders the uneasy job of searching for solutions, advising, mentoring, listening, hoping, reassuring and . . . working with my father's manuscripts. All the while she continued to write her own prose, publish, and, last but not least, follow Russian politics with her characteristic careful precision. On many an occasion Marina and I worked on the same projects. Thinking of you, Marina, my father used to recite lines from one of Pasternak's poems: "And the secret of your enchantment is inseparable from the puzzle of life." I thank you, Manechka, and my brothers Gregory and Jamie, for the genuine friendship of our family that continues to sustain every one of us.

And then there is the family of Francis and Tess Corrigan, and their children, James, Madeline, Edward and Brendon. Thank you ever so much for your support and love. To my brothers and sisters-in-law and their families—my deepest gratitude. There is also that very singular crew—Kevin Corrigan and our children, John, Yuri, Maria, and Sarah, our daughter-in-law, Arielle, and John's love, Peggy Lee. Kevin is the only person I know who found Pasternak's "Letters from Tula" to be a page turner, and his advice and love brought me through many battles with the world outside and with myself. Kevin's dedication to philosophy and his unfailing kindness ensured throughout that we had a genuine home and that an intellectual conversation linked us all. Maria, a particular thank you for your help in preparing this manuscript and for embracing Zhenya Luvers who taught you, Sarah, and me many a lesson.

The young Pasternak's first pen-name was Reliquimini, which means in Latin "you are in debt." Having finished this book, I find myself in debt to so many, and I translate that debt as a gift of love. Thank you.

Introduction

The principal aim of this book is to expand and redefine an area in Slavic Studies that has, quite inexplicably, suffered from critical neglect for at least a quarter of a century—the innovative art of Boris Pasternak's early prose, interdisciplinary to its core. Completed by the end of 1918, only three of these early fictional works—"The Mark of Apelles," "Letters from Tula," and *The Childhood of Luvers*—found a publisher. These narratives represent, however, a much more extensive corpus of work that Pasternak wrote after he had abandoned his philosophical career, which, as he had himself reported, could have kept him in Germany as a university professor, working side by side with the much-respected Hermann Cohen. While my primary focus will be the three published stories, their investigation will necessarily involve Pasternak's other writings, including his earlier philosophical notes and his fictional, critical, and autobiographical works. The relation between poetry and prose requires, in my view, a somewhat different study, and for this reason the discussion of Pasternak's poetry, though important, will be kept to a minimum. Already as a young poet, Pasternak dreamt about writing prose, and my investigation aims to capture and elucidate his thought in this regard.

The creative explosion of Pasternak's fictional writing, so soon after his farewell to philosophy, promises a feast of thought and exploration, yet this promise somehow evades the investigator's grasp. The notorious complexity of these early narratives, and their author's later proclamations of his antipathy toward their experimental and puzzling artistry, effectively broke Pasternak's prose world into two discrete periods: the early avant-garde Pasternak, and the later Pasternak of *Doctor Zhivago* and other works. This division, however, has hurt the study of both periods; it makes the Pasternak of *Zhivago* appear today, after the political storms of his own time have subsided, almost banal in the eyes of the elite postmodern *cognoscenti,* while the enigmatic quality of his early vision remains curiously isolated from the rest of his writing. This book takes up the challenge of Pasternak's early philosophical fiction and links it to the seemingly straightforward and spare prose of his later years.

How critical is this quest for a new reading of his works? On the one hand, the scarcity of new interpretative approaches has not been accompanied by a lack of fame or popularity on either side of the Atlantic. Half a century after his death, Boris Pasternak is read widely around the world and remains one of the handful of twentieth-century Russian writers who have become part of English-speaking culture, both as the author of *Doctor Zhivago* and as a much-translated poet. His life-story continues to fascinate (or at least entertain) the reading public; new translations of his famous novel enter the market; archival materials and biographies are prepared for publication on an ongoing basis; and productions of *Zhivago* and documentaries about Pasternak, the rebellious Soviet author, appear with surprising frequency. On the other hand, these trajectories of success do little to dispel the puzzling aura of "one of the most mysterious authors of the twentieth century" (Fleishman 1980, 7),[1] and if the absence of innovative approaches to Pasternak has not affected the writer's reputation with the general public, it has significantly dampened the enthusiasm of Pasternak scholars and obscured the writer's significance in the eyes of students of philosophy and cultural studies. Like his hero Tsvetkov in *The Childhood of Luvers,* Pasternak is in danger of becoming a stranger, "postoronnyj," not only to the development of contemporary art and literary theory, but also to the very core of intellectual intercultural discourse—namely, a stranger to the links and bridges between literature, philosophy, and psychology, disciplines that interested him so profoundly at different stages of his life.

There cannot then be a better time to start the project of addressing this critical impasse. The Neo-Kantianism of the Marburg school, central to the

---

1. To broaden the sphere of critical inquiry, Lazar Fleishman has urged for a more contextual reading of Pasternak's early work, warning in 1980 that "the major poet of the twentieth century appears immersed in a cultural vacuum, sparsely decorated by the magnificent portraits of Mayakovsky, Cohen, Skriabin and Rilke" (Fleishman 1980, 7). In 1996, he reiterated the challenge to criticism presented by Pasternak's "singular individual qualities" [неповторимо индивидуальные особенности] (Fleishman *Lehrjahre* 12).

cultural world of the Russian Silver Age, was overshadowed for almost a century by the philosophy of Martin Heidegger and by the Frankfurt School, but this period of neglect has definitely ended. The major impediment for the writer's literary investigators—Pasternak's intense philosophical training—can now be addressed alongside new scholarly works dedicated to the thought of Hermann Cohen. In other words, the chasm that divided Pasternak's early and later periods in the eyes of his critics and readers can now be re-evaluated in the context of new scholarly approaches to the Marburg philosophical school. A recent publication of Pasternak's student *konspekty* from both Moscow and Marburg—the two volumes of *Boris Pasternaks Lehrjahre: Neopublikovannye filosofskie konspekty i zametki Borisa Pasternaka* (1996)[2]—has begun to dissolve some of the more inscrutable problems surrounding that "most shadowy and mysterious period of his life" (Fleishman *Lehrjahre* 11). Not only does the availability of Pasternak's actual notes provide a factual comparative basis for determining Pasternak's interests; the publication also makes it possible for "the philosophical work of Pasternak to enter into the context of the intense ideological battles taking place in the Russian culture of the Silver age" (Fleishman *Lehrjahre* 11).

How crucial then was that early philosophical period, and can it provide significant help in a new reading of Pasternak's early fiction? In the 1909–10 academic year, the twenty-year-old Pasternak began his studies in philosophy at Moscow University and, in the spring of 1912, drawn to Neo-Kantianism like the rest of Russia's cultural elite, he traveled to Marburg to study with the famous Neo-Kantian philosophers of the day, Hermann Cohen and Paul Natorp (having examined with great precision their works prior to this journey). Pasternak's Marburg pilgrimage was, therefore, not a trifling endeavor, but a consciously defining choice, highly ambitious in its aims: he sought to establish a theoretical foundation for all scientific disciplines and for philosophy in general in order to explain "the aesthetics of those who were the mentors of his generation in literature" (Fleishman 1990a, 29). For a trip of such significance, nonetheless, it was surprisingly short-lived: he set out for Germany on April 21, but after a concentrated period of study and several highly successful presentations in seminars, he resolved to leave philosophy. The decision was as abrupt as it was irrevocable: on July 5 he was still considering joining Ernst Cassirer in Berlin, but on July 17 he confirmed to his friend Alexandr Shtikh the news that was announced to family and friends a week

---

2. Sendelbach aptly articulates the gratitude of every Pasternak scholar to this invaluable publication, which, in her assessment, changes the very field of Pasternak's studies: "In other words, this collection gives the reader insight into the mind of Pasternak and into the minds of those who helped shape it: his philosophy professors" (2001, 764).

earlier: "I am unwell. I am putting an end to philosophy" (*PSS* 7:124). For another year, Pasternak continued his philosophical studies half-heartedly in Moscow, but his choice of profession after Marburg was firm: he was to be a poet and a writer.

In spite of the abruptness of his decision and his habitual evasiveness about his philosophical studies, the archival data collected by scholars is incontrovertible: the writer's grasp of philosophical issues was genuine and deep.[3] Yet the editors of the two volumes of the *Lehrjahre* are cautious in their expectations. Not only do they assess previous scholarly attempts to locate the key to Pasternak-the-writer in philosophy in Kant, Bergson, Cohen, and Husserl as "one-sided" and even "mistaken" (Fleishman *Lehrjahre* 10); they also do not sound overly optimistic about the possibility of establishing any direct correspondences between Pasternak's philosophical notes (which identify the texts and textbooks he studied and loved) and his literary work. Their caution in this regard is sensibly motivated: "This theme [the demonstrable content of Pasternak's philosophical studies] cannot be mechanically or straightforwardly connected with another question, that of Pasternak's poetic sensibility. His philosophical readings were only a part, and quite possibly not the principal part, of his unified *Weltanschauung*" (Fleishman *Lehrjahre* 13).

On balance, this assessment may in fact be too restrictive, since such caution should also extend to all relationships of Boris Pasternak to his mentors and artistic predecessors, even, for example, to the German poet he so admired, Rainer Maria Rilke.[4] None of Pasternak's intellectual interests, whether well documented or still circumstantial, can be mechanically applied to his work, and no static comparison between him and other authors, literary or philosophical, can provide fruitful avenues for investigation. At the same time, the path to his dynamic and transformative engagement with other artists and thinkers is difficult to demonstrate conclusively. In 1923, Yevgenij Zamyatin, a highly perceptive critic and a brilliant artist in his own right, observed that even among the experimental and gifted apprentices of the Sil-

---

3. Sendelbach emphasizes the importance of the publication of *Boris Pasternaks Lehrjahre* to a full understanding of Pasternak's output: "The breadth and depth of this collection reminds the reader that Pasternak was not merely a dabbler in philosophy but rather a scholar of it, and a prolific one at that. To understand better Pasternak the writer is to understand Pasternak the philosopher" (2001, 764). Livingstone comments upon the importance of the two volumes: "No matter that the very ardor with which he studied philosophy suggested the romantic: he could have become the professional philosopher. One realizes with a certain shock that he was exceptionally good at it; the notes are 'first class'" (1998, 946).

4. On the inconclusiveness surrounding Rilke's role in Pasternak's work, see Fleishman *Lehrjahre* 12.

ver Age, the prose of Boris Pasternak had "neither kith nor kin" [без роду и племени].[5] Lazar Fleishman, assembling the archival materials of Pasternak's world in the 1920s, commented upon the deep-seated consensus among Pasternak investigators that the writer's creative life took place in "isolation from the concrete 'immediate' details of the literary and cultural life of his time," so much so that Akhmatova was to exclaim on many occasions: "He does not read any of us" [Он никого не читает] (1980, 7). This apparent artistic isolation of the early Pasternak is further reinforced by surviving anecdotal recollections depicting his communicative eccentricities. In the recent popular biography of the poet, Dmitry Bykov, for example, deftly employs Fazil Iskander's remark that a conversation with Pasternak, the young author, was akin to an exchange "with a very interesting drunk" (2007, 57), a sentiment that permits Bykov to dismiss the poet's early prose as "subjective, fragmentary, and resisting understanding" (434). Indeed, the portrait of the early Pasternak (as well as any evaluation of his prose) has been molded into the image of a young passionate artist unable to communicate in a coherent manner, who instead only "hooted or droned" with intonations simultaneously "wild, joyful and astonished" (54).

In clarifying Pasternak's philosophical range in his early stories, one of my aims is to address this reductive portrait—its picture of absent-minded exuberance—by shedding light on the reasons behind the writer's characteristic evasiveness in discussing influences on his art. Highly telling in this context, for instance, is the ambition Pasternak ascribes to his protagonist Yuri Zhivago who "ever since his schooldays [. . .] had dreamed of composing a book about life which would contain, like buried explosives, the most striking things he had so far seen and thought about" [Он еще с гимназических лет мечтал о прозе, о книге жизнеописаний, куда бы он в виде скрытых взрывчатых гнезд мог вставлять самое ошеломляющее из того, что он успел увидать и передумать] (*Zhivago*, 65; *PSS* 4:66). The emphasis upon "*buried* explosives," made up of the most treasured past thoughts and experiences, speaks of prose as the painstaking creation of a carefully hidden subtext, wide-ranging and highly provocative in its after-effects. Nor does this subtlety of evasiveness disappear when Pasternak, in the post-Revolutionary period, loses much of his "joyful hooting." Even though Pasternak, after the 1930s, rejected the unnecessary complexity of his earlier works,[6] a recognition

---

5. Zamyatin's review of "Detstvo Luvers" was published in "Novaja russkaja proza," in *Russkoe Iskusstvo* 2–3 (1923): 56–57. In English "The New Russian Prose" was published in *A Soviet Heretic: Essays by Evgeny Zamyatin,* ed. and trans. by Mirra Ginsburg (Chicago: University of Chicago Press, 1970), 100.

6. See Pasternak's characterization of his early writing in his reference to *Safe Conduct*

of influences did not become more transparent or straightforward in his later writings. Indeed, throughout his career, whether his style was simple or complex, the conceptual frames of his works remained a challenge for his readers and critics.

In examining Pasternak's works in the light of philosophical themes, this book does not seek to isolate all, or even a significant part, of his artistic predecessors in philosophy. Instead its main task is much more critical to the overall scholarly enterprise. In its quest to expand the range of Pasternak scholarship, this study seeks to demonstrate the deeper conceptual pathways that transformed the young pre-Revolutionary author, a major figure of the Russian avant-garde, into a popular, accessible, albeit politically uncontrollable novelist. This book argues that the materials of his Moscow and Marburg studies help best to illuminate the most difficult aspects of his thought—his formidable capacity to reshape radically the very thoughts and ideas that moved him most deeply. In other words, his studies of philosophy are viewed as an invaluable tool in finding access to the dynamic intensity of Pasternak's thought as he, in the act of writing, worked with other writers.

Recognition of the transformative character of Pasternak's thought explains best, in fact, the young writer's deep-seated evasiveness and carefully nurtured evocation of mystery and dislocation.[7] As late as 1930, in the very first pages of *Safe Conduct,* Pasternak acknowledged that the ever-widening gap between himself and his audience constituted more than a passing fancy or an accidental occurrence; this gap was the very precondition for writing prose. In order to compose a longer work, he needed to outdistance his predecessors and readers both temporally and spatially:

> He [the reader] [. . .] likes those places beyond which his walks have never taken him. He is immersed in forewords and introductions, but for me life has revealed itself only at the point where he tends to sum things up. Even without mentioning how the inner articulation of history was thrust upon my understanding in an image of unavoidable death, I only came completely alive, within life itself, on those occasions when the dreary simmering of ingredients was done and, having dined from the finished dish,

---

being "spoilt by unnecessary mannerism, the common fault of those years" [книга испорчена ненужной манерностью, общим грехом тех лет] (*Remember,* 19; *PSS* 3:295).

7. In one of the most recent studies of Pasternak's early prose, Jensen summarizes the author's narrative strategies, basing his argument on the *Childhood of Luvers:* "With the double paradox the author emphasizes that the enchantment and warmth of the story are achieved not by the closeness between the author and his protagonists but, by contrast, through alienation and distance" [занимательность и теплота рассказа обусловлены не близостью рассказчика к героям, а, напротив, отчуждением и дистанцией] (2006, 299).

a feeling equipped with all conceivable spaciousness tore loose from its moorings and escaped to freedom. (*CSP* 23)

Ему [читателю] по душе места, дальше которых не простирались его прогулки. Он весь тонет в предисловиях и введеньях, а для меня жизнь открывалась лишь там, где он склонен подводить итоги. Не говоря о том, что внутреннее члененье истории навязано моему пониманью в образе неминуемой смерти, я и в жизни оживал целиком лишь в тех случаях, когда заканчивалась утомительная варка частей и, пообедав целым, вырывалось на свободу всей ширью оснащенное чувство. (*PSS* 3:150)

The style of this passage may well index Pasternak's youthful arrogance, but it also foregrounds his unusual manner of understanding influences, traditions, and patterns of relation with his reading public.[8] The startling reference to death indicates emphatically that the very process of absorption of influence is in Pasternak's case a radical metamorphosis that reshapes and erases the discontinuous elements of the past. Similarly indicative is the writer's comparison of his own work to the image of a soaring bird that has fed on the dishes of the past and now breaks free. The image captures quite ingeniously the state of puzzlement and uncertainty of his critics, for it celebrates the writer's well-planned escape, precluding in its flight any painstaking critical attempts to trace areas of influence or intertextual contexts for his thought.[9]

The underlying problem of Pasternak's prose (and this includes all of his work) is by no means trivial, for there is a formidable gap, carefully protected by the writer himself, between his passionate affirmation of allegiance to certain artistic figures and the absence of easily demonstrable lines of apprenticeship and influence, a problem that extends to his studies of philosophy but that is by no means limited to them. For instance, in the poem "Lofty Malady," written in the turbulent 1920s, Boris Pasternak promised "to leave the stage" together with the pre-Revolutionary cultural milieu of Russia and pledged an unshakable loyalty to its art,[10] but as it so happened, he did not abandon the

---

8. See in Fleishman: "Pasternak is frequently presented as standing outside of the literary conflicts, arguments and battles, inhabiting a higher plane or passively observing them" (1980, 7).

9. Fleishman, for example, expresses uncertainty that the key to the startling originality of Pasternak can, in fact, be located in Rilke (Fleishman *Lehrjahre* 12). See here Barnes (1972), Livingstone (1983), and Gifford (1990).

10. Cf. "I am speaking about the whole milieu, with which I meant to leave the stage, and to leave the stage I will. There is no place for shame here" [Я говорю про всю среду, / С которой я имел в виду / Сойти со сцены, / и сойду. Здесь места нет стыду] (*PSS* 1:255–56).

stage at all, nor was he to vanish in the decades that followed: he was destined to belong to that smallest group of Russian artists who not only outlived the worst of the purges, executions, and war-time devastation, but survived honorably and fruitfully. Still, the same pledge of allegiance was reiterated by the writer throughout his career. At the acme of his international success in the late 1950s, during the major political crisis surrounding the publication of *Doctor Zhivago,* Boris Pasternak continued to emphasize his deep identification with the cultural world of the Russian Silver Age, insisting that "his artistic taste had been formed in his youth and [that] he remained faithful to the masters of that period" (Berlin 2004, 222). The concrete reality of this identification of his tastes offers the point of departure for what becomes the subject matter of this study.

Chapter One, "The Character of Philosophical Influence in Pasternak's Early Prose," addresses the causes of the puzzling evasiveness of Pasternak's manner of acknowledging influences, in general, and philosophical influences, in particular, by juxtaposing his recollections of his Marburg period in *Safe Conduct* with surviving archival materials from the period.

Chapter Two, "Similarity and Contiguity in Pasternak's Early Poetics and Their Philosophical Underpinnings," clarifies Pasternak's debt to philosophy through a discussion of the metaphor–metonymy opposition, first applied to Pasternak's prose by Roman Jakobson in 1935. The chapter recognizes that Jakobson's analytical *tour de force,* a masterful blend of theory and criticism, still holds the status of the reigning scholarly perspective,[11] even though critics, on many occasions, have tended to balk at his conclusion that Pasternak's metaphors and symbols are not "what determines and guides his lyric theme" (Jakobson 1969, 141). Chapter Two questions Jakobson's findings by arguing that it was Pasternak in 1913, in fact, who first proposed the opposition between contiguity and similarity, borrowing his terminology from David Hume[12] and expanding its problematics in the context of Immanuel Kant's

---

11. For the historical context of Roman Jakobson's "Marginal Notes on the Prose of the Poet Pasternak" of 1935, see Barnes's account of the appearance of *Safe Conduct* in Czech (1998, 111). In his "Afterword" to the Czech edition, Jakobson proposes his famous opposition between metaphor and metonymy, which, according to his argument, shaped the styles of Mayakovsky and Pasternak respectively. Pasternak himself, of course, always insisted that the Russian symbolists had a profound influence on his writing: "The depth and charm of Bely and Blok could not but be revealed to me. Their influence was combined in a singular way with a force that went beyond mere ignorance" [Глубина и прелесть Белого и Блока не могли не открыться мне. Их влияние своеобразно сочеталось с силой, превосходившей простое невежество] (*CSP* 31; *PSS* 3:159).

12. For Hume, ideas derived from perceptions and based on experience are organized according to *"resemblance, contiguity in time or place, and cause and effect"* (*An Enquiry Concern-*

criticism of Hume's materialism. By taking careful account of Pasternak's philosophical notes, early reviews, and pamphlets, including "The Wasserman Test," the chapter argues that Pasternak himself never conceived of the relationship between similarity and contiguity, or metaphor and metonymy, as a stark contrast. Rather, he viewed this opposition as the poles of a changing continuum of relationships with language, characteristic of any genuine poetic inner work, wherein metonymy, or association by contiguity, constitutes a basis of the poetic process from which metaphoric relationships necessarily emerge. By clarifying Pasternak's early ventures in poetic theory, the chapter creates a heuristic philosophical dictionary, if not to enumerate the philosophical preoccupations of the writer (a rather meaningless goal), then at least to prepare a context for the analysis of his early narratives.

Chapter Three, "Arguing with the Sun in 'The Mark of Apelles,'" initiates a philological analysis of Pasternak's early fiction. This chapter is dedicated to the study of a story written in 1914 that has defied critical analysis or understanding. Heinrich Heine, its mysterious protagonist, is understood not as a poetic wanderer who bears a famous name, but as an atemporal "apriorist of lyricism," entering into the darkness of the night out of unlimited time and space and realigning reality by the force of his personality and talent. The chapter examines the major (and heretofore ignored) interplay between light and shadow in the story, pointing to Pasternak's masterful rendition of Plato's cave, where the endangered human being, however, is no longer the philosopher, but the poet. This is, indeed, a significant substitution to which Pasternak returned, not only in his poem "Hamlet," but also throughout his life.

Chapter Four, "'Letters from Tula': 'Was ist Apperzeption?'", is one of the central chapters of the book. It seeks to illustrate Pasternak's ability to transform a philosophical argument into an artistic space of multiple interrelations rather than simply arguing the specific philosophical issues at hand. Addressing the perplexing narrative of "Letters from Tula," this chapter introduces the central role of the Kantian theory of apperception, a subject on which Hermann Cohen, according to Pasternak's recollection of his time at the Marburg school in *Safe Conduct,* drilled his students with particular fervor. Pasternak's revision of Kant is approached as a key to the narrative's organization, further augmented by Hermann Cohen's emphasis on the role of the "other" in the autonomous development of the self. Cohen's correction of Kant is addressed as a major philosophical paradigm-shift, understood and implemented by Pasternak as one of his boldest artistic experiments, anticipating, in fact, Jorge

---

*ing Human Understanding, 1.3 ¶ 3–4; 2007, 20). Hume in his later works approaches "cause and effect" as contiguity in time. See Chapter 2.2.

Luis Borges (a writer influenced, incidentally, by another Marburg student, Ortega y Gasset).

Chapter Five, "Contextualizing the Intellectual Aims of 1918: From 'Letters from Tula' to *The Childhood of Luvers*," examines Pasternak's letters, diaries, and excised chapters (from *Luvers*) written in 1918, while addressing his shift of perspective from the consciousness of the poet to that of a growing girl. Deepening the analysis of Pasternak's meditation on the limitations of Kantian theory of apperception, the chapter addresses human developmental psychology as reflected in the thought of Cohen's closest colleague, Paul Natorp. Pasternak's 1910 sketch, "Ordering a Drama," is examined in this context for its particular emphasis on three levels of awareness, and the chapter suggests that *Luvers* not merely integrates all three levels into its construction, but also develops the pivotal role of the "other," a singular theme of Hermann Cohen's ethics. This fifth chapter operates, therefore, as a theoretical context for the novel approaches to *The Childhood of Luvers* worked out in the next two chapters.

Chapter Six, "'The Long Days' in *The Childhood of Luvers:* Chronology of a Permeable Self," is dedicated to an analysis of the first part of the novella. While comparing the construction of the narrative to the two levels of the earlier sketch, "Ordering a Drama," the chapter shows Pasternak's careful employment of the contiguous series (a device that Jakobson describes as metonymy). These devices show the emergence of consciousness (a contiguous relationship with the inanimate world) and the birth of soul (a contiguous relationship between the child's psychological formation and natural/physical processes), and they also prepare the context for the crucial metaphorical transformations in the second part of the narrative. In order to clarify further these carefully structured tropes, the chapter concludes with Table 1, Chronology of a Permeable Self: "The Long Days" of *The Childhood of Luvers*.

Chapter Seven, "'The Stranger' in *The Childhood of Luvers:* Disruptions in Chronology and the Collision with Other Worlds," explores the emergence of new metaphorical tropes, which frame the parallel emergence of the human self—the development of the personality of the future adult. As the growing girl begins to observe the spirit that enters from outside—"an other," Stranger or *Postoronnyj*—Pasternak's tale becomes an intertextual reversal of the story of Lermontov's *Demon*. Moreover, Zhenya's reaction to Tsvetkov is not only a restructuring of Tamara's suffering in the presence of the invisible Demon (in Lermontov's poem), but also a reflection of Alexander Scriabin's influence (and that of his music) on the formation of the early Pasternak. The presence of Tsvetkov in Zhenya's life, resonating with echoes of Heine's appearance in "The Mark of Apelles" and the role of Tolstoy in "Letters from Tula," demonstrates Pasternak's own emergence as a highly complex writer, able to crown his early metonymies with carefully thought-out and, indeed, breathtaking metaphoric structures. This chapter also concludes with *Table II: Disruptions of Chronology and the Collision of Multiple Worlds in "The Stranger,"* which reflects the transformation of metonymic relations into metaphors whose carefully constructed and increasingly complex worlds, nestled within each other, describe the maturation of the intrinsically artistic personality of the young Zhenya Luvers.

The Conclusion, "Pasternak's Symbolic World: Prose and Philosophy," summarizes the findings of this study. It also addresses Pasternak's apparent and well-documented dislike of his early prose and identifies this problem as located not merely in his complex narrative style, but also in his belief in the exalted position of the spirit of the "other," understood in his youth as vestiges of the sublime world that enter, realign, and eventually undermine the mundane world. My analysis traces Pasternak's growing resistance to these spirits of the sublime, a theme that once again is central to the aesthetics of the Kantian and Neo-Kantian school. I suggest that in his later narratives Pasternak no longer embraces the sublime roles of these carriers of the *a priori* spirit, but instead expands the role of nature and of its resonance as coextensive with the domain of the soul—as, for example, in the first chapters of *Zhivago*, it is not Tsvetkov, Heine, or Scriabin, but the snowstorm that acts as a threatening *a priori* guest knocking on the window and awakening the young Yuri Zhivago, calling him into his future.

My aim throughout is to develop, on the basis of these earlier stories, a set of questions that can be fruitfully applied to Pasternak's writing as a whole, his collection of "buried explosives." In other words, the complexity of his early writing will be approached throughout as a necessary means of uncovering some of the most significant and recurrent networks and patterns of thought that will never disappear from Pasternak's writings.

1

The Character of Philosophical Influence in Pasternak's Early Prose

Mikhail Bakhtin, who never traveled to Marburg, spoke of Hermann Cohen as a formidable force in his own formation: "this was an extraordinary philosopher, who simply had an enormous influence on me, an enormous influence" (Duvakin et al., 1996, 36). No such sentiment or any other clear-cut evaluation of Hermann Cohen was ever expressed by Pasternak, even though his first awareness of Marburg as a probable point of destination for his studies is presented in *Safe Conduct* as a seminal event, saturated with mythical undertones. In *Safe Conduct,* after Dmitry Samarin[1] advises Pasternak in a cold and semi-abandoned Café Grec[2] to study with Cohen, the surrounding snowstorm intensifies and begins to draw circles of infinity. The snowflakes, whirled by the wind, fall to the ground in the shape of a figure eight (or, from another angle, of infinity), recalling in their move-

---

1. For Dmitry Samarin's life and his role as a possible prototype of Yuri Zhivago, see Polivanov (2006, 450–66).

2. There is a somewhat hidden relationship between Pasternak's mention of Café Grec and John Keats's "Ode on a Grecian Urn," established by Pasternak's line, "I could not stop thinking of what I had heard, and I grieved for the little town that I thought I was no more likely to see than my own ears" [Я не мог позабыть о слышанном, и мне жалко было городка, которого, как я думал, мне никогда, как ушей своих, не видать] (*CSP* 36; *PSS* 3:166), and its implicit reference to Keats's famous "And, little town, thy streets for evermore / Will silent be; and not a soul, to tell / Why thou art desolate, can e'er return" (309).

ment the gathering of seamen's hawsers and nets and announcing the young man's initiation into a long if somewhat intangible journey:

> The weather had changed. A wind had risen and begun lashing down a February sleet. It was falling to the earth in regular windings like a figure eight. This was how men piled up hawsers and nets in wavy layers, swinging stroke upon stroke. [. . .] I could not stop thinking of what I had heard, and I grieved for the little town that I thought I was no more likely to see than my own ears. (*CSP* 36)

> Погода переменилась. Поднявшийся ветер стал шпарить февральскою крупою. Она ложилась на землю правильными мотками, восьмеркой. Было в ее яростном петляньи что-то морское. Так, мах к маху, волнистыми слоями складывают канаты и сети. [. . .] Я не мог позабыть о слышанном, и мне жалко было городка, которого, как я думал, мне никогда, как ушей своих, не видать. (*PSS* 3:166)

After such a haunting and promising overture, the absence of any clear reference to Cohen's philosophy or direct acknowledgement of his intellectual influence either in *Safe Conduct* or elsewhere is puzzling, all the more so because in Marburg Pasternak did not merely study philosophy—he engaged with it wholeheartedly and succeeded in receiving, as he was also careful to point out, the School's highest acclaim.[3]

While this avoidance of the question of Cohen's actual teaching is not Pasternak's only silence about his own philosophical interests, it is, nonetheless, startling. No investigator of Pasternak's early prose would deny Pasternak's indebtedness to Neo-Kantianism or forget to stress the importance of his studies in Marburg. At the same time, a strange hollowness characterizes critical efforts to locate Pasternak's philosophical precursors.[4] As Fleish-

---

3. In his letters to Aleksandr Shtikh, on July 17 and 19, 1912, Pasternak emphasized, quite pointedly in fact, that he was not only invited to Hermann Cohen's house, but also offered to remain at Marburg University as a professor (*PSS* 7:124–29).

4. See, for example, de Mallac's tracing of the "dichotomies pervading the Kantian philosophical system" in Pasternak's art (1979, 426), Gifford's claim that "philosophy is an adjunct" to Pasternak's poetry and prose (1977, 27), or Muchnic's insistence that Pasternak while becoming "an apostate philosopher" still "retained the interest of the discipline he has renounced" (1961, 390). Equally telling in this regard is de Mallac's conclusion that the role of philosophy for the poet was secondary to issues of the heart: "Of all the experiences that were to have an impact on Pasternak in Marburg, however, the most powerful was that of rejected love" (1981, 65). Since de Mallac always insisted on the philosophical context of Pasternak's work, this conclusion emphasizes the uncertainty that characterizes the process of locating or arguing for influences in Pasternak's work.

man succinctly observes in his "Introduction" to the publication of Pasternak's philosophical *konspekty,* the quest to elucidate Pasternak's philosophical thought is invariably undermined by the poet himself: "[T]he deep interest in philosophy was acknowledged by him in *Safe Conduct.* But having described his studies, Pasternak left his readers uncertain in which of the philosophical schools one should search for the 'philosopher's key'" (*Lehrjahre* 12). Moreover, this puzzling evasiveness was a life-time characteristic of the writer. When, for instance, in *Doctor Zhivago* Pasternak drew the portrait of a philosopher who would have a life-long influence on the novel's hero Yuri, he was careful to ensure that Nikolay Nikolayevich Vedenyapin belonged to no school of thought, that he was influenced by Tolstoy much more decisively than by Kant, and that even in the Moscow University of the time he walked alone:

> Soon he was to take his place among contemporary writers, university professors and philosophers of the revolution, a man who thought about all of their questions, but had nothing in common with them except their terminology. All of them, without exception, clung to some dogma or other, satisfied with words and superficialities, but Father Nikolai had gone through Tolstoyism and revolutionary idealism and was still moving forward. He thirsted for something new. (*Zhivago* 7; trans. altered)

> Скоро среди представителей тогдашней литературы, профессоров университета и философов революции должен был появиться этот человек, который думал на все их темы и у которого, кроме терминологии, не было с ними ничего общего. Все они скопом держались какой-нибудь догмы и довольствовались словами и видимостями, а отец Николай был священник, прошедший толстовство и революцию и шедший все время дальше. Он жаждал нового. (*PSS* 4:10)

Any possible philosophical precursors to Vedenyapin's thought are, thus, carefully and decisively obliterated.

What are the underlying causes of this habitual pattern of *misdirection* in Pasternak's discussions of the role that philosophy might have had in his formation? Marina Tsvetaeva, in "My Pushkin," insisted that she loved couples (fictional and living) most when they separated,[5] and Pasternak is both

---

5. Cf.

> Neither then, nor afterwards did I ever love when there was a kiss of greeting; always when there was a farewell of parting. I never loved when they sat together; always when they walked apart.
> [. . .] If afterwards, a whole life long, and to this day, I was always the first one to write, the first one to stretch out my hand and my arms, not fearing judgment,

emphatic and yet evasive in his employment of descriptions of intellectual and artistic influences as departures and farewells.[6] In this chapter I will accept Pasternak's challenge in this regard and then go on to examine his famous yet obviously unsatisfactory account of leaving philosophy that follows the equally puzzling break-up with music in *Safe Conduct* (1.1–1.2) and to compare these passages with Pasternak's philosophical diaries and the archival data from his time in Marburg (1.3), which includes the letters he wrote to his family and friends during the destiny-altering July of 1912.

The celebrated passages of *Safe Conduct* that explain Pasternak's irrevocable decisions to leave both Scriabin and Cohen, as well as the factual information that has been assembled, are, for the most part, familiar to Pasternak's readers.[7] The key, however, lies in approaching his recollections not as straightforward explanations, but as instances of covert, even cunning subterfuge (1.4.)—as episodes whose tropes are guided by an intricate narrative strategy revealed when set beside the straightforward evidence of the poet's archival data.[8]

---

it is only because at the dawn of my days, a Tatyana in a book, lying prone, by the light of a small candle, her braid tousled and thrown across her breast, before my eyes, did what she did. [. . .] A lesson of courage. A lesson of pride. A lesson of fidelity. A lesson of fate. A lesson of loneliness (Tsvetaeva 1980: 336–37).

[Я ни тогда, ни потом, никогда не любила, когда целовались, всегда - когда расставались. Никогда не любила - когда садились, всегда - когда расходились.

[. . .] Если я потом всю жизнь по сей последний день всегда первая писала, первая протягивала руку — и руки, не страшась суда — то только потому, что на заре моих дней лежащая Татьяна в книге, при свечке, с растрепанной и переброшенной через грудь косой, это на моих глазах — сделала. [. . .] Урок смелости. Урок гордости. Урок верности. Урок судьбы. Урок одиночества] (Tsvetaeva 1979 2: 261–62).

6. In this work, I have intentionally avoided discussing Rilke's influence, not because it is unimportant, but because the philosophical context, examined here, makes Rilke's influence all the more profound and significant and requires a very careful examination focused on philosophy and Rilke. However, in discussing the influence of the departed—or influence in absence rather than in presence—Rilke must be cited. See here Leishman's summary of Rilke's meditation in writing *Duino Elegies*: ". . . he needed continual reminders of the human past and of intense human living, and yet, at the same time, to be free from distracting personal encounters. Surrounded, as it were, by spirits of the departed, by objects that recalled a long line of users and lovers, by a present that melted into the past and by a past that melted into the present, he could more easily achieve, more easily invoke . . ." (Rilke 2008, 48–49).

7. Critics used to believe, at first, that *Safe Conduct*'s account of Pasternak's relationship with Scriabin and Cohen was historically precise, but in the last two decades it has become clear that his recollections are often less than exact. Thus, Pasternak's leaving music was not as abrupt as he claimed, and the dates of Cohen's invitation and offers were not in June 1912—the month of Pasternak's first love, Ida Vysotskaya's visit (E. B. Pasternak 1989, 111–15 and 156–62).

8. A complex account of Pasternak's evasiveness, prompted by political consideration, in

1.1 *Safe Conduct:*
Farewell to music and the soul's stretched wings

Though *Safe Conduct* provides—on the surface—a somewhat muddled and poetically confusing context for the poet's abrupt decisions in changing his intellectual goals, the juxtaposition of the two modes of farewell—to music and to philosophy—clarifies, however covertly, the future role that philosophy was to play in Pasternak's life. Krystyna Pomorska, after a careful investigation of *Safe Conduct,* concluded that the underlying patterns or "invariants" in Pasternak's relationships with either the composer Alexander Scriabin, or the philosopher Hermann Cohen, or eventually the poet Vladimir Mayakovsky, remain unchanged: "Everything [. . .] ends up in defeat" (Pomorska 1975, 66). However, defeat is apparent only on the surface: in each circumstance of departure, Pasternak structures the narrative to imply that his decisions, no matter how apparently reckless and erratic,[9] are indicative of some deep inner processes, incomprehensible and disturbing to any onlooker, but concealing an intensely personal and joyful exaltation. Nor are the two visions of the future experienced during his departures from music and philosophy identical. In fact, their differences, subtly introduced, signal some of the key themes[10] of Pasternak's art, namely, his work with his precursors and his manner of accepting, rejecting or concealing influences.

Pasternak's decision to abandon music is accompanied by a highly specific set of images, including the evocation of the "winged will"—the intimation of a growing readiness for flight and the birth of a free self no longer humbled by self-inflicted subjugation:[11]

---

writing *Safe Conduct* is found in Clowes (2002). For a contrasting viewpoint on the straightforwardness of *Safe Conduct,* see Bykov: "there was an honest conversation about the time and oneself" (2006, 434).

9. Pasternak's seemingly nonchalant description of his return from Scriabin's home indicates that his journey takes him through side streets, not ready as yet to merge with the main road: "I went along side streets, crossing over more often than I needed to" [Я шел переулками, чаще надобности переходя через дорогу] (*CSP* 28; *PSS* 3:156). Pomorska (1975) overlooks this subtheme.

10. As Pasternak points out, on taking leave of Scriabin his emotions were contradictory: "Something was mounting up in me. Something was tearing and trying to get free. Something was weeping; something was exulting" [Что-то подымалось во мне. Что-то рвалось и освобождалось. Что-то плакало, что-то ликовало] (*CSP* 28; *PSS* 3:155). In describing his break with philosophy, he stresses his ardor, rather than his dislike: "I *lived* my scientific studies more powerfully than their subject required" [Я *переживал* изученье науки сильнее, чем это требуется предметом] (*CSP* 51; *PSS* 3:182–83; emphasis added).

11. About Pasternak's overcoming in himself "Scriabin's superman" and its accompanying winged flight, see Zholkovsky, who notes that in Pasternak's later period the emphasis is on falling from the clouds rather than flying upwards (1994, 285). Nonetheless, while the image of

But music was to me a cult, that is, the destructive focal point at which everything that was most superstitious and self-abnegating in me gathered, and therefore every time *my will took wing* after some evening inspiration, I hastened next morning to humble it again by recalling this defect. (*CSP* 26; emphasis added)

Но музыка была для меня культом, то есть той разрушительной точкой, в которую собиралось все, что было самого суеверного и самоотреченного во мне, и потому всякий раз, как за каким-нибудь вечерним вдохновеньем окрылялась моя воля, я утром спешил унизить ее, вновь и вновь вспоминая о названном недостатке. (*PSS* 3:153)

The turbulent expansion of the soul's will is suggested, rather than stated, in the description of Pasternak's mood as he leaves Scriabin's home; the whole occasion is tightly contained within a quickly flowing paragraph, ever more resonant because of its brevity and restraint. First, Pasternak mentions, as if in passing, the intensity of the emotions that cause his soul's turbulence: "no matter how exciting the news I was taking [to the people at] home, *my soul was disquieted*" [как ни возбуждала весть, которую я нес домашним, *на душе* у меня было неспокойно] (*CSP* 28; *PSS* 3:156; emphasis added). Through a careful choice of words and the reiterated emphasis on "soul," the process of decision making implies not so much the defeat of former dreams[12] as an emergent new inner state of the soul's development, with its energy beginning to affect the surrounding world. The force of this new energy is felt at this point only by Pasternak himself, as the decision, still deeply private, begins to expand into the neighboring space, propelled by the semi-conscious anticipation of a future triumph over the surrounding landscape—Pasternak's birth city, Moscow:[13]

Yet the consciousness that this very sadness was something I would never be able to pour into anyone else's ear, and that, like my future, it would stay below, in the street with all Moscow, my Moscow, mine at this moment as never before—this consciousness more and more resembled happiness. (*CSP* 28)

---

spreading wings enters through the figure of Scriabin, it continues throughout Pasternak's work in the images of the bird, pilot, and flight.

12. See Pomorska's argument to the contrary (1975, 66ff).

13. This sense of unity with Moscow is picked up by Bykov: "Pasternak recollects in *Safe Conduct* that Moscow seemed to belong to him" (2006, 36).

Но все больше походило на радость сознанье, что именно этой грусти мне ни во чьи уши не вложить и, как и мое будущее, она останется внизу, на улице, со всей моею, моей в этот час, как никогда, Москвой. (*PSS* 3:156)

His future as a poet is at this point only implicit, but if Moscow shows at the beginning of the passage its independent "single-souledness" [единодушие московской ночи] (*CSP* 28, trans. altered; *PSS* 3:156), later that night Moscow already belongs to the poet in some not too distant triumph, for the city is beginning to partake in his new state, with the old "world" broken and transformed: "Entirely without my knowledge, a world was melting and crackling in me that only a day before seemed inborn forever" [Совершенно без моего ведома во мне таял и надламывался мир, еще накануне казавшийся навсегда прирожденным] (*CSP* 28, trans. altered; *PSS* 3:155).[14] The soul's capacity to dissolve into space as a triumphant, all-embracing reverberation (a characteristic trope of Pasternak[15]) is, thus, suggested—subtly, but surely—during his instinctive turning toward his real vocation.

The wings of the will [окрыление воли] found in this intimation of his future victorious embrace of Moscow in *Safe Conduct*[16] is a traditional image for the unfettered soul.[17] Resonances of this image are everywhere in Pasternak's depictions of the role of poetry in his life. The exhilaration of flight is reflected in the titles (as well as the poems themselves) of his first poetic volumes—*The Twin in the Clouds* [Близнец в тучах] (December 1913) and *Over the Barriers* [Поверх барьеров] (1914–16). The full spread of wings in flight as a challenge to death appears in the famous "program" poems written

---

14. I argue for a very similar employment of the concept of the expanding "soul" in *Luvers* when the ice on the Kama River melts and breaks (see Chapter 6 of this book).

15. Evgenij Pasternak argues that while the symbolists used the trope of correspondences, Pasternak employed the suggestion of "dissolution" or "dissolving": "The formula 'Everything that perishes is only a reflection [or copy],' which played in its time such a major role in the theoretical works of symbolism, became for Pasternak a process of the temporary dissolving into the eternal [. . .]." [Формула "Все преходящее—только подобие," которая играла в свое время такую большую роль в теоретических построениях символизма, приобрела у Пастернака смысл перехода временного в вечное] (1997, 662).

16. The unfettered spreading of wings is intimated also in Pasternak's comparison between his own creative preferences and those of his readers that opens *Safe Conduct*: "I only came alive completely on those occasions when [. . .] a feeling equipped with all conceivable spaciousness tore loose from its moorings and escaped to freedom" [я и в жизни оживал целиком лишь в тех случаях, когда [. . .] вырывалось на свободу всей ширью оснащенное чувство] (*CSP* 23; *PSS* 3:151)

17. Psyche literally means "butterfly" In Greek. There is, of course, a further parallel with biblical and Platonic notions, namely, the wings of the dove in the Bible (Old and New Testament) and the wings of the psyche in Plato's *Phaedrus*. For Solovyov's adaptation of the Platonic winged soul, see also Kornblatt (1992, 35–50).

at very different times in his career: "Mature archer, cautious hunter" [Рослый стрелок, осторожный охотник] (1928) and "Night" [Ночь] (1956). The theme persists in *Zhivago's* "August" (1953) with its evocative last stanza: "Farewell, the flight of the fully stretched wing, the free stubborn intensity of flight" [Прощай, размах крыла расправленный, / Полета вольное упорство] (*PSS* 4:531). The admission that the fall abruptly stops life-long flight is implied in one of his last poems, "God's World" [Божий мир] (1959): "I too have fallen from the clouds" [Я ведь тоже упал с облаков] (*PSS* 2:195). And, more specifically, in "God's World," Pasternak muses that it is no longer he but his book that is engaged in flight, reaching across continents to awaken readers all over the globe. In his fallen state, however, he himself can only follow in the footsteps of the foxes and cats, a reference both to the animal kingdom and to the instincts of his neighbors, other writers in Peredelkino (and, quite possibly, to his own instinctive ability—tame and yet cunningly feral—to survive catastrophe and to live a little longer):

> By the footsteps of cats and the footsteps of foxes,
> By the cats and foxes' footsteps
> I return with a stack of letters
> To the house where I'll give my joy its free will.
>
> Mountains, countries, borders, lakes,
> Peninsulas and continents,
> Discussions, reports, reviews,
> Children, youth and old men. . . .
>
> [По кошачьим следам и по лисьим,
> По кошачьим и лисьим следам
> Возвращаюсь я с пачкою писем
> В дом, где волю я радости дам.
>
> Горы, страны, границы, озера,
> Перешейки и материки,
> Обсужденья, отчеты, обзоры,
> Дети, юноши и старики.] (*PSS* 2:195)

Thus, the impulse toward unfettered flight—that is, his turn toward poetry—is already firmly established in his first autobiographical account, where the decision to leave music is linked to the soul's expansion, with its potential commanding energy carefully acknowledged.

1.2 Seeing the fate of philosophy "in the flesh"

What is no less remarkable is that the image of expanding liberated wings, for all its direct links to Plato, Neo-Platonism, and Vladimir Solovyov,[18] neither guides nor informs Pasternak's recollection of his departure from Marburg University, where he was formally registered in two seminars, one with Nikolay Hartmann on Leibniz and the other with Hermann Cohen on Kant.[19] As we shall see below, *Safe Conduct* provides for its readers, in place of the intimation of the soul's wings, a new case of carefully constructed narrative subterfuge—an ingenious portrayal of an intellectual chasm between the two schools of philosophy that occupied Pasternak's thoughts in Marburg. While, on the surface, the content of his studies is obscured by the nonsensical contradictions of the narrative, the reader's perception is clearly jarred when Pasternak claims with startling nonchalance that he withdrew from both seminars, abandoned Cohen (whom he had ardently praised in both *Safe Conduct* and letters written just a few days prior to the abrupt decision),[20] and changed

---

18. See Pasternak's notes on *psyche* in Plato as the inextinguishable impulse for movement in *Lehrjahre*:

> Psyche = the beginning of self-directing movement. (The animate differs from the inanimate by the fact that it carries in itself the source of its own movement.) Psyche (as independently moving) *always* moves, cannot stop itself; its life is inextinguishable. Psyche is the beginning of movement of other objects; consequently it itself cannot have a beginning. One cannot conceive an end of unconditional movement. Ergo—it is immortal. [*Psyche* = начало самоопределяемого *движения*. (Одушевл[енное] отлич[ается] от неодушевл[енного] тем, что носит в себе источник своих движений). *Psyche* (как самостоятельно движущееся) движется *всегда*, не может сама себя остановить; ее жизнь неистребима. Psyche начало движения других предметов, след[овательно] не мож[ет] само иметь начало. Немыслимо прекращение безусловного движения. Ergo—бессмертна"] (*Lehrjahre* I:361; emphasis in original).

This understanding of soul is, of course, the same one that proved so highly influential for Solovyov's concept of soul under the influence of Eros: "When Eros enters into an earthly being, he at once transforms it; the lover feels within himself a new power of infinity; he has received a new and great gift. But here inevitably arises the rivalry and struggle of two parts, or tendencies, of the soul—the higher and the lower; which of them will capture for itself and turn to its advantage the mighty power of Eros [. . .]. The sensuous soul drags down the winged demon and blindfolds him, in order that he should maintain life in the empty sequence of material phenomena . . . " (Solovyov 2000, 242).

19. See Fleishman *Lehrjahre* 82ff. See also Tropp (1996, 151) and Clowes (2002).

20. In a letter from July 5, 1912, Pasternak writes: "Yesterday there was a banquet in honor of Cohen. It was a grand celebration, warm, inspiring, with excellent food, light, a multitude of people. I clinked my wine glass with him" [Вчера был банкет в честь Когена. Было торжественно, тепло, вдохновенно, вкусно, светло, многолюдно, обширно. Чокался с ним] (*PSS* 7:116). In the same letter Pasternak praises Cassirer and plans to join him in Berlin, particularly because Cohen is also moving there.

his career path because of . . . a disorder in his room, an intense and single-minded immersion in his studies.

Puzzles associated with this destiny-altering decision increase exponentially in the light of new scholarly findings, all pointing to the formidable depth of Pasternak's philosophical engagement.[21] Pasternak's depiction of his room in Marburg reflects this atmosphere of deep concentration, even though he proceeds to contextualize his chaos of opened books with a startlingly non-Kantian concept—an organic vegetative thinking [растительное мышление] that had begun its independent life both in him and in his room:

I *lived* my scientific studies more powerfully than their subject required. A vegetable kind of thinking dwelt in me. Its peculiarity was that any secondary idea would boundlessly unfold in my interpretation of it and start demanding sustenance and attention, so that when under its influence, I turned to books, I was drawn to them not from interest and knowledge but by the wish to find literary references in support for my idea. And despite the fact that my work was being accomplished by means of logic, imagination, paper and ink, I loved it most for the way in which in the course of the writing it became overgrown with a thicker and thicker ornamentation of comparisons and quotations from books. And because, with the limited time available, I had at a certain stage to give up copying pieces out and had begun, instead, simply leaving the authors open at the pages I needed, a moment arrived when the theme of my work had materialized and the whole of it lay visible to the naked eye from the doorway of my room. It spread across the room in the likeness of a tree fern, heavily unfurling its leafy coils on my desk, divan, and windowsill. (*CSP* 51–52; emphasis in original)

Я *переживал* изученье науки сильнее, чем это требуется предметом. Какое-то растительное мышленье сидело во мне. Его особенностью было то, что любое второстепенное понятье, безмерно развертываясь в моем толкованьи, начинало требовать для себя пищи и ухода, и когда я под его влияньем обращался к книгам, я тянулся к ним не из бескорыстного интереса к знанью, а за литературными ссылками в его пользу. Несмотря на то, что работа моя осуществлялась с помощью логики, воображенья, бумаги и чернил, больше всего я любил ее за то, что по мере писанья она обрастала все сгущавшимся убором книжных цитат и сопоставлений. А так как при ограниченности срока мне в известную минуту пришлось отказаться от

---

21. Cf. Sendelbach (2001, 764).

выписок, взамен которых я просто стал оставлять авторов на нужных мне разгибах, то наступил момент, когда тема моей работы матерьялизовалась и стала обозрима простым глазом с порога комнаты. Она вытянулась поперек помещенья подобьем древовидного папоротника, налегая своими лиственными разворотами на стол, диван и подоконник. (*PSS* 3:182–83)

For all its apparent naïveté, this passage crystallizes a formidable strategic trope. As observed above, the depiction of organic, intertextual, multi-referential thought processes undermines, however implicitly at this point, the non-organic principles of Kantian and post-Kantian philosophies of mind. Spreading like a menacing, dragon-like, preternatural wilderness, the book fern of expanding intellectual interests overtakes the larger parts of the room—a rhizome-rootedness of unfurling coils, requesting additional food, "materializing," as Pasternak claims, "the theme of his work"; and this means that the intellectual content of Pasternak's two seminars in Marburg battles for his attention like a Leibnizian "organic body"—a "natural automaton, which infinitely surpasses all artificial automata" (*Monadology* §64; Cahn, ed. 2002, 595)—and presents a threat to any Kantian abstraction of intellectual thought.

This implied contrast between the organic fern and non-organic thinking is never to disappear from Pasternak's thought, and even a cursory glance over Pasternak's future imagery suggests a firm preference for uniting organic and non-organic modes of thought and viewing them as one process, rather than for distinguishing between them. For instance, Yuri Zhivago's love for Lara becomes all the more piercing because of her ability to read "as if reading were not the highest human activity, but as if it were the simplest possible thing, a thing that even animals could do" [Она читает так, точно это не высшая деятельность человека, а нечто простейшее, доступное животным] (*Zhivago* 291; *PSS* 4:291). In *Safe Conduct* this potential for continuity between intelligible reality and nature, in spite of the brevity of the quickly sketched image, presents a remarkable anticipation of what modern philosophers Gilles Deleuze and Félix Guattari in *Rhizome* will call, in their own opposition to Kant, "the triumphant irruption of the plant in us" (1987, 12).

In depicting the expanding book-fern that threatens the peacefulness of the room, Pasternak is far from being a naïve innocent, blithely unaware of the contradictions in his own recollections. On the one hand, he makes his readers believe that he abandoned philosophy because of his room's chaos, which, when remembered, triggered a sense of premonition: "And when in my journey I saw this room in my imagination, I was really seeing in the flesh my philosophy and its possible fate" [И когда дорогой я видел в воображеньи мою комнату, я, собственно говоря, видел во плоти свою философию и ее вероятную судьбу] (*CSP* 51–52; *PSS* 3:183). On the other hand, his intriguing statement of "seeing in the flesh" the future of his philosophy can just as easily signify not the abandonment of philosophy, but the discovery of a new philosophical pathway, tangibly present in its initial rhizomic irruption. This latter reading is all the more plausible because the fern is an embodiment of a constant cross-referencing between philosophical ideas and literary notes and texts [литературные ссылки]. The instinctive rightness of this new pathway is also supported by the obvious linguistic pun, or resonance between "vegetative consciousness" [растительное мышление] and Pasternak's own last name with its vegetable connotations meaning *parsnip* in Russian.[22] The fern of books then can be understood as indicating an immediate and positive awareness, even a premonition on Pasternak's part, that this newly emergent vegetative growth of his "philosophy in the flesh," possessing all the qualities of a stubborn Darwinian survivor, will not abandon philosophy, but will take on a highly specific form of philosophizing, instinctive to him and no one else.

The book fern, then, is not so much a reason for leaving philosophy, nor is it a life-altering symbol of his chaotic habits, but rather it is the announcement of a new manner of philosophical engagement.[23] And while the suggestion of the leaves spreading from philosophy to literature is both implied and obscured by the wildness of organic-intelligible life (preternatural, with no clear point of origin and no visible end in sight), the growing "vegetative" book-plant,[24] certainly a highly nuanced challenge to the Neo-Kantianism of Marburg, replaces the earlier intimation of the soul's wings tightly bound, but demanding their freedom in passages associated with music and the overpowering brilliance of Scriabin.[25]

---

22. On Pasternak's "idiostyle," his play with the vegetative connotation of his name and its multilayered reference—"poet, plant, poem"—as well as a dual meaning of a leaf (leaf and page) in his poetry, see Fateeva (2003, 62ff). See also Bykov's echo of Pasternak's family conversations concerning Pasternak's falling in love in 1917 with Elena Vinograd, the bride of Sergei Listopad, who also happened to be Pasternak's friend: "an almost comical coincidence of the garden vegetable falling in love with the orchard fruit" [почти комическое совпадение фамилий—огородное растение влюбилось в садовое] (2006, 136).

23. For an alternative interpretation that Pasternak is actually abandoning philosophy once and for all, see Björling (2006, 298ff).

24. About Pasternak's poetic theme, his "auto-metaphor" of "putting soul into leaves and greenery," see Fateeva (2003, 62).

25. See Björling's argument for the centrality of metaphors in Pasternak as an overlap of temporal and atemporal sensibility. Her focus upon the image of the fern emphasizes, in contrast to my reading, Pasternak's abandonment of philosophy rather than the emergence of its newly transformed state: "Vegetative thinking implies not the abstract space of logical thinking but a physical space invaded by the unruly growth accomplished in time. Pasternak's inability to remain in the logical space of concepts is expressed through the metaphor of a grotesque plant

1.3 Between Leibniz and Neo-Kantianism
Archival data and Boris Pasternaks Lehrjahre

Since the implicit philosophical dilemma of unity-opposition between nature and intellect underlies his explanation for leaving Marburg, Pasternak must have been aware that there were at least as many precursors of this "intelligible tree" as the number of leaves and pages spreading around the room. A partial list includes the Neo-Platonic view that Nature's meditation is expanded by intellectual contemplation,[26] Kant's exploration of multiple causality in the image of tree leaves,[27] and, more specifically, the examination of nature and instinct in Spinoza and Leibniz[28] that in turn inspired all the Romantic thinkers,[29] including Schelling's *Naturphilosophie* and Goethe's *Metamorphosis of Plants.* For Pasternak, however, the image also possessed a more focused intellectual context, directly reflecting his work (and its implicit contradictions) for his seminars on Leibniz and Kant.

Prior to Marburg, Pasternak had already experienced a tension between his earlier admiration for Leibniz and *Naturphilosophie,* an interest inspired by his Moscow professor Gustav Shpet[30] and his subsequent immersion in Neo-

---

growing uncontrollably within the space of the confined room. The metaphor conveys the fact that even when engaged in logic and philosophy, Pasternak was unable to be still and settle in the timelessness of ontological discourse" (2006, 298). See here also Fleishman's argument that for the early Pasternak philosophy and poetry were intertwined (1993, 59–74).

26. One locus classicus is Plotinus' treatise on Nature, Contemplation and the One, *Ennead* 38 [30 in chronological order], vol. 3, see especially chapter 10.

27. Grene and Depew term this Kant's "subscription to epigenesis": "One part can certainly trigger off the development of another in a causal sequence under external environmental conditions. [. . .] But in a living thing the existence and balanced functioning of each part still seems to depend on the prior or concomitant existence of all the other parts, as the leaves of the tree, for example, depend in their existence on its branches, but the branches in turn depend on the leaves" (2004, 97).

28. See Dorzweiler's examination of the influence of Leibniz's philosophy on Pasternak (1993, 25–31).

29. Historians of philosophy habitually emphasize that the father of *Naturphilosophie* and Schelling's *Philosophie der Natur* was clearly Leibniz, "the darling of the Romantic age": "The great ancestor of the organic concept of nature was that old Erzfiend of Cartesianism: Leibniz. It was not the exoteric Leibniz of the monadology who made the mental and physical distinct realms, but the esoteric Leibniz of the monadology, who made matter only an appearance of vital force. It was no accident that Herder and Schelling, self-consciously and explicitly, revived Leibniz. Ironically, the arch dogmatist, so recently interned by Kant, had now been resurrected. Leibniz's hour had finally come; despite the baroque *peruke,* he had become a darling of the Romantic age" (Beiser 2004, 141). See here Evans-Romaine's chapter on "Pasternak and German Romanticism" (1997, 1–43).

30. As Fleishman observes, Gustav Shpet was a follower of Leibniz, and he opposed Kant, crediting his thought with the initiation of such philosophical directions of modernity as "empiricism, subjectivism, relativism, etc." As far as Plato was concerned, Shpet considered Leibniz

Kantianism.[31] Pasternak was also acutely aware of the philosophical debates concerning the possibility of continuity, or lack thereof, between the acts of the mind and the content of nature. In this regard, his letters from Marburg in June and July of 1912 provide an illuminating context; they clarify, first of all, that his decision to leave Marburg matured literally between his two final presentations ("рефераты на семинарах"): the first of these was delivered on June 27 at Hartmann's seminar, where Pasternak spoke of Leibniz (*PSS* 7:113), and the final presentation, on the ethics of Kant, was received by Cohen particularly warmly on July 8 (*PSS* 7:117)—by which time the decision to leave had already been made. As Fleishman is careful to point out, Pasternak's most unpleasant experiences were directly connected not to Cohen's course, but to Nikolai Hartmann's seminar on Leibniz: a particularly "acute distaste" was expressed by Pasternak at the time of his own presentation (Fleishman *Lehrjahre* 83ff). In his letter to Alexandr Shtikh (dated June 27), Pasternak questioned Hartmann's approach to Leibniz and praised his "old" Moscow understanding of Leibniz, warmly reiterating his support for Herbart's readings as preferable by far to Hartmann's interpretation:

I did give my presentation about Leibniz. It was a complicated matter: the professor did not allow me to develop those thoughts where I am—if not particularly original—at least trying to reconstruct a careful and singularly correct understanding of Leibniz that was given at one time by Herbart.

О Лейбнице я прочел. Сложно: проф. не дал мне развить тех мест, где я если не оригинален, то, во всяком случае, стараюсь восстановить тонкое и единственно правильное понимание Лейбница, которое в свое время дал Гербарт. (*PSS* 7:113)

What those places were in which Pasternak considered himself knowledgeable may remain unclear, but his *Lehrjahre* and the notes pertaining to 1910 and 1911 (when his dedication to Leibniz was at its height[32]) are explicit:

---

to be a philosopher dedicated to the potentiality implicit in Platonism, while he saw Kant as empowering all the negative pathways toward Plato. See here Mikhail Polivanov (1993) and Fleishman *Lehrjahre* 25ff.

31. Just a few days earlier, Pasternak was still hopeful that Cohen's Neo-Kantianism would be centrally important for his future. In his letter of June 5, 1912, he wrote, "I should forget all Leibniz(es) and math and philosophy as a general subject, and study only his [Cohen's] system" [мне надо плюнуть на всяких Лейбницев и математику и философию как предмет вообще—и отдаться исключительно изучению его системы] (*PSS* 7:105). A similar view was expressed in the letter to his parents of June 22, 1912 (*PSS* 7:113 n. 2).

32. On the importance of Leibniz for Pasternak in 1910–11, see Fleishman *Lehrjahre* 25–28. Pasternak's own recollection of the doctoral dissertation on Leibniz emerges in the

Pasternak, following Herbart,[33] was taken with the spiritual unveiling of ideas through nature's material content by means of the aggregation of monads. The former involvement with Leibniz via Herbart was, therefore, primarily concerned with the dynamic continuity, even progression, of spirit and soul in our physical "organism":

> Leibniz is a monist. The monads are spiritual indivisible units, which have an inner reality: the capacity of presentment. [. . .] Monads are spiritual atoms. Our organism is a complex of monads within a hierarchical relationship. The monad of the soul is primary. The monad of the soul is a simple substance; it is indivisible.
>
> Herbart: realities. One of these realities is soul.

> Л<ей>бн<и>ц—монист. Монады духовн<ые> непротяж<енные> единицы, которым присуще внутр<енние> состоян<ия>: способн<ость> пр<е>дст<а>вл<ения>. [. . .] Монады—духовн<ые> атомы. *Организм наш = комплекс монад с иерархич<еским> отношением.* Монада души господствует. Мон<ада> души—прост<ая> субстанция—неразрушима.
>
> Гербарт: реалии. Одна из реалий душа. (*Lehrjahre* I:174)[34]

Further, in *Lehrjahre* this thought is articulated by means of images already anticipating the book fern of Marburg's room. Thus, when Pasternak speaks of Leibniz and illustrates the progressive continuum of the spiritual essence through physical materiality by means of a conglomerate of monads, he draws an arresting picture of the multi-voiced and multi-willed interchange of creatures and creations. The preternatural book-fern with authors speaking both to each other and to the new apprentice is here potentially present:

---

context of the life-altering meeting with Samarin in Café Grec, when "a piece of Hegelian infinity stretched itself across the pavilion" [Поперек павильона протянулся кусок гегелевской бесконечности], and Samarin himself "had leapt from Leibniz and mathematical infinity to the dialectical one" (*CSP* 36; *PSS* 3:165). In *Safe Conduct,* Pasternak notes that in the eighteenth century Lomonosov came to study with Leibniz's disciple Christian von Wolff.

33. Johann Friedrich Herbart (May 4, 1776–August 11, 1841) was a German philosopher whose interpretations of Leibniz influenced Neo-Kantian views of psychology and education. See Davidson (1906). While studying in Moscow, Pasternak worked with the textbook *Introduction to Philosophy* [Введение в философию], written by G. I. Chelpanov, a colleague and a friend of Shpet.

34. The marks in the quotation are in keeping with those chosen by the editors of *Lehrjahre* that indicate abbreviations in Pasternak's original notes.

The world is a gathering of the wills of the different levels of complexity [. . .]. Consequently nature is a self-disclosure of the spirit: the external part of the cosmic world is matter; the internal—feelings, attractions, spiritual creativity. [. . .] Nature is a self-reflective spirit, reaching its consciousness in the human being. The difference of complexities between different willful units. [. . .] The goal of life—is a realization of the spiritual in nature, the outflow of spirituality, a transformation of nature into the substratum for the achievement of spiritual goals.

Мир—совокупн<ость> воль различн<ой> степени сложности [. . .]. Отс<юда> природа—самораскрытие духа: внешн<яя> стор<она> космич<еского> мира—материя; внутренн<яя>—чувств<а>, влечен<ия>, духовн<ое> тв<орче>ство. [. . .] Природа = дух сознающий, достигающ<ий> самосознания в человеке. Различие сложности межд<у> отд<ельными> волев<ыми> единицами. [. . .] Цель жизни—реализация духовности в творчестве, распростран<ение> духовности, превращение природы в субстрат для достиж<ения> духовн<ых> целей.] (*Lehrjahre* I:185–86)

There is, then, a notable similarity between the content of these Moscow notes and the picture of the Marburg room that gives material evidence, not merely of the state of chaos during Pasternak's studies, but also of his acceptance of the Leibnizian model of "Nature as a self-reflective spirit, reaching its consciousness in human beings," a model so influential for Schelling, Goethe, and other Romantics.[35]

Might one then conclude that Pasternak decided to embrace Leibniz's understanding of the continuum between nature and intellect and because of this abandoned Neo-Kantianism?[36] According to scholars who have examined Kant's attitude to Leibniz, in the *Critique of Pure Reason* Kant was particularly averse to Leibniz's organized continuum, his "marked enthusiasm for the notion of an infinity of infinitely small systems organized into functionally differentiated parts"; Kant, for example, rejected as "unthinkable" Leibniz's view that this organization could go on to infinity (Kant 1781 [A], ¶ 526; 1787 [B], ¶ 554) (Grene and Depew 95). While there is no indication that Pasternak

---

35. Pasternak's own thoughts on the matter are skillfully articulated: they constitute a material structure made up of distinct units that can, of course, be dismantled, but not without profoundly reorienting the poet's primary intellectual landmarks.

36. Indeed, Pasternak had to know that Leibniz's notion of the unification and mutual address of human wills though the intelligible forces of nature, or material monads, was not well received by either Kant or his followers.

after Marburg became an exclusive apprentice of Leibniz, there is considerable support for the idea that in the debate about the relationship between nature and intellect, Pasternak sided with Leibniz and the Romantics,[37] and that this decision meant for him the choice of a literary path. His letter to Shtikh of July 8—written just after his final presentation for Cohen—opens with rather telling praise for Shtikh's own letter, as Pasternak speaks of nature and natural growth that together give birth to human life and thought in a manner reminiscent of a living cell dividing itself into new, independent but interconnected units. Thus, in his compliment to Shtikh, one can see botany, writing, and life as an infinitely divisible and yet unified organic whole: "Your letter is a botanical garden, out of which life has separated itself, awash in a still palatably-steaming layer of nature" [Так, твое письмо—ботанический сад, от которого отделилась жизнь—со всем парным налетом природы] (*PSS* 7:117).

However, the presence of Gottfried Leibniz is palpable not only in the tone and imagery of this momentous letter of July 8. Pasternak, in fact, admits unequivocally that as far as his future, as-yet-unwritten poetry is concerned, his overall preference and love are not far from Leibniz. In deciding to leave Marburg because he had come to Cohen too late, but still having accepted Cohen's dinner invitation, Pasternak emphasizes that if he were ever to publish poetry, he would dedicate it "to the philosopher of the infinitesimal method." For most scholars the reference is to Cohen and his 1883 work *Das Prinzip der Infinitesimalmethode und seine Geschichte* [The Principle of the Infinitesimal Method and its History],[38] and the focus of the letter does suggest that Cohen's personality here dominates Pasternak's thoughts, and yet the supposed reference to a book written by Cohen thirty years ago is perplexing:

> It is vexing that it is too late. I will not be his student. But I will go to his dinner. And if I ever publish any poems, *I would dedicate them to the philosopher of the infinitesimal method*, and for the sake of this—since I have no poems of my own—I would even steal, all the conflictual combination of these words notwithstanding. 10 years ago Gavronsky, Harmann, etc., etc. studied with him. Now I will go to dine with him. It doesn't matter. It's vexing.

37. Dorzweiler (1993) makes a persuasive argument that Leibniz's influence on Pasternak was considerable and, possibly, decisive as far as philosophy is concerned.

38. See Kudriavtseva's note (2001, 64 n. 3) that Cohen's work of 1883 dealt with the infinitesimal method. What she forgets to mention is that Cohen deals with Leibniz in this work. As Poma points out in her work on Cohen, the infinitesimal method of Leibniz reached its full potential not only "in its application to algebra and geometry" and to "problems of mechanics," but also "this method is revealed as a principle of the reality of nature" (1997, 39–40).

Это досадно,—что поздно. Я не буду его учеником. Но я пойду к нему на ужин. А если бы я когда-нибудь издал стихи—*я посвятил бы их философу инфинитесимальной методы*; и ради этого, за неимением собственных—я пошел бы даже на кражу во всей противоречивости этого словообразования. Десять лет назад у него учились Гавронский, Hartmann, etc. etc. Я мог бы стоять среди них. Теперь я пойду ужинать к нему. Ничего, ничего. Это досадно. (*PSS* 7:118; emphasis added)

Much more telling is the fact that Cohen's study of the infinitesimal method was an engagement with Leibniz, who is known much more widely as the founding philosopher of the method in question,[39] and this makes Pasternak's reference in the letter highly ambiguous, unless his allegiance to Cohen is linked to that aspect of Cohen closest to Leibniz. In the very next paragraph, in fact, Pasternak proceeds to contrast the objective method of philosophical self-discipline with the spirit and creativity of Romanticism. His real self, Pasternak suggests, is still there in the late summer of 1910, even though from that point on he forbids himself any outright acceptance of Romantic imaginative creativity:[40]

And the vexation can only grow when . . . Marburg . . . Cohen . . . 1912 . . . —when, as I say, this combination of words enters into a belated connection with August 1910 in Spasskoe . . . after St. Petersburg . . . with the project of radical "self-reeducation" for the sake of entry into the world of Olia and her father, and so on. Distancing myself from romanticism and the creative, again and again, creative fantasy—objective judgment and strict discipline—all of this began for me with that laughable decision. It was an error.

Как же увеличивается досада, когда . . . Марбург . . . Коген . . . 1912 . . .—когда, говорю я, это сочетание входит в непредвиденную—запоздавшую связь с . . . августом 1910 . . . в Спасском . . . после Петербурга . . . с проектом коренного 'самоперевоспитания' для сближения с классическим миром Оли и ее отца etc. Отдаление от

39. Leibniz is known to students of philosophy as the founder not only of "infinitesimal geometry," but also of "the theory of infinitely small and infinite quantities [. . .] the theory of quantified indivisibles" (Knobloch 2002, 59).

40. See here the recurrent argument of historians of philosophy that the father of *Naturphilosophie* and Schelling's *Philosophie der Natur* was clearly Leibniz, "the darling of the Romantic age" (Beiser 2004, 141).

романтизма и творческой и вновь творческой фантастики—объек-
тивизация и строгая дисциплина—начались у меня с того комиче-
ского решения. Это была ошибка. (*PSS* 7:118–19)

It is characteristic of Pasternak that the role of Leibniz, the original "philosopher of the infinitesimal method" and the father of Romanticism and
Naturphilosophie, should not be named, just as the authors of the books in
Pasternak's room in Marburg remain anonymous; Leibniz-Cohen's "infinitesimal" influence lives in the prism of other voices and traditions—an erup-
tion of mind working as part of nature that permits Pasternak to abandon
his self-imposed discipline and to accept his own long-suppressed "wish to
find literary references in support" of philosophical ideas [я тянулся [. . .]
за литературными ссылками] (*CSP* 51; *PSS* 3:183). Leibniz's influence on
Romantic poets and philosophers alike is a case in point; it proves to the ques-
tioning glance of Cohen that literature can be a worthy interlocutor for philosophy, and for Pasternak such a path was not only possible and passionately
desirable, but also organically instinctual.

1.4 The multi-voicedness of philosophical themes searching for literary nourishment

The interdependence of mind and nature has been one of the most easily
identifiable Pasternakian themes, an artistic signature of sorts prevalent ever
since the writer returned to Moscow, a city where poets can be philosophers
and philosophers poets.[41] In 1913, in the poems "Eden" [Эдем] and "Of the
Forest" [Лесное], Pasternak characterizes his own voice as a participant in the
forests' conversation:[42] "I entered as a historical face into a family of forests"
[Я историческим лицом вошел в семью лесин] (*PSS* 1:64);[43] he is also a
direct expression of intense but mute organic processes[44]—an articulation of
the as-yet inaudible wetness of grass or the thickness of leaves in an impenetrable forest:

---

41. On the exceptional cross-fertilization between literature and philosophy, see Fleishman
Lehrjahre 28–47.

42. On this signature theme in Pasternak, see Fateeva (2003, 62–63) and Pollak (2006,
94–115).

43. This line appears in the later version of "Eden," "When to the Lyre's Labyrinth" [Когда
за лиры лабиринт] (*PSS* 1:326).

44. A similar stance is clearly evident in yet another early program-poem "Spring" [Весна]
(1914), where poetry, a sponge left between the wettest and freshest greenery, expresses the
inaudible voices of nature abandoned into itself (*PSS* 1:90–92).

Lacking words—the hundred-headed woods is
Sometimes—a chorus; sometimes—a solitary someone . . .
I am the conversation of anonymous lips,
I am the pillar of ancient dialects.

[Лишенный слов—стоглавый бор
То—хор, то—одинокий некто . . .
Я—уст безвестных разговор,
Я—столп дремучих диалектов.] (*PSS* 1:327)

It is in prose, however, that this evocation of writing as an intelligible maturation of the forces of nature, reflected in the multitude of human interlocutors,
finds its clearest and most articulate expression.

"Some Propositions" [Несколько положений] (1918, 1922) compares the
birth of the "book" to the rustle of a great number of treetops, all awakened
into conversation. It is also in these "programmatic" passages of 1918 that
Pasternak claims that the manuscript of his dreams (as preternatural as the
fern in Marburg) is infinite; born together with life itself and made up of the
voices and observations of many testimonies, the book asserts its "rootedness"
not merely in natural instinct, but in the indelible, intellectual, and ultimately
spiritual impulses of human beings:

Without it [the book] there could be no continuation of a spiritual kin. *It
would have become extinct.* The apes have never possessed a book.

The book was written. It grew, increased in intelligence, became
worldly wise [. . .]

Life has not just begun. Art had no beginning. [. . .] No genuine book
has a first page. Like the sighing of the forest, it is born goodness knows
where, and it grows and rolls along, arousing the thick backwoods, and
suddenly, at its darkest, thunderstruck, and panicked moment, it reaches
its goal and speaks out at once from every tree top. (*CSP* 260; trans. altered;
emphasis added)

Без нее духовный род не имел бы продолжения. Он перевелся бы.
Ее не было у обезьян.

Ее писали. Она росла, набиралась ума, видала виды,— и вот она
выросла и—такова. [. . .]

Жизнь пошла не сейчас. Искусство никогда не начиналось.
[. . .] Ни у какой истинной книги нет первой страницы. Как лесной
шум, она зарождается Бог весть где, и растет, и катится, будя запо-

ведные бредни, и вдруг, в самый темный, ошеломительный и пани-
ческий миг, заговаривает всеми вершинами сразу, докатившись.
(*PSS* 5:24–25)

This characteristic merging between intellect, nature, and the world of past
and future is evident many years later in *Doctor Zhivago*, in the sketch of the
library room in Yuriatin. Pasternak, in fact, expands within a new setting the
earlier tropes of the gathering of treetops in "Some Propositions" and of the
book-fern in *Safe Conduct*. Drawing together many voices, presences, and
realities of different wills and intensities, Yuriatin's library enriches the writer's
earlier plateau with a communion—"the bustling intersection"—not only of
open books and thoughts, but of the sun, houses, streets, lives, and people,
imagined and real, from near and far:

> Now, as the reading room gradually filled with local people, some sitting
> down near to him and others farther away, he felt as if he was getting to
> know the town by standing at one of its bustling intersections, and as if not
> only people but also the houses and the streets in which they lived were
> coming into the room.
>
> However, from the window one could also see the actual Yuriatin, real
> and not imagined.
>
> [. . .] The crowd of readers did not distract him. He had had a good
> look at his neighbors; those on the left and right were fixed in his mind, he
> knew they were there without raising his eyes and he had the feeling that
> they would not leave before him, just as the houses and churches outside of
> the window would not move from their places.
>
> The sun, however, did move. (*Zhivago* 288; 290)

И когда на его глазах зал постепенно наполнялся юрятинскими
жителями, садившимися то поодаль от него, то совсем по сосед-
ству, у Юрия Андреевича являлось чувство, будто он знакомится
с городом, стоя на одном из его людных скрещений, и будто в зал
стекаются не читающие юрятинцы, а стягиваются дома и улицы, на
которых они проживают.

Однако и действительный Юрятин, настоящий и невымышлен-
ный, виднелся в окнах зала.

[. . .] Людность зала не мешала ему и не рассеивала его. Он
хорошо изучил своих соседей и видел их мысленным взором справа
и слева от себя, не подымая глаз от книги, с тем чувством, что состав

их не изменится до самого его ухода, как не сдвинутся с места церкви и здания города, видневшиеся в окне.

Между тем солнце не стояло. (*PSS* 4:287; 289)

Most prominently, however, Pasternak's view of the interconnectedness of natural, vegetative, intellectual, and spiritual processes is given its fullest articulation in the Tolstoyan passages of *Doctor Zhivago*,[45] especially when Yuri Zhivago argues that history, always in movement, develops according to the often invisible laws of the "vegetative kingdom" in its reach upwards:

> He reflected again that he conceived of history, of what is called the course of history, not in the accepted way but by analogy with the vegetable kingdom. [. . .] [I]n only a few days in spring the forest is transformed, it reaches the clouds, *and you can hide or lose yourself in its leafy maze*. (*Zhivago* 453; emphasis added)

> Он снова думал, что историю, то, что называется ходом истории, он представляет себе совсем не так, как принято, и ему она рисуется наподобие жизни растительного царства. [. . .] Весной в несколько дней лес преображается, подымается до облаков, *в его покрытых листьями дебрях можно затеряться, спрятаться*. (*PSS* 4:451)

With such powerful echoes of *Naturphilosophie* and its themes, Pasternak's indirectness in presenting his philosophical indebtedness becomes less perplexing. The literary examples, drawing upon these philosophical themes, not only clarify the precise pathways of his relationship with philosophy, but also demonstrate the ever-growing number of participants in such vision and conversation.

"Life has not just begun. Art had no beginning. [. . .] No genuine book has a first page" [Жизнь пошла не сейчас. Искусство никогда не начиналось. [. . .] Ни у какой истинной книги нет первой страницы] (*CSP* 260, *PSS* 3:25), Pasternak observes in "Some Propositions" in 1918. His protagonist Yuri, returning from the war in 1918, speaks about the colossal nature of impending events, emphasizing that they too have no single cause and no single author. Like all major living phenomena, processes of great significance have multiple causality and are similar in this to the elemental forest or clouds in the sky:

---

45. See particularly Boris Gasparov (1992a) on the role of Leo Tolstoy in Pasternak's prose.

It is petty to explore causes of titanic events. They haven't any. It is only in a family quarrel that you look for a point of origin—after people pull each other's hair and smash the dishes they rack their brains trying to figure out who started it. What is truly great is without beginning, like the universe.

[. . .] The new order of things will be all around us and as familiar to us as the woods on the horizon or the clouds over our heads. (*Zhivago* 182; trans. altered)

Мелко копаться в причинах циклопических событий. Они их не имеют. Это у домашних ссор есть свой генезис, и после того как оттаскают друг друга за волосы и перебьют посуду, ума не приложат, кто начал первый. Все же истинно великое безначально, как вселенная. Оно вдруг оказывается налицо без возникновения, словно было всегда или с неба свалилось.

[. . .] Наставший порядок обступит нас с привычностью леса на горизонте или облаков над головой. (*PSS* 4:180–81)

In other words, Pasternak's position, firmly adopted in Marburg, on the continuity between the overlapping relationships of thought and nature, appears to have been accompanied by the major artistic challenge he set for himself: to portray the relationship between ideas and actions as engendered by a multiplicity of causes and influences, by generations of thinkers, natural processes, and historical events.

Pasternak left Marburg, then, not to return to Gottfried Leibniz, but to escape the confines of a single philosophical school; his book-fern was a weed, and it grew freely only among texts whose number could not be itemized. His acceptance of the organic character of intellectual events necessitated an artistic program within which underlying philosophical principles could never be isolated, named, or categorized as single causes or influences; their attractiveness lay in their ability not to unveil the pages of some philosophical textbook, but to gather instead a living world of dynamic interlocutors. In the same manner, the influence of the philosopher-uncle Nikolay Vedenyapin on Pasternak's young protagonist Yuri, in contrast to his effect, for example, on Misha Gordon, was one of unlimited freedom: "Yuri realized the great part his uncle had played in molding his character. [. . .] Yuri advanced and became freer under the influence of his uncle's theories, but Misha was fettered by them" [Юра понимал, насколько он обязан дяде общими свойствами своего характера. [. . .] Юру дядино влияние двигало вперед и освобождало, а Мишу—сковывало] (*Zhivago* 65–66; *PSS* 4:67). Similarly, Pasternak's turn to art in 1912 was, first and foremost, an "unfettered" reaction to philosophy—the discovery of literary form as a multiplicity of addresses, engaged in an ongoing dialogue and situated from the outset within the fullest range of philosophical questions.

Although the evidence provided by his philosophical *konspekty* goes, to some extent, against the overall principle of the author's project—the unfettered evocation of an open-ended exchange of philosophical questions—the publication of *Pasternaks Lehrjahre* from his Moscow and Marburg studies is a powerful ally for anyone who wishes to examine the philosophical themes in Pasternak's *oeuvre*. Side by side with his early prose works, these philosophical notes help to explain more fully what Pasternak as a writer learned from his philosophical studies—how to evoke a chorus of philosophical positions—directly, without preface or ornament.[46] In this context, his student notes are a rare treasure, and not only because they reveal in detail the contents of his philosophical training. The greater value of the notes is in the access they grant to the expanding conversations between Pasternak the philosopher and Pasternak the literary artist.

In what follows, I will offer new readings of Pasternak's short stories through 1918, the year in Russian history when the world of Imperial Russia was to disappear forever. 1918 is also recreated in *Doctor Zhivago* in the chapters "Farewell to the Past" and "The Moscow Encampment." In these chapters, the Russia of the past does not depart without a last significant conversation between Yuri, already a published poet dreaming of a future prose work, and his philosopher uncle Nikolay Vednyapin. As the two men face each other at this major historical crossroads, the topic of their conversation is left characteristically open-ended, but their meeting reinforces the kindredness of the two elemental forces—poetry and philosophy, without whose mutual address each interlocutor would be weaker and less comprehensible:

> Theirs was a meeting of two artists, and although they were close relatives, and the past arose and lived again between them [. . .] the moment they began to speak, all other ties between them vanished, their kinship and dif-

---

46. In her analysis of the role of nature in *Zhivago*, Witt argues that Pasternak follows Solovyov's bringing together of Schelling and Darwin, since the Russian philosopher tended to draw "many examples from the works of 'the great Darwin'" (2000a, 116) and, together with Schelling, viewed "art as a kind of continuation" of nature, with Solovyov particularly stressing art's role as an evolution "carried on by humanity" (2000a, 116). It is possible, however, to expand Witt's list of philosophical references to include Leibniz (a major influence on Kant) among the unnamed voices that passed through Yuri's mind when "Darwin was next to Schelling, the butterfly that had just flown by next to modern painting and Impressionist art" (*Zhivago* 346).

ference of age was forgotten, all that was left was the confrontation of the elemental forces, of energy and principles. [. . .]

Their talk was full of exclamations, they paced excitedly up and down the room [. . .] deeply moved by the exalting discovery of how completely they understood each other. (*Zhivago* 178)

Встретились два творческих характера, связанные семейным род-ством [. . .] но едва лишь речь зашла о главном, о вещах, извест-ных людям созидательного склада, как исчезли все связи, кроме этой единственной, не стало ни дяди, ни племянника, ни разницы в возрасте, а только осталась близость стихии со стихией, энергии с энергией, начала и начала. [. . .]

Оба поминутно вскрикивали и бегали по номеру [. . .] потря-сенные доказательствами взаимного понимания. (*PSS* 4:176–77)

The passage has potent autobiographical resonances. By 1918, Boris Pasternak could already claim considerable accomplishments in his open-ended prose, which constituted itself as an ardent conversation between literature and phi-losophy, not unlike the spirit of the episode between Vedenyapin and Zhivago.

Like his protagonists' conversation, Pasternak's narrative approach to philosophy does not involve single and discrete parts or occasional "micro"-themes that might inform his stories' intellectual content. His emphasis on the dialogic content of ideas, on a multitude of voices, a "maze of leaves," suggests that philosophical themes operate as large-scale narrative frames—as ideas and questions in open-ended dialogue. Pasternak's narrative strat-egy, therefore, is propelled neither by a detailed unveiling of causal relations between protagonists nor by explicit philosophical digressions. The text gains momentum through a series of powerful metaphoric images that subsume a multi-layered philosophical context so fully that it appears erased in this new transformation. Only a certain eccentricity signals this covert strategy. Thus, the deeper processes underlying his farewell to music are signified by a fleet-ing suggestion of expanding wings, and a chaos of opened books, both philo-sophical and literary, is offered as an explanation for leaving Marburg.

Uniquely, in fact, Pasternak's narratives acquire their fuller significance within a wide sphere of textual resonances, and this includes a philosophi-cal substratum, suggested rather than spelled out in a fleeting and seemingly absent-minded way. As I will argue in Chapter Two, this manner of writing undermines the validity of Jakobson's conclusion that Pasternak's attempts at metaphor tend to make his narratives "banal and unoriginal," even while the author defends "in theoretical digressions his right to triviality" (1969,

149). Rather, Pasternak's writing presents serious challenges for his literary investigators, who can compete neither with the depth and initial ardor of his philosophical training, nor with his ability to choose images that for all their natural embeddedness in the text signal not one, but a manifold of philosophical voices.

For all of the above reasons, the examination of Pasternak's early stories in the context of his philosophical interests points to a highly important piece of a larger puzzle, since his engagement with philosophy must be approached as inseparable from the tales themselves. The availability of his philosophical notes permits his critics to grasp more surely the direction of his interests, which are transformed almost without trace within his fictional prose. Bringing together philosophy and his prose narratives presents an opportunity to uncover some of the significant and recurrent networks or patterns of thought that will never disappear from Pasternak's writings. Consequently, as I shall argue in subsequent chapters, a detailed unearthing of these networks goes a long way toward elucidating these more hidden path- or rootways within the multi-voiced maze of his thought.

2

Similarity and Contiguity in Pasternak's Early Poetics and Their Philosophical Underpinnings

In *Safe Conduct,* Pasternak presents a rather curious list of the philosophers who occupied his thoughts during his university studies in Moscow and Marburg: "Along with some of my acquaintances I had connections with 'Musaget.' From others I learned of the existence of Marburg. Kant and Hegel were replaced by Cohen, Natorp, and Plato" [Вместе с частью моих знакомых я имел отношение к "Мусагету." От других я узнал о существовании Марбурга: Канта и Гегеля сменили Коген, Наторп и Платон] (*CSP* 31; *PSS* 3:159). Plato appears at the end of the series (prominently and non-chronologically, even in terms of the order of Pasternak's studies[1]) and, in Pasternak's characteristic manner, is never mentioned in *Safe Conduct* again, while such philosophers as David Hume, Pasternak's major early work on "The Psychological Skepticism of Hume" notwithstanding, are omitted altogether.[2] In this case Pasternak's habitual obliqueness had straightforward political underpinnings: in 1930, in spite of the prevailing ideological materialism, he clearly and somewhat eccentrically (his lifelong manner was to appear eccen-

---

1. Pasternak studied Plato with Lopatin in 1909–10 and in seminar-form with Kubitsky in 1910–11 *(Lehrjahre* I:353, 366) and later referred to Plato in the context of Cohen's work (spring 1911 [*Lehrjahre* I:356]). Nonetheless, he singles out Plato as the major influence before his trip to Marburg. See also Fleishman's note on the singularity of this notation in *Lehrjahre* 129 n.49.

2. The most probable date of Pasternak's work on his thesis [реферат] dedicated to David Hume is spring 1911 (Fleishman *Lehrjahre* 121).

tric while saying exactly or almost exactly what he wanted) recollected in a public forum his youthful immersion in philosophical idealism,[3] foreground-ing "Musaget,"[4] Hegel, Kant, Neo-Kantiantism, and particularly Plato as his key influences in the pre-Revolutionary years. This memory, as we shall see, was by no means a superficial reminiscence.

Some important aspects of Pasternak's employment of philosophical con-cepts have been brought to light by the debates that have followed Jakobson's seminal appraisal of Pasternak as the "master of metonymy" (1969, 149),[5] an appraisal that tends to co-exist in criticism with what is essentially its coun-ter-argument, namely, that Pasternak's roots are in Symbolism.[6] For Jakob-son, metaphors—and, by implication, symbols (Jakobson wisely abstains from

---

3. The Soviet critics were not amused. *Safe Conduct* was banned in 1933, and in 1931 the confiscation of a number of the issues of the journal *Red Virgin Soil* [Красная новь] was believed to have been caused by the publication of Pasternak's memoirs (Blum 2003). For a thorough account of Soviet criticism's rejection of the memoirs, see Fleishman (1984, 55–57) and *PSSCom* 3:553. In Fleishman's view *Safe Conduct* made Pasternak's confrontation with the official line both "clear and inescapable" (1984, 55).

4. Cf.: " . . . 'something like an academy' . . . was formed around the Musaget publishing concerns when it opened in the autumn of 1909. A special attraction of the Musaget gatherings was their Germanic bias" (Barnes 1989, 95 and 121 ff.), and Fleishman *Lehrjahre* 143ff. See further Davydov (2009, 8ff).

5. Vuletić carefully sketches the uneasy nature of Jakobson's gradual acceptance and re-evaluation of Pasternak's role in Russian modernism (2004, 483–86).

6. As scholars engage in the metaphor–metonymy discussion, the question of whether Pasternak's roots lie in Symbolism or in avant-garde Futurism inevitably arises. Pasternak's pre-Revolutionary acquaintance Feodor Stepun, who is minimally interested in Pasternak's use of metonymy, is emphatic about Pasternak's roots in Symbolism: "Let me add that Pasternak's philosophical and atmospheric affinity for the Symbolists is indirectly indicated by the fact that when in the third part of his *Safe Conduct* . . . [he] identifies the force that kept them afloat as the art of Aleksandr Blok, the leading poet of Russian Symbolism, and of Andrey Bely, author of a voluminous work on Symbolism and, without any doubt, its most remarkable writer, as well as the art of Skriabin, whose association with Symbolism is attested to by Vyacheslav Ivanov, and, finally, of the most popular actress of the era, Vera Komissarzhevskaya, who, rather than por-traying on the stage visible reality, strove to embody the invisible" (1962, 49). For other views on the subject, see Victor Erlich's conclusion that Pasternak's metonymy is a version of metaphor (1979, 281–88), M. Gasparov's quantitative analysis of the poetry of Mayakovsky and Pasternak that disputes Jakobson's position (1995), Fateeva's introductions of "metatropes" (or intertextual tropes) in her analysis of Pasternak (2003, 17–19), as well as Vuletić's careful argument against Jakobson's position. Thus, the debate regarding Pasternak's range in image construction is only gaining momentum. According to Kling, for instance, "the conversation between Pasternak and symbolism lasted almost for a century" (1999, 37), and he questions Fleishman's placement of Pasternak within Futurism (2002). Faryno speaks of metaphoric Pasternak (1993); Gorelik, of Pasternak's post-symbolist mythopoetics (2000). Others, like Rudova, see Pasternak's style as reflecting cubo-futurist painting with "metonymy so abundant [. . .] that the reader is forced to follow the connections between things, whereas things as such fall out of the picture altogether" (1997, 60–61).

making this interrelation clear)[7]—"are not what determines and guides [Pasternak's] lyric theme" (1969, 141). Jakobson's judgment has never been disputed on theoretical grounds, and so it remains both piercingly apt and yet problematic. For instance, Pasternak's understanding of an individual (as well as his or her role in the surrounding world) is obscured by the debate. Since metonymy, in Jakobson's evaluation, implies a weakened role for the human subject,[8] Pasternak's style, rich in metonymic constructions, contrasts with the main focus of his philosophical studies—the emergence of the individuality and self-consciousness: "All of Pasternak's studies during his university years proceeded under a banner of 'self-consciousness.' This term [self-consciousness] appears everywhere, not only in his philosophical notes but in his early literary drafts and correspondence" (Fleishman 1990a, 29). Fyodor Stepun, a leading figure in Musaget (remembered by name in *Safe Conduct*), was certain that Pasternak's prose reflects principles that "appear in Kant as 'the transcendental subject,' in Fichte—as the 'absolute I,' and in Hegel as absolute spirit" (Stepun 1962, 48), but the interconnection between such a judgment and the metonymic worldview is not easily drawn. Stepun's position is instructive, in fact, in allowing a metonymic Pasternak[9] to accompany Pasternak the Symbolist:[10] having accepted Jakobson's position, Stepun goes on to insist that

---

7. Jakobson is aware that Pasternak traces his ancestry to the Symbolists, but he argues that "Pasternak, who conceives as his literary task the continuing of Symbolist tradition, is aware that out of his efforts to recreate and perpetuate the old the new art is always arising" (1969, 137). The conclusion that should be drawn from Jakobson's positions—that in Pasternak metonymies predominate not only over metaphors, but also over symbols (which are, in fact, intertextual metaphors)—remains blurred in criticism, for no one would want to arrive at such a blatantly false conclusion. Fateeva's work with "metatropes" reflects her view that Pasternak does not accept ready-made symbols, but creates his own mythological codes (2003, 17–21); it also permits her to bypass the metaphor–metonymy conversation altogether. Thus, the acuteness of Jakobson's observation invalidates attempts to problematize his position, "that overcoat out of which other commentaries" on Pasternak have emerged (Malmstad 1992, 302).

8. See, for instance, Erlich, in analyzing the poem "Marburg," who refers to Jakobson's "sharp analysis" while noting that the subject is not weakened or turned into a passive presence but equated with the objects of his surroundings (1979, 282).

9. Stepun accepts Jakobson's premise and simultaneously reverses it by insisting that the poet's imagery expands the self: "Pasternak's poetry, on the other hand, though not immune to the metaphor, abounds, in Jakobson's words, 'in metonymic sequences.' To simplify though, I hope, not to distort Jakobson's interesting observation, one might say that in Pasternak the range of associations is virtually boundless since it is not restricted by the principle of similarity and contrast. [. . .] Jakobson notes that at the first glance the associative downpour of Pasternak's verse may appear to drown out the poet's 'I.'" Actually, Stepun argues, Pasternak's most bizarre images are metonymic companions, if not reflections, of the poet's self (1962, 51ff).

10. Stepun, with all his sensitivity to Pasternak's Neo-Kantian roots, insists that "Symbolism" in Pasternak's case by no means cancels out his closeness to the avant-garde, but stresses his "Expressionism" rather than Futurism: "By positing Pasternak's innermost bond with the Symbolists I do not mean to call into question his association, to be exact, the association of the

the early Pasternak with his "every metaphor" points to "the world's hidden mystery" presenting in this "a nearly literal echo of V. Ivanov's [. . .] theory of religious symbolism" (Stepun 1962, 48).

However distinct the diverse critical positions are, Jakobson's view remains a formidable reality to confront—a seminal analysis of a virtuoso theoretician that has profoundly affected the direction of Pasternak criticism, endowing it with much excitement, but also leaving it in a critical quandary. For there is a further problem to consider: the essential framework of Roman Jakobson's 1935 essay closely resembles Pasternak's own distinction between similarity and contiguity [ассоциативная связь по сходству или по смежности] in "The Wassermann Test" [Вассерманова реакция],[11] his fiery review of Vadim Shershenevich in 1914. Since this polemical essay was not reprinted in Soviet Russia during the author's lifetime, Pasternak critics and readers were unaware for decades of the intriguing interconnection between Pasternak's theoretical pronouncements and Jakobson's subsequent remarks. A direct line of influence from Pasternak to Jakobson and then to the subsequent criticism is noted by Livingstone, who echoes in this regard an emerging critical consensus: "[Pasternak's] distinction between, on the one hand, metaphor based on contiguity [. . .] and, on the other hand, metaphor based on similarity between things or ideas, has been taken up by Roman Jakobson and, after him, by a number of scholars, who find Pasternak's own verse characterized by metonymy" (*MG* 70). Pasternak himself, then, rather than Jakobson, becomes the principal source of the metaphor–metonymy paradigm, even though Pasternak never spoke of metonymy but of contiguity, while Jakobson equated the two notions.[12] Introducing Pasternak into the middle of

---

pre-1940 Pasternak [. . .] with the Futurist movement. [. . .] With this Mayakovsky, and with a number of his poetic contemporaries, Pasternak shared a quest and a discovery of new poetic modes that pointed beyond the Symbolist achievement. The most accurate label for these innovations is Expressionism, which at the beginning of the twentieth century became the dominant artistic style throughout Europe" (Stepun 1962, 49–51). See also Hasty's noting of "Pasternak's metaphoric explosions" and "picture-taking" (2006, 116–32), as well as Björling's view of the metaphoric early Pasternak (2006, 285–303).

11. As to the title of the essay, see Barnes (1998, 111): "The Wassermann Test" (with its title borrowed from a medical test for the presence of the antibodies against syphilis) was a vitriolic attack on the recent convert to Futurism, the former symbolist poet Vadim Shershenevich.

12. Though Hughes explains that Pasternak's support of "contiguity" in "The Wassermann Test" (1914) becomes in Jakobson's essay of 1935 (see Jakobson 1969) Pasternak's "predilection to metonymy," she avoids discussing the character of the actual historical connection between the two works: "[Pasternak,] without naming it, describes metonymy and explains his predilection for metonymic expression" (Hughes 1974, 70). Barnes, however, is more openly critical of this common theoretical stance: "the 1935 Jakobson's 'Marginal Notes on the Prose of the Poet Boris Pasternak' drew some of their ideas (without acknowledgement) from Pasternak's own article-review 'The Wassermann Test' (1914)" (Barnes 1998, 111).

the debate significantly restructures its focus: it implies a direct interrelation between Pasternak's theoretical thought and his artistic style, thus offering possibilities for analysis altogether missing when one approaches Pasternak's prose through the prism of Jakobson's judgment. Fleishman, in responding to some of these potential theoretical directions, characterizes Pasternak's "metonymic" worldview as evidence of a phenomenological stance and Husserl's influence (Fleishman 1977, 19–21) and then adds Ernst Cassirer as another probable source (*Lehrjahre* 132).[13] In so doing Fleishman acknowledges, however, a certain insoluble residue—the lack of clear philosophical precursors that could shed light on Pasternak's distinction between contiguity and similarity, and consequently elucidate the theoretical context of the writer's work with imagery (*Lehrjahre* 132–33).

In taking up the implicit challenge of this impasse in this chapter, I will argue that Pasternak's emphasis on the importance of "association by contiguity" [ассоциативная связь по смежности] in "The Wassermann Test" is based on a much broader philosophical context than most scholars suspect, a context altogether alien to Jakobson's work. To clarify Pasternak's thoughts regarding the similarity–contiguity opposition (see 2.1) is to uncover, first of all, major parallels between Pasternak's terminology and David Hume's famous classification of observations and ideas along the principles of similarity, contiguity in time and space, and causality (2.2). Hume's classification, as well as his belief that all impressions and ideas are derived from perception and are *posterior* to it, is a strictly philosophical position. Nowhere does Hume apply this opposition to poetics, while Pasternak, in his move from philosophy to poetry, readjusts his own philosophical training to a new field. Pasternak's characteristic insistence on the centrality of perception in poetic work was, therefore, reinforced (if not suggested in the first place) by Hume's philosophical analysis, even though Pasternak's attitude to Hume was also sifted through Immanuel Kant's equally famous objection to Hume—the *locus classicus* of the meeting ground between materialism and idealism in modern philosophy (2.3). "The *apriorist* of lyricism" was the characterization Pasternak chose for the Futurist poet in his essay "The Black Goblet," written roughly at the same time as "The Wassermann Test."[14] This definition points

---

13. Cf. Fleishman *Lehrjahre* 132–33: "The opposition of metaphor as similarity to metaphor as contiguity ('with its compulsory force and spiritual drama') in "The Wassermann Test" (1914) may be a far echo of the critique of the theory of abstraction of [. . .] Ernst Cassirer."

14. Pasternak's involvement in Futurism was particularly acute in 1913–15, but he published his polemical pamphlets in 1914 in the first and second editions of *Tsentrifuga*, the publication of the innovatory Futurist circle, in opposition to Mayakovsky. Cf. Livingstone: "'The Black Goblet' was Pasternak's second published article. It was preceded by one published in 1914 as 'The Wassermann Reaction'" (*MG* 69).

to Kant, who argued in opposition to Hume that not all ideas were *a poste-riori,* that is, derived from observation and experience; some were *a priori* and preceded experience.

As I will argue in this chapter, such terminological resonances were not accidental. In elucidating the implicit philosophical context and its role in Pasternak's youthful attempt at poetics, I will show that Pasternak argues for the principal role of contiguities not in order to privilege them over metaphors, but to pursue another goal altogether. In bringing together such opposed philosophical positions as Humean skepticism and the idealism of Kant (and, by extension, that of Plato), Pasternak aimed to emphasize poetry's reliance on perception and yet to preserve its link to *a priori* intuitions—an impossible task, in his view, without preserving the importance of contiguities in poetic art. This theoretical context was formulated in Pasternak's polemical essays of 1913–14 in a style that translated his philosophical training into a literary polemical discourse; on too many occasions Pasternak was stating philosophical ideas as seemingly commonplace, if idiosyncratic, assertions, and this manner of writing stymied most of his critics. It inspired, however, Roman Jakobson's famous argument of the metonymy–metaphor opposition (2.4), even though for Jakobson the implied conflict between Hume and Kant was hardly essential. All of this suggests, then, that the clarification of the difference between Pasternak's "contiguity" and Jakobson's "metonymy" constitutes an indispensable step if one is to clarify a long-lost theoretical background for Pasternak's early prose.

2.1 Pasternak's "justification through metaphor"

"The Wassermann Test," on the surface, is a vitriolic attack on Vadim Shershenevich for disregarding the "associations by contiguity" ("metonymic" or contiguous series in Jakobson's rendition) and relying instead on metaphors dictated by society's marketplace. In this polemical essay, Pasternak's writing is dynamic, highly aggressive, but opaque.[15] Only in the essay's concluding paragraphs does Pasternak unambiguously establish an opposition between contiguity and similarity (or, as he also terms it, the opposition between "proximity" and metaphor), which can be summarized as follows:

---

15. See Barnes: "His polemical article 'The Wassermann Test' (*Vassermanova reaktsiya*) was a typically oblique Pasternakian response to a commission from Bobrov which at the same time pursued issues bound up with his own creativity. The set task, in this case, was to destroy Shershenevich's credibility as a poet" (1989, 166).

a) association through contiguity or proximity [ассоциативная связь по смежности] is the essential work of the poet, for it creates the *necessary* intensity for further transformative work;

b) this work is "justified" metaphorically only when metaphors emerge out of the fermenting intensity of the poetic process, generated by the dynamism of contiguities [только явлениям смежности и присуща та черта принудительности и душевного драматизма, которая может быть оправдана метафорически] (*PSS* 5:11);

c) only consumers believe that metaphors and symbols constitute the essential poetic work, and Shershenevich has accepted this view;

d) metaphors, when not necessitated by contiguities, are products of the marketplace;

e) contiguities, the fruits of poetic observation, call forth the need for metaphors, and without that practice there is no genuine poetic work.

Although Pasternak's style may seem tortuous, his suspicion of market-place metaphors is significantly ahead of his time, for "The Wassermann Test" is one of the first theoretical works that resists the power of metaphoric relationships by emphasizing that they (when unaccompanied by contiguities) expand and reflect the extraneous codes of social conditioning and economic relations:

> Figurative imagery—this is what emerges in the understanding of the consumer as a principle of poetry. [. . .]
>
> However, even the construction of Shershenevich's metaphor is such that it is called forth not by the inner need of the poet, but dictated rather by the conditions of external usage. [. . .]
>
> The fact of similarity, more rarely—the associative link according to similarity—and never the fact of proximity—this is the origin of Shershenevich's metaphors. In the meantime the sense of necessity and inner dramatism is a characteristic of proximity, which can [then] be justified metaphorically. An independent need for association through similarity is simply unthinkable. However, such and only such association can be necessitated from within.

> Фигуральная образность, вот что связывалось всегда в представлении обывателя с понятием поэзии. [. . .]
>
> Однако и строй метафоры Шершеневича таков, что не кажется она вызванною внутренней потребностью в ней поэта, но внушенную условиями внешнего потребления. [. . .]

Факт сходства, реже ассоциативная связь по сходству и никогда не по смежности—вот происхождение метафор Шершеневича. Между тем только явлениям смежности и присуща та черта принудительности и душевного драматизма, которая может быть оправдана метафорически. Самостоятельная потребность в сближении по сходству просто немыслима. Зато такое и только такое сближение может быть затребовано извне. (*PSS* 5:10–11)

Such an approach to metaphor, novel in 1914, has become since the 1980s a mainstay of literary analysis.[16] By contrast with the contemporary (or post-structuralist) position, however, Pasternak does not resist metaphor as such; rather he points to a poetic process within which metaphors can be renewed or "justified" as part of the poet's contemplative attention to locality, to its proximate, immediate (or contiguous) phenomena.

The conclusion that metaphor must be necessitated from "within" by the expanding "associations through contiguity" (that reflects the phenomena grasped by the poet's perception) is carefully prepared throughout the essay. Shershenevich's metaphors are indicative, Pasternak claims, of the poet of marketable ideas, not of the poet-nurturer or poet-developer; the world Shershenevich represents lacks "the intimacy of the individually fostered device" developed in "the lyrical space of the initial conception" [лирик[и] замысла согретого интимностью лично взлиеянного приема] (*PSS* 5:6). Shershenevich's metaphors, therefore, point to the external fashion only, with poetry as a bi-product that reinforces the prevailing tastes of consumers: "the keys to Shershenevich's locks are found among the amateurs of the crowd" [ключи от Шершеневических затворов—в руках любителей из толпы] (*PSS* 5:11). The sharpness of the polemical attack must be understood as part of a much wider picture: the problem is not even that Shershenevich's metaphors, "packaged from without," lack justification from "within." Rather, contiguity and similarity in poetry should not be independent—or opposed—associative principles. The intimate work of the poet's perception, expressed through the language of contiguities, is *a pre-condition* to the discovery of the "inner hermitage," the poet's capacity for integrative contemplation, assisted by emerging metaphors. If contiguity's role is the training ground for seeing the proximate, metaphor is a lock to the deepest chambers of contemplative space where various elements of vision and experience are to be integrated and transformed.

---

16. See Jacques Derrida's proclamation: "a metaphor would be forbidden. The presence/ absence of the trace [. . .] carries in itself the problem and the spirit" (1976, 71).

This process of integration is of the highest value; all else is merely preparation for it, even though the integration cannot be achieved without all the preliminary steps:

> The lyrical agent, call it whatever you want, is, first of all, the vehicle of integration. The elements which are submitted for integration, or rather, which receive their life through it, are altogether insignificant in comparison with the integrating process itself.
>
> [. . .] One wants to compare metaphor with that ornamental lock, the key to which is kept by the poet, and, in the worse cases, with the lock through whose keyhole[17] one can look at the female hermit hidden in the stanza.
>
> Лирический деятель, называйте его, как хотите,—начало интегрирующее прежде всего. Элементы, которые подвергаются такой интеграции или, лучше, от нее только получают свою жизнь, глубоко в сравнении с нею несущественны.
>
> [. . .] [М]етафору хочется сравнить с тем узорчатым замком, ключ от коего хранит один лишь поэт, да и то—в худших случаях с замком, сквозь скважину которого разве только подсмотришь за таящейся в stanz'е затворницей]. (*PSS* 5:9–10)

The "female hermit" [затворница] of the passage gives readers pause or at least a jolt. In Pasternak's later writing the "female hermit" will be habitually connected to the presence of the immeasurable or infinite. The female hermit is either soul (as, for example, in his poem "Soul" [Душа] of 1915, where, not unlike Princess Tarakanova, the soul is "a prisoner of years" [пленница лет] [*PSS* 1:84]), or is indicative of the presence of the Muses (as in *Luvers* [затворница в песне]),[18] or of the future, still brewing and undisclosed.[19] In

---

17. Kling's (2002) argument that Pasternak is aware of Bryusov's "keys of the mysteries" is highly apt in this context: "Let us also remember a gesture towards the 'theurgists'—the essay 'The Keys of Mysteries' in *Vesy* (1904 [1]): Pasternak tries out on himself the theurgistic necklace 'of pure creativity, purified from all extra elements' art, on the basis of life" (2002, 33).

18. When Zhenya Luvers sees the three still women in black, prior to her meeting Tsvetkov, she muses: "They showed up black, like the word 'anchorite' in the song" [Они чернелись, как слово "затворница" в песне] (*CSP* 151; *PSS* 3:54). The reference to the "female hermit" here is mysterious and ambiguous. Among the multiple meanings, the reference to the hermit may also signify the "black" mistress-soul of Solomon's "Song of Songs."

19. See in *Doctor Zhivago* a sinister apprehension of the future, presented through a female hermit [затворница], the unstable mother of Evgraf: "The princess is a recluse. She lives—God knows on what—in her house just outside Omsk, and she never goes out. [. . .] And recently I've had the feeling that the house is staring at me nastily, through all its five windows, across the thousands of miles between Siberia and Moscow, and that sooner or later it will give me the

"The Wassermann Test," however, the female hermit appears without explication, disturbing and seemingly out of place. Thus, no matter what oblique connotations the image may signify in his later writing,[20] its role in 1914 is to point to the mystery that contrasts with the quickly churning images of the marketplace.

In other words, for all its polemical avant-garde bravado, "The Wassermann Test," from its first paragraph, is directed against modernity if modernity means the repackaging and reassembling of images by means of a conveyor belt and eradicating those signposts of "grey antiquity"—the signifiers of the sacred—that are still preserved in the language of the past:

In our century . . . of democratization and technology such principles as vocation and personal gift are viewed as superstitions. "Laisser faire, laisser passer" has entered in the area of artistic enterprise. [. . .] To grey antiquity one attributes such expressions, quite meaningless nowadays, as talent, feu sacré, etc. [. . .]

As always, the sign is given by the market. The reader no longer requires relationships with the thinker *Dei gratia,* just as he is no longer troubled by the question of whether the design of his textiles is woven by a Lancaster craftsman or executed by machine.

В наш век . . . демократизма и техники понятия призвания и личного дара становятся вредными предрассудками. "Laisser faire, laisser passer" проникает и в область художественного производства. [. . .] К седой этой старине нужно отнести и такие смысла лишившиеся выражения, как талант, feu sacré, и т.п. [. . .]

Как и всегда, знак был подан с рынка. У читателя нет потребности в сношениях с деятелем Dei gratia, как не занимает его вопрос о том задуман ли узор его сукна ланкастерским сукноделом или безымянно подкинут машиною. (*PSS* 5:6)

---

evil eye" [Княгиня—затворница. Она безвыездно живет с сыном в своем особняке на окраине Омска на неизвестные средства. [. . .] И вот все последнее время у меня такое чувство, будто своими пятью окнами этот дом недобрым взглядом смотрит на меня через тысячи верст, отделяющие Европейскую Россию от Сибири, и рано или поздно меня сглазит] (*PSS* 4:71).

20. As late as 1957, in the poem "After the Break" [После перерыва], the image of a hermit [затворник] is still directly linked to writing: "I estimated in my mind / That I will close off as if a hermit" [Прикинул тотчас я в уме. / Что я укроюсь, как затворник] (*PSS* 2:176). In "Behind the turn" [За поворотом] (*PSS* 2:187), the mysterious singing bird does not permit anyone to come to her threshold [и не пускает на порог / Кого не надо] as she guards the unknown certain future).

These transcendental significations, introduced at the beginning of the polemic seemingly *à propos* (thrown in as habitual expressions in French and Latin—*feu sacré,* etc., and *Dei gratia),* make their way into the text almost unobserved, protected by the apparent bluster of a debonair poet. Nonetheless, these terms, together with the mysterious "female hermit" behind the metaphoric lock, establish implicit contiguities and deepen their significance; the work of contemplative perception of the proximate refuses to banish *noumena* or a sense of *a priori* intuitions, all equally endangered by the new fashion, common in equal measure to politics, art, and the marketplace. What is being attacked, then, is not merely Shershenevich, but rather the emergence of a new social order and its outright dismissal of the hidden or sacred from the poet's vocation—a version of Futurism that Pasternak vehemently rejected from his first steps as a poet.[21]

2.2 The "unparalleled analytical clarity of Hume"[22]

The philosophical antecedents of this extraordinary argument are actually at the very center of Pasternak's philosophical studies: they emerge from his knowledge of David Hume's "association of ideas." Hume's insistence that impressions have a vibrancy of vitality, lost when they are transformed into ideas, was accepted enthusiastically in Pasternak's student notes and his letters, and yet this acceptance came with an important proviso. Pasternak's rendition of Hume was placed alongside his understanding of Plato, Kant, and Post-Kantian philosophy. Even though Pasternak's long essay on Hume has survived only in part, "The Wassermann Test" remains an important document reflecting the development of Pasternak's philosophical thought. Pasternak's terminology—for instance, his introduction of the distinction between similarity and contiguity—is a clear debt to the laws of David Hume's famous "fork" in *An Enquiry Concerning Human Understanding,* and particularly to Hume's division of subjective experience, drawn from perception, into impressions and ideas, with the latter organized by the laws of (1) resemblance or

---

21. Fleishman traces this position of 1914 all the way to a highly dangerous confrontation with Left Futurism, and the principle of "social demand" to the arts [социальный заказ] in the middle of 1920s. Thus, Pasternak's support of Vyacheslav Polonsky (expelled from *Novy Mir* in 1931 and exiled in 1932 to Magnitogorsk, en route to which he died from typhus) must be read in the context of his opposition to the market-place generated metaphors in "The Wassermann Test." See Fleishman (1980, 72ff).

22. Cf. "Аналитическая зоркость Юма не знает ничего равного себе" (*Lehrjahre* I:222).

similarity, (2) contiguity in time and space, and (3) causality (which is essentially for Hume contiguity through time):[23]

> To me, there appear to be only three principles of connexion among ideas, namely, *resemblance, contiguity in time or place, and cause and effect.* [. . .] A picture naturally leads our thoughts to the original [resemblance]: The mention of one apartment in a building naturally introduces an enquiry or discourse concerning the others [contiguity]: And if we think of a wound, we can scarcely forbear reflecting on the pain which follows it [cause and effect]. (*1.3.* ¶ 3–4; 2007, 20)

In his notes on Hume that preceded his studies in Marburg, Pasternak carefully diagrams this "fork" and supplements the diagram (noted in English) with a meditation on the causal progression from impressions to simple and complex ideas:

Ideas exist in a causal relationship from impressions; the first appearance of each idea necessarily appears as an impression; impressions are simple and complex; [. . .] simple ideas are correlated with simple impressions; complex ideas do not correlate in this manner.

Ideas в причинной зависимости (?) от impressions; первое появление каждой idea обязательно impression; простые и сложные, прост<ые> вызываются, простые ideas соответствуют прост<ым> impressions, сложные не соответствуют. (*Lehrjahre* I:209)

Thus, just as in Hume's philosophy where the power of impressions acquired through perception remains the foundation of ideas, whether the latter are analytical or imaginative, Pasternak in "The Wassermann Test" makes the world of the proximate, grasped by perception, a precondition for metaphoric processes.

---

23. See Traiger's exposition of the relationship between causality and contiguities in space and time: "It is unclear how something that has not existed for many years can suddenly cause the occurrence of the state of mind here and now; indeed, Hume himself says that a causal relationship between two things requires their temporal and spatial contiguity. . . . Even if we waive the requirement of spatial contiguity for causal relations between perceptions, we are left with the unmet requirement for contiguity in time" (2006, 49).

Indeed, in his 1910 philosophical notes, Pasternak carefully details how ideas are derived from perception through impressions, and he observes that the imagination, working from perception and expanding beyond "simple impressions," operates through the relationships of similarity and temporal and spatial conjunctions or links (in other words, contiguities):

> Fantasy (or imagination) aims to develop combinations (ideas) out of simple perceptions which do not correspond to impressions, according to a particular principle. These principles are as follows: *the relationship of similarity, temporal, spatial, and causal series.* In this, memory and imagination coincide: *both activities link simple impressions according to the same three principles.*

> Фантазия (воображ[ение]) стремится из простых perceptions образовать комбинации ideas, не соответствует impressions, по определенному принципу. Эти принципы: *отношения сходства, времен[н]ой, пространственной и причинной связи. В этом совпадают воображение и память; обе деятельности связывают простые восприятия по тем же трем принципам.* (*Lehrjahre* I:209; emphasis added)

Thus, when Pasternak in "The Wassermann Test" lays out the laws of similarity and contiguity, he has not forgotten the relationships described in his diaries as "temporal, spatial and causal series" [отношения сходства, времен-[н]ой, пространственной и причинной связи] (*Lehrjahre* I:209). Nor is he unaware of Hume's unambiguous insistence that every idea and every fantasy derives its power from perception: "Let us chase our imaginations to the heavens, or to the utmost limits of the universe; we never really advance a step beyond ourselves, nor can conceive any kind of existence, but those perceptions, which have appeared in that narrow compass" (*A Treatise of Human Nature*, 1.1.6; 2000, 49). And when Pasternak in July 1914 writes in his letters to his parents that the gift of the poet[24] is predominantly that of "sight" and not of "thinking," it is impossible to ignore his student years dedicated to Hume:

> It seems to me that the artistic gift consists in the following: in a fateful, instinctive, and unintentional manner, one must see as others think, and, vice versa, think as others perceive.

---

24. As Susanna Witt points out, "The emphasis on *seeing* in connection with creating has been observed by many scholars" (2000a, 32), as she proceeds to argue that Yuri Zhivago "writes poetry as an artist paints etudes" (2000a, 34).

Мне кажется, художественное дарование заключается вот в чем: надо роковым, инстинктивным и непроизвольным образом видеть так, как все прочие думают, и наоборот, думать так, как прочие видят. (*PSS* 7:185)

It is probable, then, that Pasternak aims, above all, to preserve the vitality of all available pathways from perceptions to impressions and ideas and that his insistence on the importance of contiguities [отношения пространственной связи] in "The Wassermann Test" must be read in this context.

The notes of *Lehrjahre* cannot be viewed, of course, as a precise indicator of Pasternak's thoughts in 1914, but the philosophical diary reflects, nonetheless, the direction of his philosophical interests as he studied Hume. The evidence of *Lehrjahre,* together with "The Wassermann Test," suggests, for instance, that Pasternak's early philosophical interests were still very much in play even after he broke with philosophy and that his emphasis on the need for the widest pathways from perception and impressions to poetic activity (with similarities never outweighing the power of contiguities) reflects Hume's insistence that all ideas, simple or complex, weaken the vitality of immediate impressions and lose that initial "force and liveliness with which they strike upon the mind" (*Treatise,* 1.1.1; 2000, 7).[25] Even Pasternak's passionate defense of contiguities in poetic work follows Hume, who observed that contiguous relationships between objects, when repeated, carry a sense of inexplicable mystery:

There is nothing in any objects to persuade us, that they are either always remote or always contiguous; and when from experience and observation we discover, that their relation in this particular is invariable, we always conclude that there is some secret cause, which unites or separates them. (*Treatise,* 1.3.2; 2000, 53)

Both in 1910 and 1914, then, Pasternak agrees with David Hume that the pathways from perception to imagination have to be all-inclusive if they are to preserve the vitality of impressions.

---

25. As Hume writes, the impressions are "all our more lively perception[s], when we hear, or see, or feel, or love, or hate, or desire, or will" (*Enquiry* 1.2. ¶ 3; 2007, 15), and ideas are fainter and weaker entering reality "when we reflect on a passion or an object which is not present" (*Treatise* 2.3.7; 2000, 275). It is in this context that Pasternak's development of Symbolism needs to be located; after Hume his path to imagination is through the vitality of impressions, not through symbols or ideas "purified from perception."

It is highly plausible, then (and here the missing, full text of the longer paper written in 1912 for Moscow University would have been most helpful), that in downgrading metaphor to a position dependent on contiguities, Pasternak imitates Hume's challenge to traditional understandings of philosophy. As Hume dismisses philosophers' habitual dedication to the primacy of ideas, a process that started with Plato, so Pasternak dismisses the centrality of metaphor, understood by "consumers" as the essence of poetry. Hume, indeed, reversed Plato's view that material reality is only a copy of "ideas";[26] he instructed philosophers that perception, not ideas, should be the subject of philosophical study: "I desire those philosophers, who pretend that we have an idea of the substance of our minds, to point out the impression that produces it, and tell distinctly after what manner that impression operates, and from what object it is derived" (*Treatise*, 1.4.5; 2000, 153). Thus, ideas as faint copies of experience are necessarily "posterior," being increasingly weaker resemblances of actual reality:

> An impression first strikes upon senses, and makes us perceive heat or cold, thirst or hunger, pleasure or pain of some kind or other. Of this impression there is a copy taken by the mind, which remains after the impression seizes, and this we call an idea. [. . .] These again are copy'd by the memory and imagination, which perhaps in their turn give rise to other impressions and ideas. So that the impressions of reflection are only antecedent to their corresponding ideas; but posterior to those of sensation, and derived from them. (*Treatise*, 1.1.2; 2000, 11)

Pasternak's indebtedness to Hume includes, therefore, a taste for a certain argumentative flamboyance, common to both thinkers. And if this flamboyance on Pasternak's part was relatively short-lived or his admiration for Hume limited, his acceptance of Hume's skepticism had much deeper roots.

In his university notes, Pasternak praises the "incomparable" analytical powers of Hume [Аналитическая зоркость Юма не знает ничего равного себе] (*Lehrjahre* I:222), but he also emphasizes Hume's "blind" dismissal[27] of what Descartes called "*connexion nécessaire*," the power of the

---

26. Cf. Plato, *Republic,* Book X, 596–601e (2005, 820–26).

27. See his characterization of Hume's "blindness" to ideas and to the formulas underlying the phenomena of nature: "The foundations of connections are minimized in status to that of the causes of combinations. He is blind in relation to the constitutive inseparability of the mathematical principles with the objects and objective facts of nature" [Основа коннексии мельчает до повода к комбинированию. Он слеп по отн<ошению> к конститутивной

ideas that arise in the mind, alike in precision and vitality to mathematical formulas, and armed with the vital power to define reality, rather than being defined by it:

> But the connection of ideas, called by Descartes "connexion nécessaire" lose in Hume their necessary nature, their inner productive mathematical verity. Although Hume cites the examples of geometric, algebraic and arithmetic relations, he does not see how these connections, independent from their immediate links to the processes of nature, are viewed all the more as constitutive of nature.

> Но и связи идей, названные Декартом "connexion nécessaire" лишаются у него необходимости, внутренней, продуктивно математической истинности. Хотя Юм и приводит как примеры отношения геометрии, алгебры и арифметики, но он не видит, как эти связи, безотносительные к бытию их образований в природе вещей, именно поэтому признаны конституировать эту природу. (*Lehrjahre* II:52)

While the emphasis on the primacy of seeing was to stay with Pasternak for the rest of his life, there is no parallel denigration of the power of ideas; instead he adds a complexity to his visual images that has no parallel in Hume. "The Wassermann Test" is indicative in this regard of the care, caution, and an admixture of cunning (hidden in the language of a Futurist debater) with which Pasternak states in 1914 his allegiance to the material proximity of phenomena grasped by perception, and yet also intimates the reality of transcendental imprints underlying the impressions of any artist who fights for the longevity of his *feu sacré*.[28] In this manner "The Wassermann Test" suggests a perilous complementarity between materiality and ideality, betraying its author's awareness of a Kantian and Post-Kantian critique of Hume's skepticism.

неразрывности математич<еских> понятий с вещами и фактами природы] (*Lehrjahre* II:52).

28. See the image of *feu sacré* in "The Letters from Tula," in Pasternak's imitation of Tolstoy: "A fashion has established itself in life, such that now there is no place left in the world where a man may warm his soul at the fire of shame; for the shame has everywhere gone damp and will not burn" [Завелся такой пошиб в жизни, отчего не стало на земле положений, где бы мог человек согреть душу огнем стыда; стыд подмок повсеместно и не горит] (*CSP* 121; *PSS* 3:28).

2.3 Perception, contiguity, and Immanuel Kant's *a priori* of time and space

For Hume, as for Locke and for empiricists generally, all thought starts in perception: "Nihil est in intellectu, quod antea fuerit in sensu" (*Lehrjahre* II:51).
For Kant, by contrast, *a priori* principles exist prior to the *a posteriori* aspects
of cognition derived through experience and impressions. As Kant famously
announces in the first pages of his *Critique of Pure Reason,* these *a priori* principles underlying perception strike one's consciousness with a force characterized by intrinsic necessity:

> But even though all our cognition starts with experience, that does not
> mean that all of it arises from experience. [. . .] Yet experience is far from
> being our understanding's only realm, and our understanding cannot be
> confined to it. Experience indeed tells us what it is, but not necessarily
> that it must be so and not otherwise. And that is precisely why experience
> gives us no true universality; and reason, which is eager for that [universal]
> kind of cognition, is more stimulated by experience than satisfied. Now
> such universal cognitions which are at the same time *recognized by intrinsic
> necessity,* must be independent of experience, clear and certain by them-
> selves. Hence they are called *a priori cognitions;* by contrast, what is bor-
> rowed solely from experience, is, as we put it, cognized only a posteriori, or
> empirically. (Kant A1; 1996, 43–44; emphasis added)

And according to Kant's most startling dictum, we would be unable to appre-
hend both time and space in specific instances without their *a priori* reality,
independent of our perception:

> Space is not an empirical concept that has been abstracted from outer
> experience. For the presentation of space must already lie at the basis in
> order for such sensations to be referred to something outside me. (Kant
> A23/B38; 1996, 27)

> Time is not an empirical concept that has been abstracted from any experi-
> ence. For simultaneity or succession would not even underlie our percep-
> tion if the presentation of time did not underlie them *a priori.* Only on the
> presupposition of this presentation can we present this and that as being
> at one and the same time (simultaneously) or in different times (sequen-
> tially). (A30/B46; 1996, 32)

As his student diaries indicate, Pasternak's philosophical training was focused to a great extent upon the synthetic character of perception which blends *a posteriori* and *a priori* phenomena. In notes taken prior to Marburg, he jots down the following characterization of Kant's time and space (this passage is only a brief example of many similar notes):

> Space and time are guided by immanent laws, which belong to the very essence of contemplative activity. Space and time are constitutive principles of every separate act of apprehension. When we free them, in abstraction, from all their sensible content, we only raise to consciousness those laws which operate in the genesis of every apprehension.

> Пространство и время имеют имманентную, свойственную самой сущности созерцательной деятельности закономерность. Пространство и время—конститутивные принципы каждого отдельного восприятия. Когда мы освобождаем их, в абстракции, от всего чувственного содержания, мы только приводим в сознание ту закономерность, которая действительна в гинезисе каждого восприятия. (*Lehrjahre* II:12)

This conception, of course, was central to instruction in the Marburg school; Hermann Cohen's exposition and critique of Kantian synthetic knowledge dealt directly with *a posteriori* and *a priori* aspects of cognition unifying in the act of apperception within a transcendental subject.

In order to honor Hermann Cohen's work on synthetic judgment, Pasternak's *Safe Conduct* presents Cohen's teaching in the following manner: prior to unfolding his own findings and demanding from students a definition of Kantian apperception (*CSP* 56; *PSS* 3:188), the great Marburg philosopher dramatizes for his students the full intensity of the battle between pre-Kantian metaphysics and Humean skepticism,[29] himself siding with Hume:

> Already I knew how on some other occasion, stealthily creeping up on the Pre-Kantian metaphysics, he would croon away, pretending to woo it, then suddenly utter a raucous bark and give it a terrible scolding with

---

29. Pasternak invariably emphasizes the dramatic gift of Hermann Cohen, in a hidden echo, perhaps, of Cohen's own view from 1906 (several years after *Kants Begründung der Ästhetik*) that drama manifests the new spirit of the age: "the peculiarity of drama is the realization of action not only by the author on the stage, but in a 'dialogue' between actor and spectator, in a spiritual exchange between the two" (Poma 2006, 91).

quotations from Hume. How, after a fit of coughing and a lengthy pause, he would then drawl forth, exhausted and peaceable, "And now, gentlemen . . . ," which meant that he had finished telling the century off, the performance was over, and it was possible to move on to the subject of the course. (*CSP* 44)

Уже я знал, как в другом каком-нибудь случае, вкрадчиво подъехав к докантовой метафизике, разворкуется он, ферлякурничая с ней, да вдруг как гаркнет, закатив ей страшный нагоняй с цитатами из Юма. Как, раскашлявшись и выдержав долгую паузу, протянет он затем утомленно и миролюбиво: "Und nun, meine Herrn. . . . " И это будет значить, что выговор веку сделан, представленье кончилось и можно перейти к предмету курса. (*PSS* 3:173)

The whole experience of Marburg in *Safe Conduct* is presented, in fact, as an experiment in synthesizing temporal and spatial sequences, open to the immediate perception, but suggesting a deeper "transcendental" and immeasurable signification. Even the town itself is depicted as resting in its depth upon the "lowland" [низина], first discovered by Saint Elizabeth on her legendary nightly walks. On these trips, the eccentric saint directed her steps toward Marburg's "unreachable" foundations and in the process established the spatial height and depth of the city's life. As she organized the space, the town began to operate, and has operated ever since, by means of the synthetic blending of chronological and non-chronological time, hidden in the town's lowest depth:

Since that time the town, establishing itself along the path of her nightly excursions, had set firm on the height in the form it had taken by the middle of the sixteenth century. But the lowland that had harassed her spiritual peace, the lowland making her break the orders of her superior, the lowland set astir by miracles as before walked fully in step with the times. (*CSP* 43)

С тех пор город, расположившийся по пути ее ночных вылазок, застыл на возвышеньи в том виде, какой принял к середине шестнадцатого столетья. Низина же, растравлявшая ее душевный покой, низина, заставлявшая ее нарушать устав, низина, по-прежнему приводимая в движенье чудесами, шагала в полную ногу с временем. (*PSS* 3:174)

In this manner Pasternak's depiction of Marburg enacts the philosophy practiced in its famous School. The atemporal layers of human perception enter not merely the town's locality; they transfix the minds of the students drawn to Hermann Cohen and his instruction.

Pasternak's notes on Hermann Cohen's *Kants Theorie der Erfahrung* indicate further work on atemporal signification. The roots of Kantian transcendentalism for Cohen, Pasternak observes, are not phenomenological; they are Platonic. In Cohen's world,[30] the Kantian *a priori* principles are synthesized through the centuries and become interconnected with the Platonic world of ideas (*Republic,* Book VII, 524–25), which are as independent of subjective impressions as the laws of mathematics and geography:

> The beginning of the history of epistemology is found in Plato's differentiation within apprehension between the processes which do not call for scientific study and those which require the contemplation of numbers and geometrical designs. The latter—"awakening"—of the mind; these turn the mind away from the sensual and direct it towards the contemplation of essence. Such an apprehension is "drawing to substance and calling up thought." [. . .] The systematization of this philosophy unites Plato and Kant.

> Начало истории критики познания лежит в Платоновском различии восприятия, которое не призывает научного рассмотрения, от такого восприятия, которое дает повод к мышлению чисел и созерцанию геометрических тел. Это— ἐγερτικὰ—разума, они отвращают от чувственного, направляя на созерцание сущего ([. . .]καὶ μεταστρεπτικῶν ἐπὶ τὴν τοῦ ὄντος θέαν) . . . Такое восприятие есть ὁλκὸν ἐπὶ τὴν οὐσίαν ἢ παρακλητικὰ τῆς διανοίας [. . .] Систематичность этой философии роднит Платона с Кантом. (*Lehrjahre* II:41)

An awareness of the *a priori* existence of transcendental principles and their forceful energy—the "contemplation of essences," which are understood in Kant as the forms of inner and outer intuition of time and space[31]—consti-

---

30. See Poma's examination of the relationship between Platonic "teaching of ideas" and Cohen's ethics: "In Cohen's view, Plato had not provided a satisfactory answer to this problem, and perhaps, no such answer is possible, but positing the problem and the way in which it is posited have an important meaning for critical philosophy" (Poma 2006, 179–80).

31. In Kant's *Critique of Pure Reason,* time is a form of inner intuition, because unlike space, it "cannot determine the outer appearances": "it does not belong to any shape or position, etc., but rather determines the relation of presentations in our inner state" (A33/B49–50; 1996, 88).

tutes an essential feature of Pasternak's artistic vision, with its idealistic, even metaphysical overtones, invariably emphasized and just as invariably masked and skillfully subdued.[32]

In "The Wassermann Test," then, Shershenevich, a misguided convert to Futurism in the eyes of Pasternak, is criticized for employing only a small part of the arsenal of image processing necessary for poetic maturation. And yet in lamenting the absence of deeper layers in Shershenevich's poetry (or the lack of transformative potential in his "lyrical activity"), Pasternak remains subtextually linked to Kant's transcendental themes. These Kantian *a priori* principles of "inner" and "outer" intuition,[33] present as an implicit subtext in "The Wassermann Test," emerge more clearly in "The Black Goblet," an article published in the second issue of *Tsentrifuga*'s "Rukonog," just after "The Wassermann Test" (Barnes 1989, 166–68). In "The Black Goblet," the relationship between perception and contiguous series is unambiguous, although the philosophical terminology of contiguity—ассоциативная связь по смежности—is not employed. Nonetheless, the leading image of this article—"*coffres volants*" traveling between centuries—implies precisely this association of contiguity of time; the tightly packaged "goods" [добро] in the flying coffers are not objects; they are temporal sequences brought into an intense proximity to each other. The Futurists, then, by contrast with Vadim Shershenevich, are proclaimed as capable of condensing these "goods" into the tightest possible content and are praised for this ability as the "apriorists of lyricism":

> The art of impressionism—the art of cautious handling of time and space— the art of packaging; the moment of impressionism—the moment of packing for a trip; Futurism—for the first time, a startling example of packing in the shortest possible time. [. . .] Generally, the movements of different speeds, observed by us, present in themselves one of the multilayered articles of all the good(s) chosen for the parcel.
>
> [. . .] Permit then the impressionism in the heart of metaphor of

---

32. Pasternak's tendency simultaneously to evoke and to "camouflage" his most startling thoughts is best described by Pasternak himself, but it is usually applied to his later period when he admits to Gladkov that he dreams about "originality unobtrusive, concealed in a simple and familiar form" (Gladkov 1977, 33). However, as I will argue in this book, this tendency is operative in Pasternak's prose from his first sketches. Partially it can be explained by his simultaneous attraction both to Hume and to Kant, and by his conviction that *a priori* aspects must underlie *a posteriori* experiences, even in his own artistic texts.

33. For Kant the *a priori* of time was grasped by "inner intuition": "Time is nothing, but the form of inner sense, i.e. of the intuiting we do of ourselves and our inner state" (A33/B49–50; 1996, 88). Space on the other hand was grasped though "outer intuition": "*Space is merely* the *form of outer intuition* . . . but not an actual object that can be intuited externally" (B457 n. 126; 1996, 460; emphasis in original).

Futurism to become the impressionism of the eternal. The transformation of temporary into eternal by means of the limited moment—this is the truest meaning of the Futurist abbreviations.

[. . .] But only with the heart of lyricism there begins to beat the heart of the Futurist, this *apriorist* of lyricism.

[. . .] Искусство импрессионизма—искусство бережливого обхождения с пространством и временем—искусство укладки; момент импрессионизма—момент дорожных сборов, футуризм—впервые явный случай действительной укладки в кратчайший срок. [. . .] Вообще, движения всех скоростей, наблюдаемых нами, представляют собою одну из многоразличнейших статей всего предназначенного к этой укладке добра.

[. . .] Позвольте же импрессионизму в сердцевинной метафоре футуризма быть импрессионизмом вечного. Преобразование временного в вечное при посредстве лимитивного мгновения—вот истинный смысл футуристических аббревиатур.

[. . .] Но только с сердцем лирики начинает биться сердце футуриста, этого априориста лирики. (*PSS* 5:13–14)

In other words, Pasternak's "Black Goblet," intriguing and unclear as the essay may be, is saturated with direct evocations of the *a priori* realities of Futurism, which employs—or so Pasternak proclaims—"the veritable lyrical expression, this truly *a-priori* condition of subjectivism" [истинная лирика, это поистине априорное условие возможности субъективного] (*PSS* 5:14). This *a priori* content of Futurism, as the movement's very name implies, is an experiment first and foremost with time, perception, and impression: "the impressionists of the eternal" discover metaphors through "the transformation of temporary into eternal by means of the limited moment." Whatever this complex polemic suggests, it clearly suggests the integration of David Hume with that of Immanuel Kant from within the intense debates that were characteristic of the Russian cultural and poetic modernist scene.

2.4 Beyond "The Wassermann Test":
Contiguities and their characterization in Roman Jakobson's essays and Boris Pasternak's early prose

Jakobson's 1935 essay "Marginal Notes on the Prose of the Poet Boris Pasternak," written initially as an "Afterword" for the Czech translation of *Safe*

Conduct,[34] argues that in Pasternak's narrative, the "images of the surrounding world function as contiguous reflections or metonymical expressions of the poet's self" (1969, 141). As critics have observed, Pasternak himself never used the word "metonymy," but his concept of contiguity definitely corresponds to Jakobson's metonymic examples (Hughes 1974, 70). Or does it? Jakobson's metonymy is predominantly a spatial concept; it embraces environment, landscape, material objects, the natural world, and the human agent, all blending with the world that such an agent observes. In Vuletić's view, Jakobson's analysis of "the most frequent cases of metonymy in Pasternak's prose" isolates the following metonymic relations: (a) objects represented by other objects, (b) objects represented by their states, (c) human beings represented by objects, (d) human beings represented by actions, and (e) the whole represented by the part and vice versa (2004, 485). Apparently, then, neither Pasternak's experimentation with time nor his indebtedness to Kant's inner and outer *a priori* intuition—which complicates the Humean division of ideas and impressions into similarity, contiguity, and causality—resonates with Jakobson's terminology and approach. Does this omission minimize the effectiveness of Jakobson's analysis?

For Jakobson, Pasternak's hero lives in a single temporal layer, and both the animation of the surrounding world and the de-animation of the acting human subject unfold on the same temporal plane:

> Pasternak's lyricism, both in poetry and in prose, is imbued with metonymy; in other words, it is association by proximity that predominates. [...]
>
> It is the same with Pasternak's poems and, in particular, with his prose, where the anthropomorphism of the inanimate world emerges much more clearly: instead of a hero it is, as often as not, the surrounding objects that are thrown in turmoil; the immovable outlines of the roofs grow inquisitive, a door swings shut with a silent reproach, the joy of family reconciliation is expressed by a growing warmth, zeal and devotion on the part of lamps. (Jakobson 1969, 141)

As a result, Pasternak's poetic self, as well as his protagonists, become an inalienable part of the landscape that the self shapes, but in which it is also

---

34. As Christopher Barnes notes, Jakobson's 1935 essay was formulated in response to the "publication of a Czech translation of *Safe Conduct* by Svatava Pirkova-Jakobson together with an afterword by her husband Roman Jakobson" (1998, 111). Barnes's perception of Jakobson's debt to Pasternak is accompanied by surprise over the fact that Jakobson never acknowledged this debt or referred his readers to Pasternak's youthful work.

encompassed: "Show us your environment and I will tell you who you are. We learn what he lives on, this lyric character outlined by metonymies, split up by synecdoches into individual attributes, reactions, and situations" (Jakobson 1969, 147). The metonymous protagonists, then, tend to be observers, rather than active agents: "the favorite transitional formula of Pasternak's lyric prose is a railway journey during which his excited hero experiences a change of locality in various ways and in enforced idleness" (Jakobson 1969, 147). Such a rendition of Pasternak's predominant stylistic characteristics is focused and precise, and yet surprisingly limited, for there exists in Pasternak's prose an equally predominant pattern of relationships that contrasts with (and complicates) the world of spatial contiguities.[35]

Pasternak speaks of space and time as both measured and immeasurable, and he develops his images in such a way that the suggestion of potentially infinite interrelations pierces the tangible contiguities of the world grasped by perception. This aspect remains Pasternak's consistent signature, and it is noteworthy that as late as 1956, in returning to the earlier poetic sketches of 1912, he wants to explain to his readers that even while his attention was directed toward making a visual picture exist on the page with the power of real-life experience, he used not colors but print, not photographs but ideas:

> I did not express, reflect, represent, or depict anything at all. [. . .] Quite the contrary, the subject matter of my poem was my constant preoccupation, my constant dream was that my poem itself should have something in it, that it should have a new idea or a new picture, that it should be engraved with all its peculiarities in the book and should speak from its pages with all the colors of its black colorless print. (*Remember* 77–78)

> Я ничего не выражал, не отражал, не отображал, не изображал. [. . .] Совсем напротив, моя постоянная забота обращена была на содержание, моя постоянная мечта, чтобы само стихотворение нечто содержало, чтобы оно содержало новую мысль или новую картину. Чтобы всеми своими особенностями оно было вгравировано внутрь книги и говорило с ее страниц всем своим молчанием и

---

35. The very word "metonymy" is actually somewhat of a misnomer, for Jakobson absorbs synecdoche into this term. A further development of this "highly influential theory" has necessitated a clarification of terms. Elam notes, "The Structuralists, including Jakobson, consider the kind of substitution at work here, i.e. of a part for the whole, as a species of metonymy, whereas the classical rhetoricians termed it *synecdoche*. It is worth insisting on the difference, since in practice synecdochic replacement of part for whole is essential to every level of dramatic representation" (1980, 24–25).

всеми красными строками своей черной, бескрасочной печати. (*PSS* 3:326)

Insisting that the poem should intensify the senses open to perception "with all the colors of its black colorless print," Pasternak makes a subtle deviation from what Hume considered the most vital elements of impressions. The image impresses most, Pasternak suggests, when an immediate sensation grows in complexity to embrace not just the present, but also the past and the future in such a manner that the actual picture can expand beyond an observation limited within a particular time and space. In the same passage Pasternak describes his poem "Venice" as a way of exhibiting the expanding series not merely of objects, or of reflections and impressions—and of their "copies" in water—but of the ever-growing number of interconnections, overtaking in intensity the actual materiality of the city, expanding as numerous impressions "on the horizon" far beyond an immediate temporal and spatial locality:[36]

> For instance I wrote a poem "Venice" and a poem "The Railway Station." The city on the water stood before me, and the circles and figures of eight of its reflections widened and multiplied, swelling like a rusk in tea. Or, far away, at the end of the tracks and platforms, there arose before me, in all clouds and smoke, a railway farewell horizon, behind which the trains were hidden, and which contained the history of relationships, meetings, and partings, and the events before and after them. (*Remember* 78)

> Например, я писал стихотворение "Венеция" или стихотворение "Вокзал." Город на воде стоял передо мною, и круги восьмерки его отражений плыли и множились, разбухая, как сухарь в чаю. Или вдали, в конце путей и перронов, возвышался, весь в облаках и дымах, железнодорожный прощальный горизонт, за которым скры-

---

36. A somewhat similar image concludes the life of Yuri Zhivago, as Zhivago sits by the window of the tram and observes people passing him and each other in close proximity, but at different speeds, indicating their lives before and after this meeting, as well as a quasi-invisible theory of relativity underlying the speed of their entrances and exits: "He tried to imagine several people running parallel and close together but moving at different speeds, and he wondered in what circumstances some of them would overtake and survive others. Something like a theory of relativity governing the hippodrome of life occurred to him, but he became confused and gave up these analogies" [Он подумал о нескольких, развивающихся рядом существованиях, движущихся с разною скоростью одно возле другого, и о том, когда чья-нибудь судьба обгоняет в жизни судьбу другого, и кто кого переживает. Нечто вроде принципа относительности на житейском ристалище представилось ему, но окончательно запутавшись, он бросил и эти сближения] (*Zhivago* 490; *PSS* 4:487–88).

вались поезда и который заключал целую историю отношений, встречи и проводы и события до них и после них. (*PSS* 3:325)

While suggesting what Hume would view as the material vivacity of actual impressions,[37] Pasternak proceeds in a direction that opposes not only Hume's dismissal of the power of ideas, but also what Jakobson would draw as a metonymic picture of his world, for Pasternak carefully blends and synthesizes the immediate picture of the city and the suggestion of the infinite meetings and separations that have already been and will be taking place on its streets.

This blending of the measured and immeasurable, the tangible and elusive, occurs not only in 1912 or in the recollections of that period in 1956. It is possible, of course, that the account of an expanding consciousness in *The Childhood of Luvers* supports Jakobson's depiction of Pasternak's metonymies (Jakobson refers to that novella frequently), but the prose of *Safe Conduct* that caught Jakobson's attention in the first place is rich with passages[38] that challenge his idea that the fragments of the landscape and the human protagonist share and exchange similar characteristics. The very first figure in *Safe Conduct*, Rainer Maria Rilke,[39] takes the same train as other passengers and speaks

---

37. In the same passage (and after speaking of the intense power of the past and future that opens far beyond the horizon), Pasternak concludes the description on a precise and realistic note, as if he is unaware of the temporal and spatial expansion that has just been created on the page: "There was nothing I demanded from myself, from my readers, or from the theory of art. All I wanted was that one poem should contain the city of Venice and the other the Brest (now the Belorussko-Baltiysky) railway station" [Мне ничего не надо было от себя, от читателей, от теории искусства. Мне нужно было, чтобы одно стихотворение содержало город Венецию, а в другом заключался Брестский, ныне Белорусско-Балтийский вокзал] (*PSS* 4:325–26). The structure of the poem "Vokzal" [Вокзал], remembered in this passage, echoes this development of immediate impressions and occurrences pointing to a wider, possibly immeasurable context. See the examination of several versions of this poem in Gasparov and Polivanov (2005, 68–73).

38. In Jakobson's rendition, the arbitrary replacement of one part for the other in the description of artistic inspiration (*Safe Conduct*, *CSP* 31; *PSS* 3:160) points to a metonymic mind at work: "To define our problem: the absolute commitment of the poet to metonymy is known [. . .] . He is replaced by a chain of concretized situations and surrounding objects. [. . .] One and a half decades later, in his book of reminiscences *Safe Conduct*, Pasternak mentions that he is intentionally characterizing his life at random, that he could increase the number of significant features or replace them by others [. . .]" (1969, 146–47). In Vuletić's view, "In limiting himself to noticing the very few types of metonymy indisputably used in Pasternak's prose and poetry, Jakobson himself never slipped into a problematic detailed analysis of figurative speech in Pasternak" (2004, 488).

39. Pasternak not only dedicates *Safe Conduct* to Rilke, but he intimates throughout these memoirs that he is only too aware of Rilke's style and vision and that he can strike Rilkean notes throughout his narrative. Pasternak, in fact, invariably approaches Rilke as a figure who can be materially accessible (or contiguous) only by an impossible or improbable chance. Pasternak's earliest mention of Rilke in his letters to his family initiates this theme. On May 17, 1912,

the language of a powerful European nation, but he appears to be an inhabitant of an unknown world, contiguous with no mortal creature:[40]

> The unknown man spoke only German. Although I knew the language perfectly, I had never heard it spoken as he spoke it. For this reason, there on the crowded platform, between two jangles of the bell, the foreign man seemed to be a silhouette among bodies, a fiction in the midst of the unfictitious. (*CSP* 21)

> [Н]езнакомец же говорит только по-немецки. Хотя я знаю этот язык в совершенстве, но таким его никогда не слыхал. Поэтому тут, на людном перроне между двух звонков, этот иностранец кажется мне силуэтом среди тел, вымыслом в гуще невымышленности. (*PSS* 3:148)

A similar pattern is evident in Pasternak's description of Hermann Cohen, a

---

Pasternak writes to his sister Josephine from Marburg that he himself is interested in objects that are not part of everyday life, the ones that have been lost or misplaced and that can be recovered only by imagination. In this context he refers directly to Rilke, for whom this world of lost objects—truth in the space recoverable only by imagination—is akin to the ground of God: "I would like to tell you to check carefully the features of your past and of your fantasies; to tell the truth of them is difficult, awfully difficult. [. . .] These are lost and, in essence, the only real things. They are owned not by a pocket, but by someone real, anxiously checking the shelves, asking the servants and calling his acquaintances. And around that which is picked up by imagination there rushes about someone's life looking for what it lost. Rainer Maria Rilke calls this God" [Мне хочется еще раз сказать тебе это: вглядывайся в свое прошлое и в свои фантазии; правду о них трудно, страшно трудно сказать. [. . .] Эти утерянные, и только они, *суть* настоящие вещи. Ими владеет не карман, а кто-то живой, мечущийся по шкафам, расспрашивающий прислугу и телефонирующий знакомым. И вот вокруг того, что подбирает воображенье, мечется чья-то потерявшая все это жизнь. Райнер Мария Рильке называет это Богом] (*PSS* 7:94–95). In 1931 in the "Afterword" to *Safe Conduct,* Pasternak describes how the realization that Rilke could actually read Pasternak's work made him feel as if he is read in Heaven. See E. B. Pasternak (1997, 389–90). Pasternak's letter to Rilke on April 12, 1926, echoes this amazement at Rilke's actually reading him, as Pasternak compares this to being read by Pushkin or even Aeschylus, that is, the poets no longer found among the living (*PSS* 7:648). See also Ciepiela's account of the Pasternak-Tsvetaeva-Rilke correspondence (2006, 178ff).

40. Pasternak's debt to Rilke himself is unmistakable in this regard and was meant to be grasped by his readers. Echoing what most critics call Malte's "Brahe heritage," Pasternak recreates, although very much in his own way, the atmosphere of the atemporal contiguous series, echoing Rilke's world of existence that knows no temporal borders. For example, Malte's grandfather, Count Brahe, lives according to his own temporal measurement: "The passing of time had absolutely no meaning for him; death was a minor incident which he completely ignored; people whom he had once installed in his memory continued to exist, and the fact that they had died did not alter that in the least. [. . .] with the same obstinacy, he experienced future events as present" (Rilke *Notebooks* 31). See also see Schäfer (1997, 193–208).

philosopher whose mind is firmly situated in a world that contrasts and even conflicts with the immediate everyday temporality of Marburg in 1912:[41]

> In his roomy frock coat and his soft hat, this university professor was filled to a certain degree with the valuable essence that in the olden times had been bottled in the heads of Galileos, Newtons, Leibnizes, and Pascals. (*CSP* 59)

> Этот университетский профессор в широком сюртуке и мягкой шляпе был в известном градусе налит драгоценною эссенцией, укупоривавшейся в старину по головам Галилеев, Ньютонов, Лейбницев и Паскалей. (*PSS* 3:191–92)

On the other hand, the personal tragedy of Vladimir Mayakovsky is presented as that of a man who is unnerved by his own ability to reach, with "medieval boldness" [со средневековой смелостью], the most ancient layers of lyricism and to speak in "the language of sectarian identifications" [языком почти сектантских отождествлений][42] (*CSP* 84; *PSS* 3:223). Frightened by the isolation inherent in the inborn gift of the visionary whose sight uncovers the temporal layers inaccessible to his contemporaries, Mayakovsky chooses, quite willfully in Pasternak's view, the adjacent neighborhood of the immediate "local" modernity and its "dwarf-like" inhabitants:

> [T]his poet took up just as hugely and broadly another, more local tradition.
> Beneath him he saw the city that had gradually risen up to him from the depths of *The Bronze Horseman*, *Crime and Punishment*, and *Petersburg*, a city in a haze [. . .]. He could embrace such views as this and yet, at the same time as these enormous contemplations, still remained faithful, almost as to a debt, to all the dwarf-like doings of his accidental clique,

---

41. Pasternak writes from Marburg to Konstantin Loks (May 19, 1912) about Cohen being a man not connected directly to his everyday environment, so Cohen's description is consistent with Pasternak's earlier verbal sketches: "Cohen is something trans-natural. [. . .] All such people, in their unbroken, hourly growth rise by their shoulders into some sky of idealism. At the feet of these crags there plays a handful of *enfants terribles*" [Коген—сверхъестественное что-то. [. . .] Все это люди, в своем непрырывном, ежечасном росте ушедшие по плечи в какое-то небо идеализма. У подошвы этого хребта чудачит горсть художественных enfants terribles] (*PSS* 7:100).

42. In fact, Mayakovsky's description in *Safe Conduct* is the precise opposite of Cohen's portrait in Pasternak's letter to Loks (see previous note). Mayakovsky chooses the local *enfants terribles*, terrified of the atemporal vision open to him. (*PSS* 3:223)

which was hastily assembled and invariably mediocre to the point of indecency. (*CSP* 84)

[О]н так же широко и крупно подхватил другую традицию, более местную.

Он видел под собою город, постепенно к нему поднявшийся со дна "Медного всадника," "Преступления и наказания" и "Петербурга," город в дымке [. . .]. Он обнимал такие виды и наряду с этими огромными созерцаньями почти как долгу верен был всем карликовым затеям своей случайной, наспех набранной и всегда до неприличья посредственной клики. (*PSS* 3:223)

Jakobson's spatial metonymies, highly characteristic of Pasternak's prose, are insufficient as analytical tools for those instances when Pasternak introduces the individuals capable of living[43] in a neighborhood that expands far beyond the tangible landscape into the atemporal depth of interrelations (that so frightened Mayakovsky). Pasternak's indebtedness to the philosophy of *a posteriori* and *a priori* sensibilities cannot provide in this context the whole of the answer, and yet this philosophical context clearly elucidates something fundamental about Pasternak's patterns of thought and image construction.

The inner world of visionaries, open to the many different layers of temporalities, dominates Pasternak's artistic tropes, but it is precisely this aspect of his writing that remains alien to Jakobson's understanding of Pasternak's use of metonymy. In his lecture to Musaget in 1913, "Symbolism and Immortality" [Символизм и бессмертие], for instance, Pasternak insisted that "the poet dedicates the apparent richness of his life to atemporal signification" [Поэт посвящает наглядное богатство своей души безвременному значению] (*PSS* 5:318), a position which on that occasion left his audience somewhat disoriented and dumbfounded.[44] Similarly, in "The Black Goblet," symbols

---

43. See Rilke's description of the state of writing in the *Notebooks of Malte Brigge:* "But outside—outside there is no limit to it; and when it rises out there it fills up inside you as well, not in the vessels that are partly in your control or in the phlegm of your most impassive organs: it rises in your capillaries, sucked up into the outermost branches of your infinitely ramified being. There it mounts, there it overflows you, rising higher than your breath, where you have fled as if to your last refuge. And where will you go from there? Your heart drives you out of yourself, your heart pursues you, and you are already almost outside yourself and can't get back in. Like a beetle that someone has stepped on, you gush out of yourself, and your little bit of surface hardness and adaptability have lost all meaning" (*Notebooks* 73–74).

44. Durylin gives the following account of Pasternak's lecture and the reaction of the musical and literary critic Emil Medtner, who was one of Musaget's founders: "Nobody understood anything, and looked at me crossways. (I organized this presentation.) Especially E. Medtner shrugged his shoulders with a smile [. . .]. The smile meant: this is highly juvenile. The poets

and images of different centuries are packaged alongside each other—as "*coffres volants,*" the flying chests or coffers—moving *en masse* into the future. This theme appears as a personal discomfort in *Safe Conduct,* when Pasternak asserts that he himself never felt at home in his immediate locality, and that this alienation included even Moscow University, where he experienced, almost as illness or feverish attraction, some other atemporal pole. This impatience, he noted, attracted the inhabitants from other worlds and "regions" into his own "small settlement" [из ее краев в свой поселок] with something of a magnetic force:

> This is why the sensation of the city never corresponded to the place in it where my life was being lived. [. . .] [w]here too, with its hundred auditoriums, the gray-green, much littered university ebbed and flowed with sound.
>
> [. . .] Had I gone to the doctor then, he would have thought I had malaria. Yet these attacks of chronic impatience could not have been cured by quinine. This strange perspiring was caused by the obstinate crudeness of those worlds—their turgid visuality [. . .]. Among them, uniting them into a kind of colony, the antenna of the universal preordainment rose up mentally. Just at the base of this imagined post came the attacks of fever. It was generated by the currents sent to the opposite pole. Conversing with the distant mast of genius, it summoned from those regions some new Balzacs into its own small settlement. (*CSP* 33–34)

> Вот отчего ощущенье города никогда не отвечало месту, где в нем протекала моя жизнь. [. . .] Там также сотнею аудиторий гудел и замирал серо-зеленый, полузаплеванный университет.
>
> [. . .] Покажись я тогда врачу, он предположил бы, что у меня малярия. Однако эти приступы хронической нетерпеливости лечению хиной не поддавались. [. . .] Объединяя их в какое-то поселенье, среди них мысленно высилась антенна повальной предопределенности. Лихорадка нападала именно у основанья этого воображаемого шеста. Ее порождали токи, которые эта мачта посылала на противоположный полюс. Собеседуя с далекою мачтой гениально-

---

particularly understood nothing" [Никто ничего не понял, и на меня посмотрели капельку косо. (Я устроил чтение.) Особенно Э. Метнер пожал плечами с улыбкой . . . Она означала: 'очень ювенильно.' Поэты—просто ничего не поняли] (1991, 54). It is significant that Pasternak, who objected to his own early style, remembered the lecture fondly and emphasized in his 1956 memoirs his success: "The paper created a stir. It was talked about" [Доклад произвел впечатление. О нем говорили] (*PSS* 3:319).

сти, она вызывала из ее краев в свой поселок какого-то нового Баль-
зака. (*PSS* 3:160–61)

Thus, there is a startling discontinuity between Pasternak's casual admission
that "the sensation of the city never corresponded to the place in it where
[his] life was being lived" (*CSP* 33; *PSS* 3:160) and Jakobson's assertion that
Pasternak's hero is invariably an observer of his environment, "experiencing a
change of locality in various ways and in enforced idleness" (Jakobson 1969,
147). Unintentionally, it seems, Jakobson redirects Pasternak's focus toward
a world of limited interrelations just when Pasternak seeks to expand them.

On the whole, the juxtaposition of "The Wassermann Test" and Jakobson's "Remarks" discloses several significant points of difference, reflective
of the characters of the two men. The main binary tenets of Jakobson's essay
are precise and clear-cut, while Pasternak's expression is pervaded by ideas
that will take him a lifetime to develop. This includes—centrally—Pasternak's
experimentation with time and temporal sequences that expand from within
the contiguous series brought together in an intense proximity. In this context, it is particularly instructive to examine yet another document—a letter
Pasternak wrote in December 1913 to his uncle, Mikhail Freidenberg, which
provides not so much an explanation of his decision to leave Marburg as an
outline of his earliest plans for his future protagonist. The young poet claims
that most of all he aspires to capture "in life or artistically" the type of person
near whom time and space open up their significance as infinite categories.
The reason Pasternak offers this explanation to Freidenberg is also noteworthy: according to this letter, his uncle exemplifies the personality that cannot
be neutralized by inanimate objects, for he is given "the gift of time," so that
his impressions can call forth the "spirit" of the city and invite both time and
the depth of space to situate themselves around his work-place and to magne-
tize every surrounding object:

> But there is a special gift granted to rare individuals that I would like to call
> the gift of time.
>
> People are caught by every present minute, which belongs to no one
> and imbues them with a general colorlessness of a particularized time—
> actuality. [. . .]
>
> However, I have met several individuals who appear to breathe with
> their own time, and for whom reading their clocks is only a concession
> to the common order. What does this signify? It signifies, first, a certain
> feature of immortality that has entered into their movement. And it also
> speaks of their kindredness with their destiny. [. . .]

It is difficult to express this reality. A happier attempt would be to find living or artistic means for my enthusiasm in front of them. And if such a task were within my means, I would necessarily think of you. I would think of your serene capacity, instinctually, to take control of that chaotic and close to dream impression, which leaves behind itself Petersburg, city spirit. [. . .] how you fantasize over your work place, in the evening, with bloodless nothingness behind your back. And how you transmit this dramatically performed life to surrounding objects, to the whole mystery of furnishings and rooms.

Дело, может быть, в особом даре нескольких редких людей, который я бы назвал дар времени.

Люди захвачены настоящей минутой, которая никому не принадлежит и обнимает их общей бесцветною средою данного времени—действительности. [. . .]

Однако я встретил несколько личностей, которые как бы дышат своим собственным временем, у которых показанья их часов, может быть, только—уступка общественному порядку. Что это означает? Это означает, во-первых, некоторую черту бессмертия, проникающую их движения. И затем это говорит о какой-то одинокой их близости со своей судьбой. [. . .]

В таких выражениях трудно дать об этом представление. Гораздо счастливее была бы попытка жизненно или художественно запечатлеть свой энтузиазм перед ними. И если бы такая задача была по силам мне, я неизменно думал бы о Вас. Я думал бы о том, как невозмутимо и с каким странным неведением об этом завладеваете Вы тем хаотическим и близким к грезе впечатлением, которое оставляет по себе Петербург, как город-дух. [. . .] как [. . .] фантазируете Вы над своими станками, вечером, с бескровною пустотой за спиной. И о том, как заражается этой, драматически разыгранной Вами жизнью мир предметов вокруг, вся эта тайна обстановки и комнат. (*PSS* 7:157)

This letter, with its emphasis on the city-spirit, on the inner layers of space and time, and on the capacity of the self engaged in thought to bring dramatic intensity into the world of objects, signifies with a startling clarity that the themes of Pasternak's philosophical studies have not been left behind. As the subject matter and the protagonists of his future work are outlined, the Kantian *a priori* principles of time and space constitute an important philosophical subtext, and admirers of Pasternak can already recognize in the text of this December letter the images of space and time that anticipate not only the future portraits of Rilke, Scriabin, Cohen, and (with some qualifications) Mayakovsky in *Safe Conduct*, but also the poetry of *Doctor Zhivago*, be it "Magdalina" for whom eternity is waiting at her desk,[45] or Christ in "The Garden of Gethsemene" who, sweating blood, clings for the last time to the piece of land on which he stands surrounded by the impenetrable and uninhabitable abysses of eternity that have come so dangerously close to him.[46] The themes and images of Pasternak's early prose works may as yet be unclear, but the next step of this inquiry is straightforward and obvious: the mysterious traveler, Heinrich Heine, appears altogether out of his apparent time and place amidst the darkness of Pisa in Pasternak's first published short story, "The Mark of Apelles."

---

45. "Oh, where would I now be, / My teacher and my Savior / If at night, near the desk / The eternity would not be waiting for me" [О, где бы я теперь была, / Учитель мой и мой Спаситель, / Когда б ночами у стола / Меня бы вечность не ждала] (*PSS* 4:545).

46. "The spaciousness of the universe was uninhabitable, / And only the garden was a place for the living. / Looking then into these black abysses, / Empty, without beginning or end, / So that the cup of death would pass him by / In a bloody sweat he begged his father" [Простор вселенной был необитаем, / И только сад был местом для житья. / И, глядя в эти черные провалы, / Пустые, без начала и конца, / Чтоб эта чаша смерти миновала, / В поту кровавом он молил отца] (*PSS* 4:547).

3

Arguing with the Sun in "The Mark of Apelles"

I n Pasternak's writing, the gift of poetry is either identified with or permeated by an energy force that lifts the world from gloom and darkness and
fills it, as it were, with fresh air. Both Tsvetaeva and Mandelstam in their
portraits of Pasternak attest to this refreshing dynamism in his poetic world,
Tsvetaeva by comparing it to pouring rain filled with sunlight [световой
ливень] and Mandelstam by noting that Pasternak's poetry could become an
effective treatment for tuberculosis.[1] What is intriguing in these poets' intuitive responses is not simply their enthusiastic description; rather, they both
name a major early theme in Pasternak that otherwise has remained unobserved in critical literature: the comparison, and even competition, between
the artist's ability to affect the surrounding world, on the one hand, and the
power of the sun and fresh air, on the other. In this chapter I will argue that
this competition, highly characteristic of Pasternak's early prose, constitutes a hidden mechanism in his first published story, "The Mark of Apelles"
[Апеллесова черта], and that the story's technical innovation includes the

---

1. Tsvetaeva's "Downpour of Light" was in itself a forceful "breakthrough" in reaction to
Pasternak's "downpour," since her essay was one of the first instances of the émigré poet praising
the Soviet poet, and it was written almost immediately after receiving Pasternak's *My Sister Life*
[Сестра моя жизнь] in the summer of 1922 (Ciepiela 2006, 82–84). Mandelstam's description
of this book in "Vulgata: Notes on Poetry" [Заметки о поэзии] (1923) points to poetry's natural capacity for healing the traumatic and hungry 1920s (Mandelstam 2:302).

inversion (or rather the reformulation) of Plato's trope of the sun as the highest good.

It is noteworthy that in *Doctor Zhivago*, while describing pre-Revolutionary cultural life in the Russian capital, Pasternak singles out the themes of competition with, or imitation of, the sun when the Tolstoyan follower Vyvolochnov dismisses with disdain the decadent preoccupations of the Silver Age as he addresses the philosopher Vedenyapin:

> Hmm. And now it's all this highbrow stuff—fauns and nenuphars and ephebes and "let us be like the sun." I can't believe it, bless me if I can—an intelligent man like you, and with your sense of humor and knowledge of people. . . . Come, now. . . . Or am I intruding into the holy of holies? (*Zhivago* 41)

> Нда. А теперь эти фавны и ненюфары, эфебы и "будем как солнце." Хоть убейте, не поверю. Чтобы умный человек с чувством юмора и таким знанием народа. . . . Оставьте, пожалуйста. . . . Или, может быть, я вторгаюсь. . . . Что-нибудь сокровенное? (*PSS* 4:43)

Even apart from the prominence and extent of this theme in the Silver Age and its powerful presence in post-Revolutionary culture,[2] images of sun and sunset, light and darkness, are hardly new in literature, and intertextual influences here are unlimited.[3] My task in this chapter, therefore, is not to situate Pasternak's artistic treatment of the sun in the cultural context of his time, but to elucidate the deeper philosophical roots responsible for his startling confidence as he entered, without apology or hesitation, into what might have appeared to be already exhausted subject matter and added to this well-established image his own artistic vision, by no means conventional or trite.

It is never easy to isolate a predominant philosophical influence (or the importance of a specific philosopher) in the work of any writer who finds

---

2. The motif of the sun and sunlight is characteristic of all Modernism (Russian and European); it is in Balmont, in Vyacheslav Ivanov, in the Futurists' 1913 opera *The Victory over the Sun* [Победа над Солнцем], with Malevich's picture for the brochure. Malevich's concept of Suprematism is to some extent a development of this theme, for the famous *Black Square* (1915) can be viewed as a total sunset, an actual victory over the sun. This theme is central for such classical images of Revolutionary culture as Gorky's Dan'ko with his "flaming heart" and Mayakovsky's 1918 "conversation with the sun." See, for example, Koretskaya (1978, 54–60); V. V. Ivanov, "Solyarnye mify" (1978, 54–60); and P. Davidson (1989).

3. Gifford, for example, sees parallels between *My Sister Life* and St. Francis of Assisi and his "Canticle of the Sun": "*My Sister Life* records a bond not unlike that of Saint Francis for whom sun and wind were his brothers, the moon and the stars his sisters" (1977, 53).

his voice in a period of intense cultural cross-fertilization. It is all the more difficult to identify these influences in the exceptionally elusive texts of a writer responding to the widest range of philosophical and literary voices.[4] To address this challenge, the analysis of "The Mark of Apelles" will be divided into three sections. The first section (3.1) will examine the theme of the sun in Pasternak's own recollection of the preoccupations of his youth—in *Safe Conduct*—with specific attention to passages dedicated to his university years and his descriptions of the birth of poetry. The consistent appearance of this "sunless" theme in Pasternak up to his "second birth" will be emphasized throughout. The second section (3.2) will extend this analysis to the discussion of Pasternak's philosophical diary and letters of 1910–13 and his proposed (and abandoned) philosophical dissertation, dedicated to "the laws of thought and the category of the dynamic object."[5] Pasternak's *modus operandi* (which he shared with Neo-Kantian philosophers)[6] of approaching Plato's "ideas" as diverse forms of energy rather than intellectual "abstractions" will be one focus of my approach. The examination of "The Mark of Apelles" in the third section of the chapter (3.3) will clarify the importance of these philosophical themes and their interconnection with the light of the sun for the overall construction of the story.

3.1 Poetry born in darkness:
Toward an unwritten philosophical aesthetics

Any critic working with Pasternak's early prose cannot ignore the writer's consistent framing of narratives with images of sunset.[7] Even apart from the

---

4. As de Mallac observes, "Pasternak occupies in his national and international literary age a place analogous to the one Goethe occupied in his age" (1981, xvii).

5. The topic of Pasternak's dissertation ("работа о законах мышления как о категории динамического предмета") was announced at the very same time as he decided to leave Marburg—in the letter to Alexander Shtikh of July 11, 1912 (*PSS* 7:121–22).

6. It is noteworthy that Fyodor Stepun, once an organizing force of Musaget, recognized in his discussion of *Doctor Zhivago* not only the Kantian roots of what he called Pasternak's transcendental aesthetics (which he thought were beyond doubt), but the wider influence of philosophical idealism. To explain Pasternak's belief in the dynamic force of art, Stepun begins by quoting Rickert's phrase—"to understand the world is to make it unrecognizable"—and then shows the complex resonance of the idealist tradition in Pasternak's writing (1962, 47–49).

7. Witt locates this theme both in *Zhivago* and in the poetic works of the later period as Pasternak's engagement with Dostoyevsky's *Brothers Karamazov* and, more specifically, Alyosha's memory of his mother's prayers and "the slanting rays of the setting sun" [косые лучи заходящего солнца] (2000a, 77–87). Witt also traces the theme of sunset in Dostoyevsky and that of "the slanting rays" to Sergei Durylin's article, published in 1928, on Dostoyevsky ("Ob odnom simvole u Dostoevskogo"). As Witt aptly observes, "Durylin's summarizing description

spectacular sunset that opens "The Mark of Apelles," the narrative frames of each of Pasternak's early stories display the same constellation of images: the rays of the sun are either departing (usually at the beginning of the story) or re-appearing (at the conclusion), and they are more often than not set against the background of a journey, its railway lines, stations, street lines, or quickly changing settings. Sometimes the image is obscure, as in the first page of *The Childhood of Luvers* when the girl is frightened by the lights of an industrial factory and by the new state of reality colored by the sunset. In "Aerial Ways," for instance, the emphasis is not so much upon the sun as upon an electric cloud that darkens the world. However, the interplay between light and darkness is always present and always significant.

In the surviving manuscripts of 1910, Pasternak's hero Reliquimini is invariably surrounded by dusk, sunset, and darkness, while sunshine is always a rare occasion, never directly named.[8] Nonetheless, Reliquimini recollected his childhood as daylight, while he conceived his youth as a sunrise that "pre-dated" his childhood and framed it:

It's growing dark. How many roofs and spires! And all of them, catching and tearing, have bent the sky down like a misty bush. (*MG* 18)

Just look at this chaos of shadows and silhouette-patches, all this buzzing and flowing thaw of blackened colors feathered with soot, look at them. (*MG* 20)

Dusk, you understand that dusk is some thousandth homeless anxiety, unbalanced and lost, and the lyricist has to find a placement for the dusk. Childhood remembered noons [. . .] youth linked itself with dawn.

---

of the 'символ заката и косых лучей' in Dostoevskij [. . .] touches upon a subject that very much occupied Pasternak—and that the two friends discussed: the question of realism in art" (2000a, 89). The major question is the dating of the friendship between Durylin and Pasternak. Fleishman (as Witt points out [2000a, 90]) speaks of the earliest period of Durylin and Pasternak's acquaintance, placing it in 1910–13, as highly influential in a lifelong friendship. Fleishman also observes that in 1911 Durylin was an active participant of Musaget and contributed (under the pseudonym S. Severny) to the volume dedicated to Francis of Assisi (1981, 228ff). Thus, it is more than possible that Durylin, who became a Russian Orthodox priest in 1918 (the same year as Sergei Soloviev and Sergei Bulgakov), discussed with Pasternak Alyosha's "oblique rays of the sun" as Pasternak first turned to his prose, adding Dostoyesky's influence to the great number of other influential contexts, including Scriabin's experimentation with darkness and light in his 9th (Black Mass) and 10th sonatas, as well as his insistence that one can look into the eyes of the sun as one listens to *Le Poème de l'extase.*

8. Livingstone notes "the twilight's erasure" of objects, so that "they begin to need forms to hold them together; so they are now god-seekers" (*MG* 57).

That is why Reliquimini's youth took place for him earlier than childhood. Youth predated Reliquimini's childhood.

Уже темнеет. Сколько крыш и шпицей. И все они, цепко обрывая, нагнули небо, как туманный кустарник, и выпустили его из рук. (*PSS* 3:420)

Вот посмотрите на этот хаос теней и пятен и силуэтов, на всю эту журчащую, проточную оттепель почерневших, оперенных копотью красок [. . .]. (*PSS* 3:422)

Сумерки, понимаете ли вы, что сумерки это какое-то тысячное бездомное волнение, сбившееся и потрявшее себя, и лирик должен разместить сумерки. (*PSS* 3:428)

Детство запомнило полдни [. . .] юность связала себя с рассветом. Поэтому юность Реликвимини настала для него раньше его детства. Юность предшествовала детству Реликвимини. (*PSS* 3:436)

If one examines the prose that followed "The Mark of Apelles," there is a consistent pattern of staging action in darkness, framed by sunrise. "Without Love" (Безлюбие, 1918), for example, starts with a blinding blizzard and signals the sun's eventual approach, measured not by hours, but by the length of the protagonists' journey:

[. . .] it was high time for the sun to rise, but the sun was still far away.

The sun was still far away. They would see it only after another five versts, after a short stop at the inn [. . .].

Then it appeared. It entered the manager's office with them, flooded over the carpet, settled behind the flowerpots. (*CSP* 131)

[. . .] и давно было уже время взойти солнцу, но до солнца было еще далеко.

До солнца было еще далеко. До солнца оставалось еще верст пять пути, короткая остановка на въезжей [. . .].

Тогда оно выглянуло. Оно вошло вместе с ними в кабинет, где оно разбежалось по коврику и, закатившись за цветочные горшки, усмехнулось [. . .] (*PSS* 3:408)

"Letters from Tula" (written in 1918) begins with a sunset:

[. . .] in the train from Moscow, a suffocating sun was borne along on the many striped bench seats. The sun was setting. (*CSP* 119)

[. . .] в поезде, шедшем из Москвы, везли задыхавшееся солнце на множестве полосатых диванов. Оно садилось. (*PSS* 3:26)

The story also ends with sunrise, which means that all the events of the story take place, explicitly, between sunset and daybreak:

The train was heading for Moscow, and an enormous crimson sun was borne along on the bodies of many sleeping passengers. It had just appeared from behind a hill, and it was rising. (*CSP* 126)

Шел поезд в Москву, и в нем везли огромное пунцовое солнце на множестве сонных тел. Оно только что показалось из-за холма и подымалось. (*PSS* 3:32)

"Detstvo Luvers" (1918) begins with the child's tearful reaction to a world so different during sunset, which she sees unexpectedly when awakened by the cat:

In those days Zhenya was put to bed early. She could not see the light of Motovilikha. [. . .] However, there was no name of determining what was happening far, far away on the bank. *That* had no name, and no precise color or definite outline. (*CSP* 133; emphasis in original)

Женю в те годы спать укладывали рано. Она не могла видеть огней Мотовилихи.[. . .] Зато нипочем нельзя было определить того, что творилось на том берегу, далеко-далеко: у того не было названия и не было отчетливого цвета и точных очертаний [. . .]. (*PSS* 3:34)

"Aerial Ways" (1924) opens dramatically with darkness stretching over the world:

When the huge lilac storm cloud rising at the roadside had silenced even the grasshoppers that torridly chirruped in the grass, and when the drums gave a sigh and their pattering ceased in the encampment, the eyes of the earth turned dim and there was no more life in the earth. (*CSP* 179)

Когда огромная лиловая туча, встав на краю дороги, заставила умолкнуть и кузнечиков, знойно трещавших в траве, а в лагерях вздохнули и оттрепетали барабаны, у земли потемнело в глазах и на свете не стало жизни. (*PSS* 3:86)

It seems, therefore, that a critical analysis of "The Mark of Apelles" or any of these earlier stories needs to be located within a wider discussion of the artistic aims guiding Pasternak's persistent evocation of the occluded sun in his earlier works.

In this examination, one cannot avoid the *Urtext* of the image in Western culture; in Plato's trope for the highest good, the sun is a simile for the universal power that brings to the material world its highest illumination and true generation:

> The sun, I presume you will say, not only furnished to visibles the power of visibility, but it also provides for their generation and growth and nurture though it is not itself generation.
>
> In like manner, then, you are to say that the objects of knowledge not only receive from the presence of the good their being known, but their very existence and essence [which] is derived to them from it, though the good itself is not essence but still transcends essence in dignity and surpassing power. (*Republic* Bk. VI, 509b–c; 1930, 744)

Moreover, for Plato the ideas with which the soul opines are charged with power and acuity in the intelligible world "where truth and reality *shine* resplendent," while the shining flow of energy recedes in darkness:

> When [the soul] is firmly fixed on the domain where truth and reality shine resplendent it apprehends and knows them and appears to possess reason, but when it inclines to that region which is mingled with darkness, the world of becoming and passing away, it opines only and its edge is blunted, and it shifts its opinions hither and thither, and again seems as if it lacked reason. (*Republic* Bk. VI, 508d5–d9; 1930, 744)

It is, therefore, noteworthy that in describing his philosophical training in *Safe Conduct* and the accompanying "birth of poetry," Pasternak is indicating his distance from Plato's most famous *topos* of the good. Carefully emphasizing that poetry's birth is awakened in the thickening atmosphere of darkness,

Pasternak prefaces this recollection with an invocation of the brightest sunshine whose rays illuminated his music studies throughout the many preceding years. Just as happens after Reliquimini's childhood and youth, the sunshine in Pasternak's inner and outer worlds departs as he turns eighteen (with the cessation of his music studies):

> Although my story has inclined this way, I have not asked the question of *what music is or what leads up to it.* I have not done so, not only because *I woke up one night in my third year of life and found the whole horizon flooded with it for more than fifteen years ahead,* and thus had no occasion to experience its problematics. [. . .] However, the same question in relation to art as such, art as a whole, in other words, in relation to poetry, cannot be passed over. I shall answer it neither theoretically nor in a sufficiently general form, but much of what I shall relate will be the answer I can give for myself and my poet. (*CSP* 30; emphasis added)

> Хотя к этому располагал рассказ, я вопроса о том, *что такое музыка и что к ней приводит,* не ставил. Я не сделал этого не только оттого, что, *проснувшись однажды на третьем году ночью, застал весь кругозор залитым ею более чем на пятнадцать лет вперед и,* таким образом, не имел случая пережить ее проблематику. [. . .] Однако того же вопроса в отношении искусства по преимуществу, искусства в целом, иными словами—в отношении поэзии, мне не обойти. Я не отвечу на него ни теоретически, ни в достаточно общей форме, но многое из того, что я расскажу, будет на него ответом, который я могу дать за себя и своего поэта. (*PSS* 3:158)

As Pasternak proceeds to describe how the sunny luminosity of music was replaced by the sun's restricted light and very limited hours of its entry into the family's home, it seems unwise to make a categorical assertion that Pasternak is here engaged in an implicit reconstruction of the atmosphere of the Platonic cave, "which has a way up to the light along its whole width" and whose "entrance is a long way up" (514a). However, this classic Platonic depiction of education in the *polis* cannot be too far away when the picture of Pasternak's philosophical studies is transformed into a full-fledged parody of Platonic apprentices searching for enlightenment. Pasternak begins this description by recollecting his younger self reading Hegel and Kant while the sun is dimmed by the walls of the adjacent houses and by his family apartment, the living quarters made up of former classrooms:

The sun used to rise behind the post office and, slipping down Kiselny Lane, would set over the Neglinka. When it had gilded our half of the house, it would make its way from dinnertime on to the dining room and kitchen. The apartment was government property; its rooms were made up from classrooms. I was studying at the university. I was reading Hegel and Kant. (*CSP* 30)

Солнце вставало из-за Почтамта и, соскальзывая по Кисельному, садилось на Неглинке. Вызолотив нашу половину, оно с обеда перебиралось в столовую и кухню. Квартира была казенная, с комнатами, переделанными из классов. Я учился в университете. Я читал Гегеля и Канта. (*PSS* 3:158)

This implicit comparison with Plato's descriptions of philosophers searching for liberation in darkness becomes all the more pronounced when Pasternak recalls the habits of philosophy students (and, more generally, his early artistic friends) at Moscow University who wake up at night and, stoically deaf to the material demands of the body, avoid sunlight altogether as they change their nights into day. In their pursuit of alternative sources of illumination and with disdain for mere unenlightened mortals,[9] they meet at the dead of night and travel as far as the railway station, Sokolniki or Yaroslav on the outskirts of Moscow—a task that for some unclear reason must be accomplished before sunrise. It is in this context that Pasternak mentions learning of Marburg— and a new liberating destination is finally singled out, with Plato explicitly identified and placed in a position of prominence equal to that of Cohen and Natorp:

Often we would get each other up in the dead of night. The reason for it always seemed of utmost urgency. Whoever was woken was ashamed of his sleep, as if it was an accidentally exposed weakness. To the fright of the unfortunate inhabitants of the house, all without exception considered nonentities, we would instantly set off—as if to an adjoining room—to Sokolniki and the Yaroslav railway crossing. [. . .] The illusion of inde-

---

9. Pasternak's irony is reminiscent of Plato's humor as he describes the arrogance of the disciples "consecrated" into the higher mysteries of higher truth. Socrates' disciple, Apollodorus, admits in *The Symposium* that he despises everyone, including even himself, who is unaware of the truths of philosophy: "Because, you know, before that I used to go dashing about all over the place, firmly convinced that I was leading a full and interesting life, when I was really as wretched as could be—much the same as you, for instance, for I know philosophy's the last thing you'd spend your time on" (173a1–3; ed. Hamilton and Cairns; trans. M. Joyce, p. 527).

pendence was obtained by means of such moderation in food that on top of everything else there was hunger too, which conclusively transformed night into day in the uninhabited apartment. . . . Along with some of my acquaintances I had connections with "Musaget." From others I learned of the existence of Marburg. Kant and Hegel were replaced by Cohen, Natorp, and Plato. (*CSP* 30–31)

Часто подымали друг друга глубокой ночью. Повод всегда казался неотложным. Разбуженный стыдился своего сна, как нечаянно обнаруженной слабости. К перепугу несчастных домочадцев, считавшихся поголовными ничтожествами, отправлялись тут же, точно в смежную комнату, в Сокольники, к переезду Ярославской железной дороги . [. . .] Иллюзия самостоятельности достигалась такой умеренностью в пище, что ко всему присоединялся еще и голод и окончательно превращал ночь в день в пустопорожней квартире . . . Вместе с частью моих знакомых я имел отношение к "Мусагету." От других я узнал о существовании Марбурга: Канта и Гегеля сменили Коген, Наторп и Платон. (*PSS* 3:159)

With this explicit mention of Plato, Pasternak presents the background for his recollections of the "birth" of poetry, which he describes as a pattern that somehow refuses to follow the motif of the Platonic philosopher liberated into the blinding light.

Thus, unlike the luminous light of his music studies, this new guiding force that directs his life at night is presented as altogether independent of the sun's energy, which, in Plato's writing, directs the soul to "the form of the good" that "is the last thing to be seen and hardly seen" (*Republic* VII, 517 b5–c; 1930, 749). By contrast, Pasternak remembers himself directed by a sunless force, one displaying its capacity to compete with all life-giving forces, including the power of the sun:

I had made friends with a girl from a wealthy family. It was obvious to everyone that I loved her. She took part in these walks only in abstract, on the lips of those more used to going without sleep and adapted to such a life. [. . .]

Love raced along most impetuously of all. *Sometimes it found itself at the head of nature and would overtake the sun.* (*CSP* 30–31; emphasis added)

Я дружил с девушкой из богатого дома. Всем было ясно, что я ее люблю. В этих прогулках она участвовала только отвлеченно, на устах более бессонных и приспособленных. [...]

Всего порывистее неслась *любовь. Иногда, оказываясь в голове природы, она опережала солнце.* (*PSS* 3:159)

The energy of poetic practice is found to have a further ability to enliven those aspects of reality, which, semi-forgotten, lag behind in the ever-expanding, darkened distance. Echoing the act of "conversion" or "turning around" of the cave prisoner who is liberated and "compelled to stand up suddenly and turn his head around and walk and to lift up his eyes to the light" (*Republic* VII 515 c7–d; 1930, 748), Pasternak offers readers his own version of "turning" or conversion—a backward glance that focuses upon a semi-forgotten series of impressions, experiences, facts.[10] The power of the sun is, thus, presented as a contrasting foil: as the sun directs the rotation of seasons, the poet, turning toward the call of ephemera disappearing in the darkness, has the independent ability to recover and invigorate these lifeless aspects of existence, imbuing them with new intensity that his eye discerns and awakens:[11]

> I shall ask myself at this point by what virtue and whereabouts in reality poetry was born. [...]
>
> It was born from the interruption of the series, from the diversity of their speed, from the way the more sluggish lagged behind and piled from the rear, on the deep horizon of memory.
>
> Love raced along most impetuously of all. *Sometimes it found itself at the head of nature and would overtake the sun. But as this happened only rarely, one could say that the force that gilded one side of the house and then began to bronze the other, which washed weather away with weather and turned the heavy winch of the four seasons, moved forward with constant superiority, nearly always competing with love,* while the remaining orders dragged along at the back, at various distances. I often heard the hiss of yearning that had not originated with me. Catching up with me from behind, it filled me with fright and pity. It issued from the point at which everyday life was torn away, and it either threatened to put brakes on reality or else begged for everyday life to be joined to the living air, which in the meantime had moved a long way ahead. *And what is known as inspiration*

---

10. See here MacKinnon (1988, 152ff.), who sees in this passage the announcement of "Pasternak's theory of art."

11. See Rudova on "making art a creative process" (1997, 70). See also Rudova's comparison of this passage to Rilke's writing on Paul Cézanne and *Notebooks of Malte Laurids Brigge* (1994, 62–73).

consisted in this turning around to look back. The most tumid, uncreative forces of existence called for a special vividness because of the distance to which they had rolled away. (CSP 31; emphasis added)

[Я] тут же и спрошу себя, где и в силу чего из нее рождалась поэзия. [...]

Она [поэзия] рождалась из перебоев этих рядов, из разности их хода, из отставанья более косных и их нагроможденья позади, на глубоком горизонте воспоминанья.

Всего порывистее неслась любовь. *Иногда, оказываясь в голове природы, она опережала солнце. Но так как это выдавалось очень редко, то можно сказать, что с постоянным превосходством, почти всегда соперничая с любовью, двигалось вперед то, что, вызолотив один бок дома, принималось бронзировать другой, что смывало погодой погоду и вращало тяжелый ворот четырех времен года.* А в хвосте, на отступах разной дальности, плелись остальные ряды. Я часто слышал свист тоски, не с меня начавшейся. Постигая меня с тылу, он пугал и жалобил. Он исходил из оторвавшегося обихода и не то грозил затормозить действительность, не то молил примкнуть его к живому воздуху, успевшему зайти тем временем далеко вперед. *В этой оглядке и заключалось то, что зовется вдохновеньем. К особенной яркости, ввиду дали своего отката, звали наиболее отечные, нетворческие части существованья. (PSS 3:159)*

The parallel with the sun is carefully maintained, even though the sun is not the force that moves inspiration. Poetry is born, along with compassion, when some as-yet-unnamed power invigorates the forgotten aspects of reality that are begging the poet to preserve them from disappearing from life.[12] And for his young self this new force, just like love, can outdistance the sun.

In the later sections of *Safe Conduct,* having described his pursuit of philosophy in Marburg, Pasternak announces that he can foresee a new theory of aesthetics. Laying its first foundations (or at least suggesting its outlines), he restates his conviction that art is intertwined with a force that shows its trajectory by displacing or transforming the objects it pierces. With a significant shift in metalanguage, Pasternak claims yet again that, as far as this process is concerned, textual devices are merely the by-products of a reality that has been transformed and reordered by this alternative power which exists alongside that of sunlight:

12. For an alternative view, see Livingstone's commentary on *Safe Conduct* (1985, 58–64).

At the beginning of *Safe Conduct* I said that sometimes love outstripped the sun. I had in mind the patency [evidential power] of feeling that every morning outdistanced the whole of the surrounding world [. . .]. *In comparison with this, even the sunrise acquired the character of a local rumor needing verification. In other words, I had in mind the patency [evident force] of a power that outweighed the evidential nature of light.* (*CSP* 54; trans. altered; emphasis added)

В начале "Охранной грамоты" я сказал, что временами любовь обгоняла солнце. Я имел в виду ту очевидность чувства, которая каждое утро опережала все окружающее с достоверностью вести [. . .]. *В сравненьи с ней даже восход солнца приобретал характер городской новости, еще требующей проверки. Другими словами, я имел в виду очевидность силы, перевешивающую очевидность света.* (*PSS* 3:186)

Thus, by comparison with this newly discovered "beam of energy," the sun's rays are relegated to the status of an inferior "news item," and, as Pasternak suggests, in all seriousness it seems, a formula for artistic power has been discovered that contrasts with the force of light:

If, given the knowledge, ability, and leisure, I were to decide now to write a creative aesthetics [. . .]. *I would show that as distinct from science, which takes nature in the section of a shaft of light, art is interested in life at the moment when the beam of energy is passing through it.* (*CSP* 54; trans. altered; emphasis added)

Если бы при знаньях, способностях и досуге я задумал теперь писать творческую эстетику [. . .]. *Я показал бы, что, в отличье от науки, берущей природу в разрезе светового столба, искусство интересуется жизнью при прохожденьи сквозь нее луча силового.* (*PSS* 3:186)

Moreover, according to this non-existent (but already conceived) aesthetics, the creative force of art [сила движущегося языка образов] affects reality as if by magnetism, while the force itself is discovered in reality and not in art. Even the transference of the metaphor found in reality (and Pasternak on this occasion employs a linguistic double-entendre—see the use of the word "pull" [тяга] in the passage below) is a testimony to the uncovered dynamism in static objects at the moment when they are transfixed by the force in question:

Art is realistic [. . .] by virtue of the fact that it did not itself invent metaphor but found it in nature and faithfully reproduced it. The *transferred* sense means nothing in isolation but refers to the general spirit of all art, just as *the parts of the altered reality mean nothing if taken separately.*

And in the configuration of the whole *pull* art is symbolic. [. . .] The interchangeability of images [undergoing displacement], that is art, is the symbol of power. (*CSP* 55; emphasis added)

Искусство [. . .] *реалистично тем, что не само выдумало метафору, а нашло ее в природе и свято воспроизвело.* Переносный смысл так же точно не значит ничего в отдельности, а отсылает к общему духу всего искусства, как не значат ничего порознь *части смещенной действительности.*

Фигурой всей своей тяги и символично искусство. [. . .] Взаимозаменимость образов, то есть искусство, есть символ силы. (*PSS* 3:187)

In this process, the immobile objects of reality are clearly neither illuminated nor changed, but rather returned to life by the animating force that sleeps in them:

How one understands what it is like for the visible object, when it begins to be seen. Once noticed, nature moves aside with the obedient spaciousness of the story, and in this condition, like one asleep, is quietly transferred onto the canvas. (*CSP* 70)

Как вдруг постигается, каково становится видимому, когда его начинают видеть. Будучи запримечена, природа расступается послушным простором повести, и в этом состоянии ее, как сонную, тихо вносят на полотно. (*PSS* 3:205)

In other words, as Pasternak claims that he is rewriting the classical philosophy of aesthetics, he still borrows from the Greeks the affirmation of the potency of contemplative "ideas,"[13] and his position contrasts altogether in

---

13. In a letter to Loks of January 28, 1917, Pasternak speaks of literary forms and clearly draws on his former philosophical position where forms as ideas are dynamic living energies: "if the form is to be created [. . .] it must be created as living, moved by an irrational self-consciousness of its self-subsistent and self-propelling organism" [если форма может быть создана [. . .] то она может быть создана только в виде живого,—иррационально осмысленного своею способностью самоподвижности организма] (*PSS* 7:314–15). This principle in Pasternak's world is so long-standing that it still resonated in *Doctor Zhivago* when

this regard with that of Hume, who claims that ideas are merely pale copies of impressions (*Treatise* 1.1.1; 2000, 7).

It is equally clear that in bypassing the imagery of light, Pasternak distances himself from the Platonic theory of mimesis. If in Plato's understanding of art as a reflection three times removed from reality, "the concave becomes convex, owing to the illusion about colors" as well as "[to] the art of conjuring and of deceiving by light and shadow" (*Republic* X, 602c8–d3; 1930, 827), then the unnamed power that in Pasternak's writings unearths the living energy of materiality cannot be discerned with the force of light, and in this it differs from all other ideas and aspects of consciousness [остальные стороны сознанья]:

> Actually, only this power needs the language of material proofs. The other aspects of consciousness are durable without this need for proof. *For them there is the direct path to the visual analogies of light: to number, precise concept, and idea. But there is nothing except the mobile or dynamic language of images,* that is, the language of attendant attributes, for power to express itself by, the fact of power, power durable only at the moment of its manifestation. (*CSP* 55; trans. altered; emphasis added).

> Собственно, только сила и нуждается в языке вещественных доказательств. Остальные стороны сознанья долговечны без замет. *У них прямая дорога к воззрительным аналогиям света: к числу, к точному понятью, к идее.* Но ничем, кроме движущегося языка образов, то есть языка сопроводительных признаков, не выразить себя силе, факту силы, силе, деятельной лишь в момент явленья. (*PSS* 3:187)

In short, although the force of poetry may be measured alongside the potency of sun, poetic power is an independent energy source. And when measured against feelings or passions, this power is found to be both wider and stronger than any of these other forces:

> When we suppose that a strong passion is depicted in *Tristan, Romeo and Juliet* and other masterpieces, we undervalue these works' content. Their theme is wider than this forceful theme; their theme is the theme of power. (*CSP* 54)

Yuri in Varykino "made a note reaffirming his belief that [. . .] form is a key to organic life, since no living thing can exist without it" [снова проверил и отметил, что [. . .] форма же есть органический ключ существования, формой должно владеть все живущее, чтобы существовать (*Zhivago* 454; *PSS* 4:452).

Когда мы воображаем, будто в Тристане, Ромео и Юлии и других памятниках изображается сильная страсть, мы недооцениваем содержанья. Их тема шире, чем эта сильная тема. Тема их—тема силы. (*PSS* 3:186)

These famous passages of *Safe Conduct* are interpreted by critics as the central aesthetic statement of the early Pasternak.[14] What has been centrally over-looked, however, is not only Pasternak's reliance in this regard upon the idealistic tradition that springs from Plato;[15] but the significance and consistency of the contrasts to the light force in early Pasternak are also underemphasized by Pasternak scholars, and as a result a major direction of his thought and image construction is altogether ignored.

How far-reaching, then, is Pasternak's opposition to the tradition of light metaphysics (and physics) in his writing? Traces can be found in a significant number of passages; they appear even in Pasternak's attempt (in what became the unfinished and unpublished Afterword to *Safe Conduct*) to explain to Rilke the difficulty of his personal life. Speaking with the conviction that Rilke would grasp the full seriousness of his predicament, Pasternak juxtaposes the beauty of the two women in his life by noting that one needs the illumination of light or of happiness to be beautiful, while the other is herself simply a force that, independent of sunshine, radically affects the world. This second type of beauty is excavated from the deepest layers of earth and in its very stony materiality needs little from the world itself, whereas the world cannot exist without it:

A smile rounded the chin of a young woman painter, pouring out its light into her cheeks and eyes. [. . .] And since she always needed this illumination in order to be beautiful, she needed happiness to be admired.

You would say that all faces share in this. Untrue—for I know others. I know a face that pierces and cuts both in grief and joy, and it becomes all the more beautiful in conditions destructive to the beauty of everyone else. Whether this woman flies upward or falls headlong, nothing affects her fearsome charm, and she needs less from the earth than the earth needs from her because she is femininity herself, taken out entire like a rough mountain crag out of the stony mines of creation.

---

14. Livingstone (2006b); MacKinnon (1988); de Mallac (1981, 340–42).

15. See here Stepun (1962, 48–49). Soviet critics were predictable in their reaction to *Safe Conduct*; immediately after its publication they accused Pasternak of counter-revolutionary "idealism" (*PSSCom* 3:523).

Улыбка колобком округляла подбородок молодой художницы, заливая ей светом щеки и глаза. [. . .] И так как она всегда нуждалась в этом освещеньи, чтобы быть прекрасной, то ей требовалось счастье, чтобы нравиться.

Скажут, что таковы все лица. Напрасно,—я знаю другие. Я знаю лицо, которое равно разит и режет и в горе и в радости и становится тем прекрасней, чем чаще застаешь его в положеньях, в которых потухла бы другая красота. Взвивается ли эта женщина вверх, летит ли вниз головою; ее пугающему обаянью ничего не делается, и ей нужно что бы то ни было на земле гораздо меньше, чем она сама нужна земле, потому что это сама женственность, грубым куском небьющейся гордости целиком вынутая из каменоломен творенья. (*PSS* 3:522–23)

In other words, the major emphasis on the dynamic power of the yet unnamed force, independent from sunlight, is undeniable, and although the theme of competition with the sun emerges in the final draft of *Safe Conduct* only in the context of the birth of poetry, one finds the notion of ideas as self-subsistent energetic centers in Pasternak's numerous student notes on Plato.

3.2 "I have dug into idealism to its very foundation"

Pasternak's initial plans in Marburg were to work on his dissertation entitled "The laws of thought and the dynamism of the material object." While the plans for his dissertation were abruptly abandoned (E. B. Pasternak 1997, 144), his notes on Plato, written throughout his philosophical training, point to this very specific interest in the energy of ideas or forms and the parallel discovery of living energy in the surrounding world.

The young Pasternak's reading of Plato is concerned almost exclusively with the dynamism and power of ideas—the energizing nature of intelligible reality and its empowering of material objects. Already in 1909–10, while studying with L. M. Lopatin, Pasternak summarizes the latter's understanding of Plato's ideas as an energy flow: the idea of the good, for instance, is the most "mighty" source attracting material objects and supplying them with its own dynamism. The word—тяга or "pull"—exercised over material objects, set out in these notes, already looks forward to the "pull" of artistic language in *Safe Conduct*:

The power and durability of the idea is directly proportionate to its capacity. [. . .] The highest, all-embracing idea = the idea of the good, beatitude

= highest living substance, with intellect and creativity, *pulling* others towards itself.

Мощность и жизненность идеи прямо пропорциональны ее объему. [. . .] Верховная, всеобъемлющая идея = идея добра, благости = высшее существо, обладающее разумом и творчеством, *притягивающее* к себе. (*Lehrjahre* I:356; emphasis added)

There is a striking consistency in Pasternak's understanding that the idea of the "good" cannot be abstract or general; ideas or forms, in contrast to "principles," are living, dynamic spiritual centers:

But ideas are alive spiritual centers. The relationship between things and ideas is directly opposed to the relationship between things and intellectual principles. Great dynamic power. [. . .] Idea as an ideal not abstractly generated by the mind, but possessing full reality. The ideal as the highest force, attracting objects to itself.

Но идеи – живые духовн<ые> центры. Отн<ошение> между вещ<ами> и идеями обратно тому, что между делами и понятиями. Мощность. [. . .] Идея как идеал, не отвлеченно порождаемый рассудком, а имеющий полную действительность. Идеал к<а>к верховн<ая> сила, притягивающая вещи к себе. (*Lehrjahre* I:356–67)

This emphasis (a position directly opposed to Hume) predates Marburg, and Pasternak's notes on Cohen prior to his trip indicate his awareness of the application of Plato's dynamism of ideas to Neo-Kantianism. In studying Cohen's thoughts on Plato, Pasternak carefully captures the transition in which the intelligible potency of thought is fused with Hegel's spirit, and even more so with Kant's *a priori* principles underlying apperception:

Cohen studies the apriori, reforming element of this spirit, which in a new way applies and enacts apperception upon the aposteriori material of science.

Cohen исследует априорный, реформирующий элемент этого духа, который по-новому апперцепировал апостериори материал науки. (*Lehrjahre* I:393–94)

His first letters from Germany indicate that he viewed Cohen's school as a direct offspring of the Platonic academy and Cohen himself as the insightful reader *par excellence* of Platonic philosophy, capable of experiencing a living energy of Plato's thought when all the preceding schools were simply filled with the silent and deadening "stuff of ideas":

> It is strange and terrifying to understand that, after Plato, the next crowd, armed for the whole world and for centuries ahead, is this smoked auditorium and this eccentric, confusing, and inspiringly clear old man, who himself shakes from this startling surprise, from this shocking miracle that history was not understood before him, and that all these centuries, stuffed so tightly with lives, with myriads of consciousness and myriads of ideas, are so uninterestingly mute precisely in the places where he is struck by clarity.

> Странно и жутко сознавать, что следующей, за Платоном, сваей, вооруженной всемирно на все века, оказывается вот эта заколченная аудитория и этот чудной, запутанный и вдохновенно ясный старик, который дрожит и сам от потрясающего изумления, от того поразительного чуда, что история была понята до него, что эти века, туго набитые жизнями, мириадами сознаний, мириадами мыслей, так тускло молчат, именно там, где его осеняет ясностью. (*PSS* 7:93)

Pasternak's notes on Cohen's *Aesthetics* indicate his further engagement with the vitality and dynamism of material reality, energized by substance, that is, by the highest vitality of ideas.[16] At which point the study of ideas capable of transforming material reality disclosed itself as simply a "safe profession" is unclear, but by the time Pasternak was thinking of joining Cassirer in Berlin, the decision to leave philosophy was expeditiously maturing, and as philosophy was losing its luster, art was promising the real grandeur of working with the dynamism of thoughts, which could uncover a parallel vitality of material reality. In his letter to Shtikh of July 11, 1912, Pasternak noted both his deep engagement with the power of thought "as the category of the dynamic object"

---

16. As the poet's studies in Marburg expand, a new theme is introduced as if in medias res: the dynamic power characteristic not merely of substantive ideas, but of hallucination, ideas as obsessions, and also of "a singular poetry," the poetry of an object signifying not so much the necessity of its transition into a higher status, but rather "indicating its readiness for this transition" (*Lehrjahre* II:118–19).

and his irrevocable and unconditional decision to leave philosophy in favor
of art:

> I have dug into idealism to its very foundation. I have started work on the
> laws of thought *as the category of a dynamic material object. This is one of
> the attractive logical themes that can pass for a harmless narcotic.* But I do
> not want the harmless. O God, how successful is this trip to Marburg. But
> I dropped it all; art—and nothing else.

> Я докопался в идеализме до основания. У меня начаты работы о
> *законах мышления как о категории динамического предмета. Эта
> одна из притягательных логических тем, которые иногда могут
> сойти за безобидный наркотик.* Но безобидности я не хочу. Боже,
> как успешна эта поездка в Марбург. Но я бросаю все;—искусство и
> больше ничего. (*PSS* 7:122; emphasis added)

The transition from philosophy to art was by no means without unexpected
twists. In presenting his 1913 lecture "Symbolism and Immortality" to "Musaget," a text where a great number of philosophical postulations was applied to
poetics, Pasternak all but silenced the group's members by his intense philosophical language.

It is equally noteworthy that in "Symbolism and Immortality" his highest
expectations for art were formulated as follows: art was a living repository of
the dynamism of ideas alongside transformed material reality. From his surviving "theses" of the lecture and his later recollection of the occasion in *Sketch
for an Autobiography* [Автобиографический очерк], Pasternak's abandoned
dissertation topic, "the laws of thought as the category of a dynamic material
object," reappears—this time as the qualitative essence of material reality that
cannot be perceived, except by living thought or the meditative perception of
the artist. Artists, he claims, leave their imprint of subjectivity as they observe,
armed only with their subjective search, the actual shifts in reality that necessarily emerge in response to the authenticity of their quest. Furthermore,
since art continues to testify to this shift of disclosure, the uncovering of quality rather than quantity in objects that constitute art, together with the artist's
subjective perception, is communicated to the audience: the artist, with his
vision freed from accidental historical features, enters eternity, gains immortality, testifying in his very engagement to the process he experiences:

> Qualities are enveloped by consciousness, which liberates them from con-
> nection with personal life [. . .]. Immortality takes possession of the con-
> tents of the soul. Such a phase is the aesthetic phase.

[. . .] Thus immortality is the Poet, and the poet is never a being, but a condition for quality.

[. . .] The reality accessible to personality permeated with the quest for the free subjectivity belonging to quality. Signs of this quest, issuing from reality itself and concentrated in it, are perceived by the poet as the signs of reality itself. The poet submits to the tendency [direction] of the quest, imitates it, and conducts himself as the objects around it. (*MG* 40–41)

Качества объяты сознанием, последнее освобождает качества от связи с личной жизнью [. . .]. Бессмертие овладевает содержанием души. Такой фазис есть фазис эстетический.

[. . .] Итак, бессмертие есть Поэт, и поэт никогда не существо, а условие для качества.

[. . .] Действительность, доступная личности, проникнута поисками свободной субъективности, принадлежащей качеству. Признаки этих исканий, исходящих от самой действительности и в ней же сосредоточенных, воспринимаются поэтом как признаки самой действительности. Поэт покоряется направлению поисков, перенимает их и ведет себя как предметы вокруг. Это называют наблюдательностью и письмом с натуры. (*PSS* 5:318)

In this equating of the dynamism of ideas with the contemplative perception of the artist, there is not a trace of the "sunless" theme which, one should note, cannot be said as easily about "The Mark of Apelles."

This puzzling story opens as Heinrich Heine, assisted by "a whole horde of leaning sunsets and leaning shadows" (*CSP* 101; *PSS* 3:6), enters altogether ahistorically the busy streets of Pisa. This mysterious wanderer opens the doors of the hotel just as the sun's rays are "slaughtered," reflecting in this a much more complex intellectual context than the competition between Pasternak and Vladimir Mayakovsky, or the portrait of the Romantic hero, embodying a metaphoric approach, opposed to the quieter "passive" metonymic artistic type, Emilio Relinquimini.[17] Employing the somewhat tortuous phraseology

17. The interpretations and discussions surrounding "The Mark of Apelles" tend to reflect Jakobson's distinction between metaphor and metonymy, an opposition that has been recast by Aucouturier (1969) as a contrast between a Romantic hero, Heinrich Heine, and a quieter "passive" artistic type, Emilio Relinquimini. In this context, the story becomes a competition between two artistic types, or, in the words of Lazar Fleishman, about Pasternak's reaction to Mayakovsky: "as Michel Aucoutier has convincingly shown, the content of the novella and its hero, Heine, are indissolubly linked with Pasternak's reflections about the theatrical nature of the poet and the theatrical essence of poetry, as well as with two conceptions of art offered in most complete form in 1931 in *Safe Conduct*. There one poet's outwardly passive mode of behavior (often characteristic of Pasternak) is contrasted to another type of poet: one who never leaves the stage [. . .] Vladimir Mayakovsky" (Fleishman 1990a, 77–78). It is amusing, however, that critics, having accepted this interpretation, on occasion mix up who is who, and Hingley,

of Pasternak in "The Black Goblet," one may suggest that the Heine of this story is "the apriorist of lyricism," emerging out of the "coffres volants" of cultural wealth (*PSS* 5:14) or, in the language of "Symbolism and Immortality," "a living soul alienated from [historical] personality in favor of free subjectivity" (*MG* 41; *PSS* 5:318). If one prefers to adopt the language of Pasternak's notes on Plato, Heine becomes a testimony to the power of immortal or atemporal human thought that continues to exert a vital influence over material reality. The topic of his abandoned dissertation—"the laws of thought and the category of the dynamic object"—becomes then an organizing idea for a literary construction whose paradoxical design is illuminated further when Pasternak the philosopher continues to assist the critical understanding of Pasternak the prose writer.

3.3 The composition of "The Mark of Apelles" and its "vertical saturation"

Indifference to the philosophical Pasternak has meant that while so many of the modernist works of major Russian authors have continued to be reassessed and discussed on both sides of the Atlantic, critical evaluations of "The Mark of Apelles" have remained frozen in time. Written in the spring of 1915, the story appeared in print only in 1918, that is, at a time when Russia was already a new country, demanding new themes and allegiances. The archival data, pointing to the editors' reluctance to publish this work, foreshadows the puzzling absence of subsequent critical engagement. After rejections from several more or less traditional journals in 1915,[18] Pasternak offered the story to Bobrov for the third volume of *Tsentrifuga*,[19] and, in the accompanying letter of December 30, 1916, cautiously explained the technical challenges in the execution of the narrative, while disclosing very little else about the goals of this execution, which "directed a lot of energy to the vertical saturations" [вертикальные насыщения] of the plot:

> In its technical aspects, "Apelles" is not at the height of modernity [. . .].
> But the story is written with excitement and upsurge. Perhaps, an excessive technical intensity due to my lack of skillfulness, excludes the enthusiastic

for instance, speaks of "Relinquimini-Mayakovsky" and "Heine-Pasternak" (1983, 44).

18. The story was "successively rejected" by *Sovremennik*, Gorky's *Letopis*, *Russkaya Mysl*, and eventually Bobrov's *Tsentrifuga*. Barnes (1989, 193–94).

19. For the complex history of Pasternak's relationship with *Tsentrifuga*, see Fleishman (1990a, 79–83).

upsurge in narrative, directing a lot of energy to the vertical saturations and leaving little for the horizontal speediness of movement.

По технике «Апеллес» не на высоте современности [. . .]. Но написана была вещь с увлечением и подъемом. [. . .] Может быть, сугубая техничность, по моей неумелости, подъем изложения исключает, отымая много сил на вертикальные насыщения и для горизонтальной стремительности их не оставляя. (*PSS* 7:299)

In the same letter to Bobrov, he also admitted that after "Apelles" his technical experimentation had been far less successful:

One thing I can say to you. From the spring during which I wrote "Apelles," I attempted more than once to take up prose, moving towards the focus on technique. And is it not because of this that my attempts are barren? That is why, in all justice, I cannot fully dismiss "The Mark of Apelles."

Одно скажу тебе. С той весны, как я написал "Апеллеса," я делал не одну попытку прозой заняться, клонясь в сторону техничности. И не в силу ли этого остались они бесплодны? Так что осудить совершенно "Апеллесову черту" я не мог по справедливости. (*PSS* 7:299–300)

Admitting the story's deficiencies, therefore, Pasternak continued to consider his efforts in writing it worthwhile.

His readers tend to disagree,[20] and the story remains as puzzling today as it must have appeared to its original reluctant readers and publishers. Certain aspects of the story, of course, are fairly straightforward. It is clear, for example, that the competition between the two rivals organizes the story's plot and signifies a "parabolic statement on the nature of art" (Barnes 1989, 195), and yet "it has been difficult," as Fleishman aptly points out, "to establish what it is that makes the types opposite" rather than the fact that "the juxtaposition as such is more important than what is being counter-posed" (Fleishman 1990a, 77).[21] What cannot be questioned are the following facts: the story's epigraph, a fictional account of the competition between two seemingly legendary rivals, Apelles and Zeuxis, directs the story's events. Emilio Relinquimini, who wrote the famous poem "Il Sangue," signs his work with a

---

20. See Levi: "The Apelles Mark is no more than a clever exercise, something less than a detective novel though more densely and intensely written" (1990, 106).

21. On the whole, Fleishman accepts Aucouturier's interpretation of the story as reflecting Mayakovsky-Pasternak completion and Pasternak's farewell to Romanticism (1990a, 77–78).

drop of blood and invites the Westphalian traveler, Heinrich Heine, to give a definition of love, by providing "an Apelles-style proof of identity" and ensuring his "membership in the aristocracy of blood and spirit" [Апеллесово удостоверение личности [. . .] принадлежность к аристократии крови и духа] (*CSP* 102; *PSS* 3:7). Having accepted Relinquimini's challenge (and Relinquimini indicates in the letter that he is the story's Zeuxis[22] [*CSP* 102; *PSS* 3:7]), Heine travels to Ferrara and arranges a meeting with Relinquimini's love, Camilla Ardenze, by claiming in an advertisement placed in the Ferrara newspaper that he possesses Relinquimini's lost notebook and is ready to give it to an interested party. After she answers the advertisement, Camilla finds Heine irresistible, and Heine, in turn, catches her passion. The contest, then, seems to have been won by Heine outright: Relinquimini's wager, a drop of blood, is defeated by Heine's act of seduction—the mark of Apelles—and yet his triumph is somewhat obscured by the abruptness of the story's ending. As Heine switches off the light, either he, or Camilla, or both lovers are enveloped by darkness. Despite all the difficulty of finding a publisher, Pasternak never corrected the uncertainty of this ending—a fact significant in itself.

Equally noteworthy, just as Fleishman indicated, is the difficulty of locating the exact nature of the competition or what is actually being "counterposed" (1990a, 77). Here, I believe, the simple fact that Pasternak was brought up in the family of an artist must have played a decisive role, for literary critics tend to overlook the legendary account of Zeuxis, repeated, as is often emphasized, "ad nauseam," by lovers of the art of painting (Marvin 2008, 50). Thus, according to the ancient legend (as well as to the famous painting by François André Vincent [1746–1816] exhibited in the Louvre), Zeuxis, when asked to paint the portrait of the most beautiful woman, Helen of Troy, worked from nature and brought together the most perfect features of five beautiful women to make one startling ideal. One may also note the rather famous story of German artist Anton Raphael Mengs (1728–1779) who loved to compare the paintings of Zeuxis and Apelles and chose Apelles for the vivacity of his colors—the hues of his palette (Marvin 2008, 126). Pasternak, who must have been aware of these accounts (and who thought that his readers would also have known these facts), clearly gives his own twist to the competition, and yet

---

22. There is a textual suggestion that Relinquimini assumes the role of Zeuxis when he challenges Heine to provide an Apelles-like definition of passion: "You must define it no less succinctly than the mark of Apelles. Remember, Zeuxis is merely curious about your membership in the aristocracy of blood and spirit" [скажите о ней так, чтобы очерк ваш не превышал лаконизма черты Апеллесовой. [. . .] вот о чем единственно любопытствует Зевксис] (*CSP* 102; *PSS* 3:7). However, the instability of the story makes such a careful reader as Barnes insist that Apelles is Relinquimini, and Zeuxis is Heine (1989, 194).

it is clear that his winner does not assemble parts, but rather transforms what is assembled—not by the materiality of colors and hues, but by his presence, his energy, and, course, the intensity of his meditative glance, all of which disappear before the light of the sun.

The ending, then, sets up a puzzle for the story's interpreter, and any successful reading must be able to explain it. No such reading of the story has as yet surfaced, but if one erases the imaginary wall between Pasternak's thoughts about philosophy and his plans for his art, there emerges an intriguing pathway to an altogether novel interpretation. It relies on the truthfulness of Pasternak's words to Shtikh that the trip to Marburg and its emerging focus on the dynamism of the objects and the energy of thought amounted to a real intellectual breakthrough: "O God! How successful was this trip to Marburg. [. . .] Art—and nothing else" (*PSS* 7:122). No longer fettered by the methodology of philosophical arguments, Pasternak was then free to bring together within his fiction such diverse principles as the highest potency of ideas and the living idea or ideal of the poet around whom all material objects shifted, moved, refused to stay in place. Introducing his mysterious Heine into the narrative,[23] Pasternak was able, therefore, to demonstrate—within an altogether new medium of expression—how the "great dynamic power [. . .] attracting objects to itself" (*Lehrjahre* I:356–67) could escape any single encircling explanation and generate a work of art where no identity can remain static. Either coming ahistorically, therefore, into Pisa or emerging from the pages of the book whose author remains unknown,[24] Heine in Pasternak's story was able to teach Relinquimini, a man of flesh and blood and an aspiring writer, what it meant to fuse "blood and spirit" and leave behind "a sign [. . .] which has since become a byword for artistry"—to make the world unrecognizable and to claim the love of what is most precious (*CSP* 101; *PSS* 3:7).

---

23. Ljunggren speaks of "The Mark of Apelles" as a "kaleidoscope of citations from the fragments about Reliquimini" inserted in the words of Heine (1984, 81). For the transition from the first prosaic sketches with Reliquimini as a protagonist to "The Mark of Apelles" with its contest between Relinquimini and Heine, see Fleishman (1990a, 77). See also Gorelik (2000, 38–43).

24. For instance, it is just possible that Heinrich Heine and Camilla Ardenze are Enrico and Rondolfina, the fictional characters who emerge from Relinquimini's manuscript (or his fictional lost notebook) and discover their life when Heine tears off one page (*CSP* 102; *PSS* 3:7). The lovers then, one after another, come to life after Relinquimini gives Heine his own "visiting card," a drop of his blood, for on later occasions they do address each other as Enrico and Rondolfina. Such a reading, however partial, indicates the disappearing line between the so-called real life and fiction, and this is further supported by the fact that Relinquimini's name offers a slight variation upon Pasternak's youthful pen-name. However, since the name of the author of "Enrico and Rondolfina" remains unclear, any explanation would remain preliminary and ready to "shift."

This textual *mise-en-abyme,* permitting only tangential interpretations in a narrative caught in motion, explains the textual confusions, a pattern that begins with the identity of Apelles' mark (or line),[25] especially when the story's epigraph is coordinated with its title. According to the epigraph's pseudo-legend,[26] Apelles' mark (or his line) provokes Zeuxis' response. In "The Mark of Apelles," however, it is Heine who answers the challenge of Relinquimini, which makes him Zeuxis,[27] a role already claimed by Relinquimini. Thus, the oscillating correspondence between Pasternak's protagonists and the heroes of the legend, of which there is no record, is intentionally imprecise; it shifts, like every other aspect of the story, around its fictional poets. If Heine is Enrico of Relinquimini's manuscript, Heine's victory suggests, by implication, Relinquimini's success, for Relinquimini, like any writer who makes his characters live, needs to remain overshadowed by them. The story's seemingly straightforward plot and its intentionally confusing epigraph are, thus, not intended in any way to dispel the mystery of Heinrich Heine, who, apart from being connected to "Enrico" of the torn manuscript, is often viewed by critics as either "a resurrected Heine [. . .] now making a second Journey to Italy"[28] (Barnes 1989, 195), or having "no relation to the real Heine" (Fleishman 1990a, 79), or "crudely identifiable with Pasternak himself" lacking "any obvious connection with his German namesake" (Hingley 1983, 44). The plot of the story should make any such absolute judgments impossible, and, indeed, in the case of Heine there are subtle indications that he reclaims not only the role of Enrico, but also the actual identity of the German poet. This important claim shifts in and out of focus: it is intentionally lost (or hidden) in the one-sided but suggestive telephone conversation with an enraged newspaper editor who, on the final page of the story, insists on knowing the name of the traveler and hears the following in response:

"I cannot think of any objection today. Heinrich Heine."
[. . .]
        "That's right."

---

25. The English translation of "Apellesova cherta" as "The Mark of Apelles" neutralizes the importance of lines and boundaries for Pasternak (see particularly Gorelik 2000, 17–26) and negates altogether the suggestion of the line in the title as "the tenuous borderline dividing art from life" (Fleishman 1990a, 78).

26. Although there are no accounts of the legend mentioned in the story's epigraph (*PSS-Com* 3:539), artists tend to compare the techniques of these painters (Marvin 2008, 126).

27. See here Barnes (1989, 194) for an opposite interpretation.

28. Mossman suggests Heinrich Heine's "Florentine Nights" as a possible source for the story (1972, 288).

[. . .]

"Very flattering to hear it." (*CSP* 117–18)

Сегодня я не вижу к этому никаких препятствий. Генрих Гейне.

[. . .]

Вот именно.

[. . .]

Очень лестно слушать. (*PSS* 3:24)

And in all circumstances, even if Heine wins the competition (and he does win the heart of the beautiful Camilla) and appears to claim for himself the name of the great poet, his triumph is given the strangest climax when in the final lines of the story the electric lights are switched off . . . unless the timelessness of the traveler proves "the patency [evident force] of a power that outweighs the evidential nature of light" [очевидность силы, перевешивающую очевидность света] (*CSP* 54; *PSS* 3:186).

Indeed, the light–darkness contrast, characteristic of Pasternak's view of art as an energy, is employed in "Apelles" as a significant part of its construction, and Heine's capacity to upset the orderly everyday routine does not minimize the fact that his appearances in the story are coordinated painstakingly with the approaching darkness. This consistent use of darkness and shadows, as well as the underlying philosophical echoes of the story, suggests that the connection to Plato's theme of the cave should not be overlooked, even if in order to demonstrate these themes, it is necessary to re-examine the narrative patterns of the story. Barnes, one of the very few of Pasternak's critics who has paid attention to the spectacular sunset of the story's first paragraph, emphasizes the scene's chronological discrepancy. Pasternak alludes to the September evening and yet dates the occasion as August 23:

On one of those *September evenings* when the Leaning Tower directs a whole horde of leaning sunsets and leaning shadows in an assault on Pisa and across the whole of Tuscany a nagging evening breeze carries the aroma of bay leaf rubbed between the fingers—on an evening such as this, why I remember the exact day perfectly well, *it was the evening of August 23* [. . .]. (*CSP* 101; emphasis added)

В один из сентябрьских вечеров, когда пизанская косая башня ведет целое войско косых зарев и косых теней приступом на Пизу, когда

от всей вечерним ветром раззуженой Тосканы пахнет, как от потертого меж пальцев лаврового листа, в один из таких вечеров,—6а, да
я ведь точно помню число то: *23 августа, вечером* [. . .]. (*PSS* 3:6)

Barnes explains the discrepancy as a singular personal note: the sunset in question refers to Pasternak's reminiscences of his own "1912 August trip to Italy" (1989, 194). However, this chronological discrepancy, reinforced by all other shifts of the realistic details of the story, may have another purpose—the intensification of the battle between the actual reality of Pisa during daylight and the poetic world, mindful that "immortality is the Poet" (*MG* 41), has descended upon the town in darkness.

From the opening paragraph, then, this opposition between the material and the poetic is developed by Pasternak as a dramatic battle: upon the disappearance of the sun, the peaceful setting of everyday reality is violently attacked by the sharpness of the growing shadows, and the scene is further unbalanced by the piercing smell of crushed bay leaves. The evening in question is so overwhelming for the senses that chronological time is thrown off its regular run (hence the chronological discrepancy observed by Christopher Barnes) and unbalanced further not only by a spectacular sunset, but by an intensification of the battle between the bleeding sun (the rose color of the sky at sunset) and dark shadows at the very moment when Heine arrives at the hotel that has been just abandoned by Relinquimini:

> The sun's last rays crept across the piazzas like partisans. Some streets were crammed with toppled shadows, while elsewhere there was hand-to-hand combat in the narrow alleyways. The Leaning Tower of Pisa tilted backwards, flailing wildly and indiscriminately, *until a giant stray shadow passed across the face of the sun.* . . . Day snapped off short.
>
> As he briskly and disjointedly informs Heine about the recent visit, the hotel footman managed to hand the impatient guest the card, with its brown congealed blotch a few instances before the sun finally set. (*CSP* 102; emphasis added)

Зарева, как партизаны, ползли по площадям. Улицы запружались опрокинутыми тенями, иные еще рубились в тесных проходах. Пизанская башня косила наотмашь, без разбору, *пока одна шальная исполинская тень не прошлась по солнцу.* . . . День оборвался.

Но лакей, вкратце и сбивчиво осведомляя Гейне о недавнем посещении, все же успел за несколько мнгновений до полного

захода солнца вручить нетерпеливому постояльцу карточку с побу-
ревшим, запекшимся пятном. (*PSS* 3:6–7)

The contest is not so much between people or colors as between the sunlight and the creeping shadows, directed by the Leaning Tower of Pisa, itself an illusion of continuous fall, an oscillation arrested at a standstill. Relinquimini leaves his challenge to Heine with the footman while the sun's ascendancy is still holding and the hope for victory is not yet abandoned: "the sun's last rays crept across the piazzas like partisans." However, as Relinquimini's blood-stained visiting card is taken up by the footman, the world shifts: "the Leaning Tower of Pisa tilted backwards" or took aim with all its strength [косила наотмашь, без разбору], "flailing wildly and indiscriminately, until a giant stray shadow passed across the face the sun [. . .] [and] Day snapped off short" [день оборвался] (*CSP* 102; *PSS* 3:6). Even then, according to the text, daylight does not accept its defeat: Relinquimini's challenge is handed to Heine while the last ray still lingers, that is, in the few instants after sunset: "the hotel footman managed to hand the impatient guest the card, with its brown concealed blotch a few instances before the sun finally set" (*CSP* 102: *PSS* 3:7).

After such an opening, with Heine linked directly to "the giant stray shadow [that] passed across the face of the sun" (*CSP* 102; *PSS* 3:6), Pasternak's central technical challenge is to ensure that Heine's actions against Relinquimini sustain the contrast, and that their duration is limited to the hours after sunset and before sunrise, so that the furious nature of the struggle will not be lost but developed. Indeed, this textual feature, while carefully veiled in the story, is painstakingly observed and even intensified within a precise chronological frame:

1. Heine accepts the challenge as the sun sets in September, on August 23, and travels to Ferrara throughout the night.
2. He travels to Ferrara through the night and rushes to the *Voce*'s office in the earliest hours of the morning before the paper goes to print. The text carefully indicates that during Heine's arrival in Ferrara and his hurried visit to the editor, limited in time because of the publication deadline, the rays of the sun are still not above the horizon and veiled further by the fog: "Ferrara! An indigo-black, steely dawn. An aromatic mist [fog] suffused with chill" [Феррара! Иссиня черный, стальной рассвет. Холодом напоен душистый туман] (*CSP* 104; *PSS* 3:10). It is during this uncertain hour that Heine manages to have an advertisement inserted about Relinquimini's lost notebook.

3. As the morning of August 24 begins, Heine sleeps in the hotel, and his deep and restful sleep is ensured by the fact that the sun's rays are firmly shut out of the room by shutters on the windows. As Heine rests, the sun's rays reach only the floor, creating an illusory carpet woven of light and darkness. Signaling this time frame, the authorial voice promises that Heine will awaken just as the carpet disappears into the victorious darkness (in other words, after the disappearance of the rays), yet in the narrative the power of darkness is gradually outpouring from within the carpet's intricate and constantly changing design. This illusory carpet—a play of light and shadows—also echoes the initial image of the sunset, the intense illusory conflict of rays and shadows surrounding the Leaning Tower. On the floor of Heine's hotel room the rays of sunlight endanger Heine; they appear to ignite an illusory fire that is transmitted through the blinds, and this fire burns the woven shadows as if they are tightly packed straw that is slowly turning into a faded, discolored, worn-out rag. The darkness wins but at a price:

> Venetian blinds in his room, warmed by the breath of the morning, *have heated up [burn]* just like the brass reeds of a mouth organ. By the window a bundle of sun rays falls on the floor like a strip of dilapidated rush matting. [. . .] An hour goes by. By now *the rush matting,* flowing across the floor in a pool of sunlight, *is packed closer together.* [. . .] Heine sleeps. The pool of sunlight contracts as if the parquet floor had soaked it up; then once *again the scorched plaited straws of matting appear growing more rugged all the time.* Heine sleeps on. [. . .] Hours go buy, drawing out just like the expanding black gaps in the matting. [. . .] The *matting fades, dims, dusts over. By now it looks like a jute doormat, rampled and twisted.* [. . .] *Heine sleeps on. Any minute now he will wake up.* (*CSP* 105–6; emphasis added)

> Жалюзи в его номере, *нагретые дыханием утра, горят, точно медные перепонки губной грамоники.* У окошка сетка лучей упала на пол расползающейся соломенной плетенкой. [. . .] Проходит час. Соломинки уже плотно прилегают друг к другу, уже солнечною лужицей растекается по полу плетенка. [. . .] Гейне спит. Солнечная лужица разжимается, словно пропитывается ею паркет. Снова это— редеющая плетенка *из подпаленых, плоящихся соломин.*

Гейне спит. [. . .] Проходят часы. Они лениво вырастают вместе с ростом черных прорезей в плетенке. [. . .] *Плетенка выцветает, пылится, тускнеет. Уже это—веревочный половик, свалявшийся, спутанный. [. . .] Гейне спит. Сейчас он проснется.* (*PSS* 3:11)

4. When the carpet disappears and the sunlight is overthrown, the heat of the late afternoon still manages to break the wheel of the barrow carrying newspapers outside Heine's window. The forces of the sun are fighting for Relinquimini, attempting, vainly, so it seems, to prevent the circulation of the paper. As the newspapers are thrown from the cart, but not damaged, Heine wakes up. In the background there is the metallic sound of his readiness to enter combat. Once again the authorial voice betrays the excitement of the fight. Aware that Heine's plan is endangered during the day, the narrator of the story intensifies the expectation of a heated conflict:

Any minute now he will wake up. Any time now he will jump to his feet, mark my words. Any minute now. Just give him time to finish dreaming his last snatch of dream.

A wheel that has dried up in the heat splits all the way to the hub [. . .]. The cart falls on its side [. . .]. Bales of newspaper spill out. A crowd, sunshades, shop windows, and sun blinds. The news dealer is carried off on the stretcher—there is a pharmacy quite close.

There you are now! Heine sits bolt upright.

[. . .] There is almost a metallic clank as his right foot is lowered on the floor. (*CSP* 106)

Сейчас он проснется. Сейчас Гейне вскочит, помяните мое слово. Сейчас. Дайте ему только до конца доглядеть последний обрывок сновиденья.

От жара рассохшееся колесо раскалывается вдруг по самую ступицу [. . .] тележка со стуком, с грохотом падает набок, кипы газет вываливаются. Толпа, парасоли, витрины, маркизы. Газетчика на носилках несут—аптека совсем поблизости.

Вот видите! Что я говорил!—Гейне вскакивает.—Сейчас!

[. . .] Чуть что не металлически брякнув, тяжело опускается на пол правая нога. (*PSS* 3:11)

5. Heine's love scenes with Camilla, who has been summoned by the newspaper advertisement, begin on the evening of August 24. Heine performs his magic seduction and falls in love at night, reversing chronological time in Room 8, which now smells of spring. Once again, just before the sunrise, still in darkness, the lovers are awakened by a telephone call that Heine answers outside his room, when he admits to the editor his lie about the discovered notebook, but claims for himself the name of the great German poet. Camilla comes out to join him in the hallway, still illuminated by the electricity of the corridor, which Heine then accidentally switches off, with the result that the lovers disappear in the darkness. The story, as already indicated, ends on this abrupt note, just as the hotel is about to be engulfed by sunrise:

> Like an automaton, Heine turns off the light.
> "Do not put it out, Enrico"—the sound of a voice came from the depths and darkness of the corridor.
> "Camilla?!!" (*CSP* 119)

> Гейне машинально повертывет выключатель.
> —— Не туши, Энрико,—раздается в темноте из глубины коридора.
> —— Камилла?!! (*PSS* 3:25)

6. The lovers exist and act only when illuminated by the night, its darkness visible by a specific source of energy that exists outside or rather alongside the world ruled by sunlight.

This dependence of the lovers' existence on darkness leaves the question of final victory wide open; the lovers disappear into the night, and Relinquimini, by the implication of his name, will remain,[29] assisted in his return by the morning sunlight.[30]

---

29. Pasternak's pen-name in 1910 was Reliquimini. Both in these early sketches and in "The Mark of Apelles" the two versions of the last names, Reliquimini and Relinquimini, are similar grammatical forms of different verbs. One of the best explanations of the transitions of meanings is found in Kagan (1996), which can be summarized as follows: "Reliquimini" comes from reliquor, relictus sum, reliquari—"to be in debt." Relinquimini, possessing both the active and passive forms—relinquo, reliqui, relictum, relinquere—means "to leave behind." "Reliquimini"—present tense, passive voice, second person plural, literally "you are in debt." "Relinquimini" is also present tense, passive voice, second person plural, and means "you are left behind" (Kagan 1996, 43–50).

30. Fleishman observes, in fact, that the protagonists, while being "the antipodes on the level of the plot, actually prove to be doubles or transformations of the same essence" (1990a, 78).

As already pointed out, "The Mark of Apelles" was not the first Pasternak story to be built around a conflict between sun and darkness. The surviving notes of "Reliquimini," written in 1910, suggest not only the overwhelming intensity of the darkness, but also the play of reflections and shadows "moving, like posies pinned on by street lamps" [движутся опадающие скопища и пучки, как бутоньерки, наколотые руками] (*MG* 18–19; *PSS* 3:420). Within these unfinished pages in this early sketch, Reliquimini dies in this setting, prefiguring in this, as Ljunggren observes, the death of Yuri Zhivago (1984, 81). Moreover, "The Mark of Apelles" was written shortly after Pasternak's lost fairy tale "The Tale of the Carp and Naphtalain" (dated to late 1913–early1914). In Lydia Pasternak's recollection, the subject of the tale that Pasternak described to Bobrov as "colorful, condensed and technical" (*PSS* 7:299) was an explicit sun-night rivalry, with the sun eventually triumphing: "It had a juxtaposition of round, heated vulgarity and savageness, embodied in the Carp, alias the sun, alias the summer on the one hand, and the pale blue, cool silkiness, moonlit princeliness of Naphtalain on the other. I think the Carp finally stole the Prince's regalia and killed him" (Barnes 1989, 193). "The Mark of Apelles" then follows upon an already visualized and established pattern, except for the fact that Reliquimini's death and the Carp's victory over the moonlit, blue, princely silkiness of Naftalene are problematized in "The Mark of Apelles"; Relinquimini challenges Heine just before the sun sets, but loses to him within 48 hours and just before daybreak. However, according to the meaning of Relinquimini's name, Heine's existence and ultimate victory are by no means final, for neither is tangible in the daylight.

The story, then, is not about triumph or victory. In his search for the artistic means to denote the force that pierces darkness in a manner comparable to the sun, Pasternak's ultimate challenge was not only to create the sun–shadow conflict and to ensure that his work registered the transformation of the surrounding reality—he must have aimed to develop these images further. It is clear, for instance, that Heine's ability to bring disturbance and intoxication necessarily overlapped with the fashionable preoccupation of the age: the conflict of the Dionysian and Apollonian forces.[31] The Dionysian forces surrounding Heine bring with them, initially at least, threatening chaos and an intensification of pressure, as one might expect from a good Futurist poet

---

31. Gorelik persuasively analyzes young Pasternak's inevitable closeness (implied in Scriabin's influence) to Nietzsche's "superman" and Apollonian–Dionysian opposition (2000, 8–9; 12) and his desire to develop his own artistic world-view (2000, 35). Nietzsche's Apollo–Dionysus dichotomy, so popular among the circle of Viacheslav Ivanov, characterized the intellectual context of the time, and yet it clarifies only partially the character of the early world of Pasternak. For the same reason, the revolutionary rhetoric of Futurists, although clearly important here, may obscure the deeper layers of Pasternak's thought.

always ready to strike a Romantic pose (Aucouturier 1969), and these themes, most immediately apparent in the story, are not its only frame. There also operates a changing rhythmical pattern, drawn as a musical modulation. On the one hand, Pasternak's Heine, alive in an atemporal Italy much later than the actual dates of the great German poet, is materialized within the narrative when the chronological sequence is broken. The city is subsumed and astonished by shadows and odors, and shaken by wind and the smell of crushed bay leaves—clearly a Dionysian touch [когда от всей вечерним ветром раз-зуженной Тосканы пахнет, как от потертого меж пальцев лаврового листа] (*CSP* 103; *PSS* 3:8). Heine's hurried departure to Ferrara is similarly portrayed against a feverish landscape with its citizens cursing Cassiopeia.[32] The town itself, Pasternak emphasizes, is disintegrating into a multiplicity of motionless existences: "And in just the same way that the inert town was dis-integrating [распадался] without objection into blocks, houses, and yards, so too the night air consisted of separate motionless encounters, exclamations, quarrels"—until it reaches the "limit of human endurance" [так [. . .] положила [. . .] ночь предел человеческой выносливости] (*CSP* 103; *PSS* 3:8–9). On the other hand, however, it is just as the chaos reaches *beyond* the limit of what is possible that Pasternak frames the picture with a remarkable line that arrests and transforms the chaos: "All this was beyond the limits of human endurance. It was possible to bear all of it" [Все это находилося за пределами человеческой выносливости. Все это можно было снести] (*CSP* 103; *PSS* 3:9).

If Pasternak searches to describe the power of the force that brings about a "shift" in material objects, he clearly does not stop on the Dionysian note. His Heine controls and directs the flickering, shimmering, and sputtering reality that he awakens—in fact, this upheaval in the surrounding reality does not reach or change the graceful, bored elegance with which the traveling poet moves through space, as if through the still eye of the storm:

> Chaos began right at this point, at this limit, an arm's length away. The same chaos reigned at the railway station [. . .]. All this was beyond human endurance. It was possible to bear all of it. [. . .]
> *A seat next to the window. A completely deserted platform made entirely of stone, of resonance* [. . .].
> Heine is travelling on an off chance. *There is no thought in his head. He tries to doze off. He closes his eyes.* (*CSP* 103–4; emphasis added)

---

32. The fact that Cassiopeia is a mythical figure who compared herself with the immortals, calling forth Poseidon's wrath reflects this mixture of Dionysian-Romantic-Futurist "storm and stress" characteristics of the story's atmosphere.

Тут же, об этот предел рукой подать, начинался хаос. Такой хаос царил на вокзале. [. . .]

Место у самого окна. В последний миг—совершенно пустой пер-рон из цельного камня, из цельной гулкости [. . .].

Гейне едет на авось. *Думать ему не о чем. Гейне пытается вздремнуть. Он закрывает глаза.* (*PSS* 3:9)

The same commanding stillness in the middle of chaotic intensity is reintroduced in the story at several key junctures, each time with a different level of intensity. In Ferrara, Heine sleeps ("dead, leaden sleep" [мертвым, свинцовым сном] [*CSP* 106; *PSS* 3:11]) while the city, closed off by the blinds, shimmers with so much life and heat that the carpet of shadows by his bed catches imaginary fire, loses its color, ages, and fades away, while outside the window the wheel of a cart with newspapers splits altogether. Both the language of curses and speaking in tongues follows Heine in Pisa ("cursing with fervent fanaticism as if uttering a prayer" [*CSP* 103; *PSS* 3:8]) and in Ferrara: "On the street people chatter, drowse; tongues wag" [на улице загова-риваются, клюют носом, на улице заплетаются языки] (*CSP* 106; *PSS* 3:11), but he himself remains unperturbed. Even when he has just enchanted Camilla, his kiss brings balance: "her body sings, extended, led on by the kiss, fettered by the kiss" [поет поцелуем влекомое, поцелуем взнузданное, вытянувшееся ее тело], even when the embrace is surrounded by "a string of Italian oaths, passionate, fanatical, as a liturgy" [Итальянская ругань, страстная, фанатическая, как молитвословие] (*CSP* 111; *PSS* 3:17).

The inward intensity of stillness in the midst of an almost elemental chaos is, of course, also characteristic of the early Pasternak's understanding of poetry; in the poems of 1913 he liked to use the double-entendre of the word "стих" ((1) to quiet things down; and (2) a poem)—to describe the birth of poetry. The poem comes into being both by awakening and quieting down elemental forces; this process is poetry as such:

And, loud you woke up and quieted down (*stikhla*)
And the dream, as the echo of the bell, was silent. ("Dream," 1913)

Вдруг, громкая проснулась ты и *стихла*
И сон, как отзвук колокола, смолк. (Сон, *PSS* 1:64; 1913)
***

And everything was quiet, and, nonetheless,
In the dream I heard a cry, and it
As a likeness of silent sign

Was still troubling the sky.

. . . .

Now it is a poem (*stikh*). ("Venice," 1913)

Все было тихо, и, однако,
Во сне я слышал крик, и он
Подобьем смолкнувшего знака
Еще тревожил небосклон.

. . . .

Теперь он *стих* (Венеция, *PSS* 1:68; 1913)
***

This means—in truth the sea is excited
And it settles into quiet (*stikhaet*), not asking about the day. ("Winter")

Значит—вправду волнуется море
И *стихает*, не справясь о дне. ("Зима," *PSS* 1:69; 1913)

It is not merely stillness, however, that Pasternak wants to capture as the ultimate effect of the presence of Heine in Ferrara. The new energy, which emerges through stillness out of darkness and chaos, implies the gift or birth of a new vision, an apprenticeship in the act of a perception that synthesizes rather than breaks apart disunited phenomena, and, given the status of the artistic act, is viewed as a force which attracts rather than radiates light.

This birth of new synthetic perception out of chaos,[33]—a study in *apperception,* a transcendental principle inherited by Hermann Cohen from Kant (but never disclosed as a theme by Pasternak)—is, thus, dramatized as transformative energy that emerges from the very depth of chaos (be it spatial, temporal or emotional) and is, in fact, the very mark of Apelles that the story conceals within its texture. The mark of true art, proof of which is demanded from Heine by Relinquimini, is precisely this: the birth of a new quality of vision in the midst of ecstatic experimentation and emotional chaos, and this vision, according to Pasternak, is both transitive and transformative, for it has to be experienced not by the poet, but by the poet's other—the perceiver. The birth of the new in the other is Heine's only hope, when he rushes instinctively to Ferrara in order to throw himself at the mercy of the totally unknown, as he bemusedly assesses the uncertainty of the situation that lies ahead:

"Something must surely come out of this. There is no sense, and in fact no

---

33. Pasternak's development of Kant's theory of apperception is discussed in Chapter 4.

point, in trying to guess the outcome beforehand. Ahead lies beguiling, but total uncertainty." [. . .]

"Something must come out of this, I am certain." [. . .]

"The mark of Apelles [. . .] Rondolfina. In twenty-four hours I doubt whether you can achieve anything. But I do not have any longer." (*CSP* 104)

"Что-нибудь да выйдет из этого. Наперед загадывать нет проку, да и возможности нет. Впреди—упоительная полная неизвестность." [. . .]

"Это—наверняка. Что-нибудь да выйдет." [. . .]

"Апеллесова черта [. . .] Рондольфина. За сутки, пожалуй, ничего не успеть. А больше нельзя." (*PSS* 3:9–10)

The mark of Apelles is a quality of vision experienced not simply by Heine but by Camilla Ardenze: it must be not an autonomous self-directed glance, but a creative and shared perception that grasps and unveils the essence of the perceived.

With all the puzzles of the narrative, Pasternak makes his Heine annunciate the identity of Apelles' mark, a sure sign, in fact, that this philosophical theme is not fully integrated in the narrative. Thus, Heine's compliment to Camilla on her capacity for seeing the essence of the situation as if in a flash sounds almost like a university lecture: "How perceptive you are! At one stroke, the mark of Apelles, you conveyed my whole essence, the whole crux of the situation" [Что за проницательность! Одною чертой, чертой Апеллеса, передать все мое существо, всю суть положения] (*CSP* 109; *PSS* 3:15). Moreover, the new gift is not a single mark or even a line, but a continuous energy flow that should not be arrested, and for this reason, Heine begs Camilla to continue, to draw the line of Apelles further, for that capacity of perception with which Camilla has been empowered is a flow that revitalizes what it touches:

> *You possess that vital vision.* You have already mastered a line as unique as life itself, so don't abandon it. *Don't break it off at me; extend it as far as it will allow. Take the line farther.* [. . .]
>
> Have you made *your line* already? (*CSP* 110; trans. altered; emphasis added)
>
> *Но вы умеете глядеть так чудотворно.* И уже овладели линией, единственной, как сама жизнь. *Так не упускайте же, не обрывайте ее на мне, оттяните ее, насколько она сама это позволит. Ведите дальше эту черту.* [. . .]
>
> Провели ли вы уже эту черту? (*PSS* 3:16)

Whatever this line is, awakened anew it initiates a process akin to an electrical current—a power force, rather than a light force. Even if Heine waited in "torment" for the force to ignite Camilla, his new vision, given to him by her glance, replaces the old coldness and theatricality: the flow of Apelles' line becomes a wave, proceeding from chapter to chapter, uniting the two lovers *through perception* and moving beyond:

> "Signora," exclaims Heine melodramatically, falling at Camilla's feet. [. . .]
> "Have you made your mark [drawn your line] already? [. . .] What torment!" he sighs in half-whisper, abruptly pulling his hands away from his pale face . . . and *glancing up* into the eyes of an increasingly confused Camilla Ardenze, *notices* to his utter amazement that . . .
> IV
> . . . that this woman is really attractive, almost unrecognizably beautiful, and that the beating of his own heart is like a rising tide gurgling in the wake of a boat. [. . .] The lazy lapping waves wash about her figure. [. . .]
> (*CSP* 110)

> —Синьора,—театрально восклицает Гейне у ног Камиллы [. . .]—провели ли вы уже ту черту? Что за мука!—полушепотом вздыхает он, отрывает руки от внезапно побледневшего лица . . . и, взглянув в глаза все более и более теряющейся госпожи Арденце, к несказанному изумлению своему замечает, что . . .
> IV
> . . . что эта женщина действительно прекрасна, что до неузнаваемости прекрасна она, что биение собственного его сердца, курлыча, как вода за кормой [. . .] и ленивыми, наслаивающимися волнами прокатывается по ее стану. [. . .] (*PSS* 3:16–17)

The mutuality of vital perception, igniting the other in a moment of transformative contact, explains the name Heine's beloved receives in the manuscript: Rondolfina, a circle or cycle which ends in every new artistic instance (Rondo-l-fina) and yet has no end, an image perhaps suggested to Pasternak by Schubert's cycle of songs written to the words of Heine's poetry.[34]

For all of these reasons, in assessing Pasternak's Heine one can suggest a new direction of critical inquiry that presupposes an entanglement of multiple influences, both philosophical and artistic, and that points to an argument

---

34. Heine's poem "Der Doppelgänger" (The Double) struck Schubert with its vision of a specter mocking a lover's agony.

not only with Kant's understanding of apperceptions, but also with Plato's idea of the good, of light and darkness, and particularly of the new role of the poet in the human community. Pasternak's Heine appears at sunset, avoids sunlight, and knows that he is about to "vanish without trace" (*CSP* 104; *PSS* 3:10), but even while embodying an accumulation of Romantic and Gothic imagery, this protagonist is definitely not a vampire who awakens at night and seduces women prone to art and poetry. The hero of "The Mark of Apelles" is conceived as a spirit "breaking out" from a layer of history with no beginning or end, and he speaks for the energy flow of temporal and spatial dimensions that are, in Kantian language, *a priori,* as he himself confides to Camilla: "There are such things as hours and eternities. A whole wealth of eternities exist, and not one of them has any beginning. At the first opportune moment they come bursting forth" [Существуют часы, существуют и вечности. Их множество, и ни у одной нет начала. При первом же удобном случае они вырываются наружу] (*CSP* 110; *PSS* 3:16). Conceived as a force located outside of time, this Heine[35] is called not merely into reality, but to a stage or a space where the themes of darkness and light, hours and eternities acquire new and possibly prophetic significance for his author.

In alluding to the darkness of the stage, Heine recaptures the absence of the sunlight associated with his presence in the story, but he also communicates a more alarming sense of impending turmoil, stemming from "real life's most dangerous places—bridges and crossings" (*CSP* 110; *PSS* 3:16). As the story seeks to portray the forces of inspiration at work, or the darkest "crossings" of culture, Pasternak articulates a new theme—the danger surrounding these fermenting "living dynamic centers" of thought. So hidden is their essence and origin that humankind needs more light to discover their secret. This is at least how Heine justifies to Camilla the theatrical nature of his own language and images as he reintroduces the conflict of light and darkness that characterizes Pasternak's story:

> Yes, it's the stage again. But why not let me stay a little in this pool of bright light? After all, it's not my fault that in real life the most dangerous places— bridges and crossings—are the most brightly lit. How harsh it is! Everything else is sunk in gloom. On such a bridge, let us say a stage, a man flares up in the light of the flickering rays as if he had been put on show,

---

35. See Bykov's summary of the interview with Evgenij Borisovich Pasternak, whose testimony possibly reflects Pasternak's own words about the novella, and are colored further by the habitual Mayakovsky–Pasternak comparison, though milder in tone. Here, in contrast to other critical readings, Pasternak's son asserts that the hero of the story is Heine himself and that the love melodrama is a pure metaphoric fiction (2007, 118).

surrounded by a railing against the backdrop of the town, of chasms and signal lights in the river bank [. . .]. (*CSP* 109–10)

Да, это снова подмостки. Но отчего бы и не позволить мне побыть немного в полосе полного освещения? Ведь я не виной тому, что в жизни сильнее всего освещаются опасные места: мосты и переходы. Какая резкость! Все остальное погружено во мрак. На таком мосту, пускай это будут и подмостки, человек вспыхивает, озаренный тревожными огнями, как будто его выставили всем напоказ, обнесши его перилами, панорамой города, пропастями и сигнальными рефлекторами набережных [. . .]. (*PSS* 3:16)

Heine's musings, introduced into the text as if in the middle of idle chatter, happen to reflect not only the danger of darkness, but also the danger of a chase, for the poet in Heine's speech is hunted down with searchlights and surrounded with rails and fences as if in siege or a narrowing cage.

It is somewhat ironic, therefore, that this image of the stage in "The Mark of Apelles" has been understood by critics (Aucouturier 1969) as akin to the artistic grimacing and showing off on the stage in "Some Propositions" [Несколько положений]—and opposed in this to a form of art that hides, according to the same passage, in darkness among spectators:

In our days it [art] has seen make-up and powder and the dressing room, and it is exhibited on the stage. [. . .] It is put on the show, whereas it should be hiding in the gallery, unrecognized, hardly aware that it cannot fail to give oneself away, and that when it hides in the corner it is stricken with translucency and phosphorescence as though with some disease. (*CSP* 259–60)

[А]в наши дни оно познало пудру, уборную и показывается с эстрады [. . .]. Оно показывается, а оно должно тонуть в райке, в безвестности, почти не ведая, что на нем шапка горит, и что, забившееся в угол, оно поражено светопрозрачностью и фосфоресценцией, как некоторой болезнью. (*PSS* 5:24)

Such an identification—Heine's poet on the stage and the art of make-up and powder of "Some Propositions"—is a serious misreading that loses the central impetus of the story. In fact, the English translations of both passages tend to mute the subtle difference in the original Russian, for the English word "stage" in both passages neutralizes the singular nuances of the original. Heine uses the word "подмостки" for a theatrical platform, that is, a word etymologically related to a bridge (мост) or crossing (переход), with the root of "bridge" (подмостки-мост) emphasizing the dangerous transitions between two spheres of reality. By contrast, in "Some Propositions" the term used for the stage is "эстрада," that is, the stage of popular culture. In contrast to the stage-performer of "Some Propositions," Heine's figure on the bridge-platform is drawn as an endangered self, a self called upon to step onto a crossing between two worlds, or rather pulled onto it, illuminated and acted upon possibly against his will—a theme intensified many years later in Pasternak's famous poem "Hamlet." In contrast to the figure of Hamlet in the later poem, the urgency of danger in "The Mark of Apelles" is unexpected, even alarming, for there appears no inherent threat to the elegant and seductive protagonist who invariably brings calm to chaos and darkness. As far as the context of the story is concerned, there is no explanation for this strangest of emphases, unless the passage, just like Pasternak's Heine (and later the figure of Hamlet in the poem) acquires its real significance atemporally and intertextually.

As argued throughout this chapter, Pasternak's story of 1915 is imbued with philosophical themes and images, and the story's conflict of light and darkness indicates somewhat fleeting allusions to Plato's cave allegory. These allusions, however (as argued in 3.1) are more significantly present in *Safe Conduct*—in Pasternak's recollections of leaving philosophy for poetry. Pasternak, in fact, argues with Plato by insisting upon the existence of the force that can compete with the force of light. Moreover, Pasternak admits in *Safe Conduct* that his decision to become a poet and a writer after studying philosophy would be altogether incomprehensible to his Marburg professor Hermann Cohen, whose raised eyebrows at this choice Pasternak describes so vividly:

What should I say to him? "Verse?" he would drawl. "Verse!" Had he not sufficiently studied the whole of human mediocrity and its subterfuges? "Verse!" (*CSP* 57)

Что я скажу ему? "Verse?"—протянет он. "Verse!" Мало изучил он человеческую бездарность и ее уловки?—"Verse." (*PSS* 3:189)

In "The Mark of Apelles," where Pasternak employs so many of the themes he discovered in Marburg, he actually counters his teacher's contempt for poetry by returning to the famous image of the cave—to that enigmatic, enlightened, and thus endangered figure of the philosopher returning into the deepening darkness.

Thus, in the words of Heine about the endangered poet, the allusion to the cave allegory signals an additional and an unexpected meaning—it recasts the primacy of philosophy as the pathway to the world of eternity, with the sun as its primary image of the good. If at the beginning of Book VII of Plato's *Republic* the enlightened figure of the philosopher having beheld the sun re-enters the cave, this newcomer becomes deeply disoriented in the new setting and is awkward in his movements:

> Now if he should be required to contend with these perpetual prisoners in 'evaluating' these shadows while his vision was still dim and before his eyes were accustomed to the dark [. . .] would he not provoke laughter, and would it not be said of him that he had returned from his journey aloft with his eyes ruined and it was not worth while even to attempt the ascent? And if it were possible to lay hands on and to kill the man who tried to release them and lead them up, would they not kill him? (Bk. VII, 517a; 1930, 749)

In alluding to this figure surrounded by the darkness of the cave, Pasternak challenges Plato as he puts art into a context and setting that Plato had reserved exclusively for his philosophers. This means that "The Mark of Apelles," among its many themes, reconsiders the ancient quarrel of Platonic philosophy with poetry.

In Pasternak the figure that stands for the atemporal and eternal, always threatened by the darkness within which he exercises his gift, is no longer the philosopher, but the poet—less awkward, more graceful and self-assured, perhaps more seductive, but equally endangered. Unconsciously, perhaps, Pasternak introduces here a theme whose authenticity goes beyond "The Mark of Apelles" and whose reality is to be tested not merely by literary critics, reluctant editors, and publishers, but by the unveiling of history itself, which, like Heine in the narrative, was moving in 1915 inexorably toward chaos and an eclipsed sun.

4

"Letters from Tula"

"Was ist Apperzeption?"

A strange fate befell Pasternak's "Letters from Tula." Among his critics the story provokes a silence almost as profound[1] as its protagonist's apprehension of the "complete physical silence within his soul": "Not an Ibsen silence, but an *acoustic* one" [в душе настанет полная физическая тишина. Не ибсеновская, а *акустическая*] (*CSP* 123; *PSS* 3:30; emphasis in original). This critical reaction, reminiscent of the equally taciturn reception of "The Mark of Apelles," has a few features characteristically its own. The dearth of interpretative approaches in the case of "Letters" is all the more remarkable since the story must have been intended to provoke debate, completed as it was in 1918 (a year not without significance in Russian history) for a collection dedicated to the ideological understanding of art.[2] Pasternak's goals for the story were ambitious, even boisterous. In a letter to his parents (February 7, 1917), he spoke of the future story steeped in theoretical discourse [там будет много теории] and emphasized his desire to separate himself from all "isms," to adopt a form akin to a diary or letters of correspondence,

---

1. Payne's observation that "nearly all of *Doctor Zhivago* is contained in embryo in this short, closely written sketch" (1961, 103) constitutes an exception, as is also the work of Gorelik (2000, 53–60), which emphasizes the story's capacity to provoke confusion even in the most knowledgeable of Pasternak's critics (53).

2. For a fuller account, see Barnes (1989, 268–69); Fleishman (1990a, 93–96); *PSSCom* 3:540.

and to mingle ideology with the "concrete" citations of fictional sources (*PSS* 7:322). The disjuncture between his conviction that the story would contain some of his most deeply felt theory, on the one hand, and what can only be called the miserly amount of subsequent debate, on the other, could suggest either a certain eccentricity in Pasternak's judgments and aims (which he as a young writer failed to communicate), or the misdirection of critical inquiry, or, again, a mixture of both options. In this chapter I argue that the story has been read for a long time in a key that is essentially unproductive and that critics have ignored many textual clues that suggest a focus on the processes involved in the coalescence between art and the moral quest in a world rapidly losing its ethical orientation.

In taking up the theoretical design of "Letters from Tula," this chapter will apply some of the philosophical themes discovered in "The Mark of Apelles" and extend them to include the Kantian notion of apperception—also a key Neo-Kantian preoccupation and the subject-matter of Pasternak's studies at the universities of both Moscow and Marburg.[3] In his portrait of Hermann Cohen in *Safe Conduct*, Pasternak foregrounds this philosophical principle as he depicts a severe Cohen asking his students "Was ist Apperzeption?" and failing those who believed it was "durchfassen" (to grasp through) (*CSP* 56; *PSS* 3:188).[4] Pasternak, as I shall argue both in this and the subsequent chapter, did not disappoint Cohen in this regard, but, like Cohen himself, did not fully share Kant's belief that all phenomenological data can be successfully synthesized within the autonomous self. Nonetheless, both Cohen and Pasternak understood only too well the force of Kant's argument that perception alone cannot unify personality and that only apperception "in contrast to perception deals with a unified consciousness, rather than with the separated contents" [Апперцепция в отличие от перцепции; единство сознания как особенность сознания, а не содержаний] (*Lehrjahre* I:268). It is clear, of course, that "Letters from Tula" cannot but be read in the context of Pasternak's primary theoretical interests of 1918—his desire to address in prose the question of what constitutes the unified human being,[5] as it is also apparent

---

3. See here Fleishman *Lehrjahre* 11:138; Vigilianskaya (2007).

4. Pasternak was rarely given to nonconsequential descriptions without an underlying emphasis on the importance of the theme he was conveying (even when on the surface he appeared to be merely chatting). In fact, the appearance of mere chat is often his favorite method of introducing a major theme.

5. Barnes emphasizes that the overall goal of Pasternak in 1918 was working on his "projected book of articles on man," *Quinta Essentia* (1989, 256). See also Pasternak's insistence in "Some Propositions": "By its feeling, through its spirituality, prose seeks and finds man in the category of speech" [Чутьем, по своей одухотворенности, проза ищет и находит человека в категории речи] (*CSP* 261; *PSS* 5:26).

that in pursuing this interest he could not bypass the principal direction of his university training, that is, the question of apperception and the Kantian emphasis that a unified personality emerges only on the level of the transcendental ego and can never be inferred simply through the data supplied by perception.[6]

My argument throughout seeks not merely to establish Pasternak's employment of Kant's theory of apperception in his narrative design (4.1–4.2), but also to demonstrate the writer's argument with Kant and his own emerging emphasis on the importance of creativity and play for others in the process of the conscious synthesis of impressions, be it the case of his story's protagonists or the contrasting case of the obnoxious "film actors" from Moscow (4.3). The difficulty of the topic, as in all arguments concerning the philosophical Pasternak, remains that of direct access and demonstrability: critical thought must find a way to elucidate philosophical influences even though Pasternak never explains the philosophical direction of his thought. He may have mentioned the emphasis on "theory" in his letters to his parents (*PSS* 7:322), but what he demonstrates in art *must be read by others,* not proclaimed by the author.[7] And yet unless the philosophical subtext of Pasternak's thoughts on apperception—deepened by Cohen's thought on the necessity of bringing together citizenship, philosophy, and art—is unveiled, the story's principal importance in Pasternak's thought is lost altogether (4.4), and this loss is colossal, for the story contains an admission of one of the deepest realignments in Pasternak's life. Therefore, this step—toward the traces of a self-erasing philosophical subtext—needs to be firmly taken, for Pasternak's interests in the mysteries of perception also explain to a remarkable degree his lifelong interest in Lev Tolstoy, who was not merely the *genius loci* of Tula, but also a man of many tasks and responsibilities, ready to sacrifice beauty for the sake of morality and justice, and yet possessing a singular all-uniting gift—"the passion of creative contemplation" [страсть творческого созерцания]—a gift that, as we shall

---

6. This interest also directed his plans during his work on *The Childhood of Luvers* (cf. the account of his philosophical interests in 1917–18 in Chapter 5 (5.1)).

7. In terms of explaining his aims, Pasternak, for many years and particularly in his youth, was exceptionally tight-lipped. In a short essay, published in 1928, in *Chitatel' i pisatel'* (4–5): 4, he formulates this best: "Now about the reader. I require nothing from him and have only great wishes for him. The arrogance and egoism that lie at the base of a writer's appeal to his "audience" are alien to me and beyond my comprehension. [. . .] Very probably, I like the reader more than I can say. Like him, I am reticent and uncommunicative, and unlike most writers, I cannot conceive of any correspondence with him." [Теперь о читателе. Я ничего не хочу от него и многого ему желаю. Высокомерный эгоизм, лежащий в основе писательского обращения к "аудитории," мне чужд и недоступен. [. . .] Вероятно, я люблю читателя больше, чем могу сказать. Я замкнут и необщителен, как он, и в противоположность писателям переписки с ним не понимаю] (*CSP* 267–68; *PSS* 5:220).

see further, is not without some bearing upon Pasternak's struggle with the synthetic capacity of apperception in "Letters from Tula" (4.2; 4.5).

4.1 "Was ist Apperzeption?"
Finding a fruitful approach to "Letters from Tula"

There is no need to debate the accepted biographical fact that Pasternak's Neo-Kantian training was deep and genuine, and that it reflected the intellectual language of the time. In Fleishman's words, the "wide use of neo-Kantian terminology in literary battles, in the purely literary press, contributed to further dissemination of the ideas of the Marburg school among the Moscow artistic elite" (Fleishman 1990a, 28). Furthermore, as Fleishman aptly observes, Pasternak's particular interest was always in aesthetics and philosophy, which he approached with ambitious zeal: "Just as his transfer to the university's philosophy department was provoked by Pasternak's efforts to surpass Skriabin in this sphere, his zealous study of the Marburg philosophers originated in his desire to understand more fully the aesthetics of those who were the mentors of his generation in literature, Andrei Bely and the other symbolists" (1990a, 29). Christopher Barnes equally emphasizes Pasternak's enthusiasm for Neo-Kantianism, a philosophical direction which, he stresses, prevailed in Moscow both in "the Musaget philosophical circle run by Fyodor Stepun, who was a follower of the Freiburg Neo-Kantian, Heinrich Rickert" (1989, 121) and among university "students and younger lecturers [steeped in] the teachings of Henri Bergson, German Neo-Kantianism, and the phenomenology of Edmund Husserl" (122).

It is equally true, however, that all the critical emphasis upon Neo-Kantian influences in Pasternak is usually focused upon the phenomenological *Wesensschau* of Husserl—the elimination of the sharp divide between observer and observed.[8] The erasure of the demarcation line between subject and object, so helpful, according to scholars, for understanding *The Childhood of Luvers*,[9] does surprisingly little for "Letters from Tula." Indeed, writing a story for a volume dedicated to ideologies of art should have given Pasternak a rare opportunity to demonstrate his mastery of philosophical themes within

---

8. In this respect there seems to exist an established critical consensus, reinforced by Barnes as he echoes Fleishman's judgment: "In Lazar Fleishman's paraphrase of Husserl: 'Intuitive recognition preserves the object in its authenticity. Man does not perform the act of cognition, but lives within it. It is not I who must speak about the object, about existence—the object and existence must speak about themselves'" (Barnes 1989, 122).

9. See Fleishman (1977, 19–21).

a new political setting and, perhaps, to establish his own trail-blazing path in aesthetics, but nothing happened, even though critics to this day remain polite and sympathetic toward the story that, in speaking about some unknown film actors making some unknown film, apparently settles the author's unending score with Mayakovsky—and all of this in the catastrophic 1918 (Barnes 1989, 268). For all the critical forbearance, however, "Letters from Tula" appears in critical accounts to thematize only the banal:[10] the poet of the story, heart-broken and overly emotional over his separation from his beloved, complains about film actors as "he finds himself involuntarily associated with their play-ing the genius and their declamatory gestures and phraseology," while the story's elderly actor, depressed with filming, returns home and "begins playing through to himself one of his old roles" (Barnes 1989, 267–68). Aside from the opposition between the poetic and the dramatic, the authentic and the preten-tious, the story displays a new "moralizing tendency" (Fleishman 1990a, 94), unusual for Pasternak; the writer does, indeed, appear to claim high moral ground,[11] following in this the example of Tolstoy: "Indeed, this is Tula! [. . .] This is an occurrence on the *territory of conscience*" [Ведь это Тула! [. . .] Это случай на *территории совести*] (*CSP* 119; *PSS* 3:29; emphasis in origi-nal). If Pasternak's supposed intention of developing "much theory" within a narrative is realized in this handful of commonalities, Pasternak, the prose-writer, must have been an exceptionally pedestrian thinker and a personality radically different from the groundbreaking poet of *My Sister Life*.[12] It is all the more disconcerting then that Pasternak himself, at least in 1918, was so unaware of these obvious shortcomings that he continued to push on with the publication of this prose work for several years, long after the plans for the initial theoretical volume were suspended.

The interpretative picture changes significantly, however, when the Pla-tonic themes of "The Mark of Apelles" are viewed as relevant to the analy-sis of the "Letters," and the story's vigor increases even more dramatically when Pasternak's "Neo-Kantianism" is expanded beyond phenomenological subject-object blending to reveal instead a spectacular study in apperception. The importance of the principle of apperception for the history of philoso-phy is by no means minor: Kantian apperception presupposes the existence

10. Even Gorelik's insistence that the story actively asserts the necessity of the artist to forego his personal interests in order to enter his surroundings (2000, 60) cannot break the spell of lukewarm critical regard.

11. Mossman (1972, 289–80).

12. The story took shape while Pasternak was working on *My Sister Life* (Barnes 1989, 267–68), and when it was finally published in 1922, just after *My Sister Life* (Fleishman 1990a, 111), the success of his poetry far outweighed the success of the prose.

of the transcendental ego, which alone can unify consciousness, and without whose capacity for synthesis the multiple data infused by the *a priori* and *a posteriori* phenomena supplied by perception remain merely a disunited flow. The reality of apperception was central to Hermann Cohen and the Marburg school, where Cohen's dream of developing a logical investigation of synthetic unity in self-consciousness was realized in setting out the formal categories of apperception for the *a priori* principles of space and time.[13] In Cohen's rendition of Kantian principles, the unity of synthetic judgment (the blending of *a priori* and *a posteriori* aspects of perception) presupposes the manifold data of *a priori* categories in and through experience, a "rhapsody of perception" to be processed and unified in the individual consciousness:

> For our conception, the essential point of the *a priori* lies solely in the fact that it contains the formal condition of experience. As a consequence we only uphold "synthetic unity in the connection of the manifold" as an *a priori* category. For experience in general is not possible without this. By means of it, the "rhapsody of perceptions" becomes "synthetic unity of the phenomena." (*KTE* 101; trans. Poma-Denton 11)

In the criticism of Pasternak's early poetry, including *My Sister Life,* written for the most part just before "Letters," the glorification of the poet's gaze as it adjusts between eternity and history has been attributed to the poet's ecstatic temperament, to his characteristic manner of coordinating between the upper and lower spheres within the lyrical subject (Zholkovsky 1978; 1994, 286–87; Fateeva 2003, 176–79). However, this pervasive emphasis on the synthesis between the infinite and the finite in spatial and temporal landscapes can also be understood as a reflection of his deeply rooted interest in the laws of apperception—a synthetic blending of the *a priori* and *a posteriori*[14] made proverbial by his poetry:

---

13. See here Cohen about the a priori nature of categories: "Although not a Kantian expression, it can be in the spirit of Kant to observe: how space is the form of outer intuition and time that of inner intuition; thus transcendental apperception is the form for the categories. Self-consciousness is the transcendental condition under which we produce the pure concepts of understanding. Synthetic unity is the form that, as a common element, is at the base of all the single types of unity thought in the categories" (*KTE* 144; trans. Poma-Denton 11–12).

14. It is with similar interests that Pasternak will endow his young Yuri Zhivago: Yuri, qualified in general medicine, "had a specialist knowledge of the eye," and his pursuit of "the physiology of sight was in keeping with other sides of his character—his creative gifts and his preoccupation with imagery in art and the logical structure of ideas" (*Zhivago* 79: *PSS* 4:80).

Through the window I'll call out to children
What millennium, my dear ones,
Is presently in our yard?
      ***

My dear—it's horror! When the poet loves,
The unshackled god is infatuated,
And chaos crawls out into the light
As in ancient times.

Tons of fog make his eyes tear up.
He is covered by it. He seems like a mammoth. (1917)

Сквозь фортку крикну детворе
Какое, милые, у нас
Тысячелетье на дворе?
      ***

Любимая—жуть! Когда любит поэт,
Влюбляется бог неприкаянный,
И хаос опять выползает на свет,
Как во времена ископаемых.

Глаза ему тонны туманов слезят.
Он застлан. Он кажется мамонтом. (*PSS* 1:155; 1917)

Apperception, synthetic wholeness, the transcendental ego in its comprehension of *a priori* categories, transcendental consciousness with its intuitive grasp of the "*a priori* of synthetic wholeness" [a priori синтетических единств] (*Lehrjahre* II:88)—these themes are all-pervasive in Pasternak's student diaries, and his notes dedicated to Cohen's treatment of "synthetic judgment" are particularly illuminating in this regard. However, precisely where the Neo-Kantians, following Kant, see the unity of consciousness emerging from all "the forms of perception," Pasternak suggests a contrast (and later contradiction) between synthetic consciousness and the logical "forms of thought processes." In his view, it is precisely out of this contradiction that there emerges a living spontaneous unity of receptivity, an *a priori* "transcendental" potential of consciousness:

[T]here is an antagonistic meeting of creativity in its potential (not the analyses of creativity, but creativity as such) with the judgment regarding the material object, and through the soil of this antagonism there awakens in us creativity in its different forms—as an aspect of antagonism between the associations of judgments and transcendental synthesis.

[Е]сть антагонистическая встреча творчества в потенции (не суждения о творчестве, а творчество) с суждением об объекте, на почве которого в нас [?] это творчество так или иначе пробудилось, в роде антагонизма между ассоциацией представлений и трансценд[енталь]ным синтезом. (*Lehrjahre* II:139–40)

What was for Pasternak-the-student, then, the overlap between transcendental synthesis in consciousness and transcendental metaphysics (spearheaded by his own study of multiple philosophical approaches, including those of Plato, Kant, and the Neo-Kantians) becomes in Pasternak-the-writer one of his most characteristic themes—the adjustment of the perception of the inhabitants of eternity, the "*a priori* lyricists," to the particularized historical setting. Whether or not unified consciousness emerges as a result of this adjustment remains very much an open question, but what is always emphasized in Pasternak is the need to address the antagonistic contradictory data by means of engagement in creative work.[15] The aesthetic and ethical, imitative and passionately personal do not want to cohere unless they challenge creativity, and the effort to find the answer to the gaps between them[16] is an

---

15. In *Zhivago*, the antagonism between a priori and a posteriori manifests itself directly, and not as covert, albeit crucial, philosophical content. The reality of death seems to stand out as a gap or contradiction—a mysterious challenge addressed to the synthetic consciousness. In responding to this call, the philosopher Vedenyapin speaks of the work of time and memory in creating a second universe, called human history: "he developed his old view of history as another universe, made by man with the help of time and memory in answer to the challenge of death" [он развивал свою давнишнюю мысль об истории как о второй вселенной, воздвигаемой человечеством в ответ на явление смерти с помощью явлений времени и памяти] (Zhivago 66; *PSS* 4:67). Young Yuri, influenced by Vedenyapin, senses this "presence of mystery tangible in everything" [присутствие тайны чувствовалось во всем] when working as a medical student in the anatomic theater (*Zhivago* 66; *PSS* 4:66) and realizes that "art has two constant, two unending concerns: it always meditates on death and thus always creates life" [Сейчас, как никогда, ему было ясно, что искусство всегда, не переставая, занято двумя вещами. Оно неотступно размышляет о смерти и неотступно творит этим жизнь] (*Zhivago* 90; *PSS* 4:91).

16. Pasternak's love for *Hamlet,* the play and its protagonist, was fueled by the fact that Hamlet answers the gap in reality and that being called by this contradiction in life, by the eternal conveyed by chance, he finds strength to respond: "[W]hen appearance and reality are shown to be at variance—to be indeed separated by the abyss—the message is conveyed by supernatural means [. . .]. What is important is that chance has allotted Hamlet the role of judge of his time and servant of the future" [Когда обнаруживается, что видимость и действительность не сходятся и их разделяет пропасть, не существенно, что напоминание о лживости мира приходит в сверхъестественной форме [. . .]. Гораздо важнее, что

invitation issued by what Pasternak will eventually call "the drama of high destiny, a life preordained to a heroic task" [драма высокого жребия, заповеданного подвига, вверенного назначения] (*Remember* 131; *PSS* 5:75). If one applies such a perspective to "Letters from Tula," the story—banal and seemingly self-absorbed—displays unexpected cohesiveness, depth, and thematic richness, suggesting new and fruitful spaces for analysis.

4.2 Between love and art in the world of reflections:
The adjustment of the protagonists' gaze

The sublunary world of the story, in which a nameless poet bemoans his lonely state and an aging actor[17] tries to act out an eccentric scene in his room, can now be approached as a space characterized by multiple crossings and pathways between unknown destinations. In Plato's philosophy the material world is made up of reflections only (imitations of ideas); in Hume's language, this landscape of vital impressions is imbued with contiguities and similarities, both spatial and temporal; in Kant, the disparate and contradictory phenomena presented to perception demand an integration at the deepest, transcendental level of consciousness. At the opening of "Letters from Tula," human beings are in transit; they seek to understand their particular locality through a multitude of reflections, with every subject reflected in the other.[18] All the while, some major and as yet unspecified event, already in the past, continues to pervade both the present and the future:

> The sun was setting. A bridge with the inscription "Upa" sailed across a hundred carriage windows at the very instance when the stoker [. . .] discovered the town [. . .] through the roar of his own hair and the fresh excitement of the evening saw it speeding to meet them.
>
> Meanwhile people over there were greeting one another in the street and saying, "Good evening." To this some added, "Have you been there?" "No, just going," others replied. "You're too late," they were told. "It's all over." (*CSP* 119)

волею случая Гамлет избирается в судьи своего времени и в слуги более отдаленного] (*Remember* 131; *PSS* 5:75).

17. There is no historical or fictional figure with this name, and therefore Savva Ignatievich has no intertextual references—this explains the choice for the name. The poet of course is without a name. Thus the protagonists belong to this text and no other.

18. Cf. Pasternak in the poem "Marburg" about the world of stone open to his eyes: "And all of these were merely likenesses" [И все это были подобья] (*PSS* 1:110).

Оно садилось. Мост с надписью "Упа" поплыл по сотне окошек в ту самую минуту, как кочегару [. . .] открылся в шуме его собствен-ных волос и в свежести вечернего возбуждения, в стороне от путей, быстро несшийся навстречу город.

Тем временем там, здороваясь на улицах, говорили: "С добрым вечером. " Некоторые прибавляли: "Оттуда?"—"Туда, "—отвечали иные. Им возражали: "Поздно. Все кончилось." (*PSS* 3:26)

In Fleishman's view, Pasternak the philosopher was never a docile or obedi-ent thinker: "the independence and originality of Pasternak was expressed not only in the character of his literary *débuts*, but in his philosophical studies" (Fleishman *Lehrjahre* 14). The same critical temperament can be seen at work from the very first passages of the story, for if Pasternak here is commenting upon the life of the prisoners in the cave, all of whom live in the neighbor-hood of reflected rather than real events and objects, his depiction is more positive than a Platonic world of shadows. Pasternak's emphasis on communal reflections as a means of communication also introduces, and does so with an assured touch, a serious conflict with Kant—undermining in the very first paragraph (and promising to continue to do so in the future) the autonomy of transcendental consciousness and presenting instead the data of percep-tion as essentially a shared experience. On the whole, however, in relation to Pasternak's technique in "The Mark of Apelles," the frame, suggestive of the cave allegory with its reflections and shadows, signals the presence of an endangered, possibly disoriented figure at the center of the setting, and this, indeed, proves to be the case. The story, in two parts, presents in each segment a different kind of disorientation and a different kind of protagonist, the poet and the old actor, one at the beginning and the other at the end of his artistic (and earthly) life.

"Now if he should be required to contend with these perpetual prison-ers in 'evaluating' these shadows while his vision was still dim and before his eyes were accustomed to the dark [. . .] would he not provoke laughter, and would it not be said of him that he had returned from his journey aloft with his eyes ruined?" (Bk. VII, 517a; 1930, 749), Socrates observes in the *Republic* about the state of the philosopher who returns to the cave from the sunlight. "You possess that vital vision. You have already mastered a line as unique as life itself, so don't abandon it" (*CSP* 110; *PSS* 3:16), exclaims Heine to Camilla in "The Mark of Apelles," himself struck that this woman appears as if anew before his eyes. "What misery to be born a poet! What torment is imagination! Sunshine in beer. Sunk to the very bottom of the bottle. [. . .] Oh my dear, they are all strangers around me. [. . .] Why they think it is their sun they sip

with milk from their saucer" [Какое горе родиться поэтом! Какой мучи-
тель воображенье! Солнце—в пиве. Опустилось на самое донышко
бутылки. [. . .] Ах, родная, все чужие кругом. [. . .] Ведь они думают,
свое солнце похлебывают с молоком из блюдец] (CSP 120; PSS 3:27),
writes the young poet to his beloved in "Letters from Tula," clearly unable to
adjust his vision and distinguish clearly between what is near and what is "far
far away, beyond the horizon" [очень, очень далеко, за горизонтом] (CSP
120: PSS 3:27). "Some modern movements have imagined that art [. . .] can
be resolved into means of representation, whereas it is composed of organs of
perception. It should always be one with the audience and have the clearest,
truest, most perceptive view of all" [Современные течения вообразили что
исскуство [. . .] может быть разложено на средства изобразительно-
сти, тогда как оно складывается из органов восприятия] (CSP 259; PSS
5:25), Pasternak observes in "Some Propositions." And in *Safe Conduct* Hermann Cohen, as already noted, fails students unable to explain the principles
of apperception (CSP 56; PSS 3:188). In short, Pasternak's early work is imbued
with the conviction that a very specific quality of perception constitutes an
integral part of the artist's power, and his allusions to Plato and Kant, as well as
his reminiscences of Cohen, suggest the key philosophical principles that are
destined to become an inalienable part of his narrative art.

"Letters from Tula" is highly significant in this context. Its theme—the
true quest of the artist, whose journey is stretched uneasily between two infinite passions, love and his all-absorbing craft, among dangerous and violent
reflections in a landscape steeped in awakened memories and criss-crossed by
trains—will later become Pasternak's signature, the landscape of Tula being
its first (not most successful but still fascinating) articulation. The application
of Kant's principles of perception and apperception clarifies the narrative's
framework, which remains otherwise obscure and perhaps unimpressive.[19]
The story's startling fragmentation[20] forbids any facile alignment; instead
it drives the narrative through seemingly contradictory aspects of vision
towards not so much an integration, but a realignment of the protagonists'
inner world. Hence, the poet and the actor, unaware of each other throughout
an apparently uneventful sleepless night, between sunset and sunrise, are not

---

19. See here Gorelik's resistance to Fleishman's "story within a story" or the "matreshka"
design of the narrative (2000, 53–54).

20. Cf. Rudova: "There are problems with spatiality: objects, places, sounds, and memories
seem somehow to co-exist in one plane. The narrative lacks smoothness and continuity. It
can serve as an excellent illustration of the ideal type of writing praised by Kruchenykh and
Khlebnikov. [. . .] The character's thought development does not follow a linear track, which
contributes to a disappearance of one-point perspective. What we get instead is a free, broken
perspective along which fragments of narration are dispersed" (1994, 100).

only disoriented and forlorn; like Pasternak's Heine, they are caught in the "crossing" between everyday reality and an atemporal world where precise historical knowledge as well as different fragmented memories embodied in the immediate landscape become both awakened and yet simultaneously dissipated. It is in order to overcome this uncertainty during the crossing that the poet has given his beloved a volume of Kluchevsky ("look it up in a textbook, my dear. [. . .] I put it in the case myself" [Дорогая, справься с учебником [. . .] клал сам в чемодан] [*CSP* 121; *PSS* 3:26]), while he himself is engaged in a futile search for a receipt from a pawnshop where the mementos from his past must have been stored.[21] In contrast to the Heine of "Apelles," the characters of this story are not famous in any way, although they do find themselves in Tula, a few miles from Tolstoy's Iasnaia Poliana, a fact that eventually "acts as a lever" for the story's poet.

The choice of Tolstoy is not accidental as far as the story's philosophical themes are concerned.[22] As late as 1956, while describing Tolstoy in his *Sketch for an Autobiography* [Автобиографический очерк],[23] Pasternak continues to attribute to Tolstoy the diverse and mutually opposed "categories" of vision that can be embraced and unified only by his massive talent:[24] "What are we to say of Tolstoy, if we must limit the definition to one characteristic only?" [что сказать о Толстом, ограничив определение одной чертой?] (*Remember* 69; *PSS* 3:322). Proceeding to emphasize Tolstoy's contradictory modes

---

21. Scholars point to the receipt from the pawnshop as a recollection of Pasternak's journey with Siniakova in 1915 (*PSSCom* 3:541). However, the image has a haunting quality: a disoriented speaker finding his way back into immediate historical setting by recalling the mementos of the past, including a history textbook.

22. Mossman senses the relationship between Neo-Kantianism and the role of Tolstoy but is uncertain where to place the focus in this regard, suggesting that in contrast to the Soviet "objective view of history," Pasternak believes that "the shadowy, subjective land of paradox and illogic was the fertile territory of new empirical discovery" (1972, 290). However, Pasternak's interest in apperception must be carefully examined, for the contradiction between unified consciousness and multiple contradictory phenomena is clearly a major theme in the story, and the width of the talent, its multiple strands that leave no room for superficiality—these themes with which Pasternak dealt throughout his life. One finds a similar emphasis on Pasternak's debt to his father because of the latter's multilayered talent (his ability to work on several sketches at once) and yet his all-unifying "eye" (see his letter to Olga Freidenberg of Nov. 30, 1948; Mossman, ed. 1982, 284).

23. The "Sketch" was written in May–June 1956 by request from Goslitizdat (*PSSCom* 3:582).

24. It is customary for critics to emphasize the role of Tolstoy's influence on Pasternak's life in 1918, owing to the effect of Tolstoy's moralizing on the tone of this story (Fleishman 1990a, 94) and the fact that "it is Tolstoy's view of art which Pasternak adopts in his next prose work, 'The Childhood of Luvers'" (Mossman 1972, 290). The contradiction between the multilayered interests and the singular insight that Pasternak always emphasized when speaking of the writer needs to be added to this list.

of thought, Pasternak foregrounds his extraordinary gift of perception, thus echoing, with a mature certainty of touch, the philosophical preoccupations of his own student years (cf. the unifying synthesis of perception in Kantian apperception) as reflected in "Letters from Tula":

> The chief quality of this moralist, leveller, and preacher of a system of justice that would embrace everybody without fear or favor would be an originality that distinguished him from everyone else and verged on the paradoxical.
>
> All his life and at any given moment he possessed the faculty of seeing things in the detached finality of each separate moment, in sharp relief, as we see things only on rare occasions, in childhood, or on the crest of an all embracing happiness, or in a triumph of a great spiritual victory.
>
> To see things like that it is necessary that one's eye should be directed by passion. For it is passion that by its flash illuminates an object, intensifying its appearance.
>
> Such a passion, the passion of creative contemplation, Tolstoy constantly carried about with himself. (*Remember* 69)

> Главным качеством этого моралиста, уравнителя, проповедника законности, которая охватывала бы всех без послаблений и изъятий, была ни на кого не похожая, парадоксальности достигавшая оригинальность.
>
> Он всю жизнь, во всякое время обладал способностью видеть явления в оторванной окончательности отдельного мгновения, в исчерпывающем выпуклом очерке, как глядим мы только в редких случаях, в детстве, или на гребне всеобновляющего счастья, или в торжестве большой душевной победы.
>
> Для того чтобы так видеть, глаз наш должна направлять страсть. Она-то именно и озаряет своей вспышкой предмет, усиливая его видимость.
>
> Такую страсть, страсть творческого созерцания, Толстой постоянно носил в себе. (*PSS* 3:322)

In "Letters from Tula," however, neither the poet nor the old actor is of Tolstoy's stature; rather, they struggle to acquire both for their art and for their alienated self "the faculty of seeing things in the detached finality of each separate moment" (*Remember* 69; *PSS* 3:322). The essential frame of the story, and possibly the deepest preoccupation of Pasternak's art, is, then, this capacity of seeing the diverse and mutually exclusive aspects of reality and yet discovering in this challenge a living, rather than unified, self. As we shall see further, aware that he is reflecting Kant's notion of apperception, in "Letters from Tula" Pasternak does not fully agree with Kant but provides his own solution to the problem of how an individual self is able to comprehend the diversity of observed phenomena.

The difficulty of adjusting perception is the opening leitmotif of "Letters." The poet, whose diary, or rather letter to his beloved, is the first fragment of the story, is oppressed, rather than invigorated, by the disjointedness of the world that meets his sight. He is also burdened by his recognition that there are separate realities of perception—communal or shared spaces with others,[25] whom this young man happens to fear and despise. Apparently in no way reminiscent of "the passion of creative contemplation, [that] Tolstoy constantly carried about with himself," the poet's observations of his surrounding world are accompanied by complaints—even horror—when he realizes that an utterly alien world enters his own through perception:[26]

> They do not realize that their flies stick in yours, or in ours. [. . .]
>
> My dear one, it sickens me! This is a display of the ideals of our age. The fumes that they produce are my own—fumes common to us all! This is the burning smell of woeful insolence and ignorance. This is my own self. [. . .] How dreadful to see oneself in others. It is a caricature of [left incomplete] [. . .] (*CSP* 120–21)

> Думают не в твоем, не в нашем вязнут их мухи [. . .].
>
> Дорогой друг! Мне тошно. Это—выставка идеалов века. Чад, который они подымают,—мой, общий наш чад. Это угар невежественности и самого неблагополучного нахальства. Это я сам. [. . .] Как страшно видеть свое на посторонних. Это шарж на (оставлено без продолжения). [. . .] (*PSS* 3:27–28)

As Pasternak remains true to his plans, set out in the letter to his parents, "to keep to the concreteness of different fictional citations of unknown authorities" (*PSS* 7:322), these fictional "authorities" are represented by a name-

---

25. A sense of similar "physical" impatience and strain is featured in Pasternak's recollection of his university years, when observing the capacity of the students' minds to be lifted only as high as the ceiling, he feels "these attacks of chronic impatience" (*CSP* 32–33; *PSS* 3:160–61).

26. See Rudova's argument (1994; 1997) that understanding Pasternak depends on seeing in his work the influence of Cubo-futurism (see also Wiegers 1999). However, the technique of montage or "projection of different objects into one plane" (Rudova 1994, 139) may also be approached not as an end in itself, but as a "rhapsody of impressions" that remain a prelude to a deeper, transcendental force emerging in the self.

less poet, whose future art is only a potential still forming, and an actor far past his prime, who, with the unlikely name of Savva Ignatievich, is definitively not to be found in any historical chronicles of Russian culture. Both men, however, shocked by the mundane, long for a lost transcendent: the poet mourns for his lost beloved; the actor dreams of the deepest artistic engagement, disconcerted that for the whole long day he has not heard the real "human speech of tragedy" [оно оставило неудовлетворенной его потребность в трагической человеческой речи] (*CSP* 124; *PSS* 3:31). As the story unfolds, the seeming uneventfulness of the night is called into question; in each case the alterations in the protagonists' inner states and, thus, in the character of their perceptions are intensely dramatic. Without conscious awareness of these processes (although registering his every emotion in his letters), the young man is preparing for his other indelible passion—his future life and art, with the layers of his memory and vision radically realigning. By contrast, the actor, unaware of the finality of his life experiences, is reorienting himself for "extraordinary stillness." Employing several sharp contrasts, Pasternak develops a narrative framework within which both protagonists of "Letters" are experiencing intense shifts between transcendental and experiential perceptions of reality, moving in this regard in contrasting directions: the poet, in his search for the transcendent, proceeds from longing for his beloved to artistic engagement, and the old actor reverses this inner journey and begins to recall anew his long lost and perhaps deepest love, aptly named Liubov' Petrovna.

In *Safe Conduct*, Pasternak speaks of the power of the lovers' passion in *Tristan* and *Romeo and Juliet* and suggests that the theme of these works is "wider than this forceful theme; their theme is a theme of force" [Тема их—тема силы] (*CSP* 54; *PSS* 3:186). Inhabiting a similar state of deepest attachment, the poet of the "Letters" initially holds on to the memory of an extraordinary personal experience. The need to return to life without his lost beloved, kindred to him in her essence, to reverse the journey from the infinite to the everyday, is overwhelmingly painful, but it can (only just) be soothed by his passion for writing:

> Oh, what anguish! I will choke it back, this raging anguish! I will choke it back, this raging anguish, I will dull the ache with verses.
> [. . .] Alas, there is no middle road. One must leave at the second bell, or else set off together on a journey to the end, to the grave. Look now, it will be dawn already when I make this entire journey in reverse—and in every detail too, in every trivial detail. And now they will all have the subtlety of some quite exquisite torture. (*CSP* 120; trans. altered)

О тоска! Забью, затуплю ее, неистовую, стихами.

[. . .] Ах, середины нет. Надо уходить со второго звонка или же отправляться в совместный путь до конца, до могилы. Послушай, ведь будет светать, когда я проделаю весь этот путь целиком в обратном порядке, а то во всех мелочах, до мельчайших. А они будут теперь тонкостями изысканной пытки. (*PSS* 3:26–27)

Biographers refer here to the incident with Nadezhda Sinyakova,[27] who left for Kharkov in April 1915 (*PSSCom* 3:541), but the profound angst of the separation and ensuing readjustment in the young protagonist's inner world (as well as the changing plans for his art) point rather to the power of a farewell described in 1930 in *Safe Conduct*,[28] where Pasternak recollects an occasion when the infinite force of unrequited love left him with his perception of material reality radically altered, an event that demanded an explicit "*crossing* into a new faith" [*переход* в новую веру] assisted by a quickly departing train:

It was the pose of a person *who has fallen down from something high that had held and carried him for a long time*, then let him go, passed noisily over his head, and vanished around the turn forever.

[. . .] *I was surrounded by changed things. Something never before experienced had crept into the essence of reality. The morning recognized my face and made its appearance for the very purpose of being with me and never leaving me.*

[. . .] The end, the end! The end of philosophy, that is, of any thought of it at all.

Just like my fellow passengers on the train, it too would have to come to terms with the fact that *every love is a crossing into a new faith.* (*CSP* 50; 53; emphasis added)

---

27. Barnes suggests either Elena Vinograd or Sinyakova as the prototypes of the poet's beloved (1989, 268). It is notable, however, that the journey with Sinyakova took place in 1915, while the poem "Marburg," which displays so many images in common with "Letters," was written in 1916.

28. It is possible, of course, that the description of farewell "among the train crossings" with Vysotskaya in Marburg is enriched *post factum* by the narrative depth of the "Letters from Tula." The echo of the "Letters" in the Marburg episode is further reinforced by the fact that the anonymous poet, just like Pasternak in *Safe Conduct,* grieves over the incompleteness of the farewell, their separation in the middle of the journey, which he describes as madness, and the necessity to return alone to Moscow. As Payne observes, "Pasternak is inclined to attribute superhuman powers to railroad stations" (1961, 101).

Это была поза человека, *отвалившегося от чего-то высокого, что долго держало его и несло, а потом упустило и, с шумом пронесясь над его головой, скрылось навеки за поворотом.*

[. . .] *Меня окружили изменившиеся вещи. В существо действительности закралось что-то неиспытанное. Утро знало меня в лицо и явилось точно затем, чтобы быть при мне и меня никогда не оставить.*

[. . .] *Конец, конец! Конец философии, то есть какой бы то ни было мысли о ней.*

Как и соседям в купе, ей придется считаться с тем, *что всякая любовь есть переход в новую веру.* (*PSS* 3:181–84)

"Letters from Tula," then, can be viewed as a careful depiction of "this crossing into the new faith," an altogether irrevocable separation between lovers taking two train journeys and going in opposite directions. As if returning to the cave, even if he needs to adjust his vision to the approaching dawn, the poet of the story is to travel alone in the morning[29]—back to the city, while she, with a volume of Kluchevsky's history,[30] has gone over her own "crossing": "So you changed the pathways, as we agreed with the guide"[31] [Ты значит перешла, как мы договорились, с проводником] (*CSP* 120; *PSS* 3:26). The poet's excruciating grief at his separation from the deepest, possibly eternal kindredness may suggest at first that he is also losing his connection with transcendence and needs to adjust instead to the world of phenomenal experience. Indeed, he undergoes singular changes: by the end of the night, the poet (described already in the third person) has forgotten not only the purpose of his journey, but also the addressee of his passionate diary (the name and address of the recipient of his letters), and has become no longer the

---

29. Cf. "I was surrounded by changed things. Something never before experienced had crept into the essence of reality. The morning recognized my face and made its appearance for the very purpose of being with me and never leaving me" [*Меня окружили изменившиеся вещи. В существо действительности закралось что-то неиспытанное. Утро знало меня в лицо и явилось точно затем, чтобы быть при мне и меня никогда не оставить*] (*CSP* 50; *PSS* 3:181). A similar emphasis is on the poem "Marburg": "I recognize the face of the morning" [Я белое утро в лицо узнаю] (*PSS* 1:112).

30. Pasternak was Vysotskaya's tutor, and the emphasis on the history textbook reflects something of the teacher–student relationship.

31. The translation here is altered from "So you changed compartments then, as we agreed, with the conductor" (*CSP* 120). Compare this passage's emphasis on the crossing with the dangerous bridge [переход] in "The Mark of Apelles": "After all, it's not my fault that in real life the most dangerous places—bridges and crossings—are the most brightly lit" [Ведь я не виной тому, что в жизни сильнее всего освещаются опасные места: мосты и переходы] (*CSP* 109–10; *PSS* 3:16).

"I," but rather a "third person" of the narrative—he.[32] Still, the sense of inner vigilance—and his link to the transcendence—is not lost; rather it has shifted from the experience of personal passion to his vocation as an artist involved in the fate of the *other,* the third person:

> The man who had been writing strolled up and down. He thought of many things. He thought of his art and how he might find the right path. He forgot with whom he had been travelling, whom he had seen off, and to whom he was writing. (*CSP* 123)

> Писавший прохаживался. Он думал о многом. Он думал о своем искусстве и о том, как ему выйти на правильную дорогу. Он забыл, с кем ехал, кого проводил, кому писал. (*PSS* 3:30)

Furthermore, there is an indication that his eyesight is beginning to find its focus even in everyday reality, but only by means of some deep realignment that focuses on his emerging art. With the gray dawn, the reader leaves the young protagonist on the platform, once more framed by the new complexity of the light and darkness motif, but ready to buy a ticket for the onward journey:

> The east was turning gray, and a perplexed and rapid dew settled on the face of all conscience, still plunged in deepest night. It was time to think about his ticket. The cocks were crowing and the ticket office was coming to life. (*CSP* 123)

> Серел восток, и на лицо всей, еще в глубокую ночь погруженной совести выпадала быстрая, растерянная роса. Пора было подумать о билете. Пели петухи и оживала касса. (*PSS* 3:30)

If in Kant the synthesis between different layers of experience can be achieved by transcendent consciousness, Pasternak, by contrast, seems to suggest that a full synthesis is impossible to achieve within an isolated self, and that art—the creation of another self, of he rather than I—reflects the ongoing and open-ended process of synthesis, initiated in Tula as a lifelong vocation. The young lyrical poet accepts the premises of this experience and the confusing contrast

---

32. Mossman notes the emphasis on the switch from the first to the third person and links this to the influence of Rilke in *The Notebooks of Malte Laurids Brigge,* where the switch between "I" and "he" is the structural device of the narrative (1972, 289). For the importance of this switch for Pasternak see also Pomorska (1975, 48).

of perspectival angles, adjusting better to everyday reality, but remaining in considerable turmoil, while the switch to the "third" person may indicate the transition to a new genre, fiction with the third person(s), rather than the first-person lyricism of poetry.[33]

The old actor's sense of the eternal, by contrast with the young poet, manifests itself from the very beginning of the narrative as his explicit and lifelong devotion to art—an aesthetic longing that starts to readmit personal memory only after a shocking meeting with an alien reality (an experimentation in violence by "film actors," understood by the old man as free fantasy—a performance that he detests and from which he is also excluded). The first indication of emotional reawakening takes place when he catches himself searching for someone to use a diminutive version of his name (Саввушка), and this need for dear ones persists until he experiences a living re-enactment of a meeting with his younger self in a deeply familiar celebration of homecoming:

> And he gave a start when after five and twenty years he heard—just as he was supposed to—from behind that other partition the beloved joyful reply: "Yes, I am at home!" . . . The old man was stifled with silent sobbing. (*CSP* 125)

> [И] вздрогнул, когда, как это полагалось, на расстоянии двух с половиной десятков лет услыхал за той перегородкой милое, веселое: 'До-о-ма' . . . Старика душили беззвучные рыданья. (*PSS* 3:32)

Furthermore, in his return to his youthful love, lost for so many years of his life behind *that* partition, the old man does not abandon his art:[34] he experiences this meeting with his younger self as a play in which he is finally a master and where he can exhibit "a skill at illusion that a colleague might be proud of on such an occasion" [с иллюзией, которая составила бы гордость иного его брата] (*CSP* 125; *PSS* 3:32). There is, then, textual indication that the old man, reversing the inner journey of the poet and finding his beloved Liubov' Petrovna *without* abandoning his artistic self, achieves the unity denied the poet. This indication appears in the story, however, as supplied through the intrusion of yet another perspective—this time, the emergence of an authorial

---

33. It is noteworthy that Pasternak's decision to write a novel is dated 1918 (the year of "Letters from Tula"): "In January 1918 at the Tsetlins' Pasternak had told Tsvetaeva of an ambition to write a novel 'with a love intrigue and a heroine in it—like Balzac,' and by the summer he was showing the first drafts of it to friends and colleagues" (Barnes 1989, 269).

34. This deeper synthesis between the personal and the artistic leads Gorelik to assert that "the old actor is the only artist of the story" (2000, 55).

voice indicating the fictional nature of the narrative: "And like *the main character*, he too was in search of physical silence. He was the only one in *the story* to find it, having made another to speak through his own lips" [Он тоже, *как главное лицо*, искал физической тишины. В рассказе только он нашел ее, заставив своими устами говорить постороннего] (*CSP* 126; *PSS* 3:32; emphasis added). The age of the old man and his shaken sense of reality suggest that this silence—this achievement of some unity between man and art—is also an indication that his life journey is approaching a stage as finite as his longing for transcendence is infinite.[35]

Without attempting to reconstruct a fuller picture of Pasternak's philosophical debt to his Neo-Kantian training in Marburg (a formidable task, necessitating in any case a very different focus of inquiry), one may suggest that Pasternak appears to accept the premises of Kant's notion of apperception in several crucial ways. First, it is clear that for Pasternak-the-writer the world does not exist outside of the mind and that the mind, in fact, constitutes the world,[36] and, second, that he, as artist, tends to employ multiple changing forms of perception and is drawn to the dramatization of processes in which the perspectives of phenomenal and transcendental "ego-consciousnesses" weave in and out of everyday reality. These multilayered and distinct spheres of perception are reflected in Pasternak's narrative in constant shifts of focus that also include, as we have seen in the case of the poet, the changing patterns of address in a movement away from the first person to a third-person narrative. Pasternak's employment of these multiple perspectives in "Letters from Tula" reflects, therefore, his intentional and painstaking thematization of what is involved in Kantian apperception; he draws a process within each of his protagonists in which the empirical data of everyday reality and longing for the eternal and infinite are being synthesized, realigned, and brought into new focus. However, if in Kant the synthetic unity of all perceived phenomena is achieved by an autonomous transcendental ego, "a permanent spiritual substance underlying the fleeting succession of conscious experience," inaccessible "to direct introspection, but rather inferred from intro-

---

35. It is Mossman's view that "the physical silence attained is figuratively that of a lifeless world bereft of an observer, deaf and muted [. . .] a silence under normal circumstances unavailable" (1972, 290). There is also a transcendent layer here, a performance in front of eternity, which in Pasternak's later poems would be more forcefully introduced, when for example, prior to the emergence of Hamlet on the stage, "the sound is hushed" [Гул затих] (*PSS* 4:515), or in "Bakhanalia": "How much courage is needed / In order to play in front of centuries" [Сколько надо отваги / чтоб играть на века] (*PSS* 4:183). The anticipation of "Hamlet" is noted in Hingley (1983, 63).

36. The theme is identified by Fleishman as the phenomenological position of Husserl (1975, 79–126; 1977, 8–13).

spective evidence" (Runes 1984, 88), one does not find a similar emphasis on autonomy in Pasternak. Reflecting upon the nature of art, Pasternak appears to revise Kant's thought and to assert instead that the multiple strands of experience cannot be synthesized in the isolated, "pure, original, unchangeable consciousness" as postulated by Kant (Runes 1984, 15), but must remain an ever-widening and living experience, inclusive of other selves—an artistic act that is always in play with the other, making "another to speak through one's own lips" [заставив своими устами говорить постороннего] (*CSP* 126; *PSS* 3:32).

The complex philosophical intertext and Pasternak's dialogical engagement with its main precepts (rather than philosophical subservience) explain the disorienting and puzzling quality of the story—its employment of a succession of radically changing viewpoints never fully synthesized in the story and nuanced so carefully[37] that they cannot be easily grasped and processed by the reader. The first essential emphasis, then, is on dislocation and confusion in perception. For instance, as the poet looks, in a highly impractical manner, for a mailbox into which he can drop the letters to his beloved who is already slowly fading from his memory, Pasternak experiments widely with constant shifts of focus from inward (suggesting a close-up of a reflection in water or of seats banging in the train, that is, registering in an almost simultaneous observation two very different locations) to outward (an emphasis upon looking from a great distance), as well as moving the perspective from above (the height of the stars) to below (the trains "lying" upon the earth as if depicted from a very high viewpoint), and crossways over a large distance, making it impossible to suggest who is looking "beyond" or why the scene is observed from so "far away":

Five hours passed. There was quite an extraordinary stillness. It became impossible to tell where the grass ended and where the coal began. A star twinkled. Not a living soul remained by the pumphouse. Water showed black through a moldering cavity in a moss-covered swamp. The reflection of the birch tree trembled there. It quivered feverishly. But this was far far away. Far far away. Apart from the birch tree there was not a soul on the road.

---

37. These separated levels of perception within a single narrative are reflected in a technique responsible for the difficulty associated with Pasternak's early prose (and often understood as Futuristic incomprehensible trans-sense or fragmentary Cubism). For a more substantial reading of Pasternak's prose, the Neo-Kantian "rhapsody of perceptions" waiting to be transformed into the "synthetic unity of the phenomena" should be introduced alongside these concepts (*KTE* 101; trans. Poma-Denton 11).

There was quite extraordinary stillness. Lifeless boilers and coaches lay on the flat earth like piles of low storm clouds on a windless night. [. . .] The Tula trolley line came up from the town. The reversible backrests of the seating banged. The last to alight was a man carrying letters, which jutted from the wide pockets of his broad overcoat. The others made their way into the waiting room. But this man remained outside of the building looking for the green letterbox. But no one could tell where the grass ended and where the coal began. [. . .] The night uttered a long-drawn-out guttural sound—then everything was silent. It was all far, far away, beyond the horizon. (*CSP* 120)

Прошло пять часов. Была необычайная тишина. На глаз нельзя было сказать, где трава, где уголь. Мерцала звезда. Больше не было ни живой души у водокачки. В гнилом продаве мшаника чернела вода. В нем дрожало отраженье березки. Ее лихорадило. Но это было очень очень далеко. [. . .] Кроме нее, не было ни души на дороге.

Была необычайная тишина. Бездыханные котлы и вагоны лежали на плоской земле, похожие на скопления низких туч в безветренные ночи. [. . .] Последний вагон Тульской конки подошел из города. Захлопали откидные спинки скамей. Последним сошел человек с письмами, торчавшими из широких карманов широкого пальто. Остальные направились в зал, к кучке весьма странной молодежи, шумно ужинавшей в конце. Этот остался за фасадом, ища зеленого ящика. Но нельзя было сказать, где трава, где уголь. [. . .] Ночь издала долгий горловой звук—и все стихло. Это было очень, очень далеко, за горизонтом. (*PSS* 3:27)

When placed, however, in the context of Kant's "transcendental apperception" (the "ultimate foundation of the synthetic unity of experience" [Runes 1984, 15]), these narrative patterns show that Pasternak as artist and storyteller portrays the capacity for expansion in human awareness, as he dramatizes the angles of perception from the viewpoints of multiple separated aspects of "ego-consciousness" and searches for an experience that can facilitate for his protagonists the need to integrate external phenomena within an emerging sense of self. In contrast to Kant, Pasternak sees art (desired by his poet) and "play" (practiced by his actor) as essential to this process, and yet he proceeds to distinguish two opposed manifestations of this process: a play calling forth inner alignment and further ongoing synthesis that uncovers moral concerns, and a bohemian, indeed fraudulent, play-acting, dependent upon imitation that misses or bypasses self-consciousness and conscience.

4.3 Searching for synthesis:
Art, play-acting, and film actors from Moscow

The disorientation in immediate historical reality, sensed by the story's protagonists, permits Pasternak to comment upon the revolutionary spirit of the time while displaying his rarely recognizable sly humor (aligned with his better-known political sense and its perilous balance of insight and caution). The uncertain sense of historical reality—the time of troubles [смутное время][38]—is drawn in the story both as a state of incomprehension (communicated to the readers), an intimation of the ongoing, disturbing acts of violence and murder, and as the subject of the film practiced by the actors. In *Doctor Zhivago*, this uncontrollable anxiety of the inhabitants of Moscow in 1918 will be identified and named in the narrative: "The inevitable was approaching. Winter was near and in the human world that very same state of death that winter brings to nature was in the air, finalized, decided upon and incessantly talked about" [Нависало неотвратимое. Близилась зима, а в человеческом мире то, похожее на зимнее обмирание, предрешенное, которое носилось в воздухе и было у всех на устах] (*Zhivago* 183, trans. altered; *PSS* 4:182). In "Letters from Tula," however, Pasternak experiments with the creation of the very spirit of anxiety through the eyes of two people, alienated by the very nature of who they are: the poet who has not yet discovered his voice[39] and the actor who is aging in an alien world. Tula, a place of major upheavals during the civil war, was to experience the revolutionary onslaught in spurts of activity and short periods of rest[40]—a network of rail-

---

38. "Letters from Tula," composed in 1918, Russia's turbulent year that followed upon the altogether unprecedented 1917, cannot be placed alongside such Revolutionary works as Blok's "Twelve" or, for instance, John Reed's *Ten Days that Shook the World* (1919). What happens instead in Pasternak's tale is, above all, an event that had already finished before it properly started and was decisive for the provinces (at the beginning of the story)—an event that needs to be grasped via reflections. As Pasternak notes in *Doctor Zhivago*, the revolution was made in the cities, which, nonetheless, suffered most from what they had engendered: "The people in the cities were as helpless as children in the face of the unknown [. . .], although it was itself the offspring of the city and the creation of city dwellers" [Люди в городах были беспомощны, как дети, перед лицом близящейся неизвестности [. . .], хотя сама была детищем города и созданием горожан] (*Zhivago* 183; *PSS* 4:182).

39. In his recent popular biography, Bykov suggests that Pasternak, in love with Elena Vinogradov, did not notice the Revolution, and quotes here the support of E. B. Pasternak in his interpretation of Gladkov's memoirs (2006, 147).

40. Tula, 200 kilometers south of Moscow, was a strategically important location for rail access because of the River Upa. In 1896, Tula became a major center for the production of armaments and weapons, and for this reason one of the centers of active Bolshevik propaganda during the Revolution. According to Soviet historians, the membership of workers in the Bolshevik party in 1917 grew from 22 people (in February) to 1500 (in October), and on October

roads and a major strategic center with its famous Tula Arms Plant [Тульский оружейный завод], but also a province in a state of uncertainty, its future determined by the country's capitals. The fact that both the poet and the old man are disturbed by film actors who appear to be playing some major historical drama of mutiny and execution should, therefore, be sifted through the unfocused lenses of this ongoing anxiety during a period of unnamed historical turmoil. The uncertainty between reflection and reality that permeates the narrative permits Pasternak to approach an otherwise dangerous political theme—the description of an arrogant crowd that has taken the action from the Kremlin to Tula, where they are now playing out some "violent" episode involving "Bolotnikov and Peter," spectacles of mutiny and execution described, the poet surmises, in the historical accounts of Kluchevsky:

> They act as if they were geniuses, declaiming and hurling phrases at each other [. . .]. They have been shooting *The Time of Troubles* in the Kremlin and in the places where the ramparts were.
>
> Read Klyuchevsky's account—I have not read it myself, but I think there must be some episode with Bolotnikov and Peter. This is what brought them to the River Upa. I find they have set the scene exactly and shot it from another bank. (*CSP* 121; trans. altered)

> Они гениальничают, декламируют, бросаются друг в дружку фразами [. . .]. Ставили «Смутное Время» в Кремле и где были валы.
>
> Прочти по Ключевскому,—не читал, думаю, должен быть эпизод с Петром и Болотниковым. Это и вызвало их на Упу. Узнал, что поставили точка в точку и сняли с другого берега. (*PSS* 3:28)

The drowning of Ivan Bolotnikov's followers in the River Upa in 1607, which, according to the poet's oblique remark, was shot by the film crew "from the other bank" with professional exactitude [точка в точку], belongs to some of the most disturbing pages of Russian history, and yet the violent content of this historical reference is overlooked, as most of Pasternak's commentators accept this strange, unfocused frame at face value, as a straightforward

---

31 the arsenal of arms was confiscated by the revolutionary committee and sent to Moscow. After that time, Tula became the center of the civil war, a process that reached its zenith in 1919 when Denikin's army descended on Tula, attempting to destroy the "principal source of the supply of the armaments for the Soviet army" or, as Trotsky termed it, "the jewels of the Soviet Republic."

account[41] of the poet's dislike of film actors.[42] However, it is equally probable that Pasternak uses the context of film and acting, as well as the historical memory of mutiny and mayhem in Tula, to develop, for the first time in his prose, an opposition between two kinds of self: the imitator, ready to copy acts of murder and violence, if these become fashionable, and the creative self[43]— and to find his original voice by approaching this contrast alongside Kant's theory of apperception.

It will be helpful to sketch, however briefly, the centrality of this theme in Pasternak's later writing. In *Doctor Zhivago* the opposition between artist and imitator appears in one of the novel's most startling scenes—Yuri's meeting with Pasha Strelnikov, once again at a railway station. The gift of the fiery revolutionary is identified as his ability to *copy*, so typical (and necessary for survival) in those turbulent years:

> This talent, which showed itself in his every movement, might well be the talent of imitation. In those days everyone modeled himself on someone else—they imitated heroes of history, or the men who had stuck their imagination by winning fame in the fighting at the front or in the streets, or those who had great prestige with the people, or this or that comrade who had won distinction, or simply one another. (*Zhivago* 249)

> Дар, проглядывавший во всех его движениях, мог быть даром подражания. Тогда все кому-нибудь подражали. Прославленным героям истории. Фигурам, виденным на фронте или в дни волнений в городах, и поразившим воображение.

---

41. Apart from the actors representing episodes of rebellion and execution, there is also the reality of the mutiny of 1607 in the name of the self-appointed "Prince" Peter (hence "the time of troubles"), re-enacted in 1918. The mutiny of 1607 near Tula was led by Ivan Bolotnikov, and Bolotnikov's army gave itself up to Prince Schuisky in October 1607 (*PSSCom* 3:541), when most of Bolotnikov's men were drowned in the River Upa. The device of ahistorical re-enactment is also reminiscent of Rilke's *The Notebooks of Malte Laurids Brigge,* in which the ghosts of the past move in and out of reality. In "Letters from Tula," however, scholars tend to see "the depressing sight of the amateurish attempts by the bunch of film actors to re-enact the 'Time of Troubles' and then pick up this record of 'history' in their suitcases" (Barnes 1989, 268). Fleishman speaks of Pasternak aiming at "Mayakovsky, who deemed it necessary to take a visible role in revolutionary affairs" (1990a, 94).

42. The acceptance of film actors *prima facie* contributes to the perception of Pasternak's early prose as highly idiosyncratic and more preoccupied with Mayakovsky's actual participation in the film versions of either *Martin Eden* (Barnes 1989, 268) or *The Young Lady and a Hooligan* [Барышня и хулиган] (*PSSCom* 3:541) than with the major historical upheavals of Russia (and Tula as its microcosm). Fleishman argues that "Tolstoy, like Pasternak, had come to consider film as a profanation of art" (1990a, 95).

43. Hingley calls this "a study of the false and genuine in art" (1983, 63).

Наиболее признанным народным авторитетам. Вышедшим в первые ряды товарищам. Просто друг другу. (*PSS* 4:248)

The significance of the episode, presenting the highly unified and concentrated personality of Strelnikov,[44] emphasizes that not all "synthesized phenomena" can awaken an independent and original (and for Kant, transcendental) self. More often than not, surrounded by so many indigestible reflections during Russia's "horrifying years," the participants of these events do not develop an original synthesizing response, but choose instead to imitate others, and survive the turbulence of reality in this chameleon-like state just as well or, perhaps, even better.[45] In *Zhivago*, in fact, Pasternak frequently returns to the declamatory, unnatural, and imitative characters of political figures, and his female heroine, Lara Antipova, even attributes the cause of Strelnikov's downfall to his inability to see through the stage rhetoric of their times and to become infected by the general societal malaise that reinforces the herd instinct of "imitators":

> [T]hey must all sing in chorus, and live by other people's notions, notions that were being crammed down everybody's throat. And then there arose the power of the glittering phrase, first the Tsarist, then the revolutionary.
>
> This social evil became an epidemic. It was catching. And it affected everything, nothing was left untouched by it. Our home, too, became infected. Something went wrong in it. Instead of being natural and spontaneous as we had always been, we began to be idiotically pompous with each other. Something showy, artificial, forced crept into our conversation—you felt you had to be clever in a certain way about certain world-important themes. (*Zhivago* 404)

> [T]еперь надо петь с общего голоса и жить чужими, всем навязанными представлениями. Стало расти владычество фразы, сначала монархической—потом революционной.
>
> Это общественное заблуждение было всеохватывающим, прилипчивым. Все подпадало под его влияние. Не устоял против его пагубы и наш дом. Что-то пошатнулось в нем. Вместо безотчетной живости, всегда у нас царившей, доля дурацкой декламации прони-

---

44. There is an emphasis in the description on the fact that Strelnikov is a completed "manifestation of will" [этот человек представляет законченное явление воли] (*Zhivago* 248; *PSS* 4:248).

45. See Witt (2000a, 97–105) on mimicry in *Doctor Zhivago*.

кла и в наши разговоры, какое-то показное, обязательное умничанье на обязательные мировые темы. (*PSS* 4:401)

This participation in history as a form of imitative role-playing constitutes a recurrent theme in Pasternak's poetry dedicated to these revolutionary years, when, for instance, he speaks of Russia's cultural pre-revolutionary milieu as performers about to leave the theatrical stage in "Lofty Malady" [Высокая болезнь][46] and Vladimir Lenin[47] as a new figure exploding onto that stage (*PSS* 1:259).

Thus, it is more fitting to suggest that the film actors, disturbing irritants for both the poet and the old actor, are, in fact, indistinguishable in their roles from the actual revolutionaries who, after their unparalleled performance in the Kremlin, continued to exercise their craftsmanship in Tula. Employing the persona of the disoriented observer, Pasternak accuses these contemporary trendsetters, political actors and the revolutionary crowd with their ideologies and "isms," of behaving like inferior actors, armed with the worst pretensions, and the poet's careful erasing of this thought in his letter indicates both his anger and a need for caution: "I have not said who they are: the worst form of the bohemians [carefully crossed out]" [Я не сказал, кто это. Худший вид богемы. (Тщательно зачеркнуто)] (*CSP* 121; *PSS* 4:29). Moreover, there is a trace of the unexpectedly subtle humor of the situation where appearances and reality blend as the young poet thinks that these performers of *The Time of Troubles* must have hidden parts of their costumes in their suitcases ("Now they have the seventeenth century stowed away in their suitcases while all the remnants linger on over the dirty tables" [Теперь семнадцатый век рассован у них по чемоданам, все же остальное виснет над грязным столом] [*CSP* 121; *PSS* 4:29]).

This humorous touch ensures that the mixture of horror and indignation at the actual scenes of violence does not automatically signal a sharp political commentary; instead, the uncertain events remain obscured, suggesting either a film narrative or the unleashing of ancient ghosts and memories locked within the surrounding landscape. The poet's observation—"The Polish

---

46. "We were a music on ice. / I speak here about the whole milieu / With which I meant to leave the stage and will do so" [Мы были музыкой во льду. / Я говорю про всю среду, / С которой я имел в виду / Сойти со сцены, и сойду] (*PSS* 1:255–56).

47. In the description of Lenin, there is an uncertainty whether the leader of the Revolution is an author, approaching his art from the standpoint of the first person: "Then having met him in reality / I thought and thought without end / About his authorship and his right / To dare from the first person narrative" [Тогда его увидев въяве, / Я думал, думал без конца / Об авторстве его и праве / Дерзать от первого лица] (*PSSCom* 1:517).

women are horrid, and the boyars' children even more dreadful" [Ужасны полячки, и боярские дети страшней] (*CSP* 121; *PSS* 3:28)—points, therefore, to the reality of actual historical events of 1607 and yet obscures the reference, for the old actor rummaging "through his own repertoire," finds "no such chronicle there" (*CSP* 124; *PSS* 3:31). The old man's terror in front of a scene of obvious execution (be it in film or in reality) is again depicted through a multitude of lenses: the old man observes an event, which he, well-trained in theater, understands as lacking a good script; he leaves the scene saddened that it is not yet a performance, but rather "some free flight of fantasy" [Старик [. . .] пошел опечаленный прочь с лужайки, когда узнал, что это вообще не пьеса, а покудова вольная еще фантазия] (*CSP* 124; *PSS* 3:31). The freedom of fantasy, however, is clearly directed toward scenes of mass murder that the old man understands again as free re-enactment of some historical drama, safely removed from everyday reality, although the battle-axes (obviously rifles) they use reflect no light:[48] "he first saw the boyars and governors milling on the far shore, and the commoners leading the bound men and knocking off their hats into the nettles, he saw the Poles clinging to laburnum bushes on the scarp, and *their battle-axes, which gave no response and no bright ring*" [Сначала, при виде бояр и воевод, колыхавшихся на том берегу, и черных людей подводивших связанных и сшибавших с них шапки в крапиву, при виде поляков, цеплявшихся за ракитовые кусты по обрыву, *и их секир, нечувствительных к солнцу и не издававших звона*] (*CSP* 124; *PSS* 4:31; emphasis added).

This covert and ambiguous identification of the imitative historical "performers" with the "bohemian artistic crowd of the worst sort" is, of course, not merely a cautious political statement or an unsuccessful artistic device.[49]

---

48. In *Doctor Zhivago*, Lara speaks about the interdependence between the daily violence of wartime and revolution and the loss of personal viewpoint. Repetition and mimicry are the root of the loss of morality: "And then there was the jump from this peaceful, naïve moderation to blood and tears, to mass insanity. [. . .] The main misfortune, the root of all evil to come, was the loss of confidence in the value of one's own opinion. People imagined that it was out of date to follow one's own moral sense, that they must all sing in chorus, and live by other people's notions. [. . .]" [И вдруг этот скачок из безмятежной, невинной размеренности в кровь и вопли, повальное безумие и одичание [. . .] Главной бедой, корнем будущего зла была утрата веры в цену собственного мнения. Вообразили, что время, когда следовали внушениям нравственного чутья, миновало, что теперь надо петь с общего голоса и жить чужими, всем навязанными представлениями] (*Zhivago* 404; *PSS* 4:401).

49. In his letter to Polonsky in the summer of 1921, Pasternak basically recreates the scene of his own aversion to the political position of the avant-garde artists that is virtually identical to the stance of the poet, and he mentions 1917 as the last year of their common journey. His own "sea sickness," that is, the mixture of nausea and horror, is mentioned in the context of the "sea of violence" [море произвола] and he puts a significant emphasis on his own "isolation" from the "originality" of the artistic crowd: "Until 1917 I had a path externally common with

Pasternak's participation in the Futurist movement was becoming ever more problematic as he began to view the world of politics and that of revolutionary futurist art as interconnected, if not ideologically identical.[50] Still in 1918, the story's employment of film actors indicates that he was still hoping that better spectacles (and actors) might soon appear on the stage—a hope that would not last long.[51] Pasternak's lifetime experience, in fact, was to observe the process by means of which ethical and aesthetic judgments in the worlds of state-sanctioned art and politics were to become based entirely upon the imitation of fraudulent principles, and as a result any pathways to the inner self and to the personal capacity for independent judgment were entirely closed. Needless to say, these patterns were in direct contrast to the Kantian view of apperception that situates true moral judgment in the autonomous transcendental self.

The relationship between art and the awakened voice of conscience, entailed in the opposition between the two types of play-acting in life and art—imitative and creative—was only to deepen in Pasternak's writing, with "Letters from Tula" disclosing his first artistic draft that also carried the most immediate imprint of his philosophical studies. Just as Heine's passage into the dark world of Pisa in "The Mark of Apelles" echoes the Platonic philosopher's return to the cave, "Letters from Tula" presents yet another page of the writer's *apologia* for art's primacy over philosophy. When put into the context of the Kantian theory of apperception, art's capacity to mediate and synthesize the deepest layers of reality[52] is theoretically grounded and demonstrated. Moreover, the focus of "Letters from Tula" on the synthetic processes of consciousness entails the obligation of the artist to address all aspects of perception presented to him, and this includes questions of morality and conscience that are necessitated by scenes of cruelty and violence imposed on the eyewitnesses. Hermann Cohen's work with Kant's "synthetic unity" and his writing

---

all, but my fatal peculiarity [роковое своеобразие] brought me to an impasse, and I alone, it seems [. . .] realized that logical end into which our era's originality in quotation marks leaves us" (*PSS* 7:371).

50. As Nerler observes, "Mayakovsky, alas, was one of the first poets who initiated the mutual infiltration between the Cheka and the writers' world" (2010, 26). See also Gordin about the "Futurists serving in the Cheka" (1993, 8)

51. See a careful account of Pasternak's alienation from Futurism in Fleishman (1980, 12–43).

52. Answering a questionnaire from the Soviet magazine *The Writers' Watch* in 1927 ["На литературном посту" 5–6], Pasternak defines the "classical" writer as a person who can synthesize reality within an approximation of a holistic vision that can be accepted as the worldview of his epoch [Под классиком я разумею писателя, который в своем творчестве дает пластическое подобие цельного мировоззрения. Классическая же литература есть совокупность таких произведений и тенденций, которые впоследствии принимаются за мировоззрение эпохи] (*PSS* 5:216).

on philosophy, law, religion, and aesthetics no longer present themselves in this context as irrelevant or "safe" meditations[53]—rather, Cohen's philosophy helps to address as if anew the traditional opposition between aesthetics and morality, or between the "beautiful" and the "good," as part of the phenomenal world open to the synthetic processes of apperception. Nor is Tula's landscape indifferent to these problems, for it remembers, as the poet too is about to recollect in the course of a single night, that its actual spaciousness had been transformed not only by Bolotnikov and "the time of troubles," but by Lev Tolstoy's writing, which testified to an irreducible "territory of conscience"—to the inescapable tension between "the beautiful" and "the good."

4.4 Between *to kalon* and *to agathon*:
Cohen's Neo-Kantianism, the fire of conscience, and Lev Tolstoy's gift of perception

Once the purpose of sharply changing perspectives is understood as a principal frame of the story (and a frame rooted in Pasternak's dialogue with the key philosophical questions of his day), the psychological realities of his protagonists lose their apparent banality, and the story's landscapes of different phenomenal perspectives no longer appear hopelessly disjointed. Rather, their disjointedness becomes a necessary precondition for the living contradictory force of creative consciousness. Like no other Russian writer of his generation, Pasternak was thoroughly prepared to address the relationship between the moral and aesthetic, and to bring into close proximity highly complex philosophical, political, ethical, and literary concerns.

The relationship between the moral and aesthetic was not only the leading frame of Kant's *Third Critique* and its insistence that universal agreement in judgments of the sublime rests on an appeal to moral feeling (§29, 265–66); these questions constituted the very kernel of the philosophy of Hermann Cohen, and, more generally, stood for the intellectual signature of the Marburg school. Cohen's own work in law and religion stemmed from his ardent loyalty to the unity of the transcendent, the sublime, and the moral, reflecting in this the Platonic affirmation of the *kalon* (the beautiful) and *agathon* (the good) as the organizing forms for the experience of the infinite.

---

53. According to his letters to Shtikh from July 8 and 11, 1912, Pasternak viewed Cohen's "logic, the idea of reality, integration, self-consciousness of the state" as a harmonious and beautiful work of genius [его логика, его идея реальности, интеграла, самосознания государства], but a safe narcotic [безобидный наркотик] (*PSS* 7:118, 122). In 1918, Cohen's "idealism," surprisingly apropos, would no longer provide a safe haven.

Cohen's stature as a thinker, his deep devotion to the reality of both transcendent categories and logical argument, need no introduction, and yet it is helpful to recollect how every step of his argument presupposes the longing of the finite for the infinite. In this longing, moral principles draw the "external or heterogeneous" infinity into the immediacy of aesthetic purity:

> The finite is not happy to remain finite, but has the courage to overcome the distance from infinity. The limitations of the finite are eliminated, there is an aspiration to elevation (*Erhebung*) to infinity. Infinity must not remain something alien, external. It may well be that it must be and remain something transcendent. This is unimportant, as long as it must not be something external or heterogenous. *But is what happens in this aesthetic sublimity (Erhebenheit) arrogant, or presumptuous (Uberhebung)? This cannot be right, since presumption is contrary to moral law, but the latter is the indispensable premise, concerning matter and method, of aesthetic purity. The sublime thrust towards infinity is not at all presumptuous, otherwise sublimity will be presumptuous as well as elevation.* (ARG I:266–67; trans. Poma-Denton 144; emphasis added)

Cohen's argument that aesthetic and cultural products belong in the moral domain opposes Marx's view of culture as by-products of economic relations, a position Cohen found particularly misleading:[54] "It is simply not true that the compulsion of nature and especially of animal nature in man produced those achievements of culture which can be only hypocritically called moral culture, and should rather be labeled economic" (*Ethic* 37; trans. in Munk 2005, 20). The loss of presumption in the "sublime thrust towards infinity" presupposes in Cohen the heavy weight of ethical self-judgment, just as the need for "the courage to overcome the distance from infinity" emphasizes the ensuing difficulty of perseverance.

Pasternak, as his student notes (and all his later work) indicate, was stirred by these views, emphasizing for himself the need to push consciousness toward new creative solutions and new boundaries, without minimizing the power of contradictory impulses (operating in "obverse proportions" and directions) and thereby inflaming consciousness and awakening creativity. Thus, he jots down the following under the subtitle "Towards Urtheilskraft–Kant" [K Urtheilskraft—Канта]:

---

54. Holzhey argues that for Cohen the man's adoration of himself would end in "anthropological naturalism," against which Cohen defends his "ethical idealism"—"the notion of a human being who makes it his task to 'eternally' perfect himself" (2005, 20).

Any construction emerging from transcendental *conditions serves as an antagonistic impulse* towards a problem only when we enter (think of) life as such, in whatever form it is presented; then the construction of the object and its non-material residue enter into an obverse relationship. The more clear is the organism, as an object of study, the less clear it becomes as a unifying life force; and only thinking of its living quality, do we break through the sphere of its object-like materiality; the sphere of experience. [. . .]

But in creativity, immanent apperceptions, the whole Milky Way of the centers of creative unities, the incomprehensibility of its inflamed systems [. . .].

Конструкция из тр[ансцендент]альн[ых] условий возможности становится антагонистическим толчком к проблеме лишь когда мы мыслим жизнь как таковую, где бы то ни было представленную; тогда конструктивность предмета и его непредметный остаток обратно пропорциональны по своей понятности. Чем яснее нам организм, как предмет познания, тем он непонятнее, как единство жизни; и тогда мысля его жизненность, мы прорываем сферу предметности, сферу опыта. [. . .] Т.е. телеологический принцип антагоничен принципу предметности. [. . .]

Но в творчестве имманентные апперцепции, целый Млечный путь центров творческого объединения, туманности их воспаленных систем [. . .] . (*Lehrjahre* II:139–40)

The notes in his *Lehrjahre* provide, of course, only a superficial demonstration of what must have been in reality a deep intrinsic conviction, reinforced by the Russian pre-Revolutionary and Revolutionary cultural scenes, that diversity is both a challenge and the fodder for a creative thinker.

In "Letters from Tula," Pasternak does little to dilute the complexity of the intellectual and moral intertext, as he brings together in the consciousness of his poet dispersed phenomenological data that are infused by the memory of his lost beloved, confusion, pangs of conscience, abhorrence of violence, revulsion, fear, shame, the need to find truth, and the need to write—all of this constituting the challenging (and necessary) preconditions for the *flame* of creativity,[55] "the whole Milky Way of the centers of creative unities, the incomprehensibility of its inflamed systems" [целый Млечный путь центров

---

55. Cohen, after Kant, saw this process in somewhat milder terms: the "rhapsody of perceptions" longing to be transformed into the "synthetic unity of the phenomena" (*KTE* 101; trans. Poma-Denton 11).

творческого объединения, туманности их воспаленных [. . .] систем] (*Lehrjahre* II:139). Contradictory data that cannot be easily unified communicate an intense pressure capable of igniting the objects it touches. In the face of deeply troubling historical events, Pasternak's poet is not only shocked, smitten, and pierced; when the difficult April night obscures all available sources of light, his conscience, unable to work through the startling contradictory data, is set aflame:[56]

> "O night; all is not over yet; scorch me to cinder; that word that thrust through all accumulated dross, burn, burn bright and clear, the forgotten, angry, fiery word 'conscience' [heavily underscored with a line that tears through the paper in places]. [. . .]
> Now for the first, for the very first, time since the distant years of childhood I am consumed with fire [crossed out]."
> Another fresh attempt. The letter remains unposted. (*CSP* 121–22)

> "Терзай, терзай меня, ночь, не все еще, пали дотла, гори, гори ясно, светло, прорвавшее засыпь, забытое, гневное, огненное слово 'совесть' (Под ним черта, продравшая местами бумагу.) [. . .]
> 'В первый, в первый раз с далеких детских лет я сгораю'" (зачеркнуто все).
> Новая попытка. Письмо остается неотосланным. (*PSS* 3:28)

Oppressed by disunity, the poet does not merely wail in self-pity ("I still understand nothing. So strange it is, so terrible" [Ничего еще не понимаю. Так странно; так страшно] [*CSP* 121; *PSS* 3:28]). The emphasis upon horror may not be, after all, so much out of place: the young poet in the story and, by extension, his young author, understand on this night—with absolute clarity—that they are destined to fulfill their vocation in hostile historical times among hostile co-travelers, from whom they are, at this point, indistinguishable: "'Colleague,' the scum had said. Yes, indeed, and he was right! Here was the witness's evidence for the prosecution" ['Коллега,'—сказал этот подонок. Да. Прав. Это свидетельское показательство обвинения] (*CSP* 122; *PSS* 3:29). This sense of reality acquires the force of a prison sentence ("the witness's evidence for the prosecution"), and the echoes from Plato's cave may not be altogether out of place. What is demanded now from the young poet is not so much a unified perception, but rather a decision to accept his alienation

---

56. For the intertextual echoes of the flaming heart, "cor ardens," tradition in the Russian Silver Age, see Proskurina (2001, 196–213).

and to suspend all the nominations and ambitions that belong to the surrounding world.[57] Thus, "a line [underneath the word conscience] that tears through the paper" [под ним черта, прорвавшая местами бумагу] (*CSP* 121; *PSS* 3:28) has turned into a fire[58] that burns "through all the accumulated dross" [прорвавшая засыпь] (*CSP* 121; *PSS* 3:28), operating in the text as a significant textual marker: burning through the protective construction of the first person, it levels the field of perception. Indicating the birth of a new genre,[59] the fire reduces to ashes Romantic self-aggrandizement (and sentimental self-pity) and brings the poet to a new artistic vision—a third-person discourse, conceived, or so it seems, as a cure for the language of his own time that so favors the presumptuous pose of the poet.[60] While reformulating the poet's future, the fire does little, however, to his surroundings, indicating that the personal call of conscience has not as yet begun its hopeless task of dispelling the oppressive "putrefaction" of the surroundings where the strips of light,[61] nonetheless, do not arrest their assault on darkness:

> While these lines were being written, nothing changed in the entire space of conscience. From it rose smells of putrefaction and of clay. Far, far away, from its farthest extremity, a birch tree gleamed and a cavity in the swamp showed up like a fallen earring. Strips of light broke from within the waiting room and [. . .] squirmished, revolting together. (*CSP* 123; trans. altered)

> Ничто не изменилось на всем пространстве совести, пока писались эти строки. От нее несло гнилостностью и глиной. Далеко, далеко, с того ее края, мерцала березка, и, как упавшая серьга, обозначался в

---

57. See Fleishman on Pasternak's disagreement with Mayakovsky about the public role of the poet (1990a, 94–95).

58. Here Pasternak brings several philosophical traditions together. The fire imagery in (and outside of) Plato's cave as well as Kant's notion of moral categories ingrained upon the transcendental ego and understood as moral imperatives, contribute here to a complex literary intertext.

59. Zholkovsky notes the correlation between flame and ecstatic awakening in Pasternak's poetry, his "transformation: passage into a new state, taking off the mask and, on occasion, metamorphosis, connected with fire" [преображение: переход в новое, срывание маски, иногда перевоплощение, связанное с огнем] (1994, 286).

60. See Fleishman's view that the poet sees in the actors "the same falseness he has detected in himself. The conclusion he reaches is devastating: he must break immediately with poetry, since it distorts the truth" (1990a, 93).

61. In "Letters from Tula" Pasternak appears to experiment with the descriptions of several forms of energy, with inflaming, magnetic, and electrifying forces: departing sunlight, the power of the train engine in the beginning of the story, the flame of conscience, a "lever that sets the whole scene in motion," the dance of compass needles, the putrefying smell of corruption, and the rebellion of the strips of light.

болотце продав. Вырываясь из зала наружу, падали полосы света на коночный пол [. . .]. Эти полосы буянили. (*PSS* 3:30)

The image of the flame of conscience, born out of the pressure of contradictory impulses within the poet and still too weak to pierce the darkness, clarifies to some extent the identity of the force that Pasternak often discusses in his work: the force, distinct from the force of light, born, nonetheless in creative perception in response to the accumulated challenging multiplicity of surrounding phenomena. Its power of ignition, its combustible intensity,[62] assisted Heine in his journey in Pisa; in the darkness of "The Mark of Apelles," as he himself attests to Camilla: "*a man flares up* in the light of the flickering rays" [человек *вспыхивает*, озаренный тревожными огнями] (*CSP* 110; *PSS* 3:16; emphasis added). In "Some Propositions," sections 2 and 3, Pasternak discusses the piercing power of phosphorescent light from within (or behind the perception) and then compares the book to the fire of conscience:

[. . .] It should always be one of the audience and have the clearest, truest, most perceptive view of all [. . .] hiding in the gallery, unrecognized, hardly aware that it cannot fail to give itself away and that when it hides in the corner it is stricken with translucency and phosphorescence as though with some disease [and that hiding and biting nails, it illuminates and blinds, from its back x-rayed by Lord God].
[. . .]
A book is a cube-shaped chunk of blazing, smoking conscience—nothing more. (*CSP* 260)

[. . .] Ему следует всегда быть в зрителях и глядеть всех чище, восприимчивей и верней [. . .] тонуть в райке, в безвестности, почти не ведая, что на нем шапка горит и что, забившееся в угол, оно порождено светопрозрачностью и фосфоресценцией, как некоторой болезнью [и что таясь и кусая ногти, оно сверкает и слепит, из-за спины рентгенируемое Господом Богом].[63]
[. . .]
Книга есть кубический кусок горячей, дымящейся совести—и больше ничего. (*PSS* 3:24)

---

62. See here the beginning of the poem "Marburg": "I shuddered, I was afire, I was switched off, I shook" [Я вздрагивал. Я загорался и гас. Я трясся] (*PSS* 1:110).
63. This image of divinely sent X-ray forces remained in Pasternak's drafts, clearly unacceptable for the Soviet press (*PSS* 5:523).

And years later, the young Yuri Zhivago, echoing this emphasis on the shared contents of perception, will attempt to prove to Anna Gromeko that the fire of thought has to be turned not into oneself, but outwards. In other words, the light of consciousness, in order not to harm itself, should not be directed toward an autonomous experience:

> Consciousness is a poison when we apply it to ourselves. Consciousness is a light directed outward. It lights up a way ahead of us, so that we do not stumble. It's like the headlights on a locomotive—turn them inward and you will have a crash.
>
> [. . .] your consciousness [. . .] your soul, your immortality, your life [. . .] have always been in others and will remain in others. (*Zhivago* 68)

> Сознание яд, средство самоотравления для субъекта, применяющего его на самом себе. Сознание—свет, бьющий наружу, сознание освещает перед нами дорогу, чтоб не споткнуться. Сознание это зажженные фары впереди идущего паровоза. Обратите их светом внутрь и случится катастрофа.
>
> [. . .] Вот что вы есть, вот чем дышало, питалось, упивалось всю жизнь ваше сознание. Вашей душою, вашим бессмертием, вашей жизнью в других. И что же? В других вы были, в других и останетесь. (*PSS* 4:69)

As one returns to "Letters from Tula," it appears plausible, therefore, that the fire of conscience and the ensuing switch to the third person (indicating alienation from the poet's old self) operate in the story as the only possible unifying step for a writer at this point in the journey, a choice simultaneously moral and artistic[64] on the path toward an ever sterner understanding of oneself and one's time.

The vision, however, is not only that of moral perseverance. As the poet pledges to his beloved, speaking of himself by now in the third person, his future art and moral stance will not be the testament of an onlooker. The observer is to become the observed, and as the object and focus of the perceptions (and judgments) of others, he will need to find inner strength, even at the price of utter loneliness and self-sacrifice, not to be one face among many, not to be lost in the crowd among these colleagues:

> He swears to you, that when he someday sees *The Time of Troubles* on the screen (it will be shown eventually, one imagines), the sequence on the

---

64. On Pasternak's "lengthy farewell to Romanticism," see Gorelik (2000, 39).

River Upa will find him *utterly alone*, if actors have not reformed by then [. . .]. (*CSP* 122; emphasis added)

Он клянется тебе, что когда-нибудь, когда он увидит с экрана «Смутное время» (ведь поставят его когда-нибудь), экспозиция сцены на Упе застанет его *совсем одиноким*, если не исправятся к тому времени актеры [. . .]. (*PSS* 3:29)

In terms of the philosophical motifs that traverse the story, the poet's decision signals an acceptance of responsibility for the world inhabited, if not by shadows, then by imitators and reflections—all of which in Plato's cave indicated danger—a situation that might well end in the philosopher's death. In Pasternak's narrative, however, the choice, once made, immediately recovers a new sense of belonging and association. In contrast to Pasternak himself, who admitted his theoretical underpinnings in his letter to his parents [там будет много теории (*PSS* 7:322]), the poet in the story—in his moral awakening—aligns himself neither with Kant's view that a "mental attunement [is] favorable to moral feeling" (*Third Critique*, §42, 298–99), nor with Cohen's upholding of "moral culture" (*Ethic* 37), but with Lev Tolstoy, who is introduced as "an occurrence on the territory of conscience, in its gravitational and ore-bearing sector" [случай на территории совести, на ее гравитирующем, рудоносном участке] (*CSP* 122; *PSS* 3:29).

Tolstoy's presence is the nourishing ("ore-bearing") force in the soil of memory in the poet's surroundings, able to transform the weight of moral responsibility into an artistic decision[65]—a possibility to emerge from the disunited data of impressions and convictions towards the authorship of a new world inhabited by the diverse viewpoints of *other* living characters, in short, a fictional narrative populated by *others*. This artistic reorientation begins with a jolt. Out of a shared layer of darkened memory emerges a re-awakened recollection of Tolstoy's funeral, as the writer's power escapes a finite sentence. For the poet, this recollection spurs the confirmed recognition of the self in a third-person narrative, a self situated among others, and not all of them alien:

---

65. Mossman speaks of the interrelationship between Tolstoy and Pasternak's "facility of vision" and art as an "act of conscience." He also quotes the following "unsent" letter of Pasternak: "the central and most undying aspect of Tolstoy, that which is greater than the teaching on Good and broader than his immortal artistic individuality (perhaps that which makes up his true being) is a new kind of inspiration" (1972, 291). Mossman identifies the addressee of the letter as Sergei Durylin. In fact, the letter was sent to N. Rodionov on March 27, 1950 (*PSS* 11:603).

At this point something new occurred—a mere trifle, *but the one that in its way shivered all the events* and all he had experienced in the waiting room up until this moment.

"The poet" at last recognizes the person strolling by the baggage office. He has seen that face before. From somewhere locally. He has seen it on several occasions [. . .]. It was when they were assembling a special train at Astapovo [. . .].

In an instant, realization now weighs in on all that has so far happened to the 'poet' in the waiting room, and *it acts as a lever to set the whole revolving stage in motion*. And why?—Indeed, this is Tula! This night is a night in Tula. Night in a place bound up with the life of Tolstoy. *Is it any wonder that compass needles start to dance here?* Such events are in the very nature of the place. This is an occurrence on the territory of conscience, in its gravitational and ore-bearing sector. There will be no more of the 'poet.' (*CSP* 122; emphasis added)

В это время происходит новое, сущий пустяк, по-своему сотрясающий все случившееся и испытанное в зале до этого момента.

«Поэт» узнает наконец прогуливавшегося по багажной. Лицо это он видел когда-то. Из здешних мест. Он видел его раз, не однажды, в течении одного дня, в различные часы, в разных местах. Это было, когда составляли особый поезд в Астапове [. . .].

Тут мгновенное соображение наваливается на все, что было в зале с «поэтом», и *как на рычаге поворачивает сцену*, и вот как. Ведь это Тула! Ведь эта ночь—ночь в Туле. Ночь в местах толстовской биографии. *Диво ли, что тут начинают плясать магнитные стрелки?* Это случай на территории совести, на ее гравитирующем, рудоносном участке. 'Поэта' больше не станет. (*PSS* 3:29)

The discovery of Tolstoy's power in a highly charged layer (a magnetic force in fact) among the multiple layers disclosed to perception—"Is it any wonder the compass needles start to dance here?" [Диво ли, что тут начинают плясать магнитные стрелки?] (*CSP* 122; *PSS* 3:29)—finally realigns these landscapes. In contrast to Kant's "synthetic unity of experience," Tolstoy's heritage does not unify the disparate elements, but makes them live and speak in an ever-widening multiplicity of characters and voices.

The inner expansion into different voices, associated with the presence of Tolstoy, explains, in turn, the structure of the story. In the second part of "Letters," the old actor is conceived of not merely as a Tolstoyan character and, thus, a tribute to Tolstoy: he is also explicitly the protagonist of a story within a story, a powerful indication that the outcome of the poet's turmoil is the act of writing with a distinct *other* protagonist who, nonetheless, comes into existence woven out by the poet from his own experience, reassembled into a new design from the poet's disjointed thoughts, emotions, and artistic attempts to speak through the voice of the other, spearheaded by the example of Tolstoy. It is in order to emphasize this creative birth that Savva's first appearance in the story[66] is accompanied by the whispers of the disheveled poet, who is finally thinking about his ticket toward his morning destination:

> It was only then that in his apartment in town on Posolskaya Street an extremely strange man finally settled down to sleep. While the letters were written at the station, this apartment had quivered with soft footsteps and the candle at the window had caught a whisper broken by frequent silences. It was not a voice of the old man, though apart from him there was not a soul in the room. It was all amazingly peculiar. (*CSP* 123–24)

> Только тогда улегся наконец в городских номерах на Посольской чрезвычайно странный старик. Пока писались письма на вокзале, номер подрагивал от легких шажков, и свечка на окне ловила шепот, часто прерывавшийся молчанием. То не был голос старика, хотя, кроме него, не было души в комнате. Все это было удивительно странно. (*PSS* 3:30)

And even though the old man, having entered the story, starts operating as an independent agent, reversing some of the themes associated with the poet, and is more successful in incorporating "otherness" than his author, both his entrance and departure from the narrative emphasize his fictional status. Eventually, the authorial intrusion announces his belonging to a fictional text, just as it celebrates the actor's ability to transform himself so fully into another self and achieve silence: "He was the only one in *the story* to find it, having made another to speak through his own lips" [Он тоже, *как главное лицо,* искал физической тишины. В *рассказе* только он один нашел ее, заставив своими устами говорить постороннего] (*CSP* 126; *PSS* 3:32; emphasis added). This shock of authorial intrusion, coming as it does at the end of the narrative, signals the need for disclosure (akin to what Shklovsky termed the "baring of the device"—обнажение приема) in a story somewhat baffling in its subtextual intensity.

---

66. See Fleishman: "the 'actor' in the second part may well be seen as a transformed 'poet' of the first part" (1990a, 94).

Pasternak in this instance states directly what he considers to be the only possible synthetic unity—the story's end, or *telos*—the artistic goal, both for the narrative, and also more generally for his own future as an artist: all the turmoil of multiple perspectives and viewpoints must finally come together not in an autonomous transcendental self, but in the birth of art—the attainment of those rare occasions when real inner silence permits another or others to speak through one's own self. His young poet, as we catch our last glimpse of him, dreams precisely about this future, hoping that his own voice will eventually give way to a very different inner state, a theater-stage for the voices of others:

> He supposed that everything would begin again when he ceased to hear himself, and when there was complete physical silence within his soul. Not an Ibsen silence, but an *acoustic* one. (*CSP* 123; emphasis in original)

> Он предположил, что все начнется, когда он перестанет слышать себя и в душе настанет полная физическая тишина. Не ибсеновская, но *акустическая*. (*PSS* 3:30)

The notion of silence at the edge of chaos was, in fact, one of the key themes noted in "The Mark of Apelles"; it also operated as a definitive theme of Pasternak's early lyrical poetry where the word "stikh" (it quieted) is used as a double-entendre for the poem, also "stikh." But here in "Letters from Tula," Pasternak speaks about the search for a new form of art—a multivoicedness of narrative, which captures the multiplicity of viewpoints, the whole range of the "rhapsody of perceptions" giving way to the "synthetic unity of the phenomena" (*KTE* 101), conceived as an artistic direction on the very ground traversed by Tolstoy. Moreover, if an acoustic silence, a potential, comes as the final desired end of multiple perspectives, then Pasternak's heteronomous understanding of "apperception" also offers a definitive correction to the Kantian theory of the autonomous self.

4.5 Tolstoy, the Tolstoyans, and the living characters of fictional space:
Autonomous transcendental consciousness versus a created living world of perceived and perceiving selves

As generally agreed by philosophers, in developing the notion of apperception Kant insists upon the autonomous unity of experience and views it as a necessary precondition for knowledge, or for any real sense of what it means to be a self:

> Kant argues that one of the most basic rules of this activity is that the self organizes its experience in such a way that it always recognizes them as *its own experience*. The rule is that we must always "synthesize" our various experiences into a unity, for we could not come to any knowledge whatever of a scattering of various impressions and sensations without this synthesis. (Solomon 2005, 277; emphasis added)

On the basis of "Letters from Tula" and the development of the themes of the story in subsequent years, it appears most likely that Pasternak, in contrast to Kant, did not believe in the possibility of an autonomous, unified, and self-dependent "ego-self," but rather conceived of synthetic consciousness as a transformative space for the birth of many voices and visions. This means that although his philosophical training supplied for Pasternak an initial way of approaching consciousness, he moved quickly into his own direction of thought. Kant's autonomous self was in some complex way contrasted with Tolstoy's example, for throughout Pasternak's life (and as late as the 1956 *Sketch for an Autobiography*) the figure of Tolstoy demonstrated for him a paradoxical contrast between a man of multiple and conflicting interests searching for a wholeness of vision and invariably coming short, on the one hand, and, on the other, a horde of followers who thought of that vision as straightforward, unified, clear, and complete.[67] Hence, the relationship between Tolstoy and his followers—"those who were the most un-Tolstoyan in the world—the Tolstoyans" [те, что было самым нетолстовским на свете,—толстовц[ы]] (*Remember* 67; *PSS* 3:320)—would signify in time a contrast between the pseudo-peacefulness of a unified consciousness, lacking any creative charge, and the powerful consciousness of the artist, characterized as an ever vigorous space for the birth of new visions and voices.

For Pasternak, therefore, the impossibility of the unification of thought into one clear, autonomous vision, even if it has the force of transcendence,[68] is of paramount importance for the writer. *Doctor Zhivago*, in its very first chapters, speaks of "one of those followers of Tolstoy in whom the ideas of a genius

---

67. See Pasternak's emphasis on Tolstoy's individuality being "beyond measure" and altogether new [«главное и непомерное», «больше проповеди добра», «шире его бессмертного художественного своеобразия», «новый род одухотворения»] (*PSS* 11:603).

68. When Pasternak speaks about artists and writers *continuing* "the Revelation of St. John" (*Zhivago* 90; *PSS* 4:91), he states his deepest belief that no living vision is complete. On "Creation as dopisyvanie," see Witt (2000a, 57–94).

who had never known peace had settled down to enjoy a long unclouded rest, growing hopelessly shallow in the process" [один из тех последователей Льва Николаевича Толстого, в головах которых мысли гения, никогда не знавшего покоя, улеглись вкушать долгий и неомраченный отдых и непоправимо мельчали] (*Zhivago* 40–41; *PSS* 4:42). Significantly in *Sketch for an Autobiography,* Tolstoy's relationship with his wife—a separate area of familial intimacy that Savva Ignatievich of Tula only begins to recollect and accept as his own in the final stages of his life—is viewed by Pasternak as essentially distinct, an area of Tolstoy's personality within which Sofia Andreyevna retains a deservedly separate, autonomous voice. Revisiting her quarrel with her husband's followers, Pasternak emphasizes the importance of her role as Tolstoy's other, as yet alienated self: by contrast with the Tolstoyans, she testifies to the full range of organic spaciousness and living contradictions in Tolstoy's world and refuses to harmonize peacefully[69] with it: "In a room lay a mountain like Elbrus, and she was one of its large, detached crags [она была [. . .] большой отдельной скалой]; the room was filled by a storm cloud the size of half the sky, and she was one of its separate lightings [она была [. . .] отдельною молнией]" (*Remember* 67; *PSS* 3:320). Moreover, these distinct spaces within personality are an indication for Pasternak that personality is living and human, and its work has not as yet been completed.

Alongside Kant's autonomy of apperception, therefore, Pasternak offers heteronomy; against the synthetic unity of experience within the autonomous, isolated consciousness, he proposes a transformative gap, or silence produced by the incommensurate—a space for art, which gives birth to another landscape or landscapes[70] and becomes a force that can influence and realign other consciousnesses. If for Kant "transcendental apperception is a linkage between spontaneity and receptivity" [Тр[ансцендента]льная апперцепция содержит соединенными спонтанность и рецептивность] (*Lehrjahre* II:89), Pasternak, as a young student, already argues with Kant in his notes that the gap in perception created by the antagonism between the transcendental *a priori* and logical thought processes cannot be easily filled: "The significance of 'the forms of perception' is unveiled in contrast to the 'forms of thought'" [Значение "форм воззрения" раскрывается в противоположе-

---

69. Moreover, there is in the same passage a significant irony directed at the modern man who expects a measured normality from the poet: "Poor Pushkin! He should have married Shchegolev and the latest Pushkiniana and everything should be perfect" (*Remember* 67; *PSS* 3:321).

70. This pattern is stated with exactness of formulation in the first lines of the poem "Hamlet": "The sound is hushed. / I stepped forward on the stage" "Гул затих. Я вышел на подмостки" (*PSS* 4:515).

нии "ф[ормам] мышления"] (*Lehrjahre* II:89). The role of this contrast or gap is to disturb and yet to awaken creative force in consciousness:

> [. . .] through the soil of this antagonism there awakens in us creativity in its different forms—as an aspect of antagonism between the associations of judgments and transcendental synthesis.

> [. . .] есть антагонистическая встреча творчества в потенции [. . .] на почве которого в нас [?] это творчество так или иначе пробудилось, в роде антагонизма между ассоциацией представлений и трансценд[енталь]ным синтезом. (*Lehrjahre* II:139–40)

"Letters from Tula," in this regard, is a unique artistic document: it actually elucidates what Pasternak means when he says he plans to write a story that contains "much theory" (*PSS* 7:323). The poet's piteous complaints about the disturbing picture that meets his sight is only the beginning of visual adjustment. The fire of conscience that can burn him to cinder "through all accumulated dross" and "tear through the paper" (*CSP* 121; *PSS* 3:322) indicates that in response to the multiplicity of challenging data crushing upon and against perception, there emerges in the darkness of Tula an alternative force, an energy, which was able in Tolstoy's case to ignite vision, "a passion that by its flash illuminates an object, intensifying its appearance" [глаз наш должна направлять страсть. Она-то именно и озаряет своей вспышкой предмет, усиливая его видимость] (*Remember* 69; *PSS* 3:322). As a result of its magnetism, this force will affect the consciousness of numerous readers.

"Letters from Tula" is only the beginning of this meditation, but this multilayered text is highly significant not least insofar as it contains a startling number of themes and images that will remain in Pasternak's art, to be transformed certainly, but never abandoned. The example of Tolstoy's death as the death of an artist, whose vision still "acts as a lever to set the whole revolving stage in motion" [как на рычаге поворачивает сцену] (*CSP* 122; *PSS* 3:29), changes the direction of the young poet's life. But what is it that he remembers most? His recollection is not merely of the dead body of an artist, surrounded by railway lines. What catches his vision is the railway lines that bring together individual consciousnesses and perceptions, impossible to enumerate and unify within a tortuous and uneven landscape, and also the multiplicity of different worlds crisscrossing in Astapovo as a final but never-ending farewell:

> It was when they were assembling the special train in Astapovo, with a freight car as a hearse, and when the crowds of strangers left the station in

different trains, which then wheeled and crossed the whole day around the unexpected turns of the tangled junction where four railroads converged and parted, returned and split again. (*CSP* 122)

Это было, когда составляли особый поезд в Астапове, с товарным вагоном под гроб, и когда толпы незнакомого народа разъезжались со станции в разных поездах, кружившихся и скрещивавшихся весь день по неожиданностям путаного узла, где сходились, разбегались и секлись, возвратясь, четыре железных дороги. (*PSS* 3:29)

In his 1956 memoirs, just after he summarizes the theses of "Symbolism and Immortality" and writes about the primacy of individual perceptions, Pasternak returns to this portrayal of Tolstoy's death and depicts again the many railway lines meeting around Astapovo and the trains which in "Letters from Tula" carried "an enormous crimson sun [. . .] along the bodies of many sleeping passengers" (*CSP* 126; *PSS* 3:33). In 1956, however, Pasternak goes directly for the hidden dynamic center of the image. Tolstoy's art is viewed as the celebration of the numerous pathways of perception, which has not merely recognized the great multiplicity of viewpoints within the larger cosmos, but made each a reality to be communicated to the world at large. So in 1956, Pasternak recollects his earlier narrative in "Letters from Tula," effectively rewriting the landscape of this "territory of conscience" with a surer hand. And even though he professes to have rejected his earlier style, he honors this important insight of 1918 by recreating the gathering of a great variety of ever-changing observers traversing Russia by means of those multi-layered and multi-directional railway lines surrounding, yet again, the reality of Tolstoy's death. All those who trespass or bypass the station are drawn into a process of a differentiated and diverse, yet continuous moment of "seeing." As they look unknowingly over the material evidence of the landscape, they are emphatically not unified, but continue to live their own lives immortalized by what has become the now departed observer, who finds his rest near the crossroads of uninterrupted communication:

It was natural, somehow, that Tolstoy was at peace and that he should have found peace by the wayside, like a pilgrim, near the main lines of communication of the Russia of those days, which his heroes and heroines continued to fly past and pass and repass, *looking through the windows* of the train at the insignificant railway station they were passing through, without realizing that *the eyes which had watched them all their lives, the eyes which had seen through them and immortalized them, had closed forever in it.* (*Remember* 68; emphasis added)

Было как-то естественно, что Толстой успокоился, успокоился у дороги, как странник, близ проездных путей тогдашней России, по которым продолжали пролетать и круговращаться его герои и героини и *смотрели в вагонные окна* на ничтожную мимолежащую станцию, не зная, что *глаза, которые всю жизнь на них смотрели, и обняли их взором, и увековечили, навсегда на ней закрылись.* (PSS 3:321)

5

Contextualizing the Intellectual Aims of 1918

From "Letters from Tula" to
The Childhood of Luvers

The year 1918 proved to be a highly significant one in Pasternak's creative life. His collection of poetry *Over the Barriers* [Поверх барьеров] was published in 1917; *My Sister Life* [Сестра моя жизнь], finally published in 1922, was subtitled "Summer of the Year 1917," which "indicated when most of its poems were written" (Barnes 1989, 228). "Letters from Tula" was completed in April 1918; by the summer of 1918 the manuscript of what is now known as *The Childhood of Luvers* [Детство Люверс] was also ready for publication. Pasternak worked on this novella as part of a larger novel, provisionally entitled *Three Names,* during the winter of 1917–18. By all accounts, he wrote "rapidly, with the same impetus that produced the lyrics of 1917 and 'Letters from Tula'" (Barnes 1989, 268). In 1918 Pasternak also completed "Some Propositions" [Несколько положений], which encapsulated his understanding of creativity, reasserted as his "credo" [две странички, за которые стою головой] to Marina Tsvetaeva during their passionate letter exchange in 1926 (May 23; *PSS* 5:683). By the fall of 1918, the deteriorating social conditions of Russia finally arrested this tremendous upswing: "underfed and in poor health" like the rest of his country, "he had survived creatively longer than some, but he now needed to find employment to help maintain the family" (Barnes 1989, 273).[1] *The Childhood of Luvers* was published only

---

1. As Barnes notes in this context, Pasternak, in a short biographical note of 1923, states that "serious creative work came to an end in 1918, and there followed a four-year interval

in 1922 in Moscow in the almanac *Our Days* [Наши дни] and was warmly received by critics (even Maxim Gorky wrote an enthusiastic introduction in the 1920s for "an American translated edition" [*PSS* 3:543]).[2] However, enthusiastic support from Russia's foremost scholars and writers does not mask the curious disjuncture between the focus of these critical assessments and Pasternak's own plans for this work, evident in several passages that were eventually excised from the published version of the novella. These "purely philosophical digressions"[3] are echoed in many of his observations, including letters to his family and friends. Chapter 5 will address this dislocation prior to an analysis of this central early work[4] in Chapters 6 and 7, focused sequentially on two parts of *Luvers,* "The Long Days" and "The Stranger."

In the passages excised from the published novella, Pasternak contrasted the artistic and philosophical touch of the artist. The philosophical touch, according to the authorial voice, has no sensual characteristics and emits no smell, but opens up from within into "clear and distinct" ideas, while the artistic touch smells of "human meat"—"noble, sacred, philosophizing, slowly liberating oneself from the pernicious power of fate" [Каким же мясом несет от идей при всяком художническом прикосновении? Человеческим. То есть: благородным. Святым, философствующем, постепенно освобождающемся от вредной власти судьбы] (*PSS* 3:515). Cartesian echoes in the phrase "clear and distinct" ideas point to the emergence of subjectivity in the history of philosophy,[5] a resonance that blends only too well with the emphasis on "human touch" and "human meat." The overall dilemma for the interpreter of *The Childhood of Luvers* stems, however, from the uncertain character of this philosophical-artistic interplay, and from the fact that although Pasternak had abandoned philosophy as a career path, philosophy's influence clearly lingered in his approach to art. The philosophical undercurrent, nonetheless, is not easy to demonstrate; he tends to "camouflage" philosophical issues[6] not by eschewing them, but rather by embedding them deeply

---

whose greater part was taken up with verse translation work on commission from TEO and World Literature publishers" (1989, 273, 443).

2. See Fleishman (1990a, 120; 147).

3. In Fleishman's view, these "digressions were injected into the original narrative, only to be deleted, apparently by the editors" (1990a, 104).

4. Pasternak names *Luvers* as his central work in the "Questionnaire of Profsoyuz of 1919" (*PSSCom* 3:542).

5. Philosophical ideas opening up "clearly and distinctly" points to the "clear and distinct" ideas of Descartes's *Meditations,* and especially to the primacy of the philosopher's clearest but most puzzling idea of infinity in Meditation 3. In "On the Object and Method of Psychology," Pasternak points to Descartes's thoughts on the Cartesian consciousness and the emergence of the subject, as replacing Aristotelian objectivity (*PSS* 5:304).

6. See Dorzweiler (1993, 25–31), and particularly his commentary on Pasternak's descrip-

within his realistic prose narrative. It is, therefore, unclear what issues of philosophy—be they the emergence of Cartesian subjectivity, a quasi-Humean emphasis on perception and impressions, Kantian apperception or its treatment by the Neo-Kantian school, or more generally images and ideas familiar from Plato—should be expected to underlie this new completed work. And all of this must have been fodder for an altogether new start in prose, so that Pasternak's statement to Marina Tsvetaeva about writing "a love intrigue and a heroine in it—like Balzac" (Barnes 1989, 269) is cited frequently in order to demonstrate Pasternak's departure from his other prose works. But was it really a departure? And, equally important, a departure from what? In 1921, in a letter to V. P. Polonsky, Pasternak admitted that in this work he had tried, in contrast to his previous prose pieces, to open his hand and share with his readers the focus of his technical and theoretical experimentation; in the same letter he also acknowledged that in the past he had kept formulations of these concerns "outside" the text, never fully explaining his goals:

> I decided to make a sharp turn. I decided I would write as people do write letters, and not in the current manner, revealing to the reader all that I think and intend to tell him, refraining from technical effects fabricated outside his field of vision and served up to him in a ready form, hypnotically. [. . .] I began to write about a heroine, a woman, with her psychological genesis and a scrupulous account of her childhood. (trans. in Barnes 1989, 270)[7]

Thus, Pasternak searched for a new start, accompanied by open-handed intellectual disclosure—a path, one may note, altogether alien to his artistic temperament.

Consequently, his desire to abandon his hitherto habitual camouflage was not realized, due either to his decision or to that of his publishers. Lazar Fleishman in the 1970s, while sifting through the drafts of *Luvers*, uncovered these singular pages, excised from the final version,[8] which announced the author's theoretical intentions, but they were—for all Pasternak's intentions—never included in the text when it was published in 1922.[9] The overall problem for

tion of Kleist's studies of philosophy in the 1911 essay "G. Fon Kleist. Ob asketike v kul'ture" (*PSS* 5:294–301).

7. The letter to Polonsky is dated "Summer 1921" (*PSS* 7:370–72).

8. See Fleishman (1975) and (1977, 18–129).

9. The novella was set to be published in the summer of 1918, but the publication was cancelled because of "the general crisis" and appeared only in 1922 (Fleishman 1990a, 104, 111). In 1921, in a letter to Polonsky, Pasternak complained about the weighty digressions in the text: "It is simplified to the extreme and filled with long digressions and asides" [перегружена

the interpreter of his prose is, thus, clear. With the exception of these passages, the early Pasternak tended not to include abstract philosophical issues or to display them as easily identifiable layers of his fictional texts. Since, however, it is the view of this study that there were never two distinct Boris Pasternaks (the philosopher and the artist), it is necessary to elucidate a deeper layer of integration in his prose between his artistic goals and his philosophical training, all the more so because Pasternak's "manner of thought always remained independent and original" (Fleishman *Lehrjahre* 133).

In such a context, the pages deleted from *Luvers* constitute an important document, and this chapter seeks, as its first step, to examine the theoretical overlap between Pasternak's asides and disclosures in earlier drafts of the novella and the philosophical themes ("много теории") of "The Mark of Apelles" and particularly "Letters from Tula" (5.1). Our next step is to examine the structure of one of Pasternak's earliest prose sketches, "Ordering a Drama" [Заказ драмы], which portrays the development of artistically gifted children, a topic of direct relevance to *The Childhood of Luvers* (5.2). The sketch was composed under the pen-name of Reliquimini in 1910, that is, one year after the beginning of his philosophical studies.[10] The chapter then proceeds to examine this earliest attempt on the part of Pasternak to speak about the child's psychological development by placing this theme into the context of his philosophical interests. His student notes on psychology and his single surviving philosophical essay "On the Object and Method of Psychology" [О предмете и методе психологии][11] are invaluable at this stage (5.3). Blending these multiple angles of inquiry adds a significant theoretical perspective, hitherto unsuspected, to established readings of *The Childhood of Luvers* (5.4) and provides a cohesive context for the analysis of the novella in the next two chapters.

5.1 The "spirituality" of prose:
"It is important to visit a person when he is whole"

In contrast to Akhmatova's characterization of Pasternak's poetry as conceived "before the sixth day of creation" or without a human being in view (Bykov 2007, 92),[12] *The Childhood of Luvers,* Pasternak's first critically acclaimed prose

---

сентенциями и длинотами] (*PSS* 7:371).

10. Pasternak "formally commenced philosophy studies [. . .] in the autumn of 1909" (*CSP* 1989, 120).

11. Fleishman dates the essay to 1912–13 (*Lehrjahre* 120–21). However, there is a possibility that the paper was written in December 1911 (*PSSCom* 5:641).

12. Lydia Chukovskaya jotted down this statement of Akhmatova's in the 1940s.

work, is dedicated explicitly to the psychological development of the person. In discussing the context of Pasternak's paper "On the Object and Method of Psychology," Fleishman emphasizes that his whole period of philosophical studies is colored by his examination of "psychology and psychologism" (*Lehrjahre* 121),[13] an interest Pasternak reaffirmed in his letter to Polonsky as late as 1921 ("I began to write about a heroine, a woman, with her psychological genesis" [quoted from Barnes 1989, 270]). Furthermore, as aptly noted by Bykov, 1918 and 1919 were years when Pasternak, moved by the complexity of revolutionary experience, was particularly taken with the idea of the human self; he suspended his work on poetry and planned a book based on his 1913 lecture "Symbolism and Immortality"[14] and then "Articles about Personhood" [Статьи о человеке], for which he considered the title *Quinta Essentia,* reflecting a premise of the Italian humanists who added the fifth element—man—to the four elements (fire, air, water, earth) found in nature (Bykov 2007, 169).[15]

Thus, Akhmatova's curt remark helps to identify, albeit unintentionally, the curious orientation of Pasternak's thought in 1918, namely, his drawing an unusual distinction between poetry and prose in "Some Propositions" (written, as observed above, also in 1918). Here he characterizes poetry's task as the search for "the melody of nature," while the primary goal of prose is for him nothing less than "finding" the individual (человек) who is then placed in the maelstrom of contemporary life. Writing, with its two poles of poetry and prose, connects nature and human beings, with the latter as the "spiritual" focus and destiny of prose:

> Poetry and prose are two polarities, indivisible one from another.
>
> Through its inborn hearing, poetry seeks out the melody of nature amid the noise of lexicon, and picking it up like some motif, it proceeds to improvise on that theme. *By its feeling, through its spirituality, prose seeks and finds man in the category of speech. And when man is found lacking in an age, then it re-creates him from memory* and sets him there and pretends for the good of mankind to have found him in the present. These two principles do not exist separately. (*CSP* 261–62; emphasis added)

Неотделимые друг от друга поэзия и проза—полюса.

---

13. Fleishman writes: "the whole period of the philosophical interests of Pasternak is colored by the discussions of psychology, psychologism, and poetic creativity" (*Lehrjahre* 121). I leave aside here Aristotle's notion of aether as a fifth, more divine element.

14. This lecture, by many accounts, was related to Pasternak's dissertation, the text of which has not survived (Fleishman 1977; *CSP* 1989, 148; *PSSCom* 5:644).

15. "Some Propositions" [Несколько положений] was a part of this projected book (*CSP* 1989, 256).

По врожденному слуху поэзия подыскивает мелодию природы среди шума словаря и, подобрав ее, как подбирают мотив, предается затем импровизации на эту тему. *Чутьем, по своей одухотворенности, проза ищет и находит человека в категории речи, а если век его лишен, то на память воссоздает его*, и подкидывает, и потом, для блага человечества, делает вид, что нашла его среди современности. Начала эти не существуют отдельно. (*PSS* 5:26)

Emerging, therefore, from the much wider context of his interest in the human being as "the fifth essence," this "proposition" may help to explain his zeal (persisting from 1918 onwards) for writing prose as well as his seemingly inexplicable emphasis upon prose's "spiritual nature" and the observation that there are ages in which the individual (человек) may not be found. This startling connection between the human being and the spirit(edness) of prose [одухотворенность] was clearly meant to be noticed.

As one searches for an explanation, the bridge between Neo-Kantian apperception and psychology may provide a plausible missing link. In "The Object and Method of Psychology," Pasternak focuses on Natorp's view that a series of impressions can be unified only by apperception, and that the whole field of consciousness belongs to apperception. Any subjective impression and, indeed, all particularized contents of experience must become subject to this all uniting principle:

Let us note that not one single content can enter consciousness without entering the act of apperception in one manner or another. [. . .]

This consideration will bring us forcefully to the sought-for principle. Indeed, the principle of connectivity is essentially a generic characteristic: this becomes clear from the fact, that apperception covers the whole arena of consciousness. In the same manner, it is a psychological principle.

Заметим, что ни одно содержание не может войти в сознание не апперцепируясь так или иначе. [. . .]

Эти соображения сильно приблизят нас к искомому признаку. В самом деле, признак связи, прежде всего—признак родовой: это явствует из того хотя бы, что апперцепцией покрывается все поле сознания. В одинаковой мере это признак чисто психологический [. . .]. (*PSS* 5:311)

Thus, the Kantian transcendental ego in the work of apperception, the major interest of Pasternak's studies in psychology, here resurfaces as a central unifying principle of human psychology and this also becomes in 1918 the characteristic of prose whose work it is to find and place the human being "in the category of speech." This philosophical resonance explains, in turn, why the very notion of prose writing appears to Pasternak not merely spiritual, but also rather an act of "spirit-creation" [о-духо-творенность] (that is, an activity possessing the literal ability to create other spirits) or "spirit-embodiment" within a "whole, but fictional individual."[16] By remaining a personal or lyrical vehicle of expression, poetry does not pursue this goal of creating other selves as clearly; it does not explicitly move, like the poet in "Letters from Tula," from the first to the third person.

Thus, it should be noted that alongside the Kantian transcendental consciousness (or transcendental ego) capable of uniting disparate elements because of its spiritual essence, Pasternak tends to see the unifying principle as essentially a creative act directed outwards. When the description of the "spiritedness of prose" is put into the context of those pages excised from the final manuscript of *The Childhood of Luvers,* the emphasis that Pasternak places in his notes on the young girl discovering her wholeness becomes much clearer. "It is important to visit a person when he is whole" [Надо заходить к человеку в те часы, когда он целен] (*PSS* 3:515), observes Pasternak, in a passage excised from the concluding pages of "The Long Days," and this emphasis on wholeness is hardly new in the writer's corpus. In fact, Pasternak's search for wholeness is often misunderstood when it is placed into the context of the cubo-futuristic "projection of different objects into one plane" (Rudova 1994, 139) or when viewed as a "chain of 'riddles' and 'solutions,'" dependent on the characters' solution of linguistic puzzles (Fleishman 1979, 48). Any solution to the series of impressions at different levels of intensity or intellectual depth and power is for Pasternak invariably an awakening of a deeper "apperceptive" self, and it is in this sense that he opposes his work in the letter to Polonsky to "the sea of violence that stands behind all our neo-aesthetism" and that afflicts him "with sea sickness" (*PSS* 7:371).

When his early prose is examined in this light, it is striking to what extent his writing is guided by the theme of grasping the human being as a unified movement—a sketch, line, or stroke that is not a "collage" or "deliberate semantic confusion" (Rudova 1994, 140)[17] but that expresses a singular feature

---

16. Barnes connects this theme, also central in "Symbolism and Immortality," not merely to Husserl, as does Fleishman, but also to Andrey Bely's use of the Kantian "transcendental subject" and Berdyaev and Frank's view that creativity involves a "supra individual form of consciousness" (1989, 151).

17. A similar view to Rudova's insistence on Pasternak's aesthetic closeness to cubo-futurism is expressed by Wiegers (1999). Olga Hasty, however, suggests, on the basis of her analysis

which can then be viewed as an organizing principle for the whole personality. "The lyrical agent [...] is first of all a principle of integration" [начало интегрирующее прежде всего] (*PSS* 5:9), said Pasternak, arguing with Shershenevich in 1913, and he never abandoned this position. When, for example, in "The Mark of Apelles," Camilla appears to succeed in her intuitive grasp of Heine, Pasternak's Heine praises (somewhat too emphatically) her capacity to grasp his nature in a unified gesture, proclaiming it to be the only artistic accomplishment worthy of Apelles' line. The gift of "vital" perception, of life itself, and the intoxication of deep love are required for drawing such a line:

> How perceptive you are! At one stroke, with the line of Apelles, you conveyed my whole essence, the whole crux of the situation. [. . .]
>
> [. . .] You possess such vital vision. You have already mastered a line as unique as life itself. [. . .] (*CSP* 110; trans. altered)

> Что за проницательность! Одною чертой, чертой Апеллеса, передать все мое существо, всю суть положения! [. . .]
>
> Но вы умеете глядеть так животворно. И уже овладели линией, единственной, как сама жизнь. [. . .] (*PSS* 3:15–16)

Consciousness in the act of creativity turned toward others, a "vital vision" enhanced and intensified by passion, had been Pasternak's antidote to the disunited layers of impressions and ideas within the individual; this act of turning discloses a permeable boundary where the holistic emergence of self can be located in his works prior to *Luvers*. As noted in earlier chapters, this theme also tends to be interwoven with images of electrified illumination, in which inspiration is presented as a flash that illuminates and clarifies the real outlines of personality.[18] As Pasternak asserts in "Some Propositions," artistic vision (or the intense dramatization of apperception, we may add) is inseparable from "some unearthly, transient, yet forever vernal thunderstorm . . . [as it begins] to spread and roar through consciousness stroke by stroke, like the convulsions of lightning on dusty ceiling and plaster" [как мах за махом, напоминая конвульсии молний на пыльных потолках и гипсах, начи-

---

of "The Black Goblet," that "Pasternak senses that for all their hyperbolized enactments of breaking with tradition, the Futurists contribute nothing essentially new to that perennial question that stymied the Symbolists of how the fleeting and the eternal are to be negotiated" (2006, 120).

18. Hasty speaks of the image of the "flash" as "the age-old quest to reconcile the fleeting and the eternal" (2006, 123). On Tsvetaeva's themes and variations of Pasternak's light in darkness, as well as his androgynous masculine-feminine self, "flooded and overwhelmed," see Ciepiela (2006, 41).

нает ширять и шуметь по сознанью отраженная стенопись какой-то
нездешней, несущейся мимо и вечно весенней грозы] (*CSP* 262; *PSS* 5:
27). And as I argued in Chapters 3 and 4, this vernal storm in the early Pasternak is aligned with the theme of artistic competition with the sun's energy
(and for this reason the theme of light or electric illumination remains an
important focus for the examination of all his works).[19]

However, these grandiose themes of "storm and stress" cannot be developed in *Luvers,* for here Pasternak is engaged in a task altogether different
from a vision accompanied by the "dance of compass needles" or "vernal
thunderstorm": the perceptions of a child cannot be imbued with, or accompanied by, either creative passion or the presence of intensive creative light,
as supplied in "The Mark of Apelles" by the genius of the wandering Heine.
"Apperception" and the "transcendental ego" in Kant indicate personal maturity, just as in Pasternak creative vision and all-transforming poetic power are
themes by definition outside the purview of the experiences narrated in the
novella.

Recalling, perhaps, his experience in writing *Luvers,* Pasternak in *Safe
Conduct* emphasizes that the perception of the child has very little to do with
the Romantic earth-shattering sublime, for the child does not experience any
Romantic aggrandizement of self and does not exaggerate the extraordinary
nature of extraordinary experiences:

> It [antiquity] was insured against this because it prescribed entirely for
> childhood the whole dose of extraordinariness contained in the world.
> And when, after taking it, a person entered with gigantic strides into a
> gigantic reality, both his strides and the world round him were accounted
> ordinary. (*CSP* 28–29)

> От этого она [античность] была застрахована тем, что всю дозу нео-
> бычного, заключающуюся в мире, целиком приписывала детству. И
> когда по ее приеме человек гигантскими шагами вступал в гигант-
> скую действительность, поступь и обстановка считались обыч-
> ными. (*PSS* 3:156)

One may suggest, then, that when compared with the earlier stories, Pasternak's thematic shift in *Luvers* is considerable: the writer must work with the
many developmental stages occurring within a protagonist who is not yet an

---

19. See Greber: "In Pasternak, as in classical mnemotechnics, an almost literal illumination
is required to light up the *imaginés* so that they become recognizable" (1997, 33).

artist, poet, or musician—stages that precede any serious artistic engagement even though childhood constitutes, according to *Safe Conduct,* an independent unity, "like a central nucleus of integration" [детство замкнуто и самостоятельно, как заглавное интеграционное ядро] (*CSP* 28–29; *PSS* 3:156).

Thus, in his second prose work of 1918, Pasternak chose a challenging subject-matter, and one where any Kantian notion of apperception could not function as a straightforward guiding principle: the growing child, and this is very clear in *Luvers,* is only learning how to synthesize her impressions and thoughts. It is possible then that it was precisely the open-endedness and incompleteness of the developmental psychological states of the child that attracted Pasternak,[20] allowing him room for artistic experimentation and innovation, all the more so because Andrey Bely, also deeply influenced by Neo-Kantianism, had just finished "his own account of a childhood, *Kotik Letaev,* [that] was serialized in the Scythian journal *Skify* (no.1, 1917 and no. 2, 1918)" (Barnes 1989, 271–72). Here, then, is the crux of the problem for the interpreter, yet it remains altogether unclear how Pasternak could have combined the portrayal of a child's developing perception with the realization of his intention to "visit a person when he is whole," especially if in his artistic exploration he was aiming to compete with Bely.

Pasternak, of course, was the first to admit this challenge. In 1917–18, as he was working on *Luvers,* he explicitly discussed—in the same excised passages—the difficulty associated with any holistic presentation of a growing self. Lamenting the previous failures of this enterprise (particularly the exclusive concentration on the issues of sex by novelists and doctors), Pasternak reaffirmed the need to encapsulate the fullest range of phenomena, apprehended by and realigned within the individual self. In fact, in labeling his approach "artistic materialism," he compared it to the judgment of a textile producer who wants to see the texture of the material as a whole and rejects any tests on isolated pieces of the fabric:

> *Physicians facilitated this task of the novelists. They concentrated the latter's attention on sexual maturation. A novelist sees a male and a female. He writes a novel and promises the reader a novel of love. A novelist must know that the one who cuts and amputates puts an equals sign between a textile product and a separate textile sample. [. . .] But this is a cheap, naively cynical, and lazily trusting materialism. The textile producer, however, checks the*

---

20. See here also Pasternak's insistence in his student notes that for the Neo-Kantian school only apperception "in contrast to perceptions deals with a unified consciousness" [Апперцепция в отличии от перцепции; единство сознания как особенность сознания, а не содержаний] (*Lehrjahre* I:268).

full product and often finds it wanting. He is not brought up on separated samples. He doubts.

Thus, we too doubt. We doubt that an animal develops according to the principles of the separated living parts, all the more so because these separated parts decay.

We doubt the correctness of the boundaries, placed by doctors to direct writers' materialism. *We doubt the value of such materialism and we doubt its satisfactory depth.* [. . .]

It is important to visit a person when he is whole.

Врачи облегчили романистам их задачу. Они сосредоточили внимание последних на созревании пола. Романист видит женщину и мужчину. Он пишет роман и обещает читателю повесть любви. Романист должен знать, что тот, кто умеет ампутировать, привык отожествлять кусок с образцом. [. . .] Но это—дешевый, цинически-наивный, лениво-доверчивый материализм. Производитель пропускает весь кусок перед собой и часто бракует. Он не воспитан на лоскутках. Он сомневается.

Мы тоже сомневаемся сейчас. Мы сомневаемся в том, чтобы животное развивалось по законам разложения животного на части, и тем более по законам разлагающегося животного.

Мы сомневаемся в правильности границ, положенных врачом материализму писателя. *Мы сомневаемся в достоинствах такого материализма, в достаточной его глубине.* [. . .]

Надо заходить к человеку в те часы, когда он целен. (*PSS* 3:514–15; emphasis added)

However, in presenting this version of the emergence of the "whole individual" whom he expected to "visit" in his novella, Pasternak blends idealist philosophy and Humean materialism, a mixture that appears under the formulation of "artistic materialism."[21] Attacking throughout the insufficient "materialism"

---

21. Athough Pasternak would later tell Polonsky that he had revealed "to the readers all that he thinks and intends to share" (quoted from *CSP* 1989, 270), he does misdirect his readers when he speaks of his own materialism. There is perhaps an unintentional confusion of terms, but a confusion nevertheless: while explaining his views as materialistic in principle, Pasternak continues to stress not so much his materialistic premises, but rather materialism's philosophical antonym—the classical idealistic position, the world of thought influenced by Platonic and Neo-Platonic arguments within which the notion of the form or idea can never be found as such in sensible reality but belongs instead to the realm of the intelligible world. According to classical idealism (if, for argument's sake, one speaks of idealism more broadly so as to avoid a Cartesian split between the finite and the infinite), the form of personhood, that is, the human

of other practitioners of the craft, Pasternak carefully places the word "soul" into the mix and emphasizes the spiritual context of his "full-blooded" commitment to the soul's material development:

> We doubt the value of such materialism and we doubt its satisfactory depth. We permit ourselves to believe that decisively *all psychological (soul's) content*—the whole without exception—*is maturing in the human soul with the same gravity* and full-blooded materiality as, with the easy blessing by a doctor, the emphasis in the novel is placed on a small sample—sex.

> Мы сомневаемся в достоинствах такого материализма, в достаточной его глубине. Мы позволяем себе думать, что весь решительно *душевный инвентарь*, весь, без изъятья, назревал и назрел *в человеческой душе* с той же тягостной, кровавой матерьяльностью, какую, с легкой руки врача, натуралистам в романе угодно сосредоточить в небольшом куске романического мяса—в поле. (*PSS* 5:514; emphasis added)

In these same excised pages[22] he admits to the reader that "the world of the human soul" will be ultimately examined in the context of the values and ideas born within it, and that the full range of the self, the whole of the personality, cannot be grasped until the self is situated in the environment of ideas that open up "clearly and distinctly" [ясно и отчетливо]. In intimating this Cartesian context,[23] Pasternak proclaims that for his work he has chosen an idea that is the most common and "nameless," while demanding from it not a philosophical, but an artistic touch:

> The most diverse, the most abstract ideas of the living person [. . .]. We speak here about the artistic touch. There still exists another—philosophical. Then the ideas do not smell, but they open up clearly and distinctly.
> To be true to our word, we will narrate presently in what circumstances there was once born, on a particular occasion, within the world of a human

---

soul, as the organizing principle of personality, remains intangible on the level of material substance; it is both invisible and indivisible in the sensible world while being in itself the principle of wholeness and the expression of the person's sacred essence. To find its material principles artistically is, thus, not a simple task at all.

22. The length of these excised passages suggests that Pasternak was aware that the reader would need further direction: one can sense here both his simultaneous desire and reluctance to give explicit articulation to the direction of his thought.

23. See n. 4 above.

soul one of the most popular and unnamable ideas. It will demand time. It will be a lengthy passage, full of facts and descriptions.

> Самые различные, самые отвлеченные идеи живого человека [. . .]. Мы говорим о прикосновении художественном. Существует другое, философское. Тогда они не пахнут. Тогда они не смеют пахнуть, но должны распахиваться ясно и отчетливо.
>
> Верные слову, мы расскажем теперь, в какой обстановке родилась однажды в такой-то и такой раз в мире человеческой души одна из распространеннейших и безымяннейших идей. Это потребует времени. Это будет пассаж продолжительный, ряд фактов и описаний. (*PSS* 5:514–15)

The crucial role of abstract ideas in the formation of the human self is also reiterated in Pasternak's letter to Bobrov of July 16, 1918 (the only surviving letter of this period that discusses *Luvers* directly). Not only does Pasternak insist in this letter that the growth of human beings and their subsequent destinies are inextricably connected with what he calls an "abstract moment," but he also states that any moral development in the life of the individual is directly related to the world of ideas, among which he chooses "the *idea* of a third person" or the independent other as *the* most significant first step:

> [. . .] the second and third portions, fastened together (as the notebooks), are all connected together by an attempt to show *how there takes shape in consciousness an abstract moment, to what it leads in consequence and how it is reflected in the character of the personality. Here it is shown through the idea of the third person.*

> [. . .] вторая и третья скрепленные порции (тетради) связаны воедино попыткой показать, *как складывается в сознании момент абстрактный, к чему это впоследствии ведет и как отражается на характере. Тут это показано на идее третьего человека.* (*PSS* 7:348; emphasis added)

This letter, then, adds further clarification to those excised statements discussed above which aimed to explain Pasternak's intention in working with *Luvers*: his task of "visiting a person when he is whole" includes the portrayal of a meeting space between the world of thought and the child's forming personality, or, in his own terms, a meeting place between abstract reality, the world of ideas, and what he calls in earlier drafts "the world of the human soul" [мир человеческой души] (*PSS* 3:515).

Such themes as personhood, the human soul, the role of ideas, and the specific idea of the "third person" can be further elucidated by recalling Pasternak's experience in Marburg and the focus of Cohen's ethics on the "person, specifically on the unity of person [. . .] born through ethics and nourished by it" (cf. Fleishman *Lehrjahre* 97). Cohen, in fact, augments Kant's view of the unified self by insisting that moral growth begins when the external freedom of the individual "is broken down in relation to an *other* person" (Gibbs 2005, 206). Cohen's emphasis upon the *other,* singled out later by Levinas,[24] denotes the conditions for the development of a moral self, that is, the self's purification of will:

> For the will and for action self-consciousness cannot mean the consciousness of the self as a unique person. This self must not so much include the other, but rather be related to him. [. . .] No one can be regarded as expanded by the other. *Both must remain standing isolated.* But precisely then they do not remain isolated; rather they are related to each other and build self-consciousness in this correlation. *Self-consciousness is in the first case determined through the consciousness of the other.* The uniting of the other with the one generates self-consciousness for the first time as that of a pure will. (*Ethics* 212–13; 10a–b; trans. Gibbs 2005, 206–7; emphasis added)

It is very probable that precisely this position—the awakening of the self's ethical dimensions in regard to the *other*—was endorsed by Pasternak and identified as "the most common and nameless idea" in the drafts of *Luvers* and named as "the idea of the third person" [идея третьего человека] in his letter to Bobrov (*PSS* 7:348).

In this manner, *The Childhood of Luvers* helps to clarify that Pasternak was one of the first writers to grasp the importance of Cohen's insight, an insight destined to become a major focus of postmodernity, even when not attributed to Cohen directly,[25] for the idea of "the *other*" is combined in Pasternak with

---

24. In current philosophical studies, there is a renewed interest in Cohen's development of the principle of the *other,* and his possible influence on Levinas. Levinas, however, saw Cohen as primarily a Platonist, but this meant that Cohen's "love" for the world of ideas was also a relationship with otherness: "Hermann Cohen (in this a Platonist) maintained that one can love only ideas; but the notion of an Idea is in the last analysis tantamount to the transmutation of the other into the Other (de l'autre en Autrui)" (Levinas 68; trans. Levy 1997, 138).

25. Levinas' concept of the *Other* may not owe any direct debt to Cohen's concept of the

an artistic awareness that the unity of the personality cannot be experienced without a creative move toward another self. *Luvers,* then, follows directly upon the philosophical preoccupations of his earlier prose, including Camilla's marvelous glance directed toward Heine, and his world effectively changed thereby and his own vision redirected both toward and because of her. In "Letters from Tula" the poet's moral growth is also signaled by the narrative switch from the first to the third person, while the story's actor triumphs when he makes "another . . . speak through his own lips" [заставил своими устами говорить постороннего] (*CSP* 126; *PSS* 3:32). One hears the development of this thematic emphasis at the closing of *Luvers* (in the story's second part, tellingly entitled "The Stranger" [Посторонний]—that is, "outside" any immediate personal boundary), when the authorial voice observes that Zhenya's significant transformation is marked not by the fact that she has experienced "sexual maturity" and fallen in love (as her tutor had assumed upon seeing a "little woman" in her bearing),[26] but by her painful stumbling upon an uncontrollable new principle, as yet unfocused (туманный) and featureless—a generalized outline of the *other* self, "a third person":

> "How is one to explain this excessive sensitivity?" the tutor reflected. Evidently the dead man meant something special to the girl. She had changed greatly. He had been explaining decimals to a child, whereas the person who had just sent him into the classroom. . . . And this was only a matter of one month! Obviously at some time the dead man had made an especially deep and indelible impression on this little woman. [. . .]
>
> He was mistaken, for the impression he imagined did not fit the case at all. But he was right in that the impression that lay behind it all was indelible. Its depth was even greater than he imagined. . . . It lay beyond the girl's control, because it was vitally important and significant, and its significance consisted in the fact that *another* human being had entered her life—a third person totally indifferent, with no name, or only a fortuitous one. (*CSP* 178)

> Чем объяснить этот избыток чувствительности?—размышлял репетитор.—Очевидно, покойный был у девочки на особом положении.

"neighbor," but, as Levy indicates, there are expanding "new vistas for a better understanding of the main ethical views of the two philosophers" and for "Cohen's and Levinas' conceptions of the other man and the stranger as a mediating idea in their understanding of man" (Levy 1997, 136–37).

26. In this, Pasternak clearly places himself in opposition to the "novelists and psychologists" and their emphasis upon "sexual maturation."

Она очень изменилась. Периодические дроби объяснялись еще ребенку, между тем, как та, что послала его сейчас в классную . . . и это дело месяца! Очевидно, покойный произвел когда-то на эту маленькую женщину особо глубокое и неизгладимое впечатление. [. . .]

    Он ошибался. То впечатление, которое он предположил, к делу нисколько не шло. Он не ошибся. Впечатление, скрывавшееся за всем, было неизгладимо. Оно отличалось большею, чем он думал, глубиной . . . Оно лежало вне ведения девочки, потому что было жизненно важно и значительно, и значение его заключалось в том, что в ее жизнь впервые вошел другой человек, третье лицо, совершенно безразличное, без имени или со случайным, не вызывающее ненависти и не вселяющее любви. [. . .] (*PSS* 3:84–85)

However, this conclusion, for all its echoes of Hermann Cohen and its spiritual and ethical overtones, appears only at the story's end—as a shock or revelation, and it remains unclear whether or not (and by what means) this principle of the *other* has previously guided both the narrative and the child's personality (or even the developing soul) toward individual unity or individualization.

5.2 "Three groups":
Three levels of reality in "Ordering a Drama"

The puzzle of the novella is deepened further by a startling resonance, frequently overlooked in critical literature,[27] between the three-layered organization of the worlds of *Luvers* and one of Pasternak's earliest sketches composed under the pen-name of Reliquimini. "Ordering a Drama" [Заказ драмы], whose composition coincides with those years when his devotion to philosophy was still wholeheartedly enthusiastic,[28] is dedicated to the portrayal of the minds of growing children. While the sketch places major emphasis on music rather than poetry (in *Luvers,* Zhenya is not a musician, but an avid

---

27. Ljunggren observes the similarity between "Ordering a Drama" and *Luvers,* the emphasis of both works on the inanimate objects as the needy recipients of the action, an image that she traces to Rilke (1984, 99–101). See also Gorelik (2000).

28. Fleishman *Lehrjahre* 120. See also *CSP*'s eloquent summation of the period: "[H]e formally commenced. His capacity for abstract thought was remarked upon [. . .]. After mastering the rudiments of a subject, he and his like-minded companions worked semi-independently in the University library and pursued their private philosophical enthusiasms" (1989, 121).

reader), the major emphasis of the narrative is upon the formation of personalities pierced (or "sewn" together) by art and thought.[29] In pre-setting the stage for the as yet unknown event of the future ("ordering a drama"), Pasternak isolates three layers of reality[30] that are not without some bearing on the construction of *Luvers:* (1) the inanimate objects of the room that live "like well-attended children" [вещи в комнате (как одаренные вниманием дети)] (*PSS* 3:458); (2) the first lyricism of music, a constant "movement with no materiality" [движение без действительности]; and (3) the spirit of the street in winter directly associated with the composer Shestikrylov (the Six-Winged One),[31] the children's tutor (*PSS* 3:460–64).

If we return, ever so briefly, to Pasternak's letter to his uncle Mikhail Freidenberg in December 1913, we will find, to our surprise, precisely the same three levels in the portrayal of Freidenberg's working space. The levels appear in a descending order: (3) Petersburg, city-spirit; (2) a *dramatic movement* of thought and engagement; and (1) the inanimate objects in his room that absorb the intensity of the man at the desk:

I would think of your serene capacity, instinctually, to take control of that chaotic and close to dream impression, which leaves behind itself Petersburg, city spirit.

[. . .] how you fantasize over your work place, in the evening, with bloodless nothingness behind your back.

And how you transmit this dramatically performed life to the surrounding objects, to the whole mystery of furnishings and rooms.

Я думал бы о том, как невозмутимо и с каким странным неведением об этом завладеваете Вы тем хаотическим и близким к грезе впечатлением, которое оставляет по себе Петербург, как город-дух.

---

29. Livingstone in translating "Ordering a Drama" says the following about these earliest sketches: "This odd, dense prose is rich in motifs characteristic of the poet's later work; here they appear in their intensest, primary form. It is clear from them that Pasternak was possessed by a single vision and was developing a single main cluster of images for it which would evolve and settle but not radically change" (*MG* 56).

30. See Livingstone: "'Ordering a Drama' sets out to construct something like a philosophical system. [. . .] Not all of this is clear, but certain things are clear enough. It is clear that the life of a particular man is needed to combine the three categories" (*MG* 59).

31. In *Safe Conduct,* Pasternak attaches the same epithets to Scriabin: "So, it was winter out of doors. The street was chopped a third shorter by dusk and was full of errand-running all day long. A whirl of streetlamps chased along after the street, lagging behind in the whirl of snowflakes" [Итак, на дворе зима, улица на треть подрублена сумерками и весь день на побегушках. За ней, отставая в вихре снежинок, гонятся вихрем фонари] (*CSP* 23; *PSS* 3:50).

[. . .] как [. . .] фантазируете Вы над своими станками, вечером, с бескровною пустотой за спиной.

И о том, как заражается этой, драматически разыгранной Вами жизнью мир предметов вокруг, вся эта тайна обстановки и комнат. (*PSS* 7:157)

Shestikrylov's portrait is, of course, considerably more dramatic than the sketch of the uncle in the letter: the composer "sews" together the three levels, while he himself is "sewn by life"; in the manuscript of "Ordering a Drama"[32] he is also a mysterious eternal figure—an almost Hegelian spirit of history in transition (as well as a literary reminiscence of Pushkin's poem "The Prophet," with its Six-Winged Seraphim).[33] Awaited eagerly by the children, surrounded by storms and lit-up windows, and dressed in fur coats, the composer is eternally in search of himself, either lifted up by music (when he becomes god-like) or descending into the lives of others[34] and, although he has a room where he teaches and performs, he does not really have a place. Not unlike Heinrich Heine in "The Mark of Apelles," Shestikrylov is a presence that belongs to infinity,[35] as he both recollects and forgets his immediate factual reality. He is essentially a unifying principle, even while being always in motion:[36]

---

32. Gorelik suggests the Nietzschean echoes (e.g., the emergence of drama, *The Birth of Tragedy from the Spirit of Music*) in the title and the overall conception of the sketch, and speaks also of the Apollonian and the Dionysian opposition (2000, 10–12). Since, in my view, Shestikrylov is a portrait of Scriabin's influence on Pasternak's childhood (Gorelik indicates as much: 2000, 9), the Nietzschean overtones should not be discounted, but in themselves they are not sufficient. Shestikrylov is a multilayered image.

33. The sleep of Shestikrylov that Gorelik reads as an Apollonian dream (2000, 13) can be also read as a reminiscence of Pushkin's "prophet" falling asleep as he meets his Six-Winged Seraphim: "And the Six-Winged Seraphim / Appeared to me at the roads' crossing / With the fingers light as sleep / He touched my eyes" [И шестикрылый серафим / На перепутье мне явился. / Перстами легкими как сон / Моих зениц коснулся он] (Pushkin 3:30).

34. Cf. Scriabin in *Safe Conduct*: "On the way home from school, the name Scriabin, covered with snow, skipped down from a poster onto my back" (*CSP* 23:150).

35. Cf. also Freidenberg's gift of time in the letter of December 1913: "But there exists a reality of a special gift of rare individuals which I would like to name as the gift of time. [. . .] However, I have met several individuals, who appear to breathe with their own time, and the indication of whose clocks is only a concession to the common order. What does this signify? It signifies, first, a certain feature of immortality that has entered into their movement. And it also speaks of their kindredness with their destiny" [Дело, может быть, в особом даре нескольких редких людей, который я бы назвал дар времени. [. . .] Однако я встретил несколько личностей, которые как бы дышат своим собственным временем, у которых показанья их часов, может быть, только—уступка общественному порядку. Что это означает? Это означает, во-первых, некоторую черту бессмертия, проникающую их движения. И затем это говорит о какой-то одинокой их близости со своей судьбой] (*PSS* 7:157).

36. In "Letters from Tula," the poet forgets or places some of his belongings in the pawnshop while traveling (*CSP* 120; *PSS* 3:27).

The three layers were being sewn together by the life of the composer, so that one whole should result; and according to which layer he was piercing, the composer Shestikrylov would at one moment be fretting and worrying, feeling the inanimate weight of guilt and need, while, at the next, uplifted, he would gaze around: "Where are the kneelers?" But most often of all, life was being stitched and embroidered by means of the composer, and together with it he would fling himself into the search for himself. [. . .] All too often he forgot he had taken himself along with him once and for all. But is it possible to bear this in mind eternally? (*MG* 28)

Жизнью композитора сшивали эти три слоя, чтобы вышло целое, и, смотря по тому, какой слой прокалывал, композитор Шести-крылов то не находил себе место и чувствовал неодушевленную тяжесть вины и нужду неодушевленную, то, вознесенный, огляды-вался: где же коленно-преклоненные? Но чаще всего композитором шили, вышивали жизнь, и вместе с нею он бросался искать самого себя [. . .]. Слишком часто он забывал, что захватил себя с собою навсегда. Но разве можно вечно помнить это? (*PSS* 3:461)

Moreover, all three levels, about to be sewn right through and coexisting in the same room, are permeated by expectation, with life as their eventual guest (Впоследствии к ним стучалась жизнь [*PSS* 4:462]).[37] The presence of the three levels is essential for the young children's instruction in art,[38] for those who "*think further than others* and become unrecognizable as a result," as they learn all the while that in order to confront the requests of all three levels of reality as themselves, they must discover their own art:

Thus. Three groups. First: a true story, reality as a great immobile legend of wood and cloth, objects in need, twilight in need, like a church parish that has grown stale from waiting. And lyricism, music, this is the sec-ond. [. . .] The first is—reality without movement, the second—movement without reality. And the third: the music down there in the snowflakes, the music of people going in and out of their homes, in brief the street's music [. . .] the movement of reality which tosses about and desponds and stretches itself over temporal layers [. . .].

So, life is the third element. And the composer Shestikrylov, who gave lessons in the winter twilight, the composer Shestikrylov, who was waited

---

37. See here Ljunggren (1984, 75–78).

38. Gorelik emphasizes the relationship between children and objects, for, like children, objects are unable to reveal their potential unaided (2000, 13).

for by his pupils in the salon a long, long time [. . .]. The Composer Shestikrylov was the surgical thread for the stitching up of the world order that was operated upon. [. . .]

Now I shall unobtrusively tell a small truth: a drama has been promised, and like all dramas it begins with a scenario, a description of objects [. . .].

Here is the scenario: twilight in the composer's apartment—and either there is no meaning in it or else it's to be followed by a drama. This was how it was in life too—there stood the inanimate principles, demanding to be set in motion, and people would start off here at a run, and some of them, and ones who always thought further than others, and more quickly became unrecognizable to their acquaintances, they endured this delicious suffering: to work, to think upon the inanimate objects. [. . .]

Later they became artists. (*MG* 28–29)

Вот. Три группы. Первое: быль, действительность, как великое неподвижное предание из дерева, из тканей, нуждающиеся предметы, нуждающиеся сумерки, как церковный зачерствевший в ожидании приход. И лиризм, музыка—это второе. [. . .] Первое— действительность без движения, второе—движение без действительности. И третье, там, внизу,—музыка в хлопьях, музыка тех, которые идут домой и из дома, словом уличная музыка, [. . .] движение действительности, которое мечется и грустит, и тянется по временам [. . .].

Итак, жизнь—это третье. И композитор Шестикрылов, дающий в зимние сумерки уроки, композитор Шестикрылов, которого долго, долго ожидали ученики в зале [. . .]. Композитор Шестикрылов был той терапевтической нитью, которая должна была сшивать оперированный миропорядок [. . .].

Теперь я украдкой скажу маленькую правду: тут обещается драма, и начинается она, как вообще драмы, сценарием, описанием предметов [. . .].

Вот тут сценарий: сумерки в квартире композитора, и они или не имеют смысла, или за ними должна следовать драма; так и было в жизни,—стояли неодушевленные начала и требовали разбега; люди разбегались здесь, и некоторые из них, те, которые думали всегда дальше других и скорее становились неузнаваемыми для знакомых—они выносили это сладостное страдание: работать, думать за неодушевленное. [. . .]

Впоследствие, они стали художниками. (*PSS* 3:460–62)

The necessity of abstract thought and of ideas that allow future artists to think for the inanimate objects in the room is therefore the ultimate destination of the children's growth: it is a crucial stage of their childhood—a time of growth and transformation.[39]

The organization of Zhenya Luvers's world is nuanced, of course, around different emphases (for example, the story's script is no longer situated within a single room, and it extends throughout every season of the year, rather than taking place exclusively in winter); yet there is a surprising number of common themes between the two texts, the most prominent of which is the question of "inanimate foundational principles" (or "reality without movement"), for which the children must think and which they need to animate[40] so that the emergence of a world of constant movement (movement without reality) can replace the static restfulness of inanimate reality. Also common to both texts is the presence of art in the children's lives, and while there is no composer Shestikrylov with his echo of Pushkin's prophetic Six-Winged Seraphim, there is the mysterious Tsvetkov, the "stranger" who emerges with "an atlas or an album" just as Zhenya reads Lermontov's "Demon" in the early fall and who disappears during a winter storm, breaking the chronological precision of the story in his last appearance.

"Thus. Three groups," Pasternak writes in "Ordering a Drama" and adds, "These three layers were being sewn together by the life of the composer" (MG 27–28). The world of The Childhood of Luvers eschews the simplicity of a three-level structure, and yet Pasternak was seriously thinking of calling the work "Three Names" (see Chapter 7.5). Moreover, both narratives start with an analysis of the children's impressions, synthesizing the presence of inanimate objects and eternal significances,[41] and both texts appear to point to thought and thinking as the transforming axis of the children's lives (one finds a similar emphasis in the portrait of Mikhail Freidenberg). In contrast to

---

39. In Pasternak's poetry Fateeva discerns two layers, or rather two circles: "the first circle of Pasternak—the initial stage set for growth," the organic processes; the second circle is the place of "Divine tragedy" where Dante's hell is inhabited (2003, 190). This pattern, characteristic of My Sister Life and The Childhood of Luvers, should be reconsidered in the context of the three-layered world of "Ordering a Drama."

40. See here Fateeva: "the category of the development in him is, in the final analysis, three-dimensional [категория трехмерна]. It is, first of all, the development along the vertical axis [. . .] synthesizing the idea of growth: natural, spiritual, historical" (2003, 111). Similarly Faryno speaks about the scale of transformation from the "material" into "spiritual" [разница позиций на общей шкале трансформаций 'материального' в 'духовное'] in Luvers (1993, 12).

41. Faryno observes the correlation between "a great immobile legend of wood and cloth, objects in need, twilight in need" and "the puzzles of the wood, wool, and metal" at the end of Luvers (1993, 12).

Hume, therefore, for whom impressions are the most vital aspects of human apprehension (see Chapter 2.2 above), Pasternak's children-protagonists in both texts not only undergo stages in the development of their perception and impressions; they also come to maturity in the context of the artistic ideas they embrace.

When all of the above is situated in the context of Pasternak's philosophical studies, this three-layered organization reverberates with deeper precision, and the world of the children can be identified as the layers of the inanimate, the world of animation, and the movement of the spirit or ideas. "Spiritualism," Pasternak wrote while at Moscow University about the thought of Leibniz, "is comprised of monads [which are] the gradation of the clarity of perception," while the human organism is "a compound of monads within a hierarchical relationship" (*Lehrjahre* I:174). While the first layer, namely, material reality apprehended through perception, is a world more than adequately grasped by Hume, Hume's model, according to Pasternak's notation, denies the existence of the monads of the soul:

Herbart: *realia*. One of the *realia* is soul.
Contemporary spiritualism: soul—spiritually simple, [. . .] unchangeable in the foundation of its occurrences, its modulation. An argumentation: the unity and self-identity of consciousness, a substance, denied by Hume, but a principle which is not analogous to impressions.

The analytical insight of Hume is incomparable. But the subject which is thus examined, cannot be approached as a fully philosophical, consciously placed dilemma [. . .].

Гербарт: реалии. Одна из реалий—душа [. . .]
Совр[еменный] спиритуализм: [душа]—духовн[ое] простое, [. . .] неизменная в основании явлений, ее модусов. Аргум[ентируют]: единство и тожество сознания, субстанция отрицаемая Юмом, но понятие, которое не соответсвует впечатлениям. (*Lehrjahre* I:174)

Аналитическая зоркость Юма не знает ничего равного себе. Однако предмет, на который она направлена, не может быть назван философскою, сознательно поставленною проблемой [. . .]. (*Lehrjahre* I:222)

And, as observed above, it is of the child's "soul" that Pasternak intends to speak in those excised passages of *Luvers,* insisting that the moment of transformation takes place while the soul is visited by the idea,[42] and if not "sewn" through by it, then at least it is so shaken that its impressions become "indelible."

The first two realities of "Ordering a Drama" suggest, then, the world of material reality and that of soul entering into the surrounding world: the process of the "inanimate" undergoing "animation." Moreover, if Hume's philosophy cannot clarify for Pasternak the world of "soul," his synopsis of Plato and the ancient Greek philosophers more than adequately make up for the gap. His *Lehrjahre* notes dedicated to Plato correspond directly to what he employs as the second stage of "Ordering a Drama"—its "movement without reality" [второе—движение без действительности] (*PSS* 3:460), already prefiguring the dynamism of animation that Pasternak employs so centrally in *Luvers*. Thus, Pasternak carefully notes in his diary the view of soul (in the Greek, Ψ[υχή]) as unceasing movement, constant renewal of content, possessing no material reality of its own and directing itself, as also in Pasternak's world, toward the world of ideas:

Ψ[υχή] = the beginning of self-directing motion (The inanimate is distinct from the animate precisely because it contains the source of its motion. Ψ[υχή] (in a self-dependent motion) moves always, cannot arrest itself; its life is without cessation. Ψ[υχή] is the beginning of movement of other objects; as a consequence it cannot have a beginning.
Ψ[υχή]—is invisible and intangible.
[. . .] Ψ[υχή] lives and moves of itself. The complex is always changing. Ψ[υχή]—turning away from sensible objects and concentration on the intelligible, elevating itself to the unchangeable, self-identical condition.

Ψ[υχή] = начало самоопределяемого движения. (Одушевл[енное] отлич[ается] от неодушевл[енного] тем, что носит в себе источник своих движений). Ψ[υχή] (как самостоятельное движущееся) движется всегда, не может сама себя остановить: ее жизнь неистребима. Ψ[υχή] начало движения других предметов, след[овательно] не мож[ет] само иметь начало. [. . .]
Ψ[υχή]—невидима и неосязаема.

---

42. Cf. the passage that is excised from the final draft: "To be true to our word, we will narrate presently in what circumstances there was once born, on a particular occasion, within the world of a human soul one of the most popular and unnamable ideas." [Верные слову, мы расскажем теперь, в какой обстановке родилась однажды в такой-то и такой раз в мире человеческой души одна из расспространеннейших и безымяннейших идей] (*PSS* 5:514–15).

[. . .] *Ψ[υχή]* живет и движется от себя. Сложное непрерывно
изменяется. *Ψ[υχή]*, отвращаясь от чувственных вещей и сосредото-
чившись на умопостиг[аемом], возвыш[ающемся] до неизменного,
тождественного себе состояния. (*Lehrjahre* I:361)

The third layer of the story in "Ordering a Drama," inhabited by the composer
of Six-Wings, a layer independent of inanimate objects and the world of animation, is actually the reality or spirit of the street, coming to pierce the silence
of the room's furniture. "The spirit," observes Pasternak in his philosophical
notes, "always comes from the outside" [Дух приходит извне] (*Lehrjahre* I:
174), obviously referring to the Aristotelian *nous thurathen* (the mind-spirit
from out of doors).[43] Moreover, the real character of a person, according to his
notes on Plato, cannot be found unless it is sought in the world of ideas and
layers of the spirit:

Ψa = Spirit, personal in a human being, his/her 'I.' It contemplates the
world of ideas. It is similar to that world.

Ψa = Дух, личн[ое] в человеке, его Я. Оно созерцает мир идей.
Подобно ему. (*Lehrjahre* I:361)

The juxtaposition of "Ordering a Drama" and Pasternak's student diaries suggests, therefore, that the children's psychological progression articulates the
following sequence: (1) the life of material objects as it is grasped by the children's perception, (2) the animating power of soul, and (3) instruction by the
Spirit from outdoors.[44] Whether a similar progression is to be found in *Luvers*
cannot be confirmed without a more careful analysis of the text, the goal of
Chapters 6 and 7.

What can be observed without further examination, however, is the fact
that apart from Freidenberg's ability to live in the presence of the city-spirit,
both *Safe Conduct* and *Sketch for an Autobiography* are explicit in their emphasis upon the power of the "spirit" [дух],[45] rather than upon psychological (or

43. For the *nous thurathen* see *De Gen. An.* Book II, ch. 3, 736b15–29. *Thurathen* also occurs later in *De Gen. An.* Book II, ch. 6, 744b21.

44. There are more than sufficient philosophical precursors for this layered eclectic world
in Pasternak, but it is also necessary to point to Mikhail Gershenzon, one of the closest friends
of Leonid Pasternak (*CSP* 1989, 251), whose opposition of the layers of consciousness into
"soul" and "spirit" must have been well known to Boris Pasternak. See Gershenzon's articulation
of this position (1918).

45. See also the image of city-spirit or *gorod-dukh* in Pasternak's letter to Mikhail Freidenberg in Dec. 1913 (*PSS* 7:157).

"soulful") reality, when Pasternak speaks about the people who influenced his deeper formation as an artist. In his description of Alexander Scriabin (as mentioned above, Scriabin undoubtedly was an actual "historical" prototype of the "Six-Winged Composer" or Shestikrylov), the theme of "spiritual" power is suggested with mild irony. Nonetheless, if in *Safe Conduct* Scriabin's name, in a demon-like manner, jumps on the child's back in wind-swept Moscow and the composer himself becomes the boy's idol rather than God,[46] then in the *Sketch for an Autobiography* Pasternak is less evasive; the "spiritual" designation of "dukh" is clearly there:

> In general he cultivated general forms of in*spir*ed lightness and unencumbered motion on the borderline of flight. [. . .] But Scriabin won me by the freshness of his *spir*it. (*Remember* 37–38)

> Он вообще воспитывал в себе разные виды одухотворенной легкости и неотягощенного движения на грани полета. [. . .] Скрябин покорял меня свежестью своего духа. (*PSS* 3:303)

Hermann Cohen's portrait in *Safe Conduct* leaves no ambiguity on this account, even though the "spirit" assisting Cohen in his movements is that of science, rather than art or philosophy:

> Talking with him was rather frightening, and going for a walk with him was no joke at all. Beside you, leaning on a stick and moving along with frequent stops, went the very *spirit* of mathematical physics, which had assembled its basic principles, step by step, by way of such a gait as this. (*CSP* 59)

> Беседовать с ним было страшновато, прогуливаться—нешуточно. Опираясь на палку, рядом с вами с частыми остановками подвигался реальный *дух* математической физики, приблизительно путем такой же поступи, шаг за шагом подобравшей свои главные основоположенья. (*PSS* 3:191)

Nor is there any uncertainty in feeling and vocabulary in Pasternak's initial attitude to Mayakovsky, whose portrait, like that of a "spiritual horizon," carefully blends the finite character of machines and the infinity and endless depth of space, open to perception:

---

46. Pasternak in *Safe Conduct* speaks of his love for music as a cult [музыка была для меня культом] and calls Scriabin "his idol" [мой кумир] (*CSP* 28; *PSS* 3:153).

Far off, locomotives roared like grampuses. At the very same unconditional distance as upon the earth was there in the throaty territory of his creation. This was that immeasurable in*spiration* without which there is no original-ity, the infinity that can open out in life from any point and in any direc-tion, and without which poetry is merely a misunderstanding that has not yet been clarified. [. . .]

I had made a *god* of him. He was a personification of my *spirit*ual hori-zon. (*CSP* 79, 81; emphasis added)

В горловом краю его творчества была та же безусловная даль, что на земле. Тут была та бездонная одухотворенность, без которой не бывает оригинальности, та бесконечность, открывающаяся с любой точки жизни, в любом направленьи, без которой поэзия—одно недоразуменье, временно не разъясненное. [. . .]

Я его боготворил. Я олицетворял в нем свой духовный гори-зонт. (*PSS* 3:218, 220)

And to Rilke in a letter of 1926 Pasternak was, perhaps, even less ambigu-ous: "I am indebted to you by the general features of my character, by the overall cohesiveness of my *spirit*ual life. You have created them" [Я обязан Вам чертами моего характера, всем складом духовной жизни. Они созданы Вами] (*PSS* 7:648; emphasis added). These evocations of a lexicon of "spiritual" gifts also point to Pasternak's careful effort to place the "mea-sureless" properties within everyday language, but the force of these portray-als explains even in retrospect what Pasternak might have meant in 1910 when he insisted that the composer Shestikrylov was the needle and thread that was sewing the children's world into one cloth—the composer clearly left an indelible impression on his pupils' psychological make-up.

5.3 The limitations of psychology:
Neo-Kantians in dispute with David Hume

Thus, Pasternak's "artistic materialism" and its evocation of spirit and infinity seem to have coalesced into an unusual genre, nourished by a highly eclectic philosophical substratum. However, how precisely did his studies of psychol-ogy assist him in his attempts in *Luvers* to reconstruct the tangible qualities of the ever more intricate and widening layers of the child's understanding? Pas-ternak's disappointment in psychology—and the ironic dismissal of its subject matter—is stated in *Luvers* by means of an authorial voice, reminiscent in this of similar evocations that were deleted from the final draft. The following pronouncement, however, was kept, placed centrally as a conclusion to the episodes of early childhood, and it contained the word "soul"—one of its first appearances in the text:

> [I]f a tree was entrusted with the care of its own growth, [. . .] it would forget the surrounding universe which should serve as a model [. . .].
>
> And to guard against the dead branches in the soul—to prevent its growth from being retarded and man from involving his own stupidity in the formation of *his immortal essence*—several things have been introduced to divert his banal curiosity from life, which dislikes working in his presence and tries every means to avoid him. *For this purpose all proper religions were introduced, all general concepts and human prejudices, and the most resplendent of these, and the most entertaining—psychology.* (CSP 135–36; trans. altered; emphasis added)

> Если доверить дереву заботу о его собственном росте [. . .] она забудет о вселенной, с которой надо брать пример [. . .].
>
> И чтобы не было суков в душе,—чтобы рост ее не застаивался, чтобы человек не замешивал своей тупости в устройство своей *бессмертной сути*, заведено много такого, что отвлекает его пошлое любопытство от жизни, которая не любит работать при нем и его всячески избегает. *Для этого заведены все заправские религии и все общие понятия и все предрассудки людей и самый яркий из них, самый развлекающий—психология.* (PSS 3:37)

In this dismissive observation, psychology is actually not badly damaged, for it is put aside together with "all proper religions" and "all general concepts and human prejudices." Nonetheless, this semi-humorous disavowal of psychology indicates Pasternak's desire in *Luvers* to inform his readers of a major gap in knowledge concerning the development of the individual self, a gap psychology is unable to fill or reach.

Pasternak's disappointment with psychology during his university years has been well documented, and his pronouncements that art is more psychologically astute than psychology [психологичнее психологии], carefully noted.[47] However, the deeper cause of his disappointment still needs to be

---

47. On Pasternak's disappointment in psychology as ultimately "subjectless," a position that contrasted with a much more optimistic assessment of the discipline's potential by his Moscow teachers, see Fleishman *Lehrjahre* 122. See also *PSSCom* 5:641–42, which contains the evaluation of Pasternak's essay "On the Object and Method of Psychology" by a renowned psychologist S. G. Gellershtein. Gellershtein's conclusion: the work of Natorp was for young Pasternak a catalyst; it directed him to address the deeper concerns of the psychological make-up of the

elucidated. According to the weight of existing documentation, the following objections were formulated by the young Pasternak during his initially fervent studies of Heinrich Rickert and Paul Natorp's *Einleitung in die Psychologie nach kritischer Methode.*[48] While his essay "On the Object and Method of Psychology" shows that he agreed wholeheartedly with the Neo-Kantian postulation that "apperception covers the whole field of consciousness" [апперцепцией покрывается все поле сознания] (*PSS* 5:311), this position also leads him, according to his diary notes, to suggest together with Natorp that psychology should make the study of apperception the content of its discipline [единство содержания . . . не в сознанности, а в ап[ерцепц]ии к[ак] *содержании*—задача психологии] (*Lehrjahre* I:268; emphasis in original). At the same time, he is aware that methodological explorations, armed with scientific categories and analytical principles, will block the metaphysical content of apperception and choose instead "consciousness" as its focus of study, while consciousness, in turn, will pose its own imponderable challenges:

[Scientific psychology], of course, critically rejects metaphysics <?>—for consciousness for psychology as a science—is a series of flowing, raw phenomena, waiting for its explanation, account, placement or description.

[Научная психология], конечно, критически отворачивается от метафизического литья <?>—для нее сознание—ряд тякучих, необработанных феноменов, ожидающих своего объяснения, учета, размещения или описания. (*Lehrjahre* I:278)

The surviving text of "On the Object and Method of Psychology" rather masks this problem, while his diary notes, for all the incompleteness and disjointedness of the note-taking process, point to his awareness of the inabilities of psychological methods to grasp spatial and temporal series as they strike consciousness. Since space and time (in their *a posteriori* and a *priori* range) challenge any mechanistic or purely analytical approach, spatial and temporal phenomena, when grasped sensually, will only intensify the impression of indefiniteness.[49] In other words, the subject-matter of psychology will resist

individual (*PSSCom* 5:642).

48. See here Loks's unforgettable portrayal of young Pasternak: "More and more often I was noticing in him some deeply seated despair, hidden behind this flow of unfinished speech, so gifted, and somehow cut from within. I began to look for the cause of this and soon found it. It was a fear of himself, an uncertainty in his chosen path" (1993, 37).

49. See here Loks's statement that, while emerging from a different context, is still highly significant: "Pasternak loved this clarity [of the university lectures], but at the same time I saw that such thinking was alien to him. In this difficult battle one could sense that a right to

the schematizations of mechanical logical quantifications, limited by "the realism of mechanical understanding." As a result, phenomena, open to consciousness *in all its fullness,* will escape analytical objectivization:

> It is impossible to explain causally sensual impressions (impossible to [deduce] psychological from physical), <cf. Natorp, 1888, S. 80> because a mechanism, as a causal system, can give only a mechanical effect, and the causal dependency is a synthetic unity of sameness. At the same time there exists an objective reality, expressed in mechanical terms—it is a measurable, quantified multiplicity of space and time. The purity of such measurements necessitates the self-identical precision of their intellectual understanding. Such understanding unifies in itself also the irrationality of time and space. But if one applies a sensual evaluation of time and space, they will appear indefinite; only intellectual understanding identifies them. But such understanding can signify and identify a certain qualitative unity [. . .] within which, on the causal side, we will be thinking by applying pure mechanistic terms. [. . .]
>
> This finality of the impossibility to convert psychological data into a physical measurement is founded upon the impossibility of analyzing the phenomena in purely objective terms.

Нельзя причинно объяснить ощущения (вообще психическое из физического), <cf. Natorp, 1888, S. 80.> т<ак> к<ак> механизм, к<ак> причиняющая система, мож<ет> дать механический лишь эффект; причинн<ая> зависимость есть синтетич<еское> единство однородности. [. . .] Объективное, выраженное в мехническ<их> терминах, есть измеренное, квантифицированное многообразие пр<о>стр<анства> и времени. Чистоту этому измерению дает идентичность и точность *понятия* в нем. *Оно* скрепляет как бы— иррациональность врем<ени> и пр<о>стр<анства>. Если остаться при чувственной оценке врем<ени> и пр<о>стр<анства>,—то они окажутся неопределенными; понятие—вот что однозначно и тоже-ственно определяет их. Но понятие мож<ет> обозначить и тожест-венно закрепить изв<естное> качественное образование [. . .] где на стороне причинного обусловления мы будем мыслить чистые механистич<еские> термины. [. . .]

Последн<ий> смысл заявляем<ой> невозможности психологиче-ское свести на физическ<ое>—лежит в невозможности разложения

---

indefiniteness was for him—a crucial question [право на неясность для него—решающий вопрос]" (1993, 37).

явления целиком на объективность. (*Lehrjahre* I:279–80; emphasis in original)

The limitations of psychology, however, go, according to his notation, much further.

In order to explore the status of personality as that of an independent self, psychology has to confront the reality of subjective understanding—the subjective "I"—which unifies initially disunited phenomena.[50] However, the content of the multiple series of impressions, the diversity of the "synthetic flow," will distract the investigation from the unified consciousness, which will need to be constantly superimposed upon the data of impressions:

> In order for the multiplicity to become consciousness, one consciousness, it is not only necessary, but is already evidently present, that the multiplicity is unified in the emotive life of consciousness and that this unity is the characteristic moment of the subjective experience. [. . .]
> This is characteristic for every 'I'; 'I itself' is denoted by the particularity, even by the solitariness of its experience, but it is based on the unified nature of such memories in one's recollections—that is—it exists as a complex interweaving of the general connections of temporal and simultaneous experiences only because this 'I' remains the same.

> Как многообразие становится сознанием, одним сознанием—необходимо; но очевидно, что оно—едино в переживании сознания и что это единство характеристич[еский] момент субъективн[ого] переживания. [. . .] Это свойственное каждому «Я» или «Я сам»

---

50. To this problem Natorp adds his own question as to whether or not psychology can be that science:

> But it is necessary to find a common principle signifying all these contents, which is capable a) to unite these contents under one task of a separate science [. . .].
> This principle—a connection between constantly complex contents: [in which] one separate elementary act is differentiated from, as well as unified with another elementary act in a temporal sequence; linked everywhere as its contents are signified by temporality and locality.

> Но требуется найти общий всем этим содержаниям признак, кот[орый] был бы способен а) объединить эти содержания под одной задачей особой науки [. . .].
> Этот признак—связь, связность постоянно сложных содержаний: отдельн[ый] элементарн[ый] акт времен[ым] обр[азом] отличается и связывается с друг[им] элем[ентарным] [актом]; связность повсеместно: все содержания простр[анственно] и времен[но] обусловл[ены]. (*Lehrjahre* I:268)

характеризовало через особенность, даже одинокость его пережи-
ваний, оно основывается на непрерывности этих воспомин[аний] в
его воспоминании, т.е. к[а]к очень сложное [complexion] сплетение
общих связей (временн[ых] и единовременн[ых]); только благодаря
этому Я—тот же. (*Lehrjahre* II:206–7)

The principle of "synthetic flow," a recurrent theme in his notes, is accompanied by the reiterated assertion that personality cannot be built up from the
summation of subjective impressions as its constitutive elements, but must
incessantly synthesize the ever new impressions that enter into the human
purview: "Selfhood (or personality) is the unity of consciousness, in which
every newly added element starts playing the role of a connecting principle" [Личность есть такое единство созн[ания], в кот[ором] каждый
последний элемент оказывается связью] (*Lehrjahre* I:276). This "synthetic
flow," however, cannot be grasped in stillness; it is realigned with the addition
of every new element, and it necessitates, therefore, the presence of a living
active consciousness [текущее сознание]:

> A personality does not consist of elements; rather there exist elementary
> and complex connections, not separate members of these mixtures: the
> non-breakable unity of subjective consciousness rests on this and only this
> paradox. [. . .]
>   This function of connectivity, its differentiated features, are character-
> ized by the processes of the flowing active consciousness.

> У личности нет элементов: есть элементарн[ые] и более сложн[ые]
> связи, но не члены этих сочленений: на этом и только на этом пара-
> доксе связи держится непрерывность субъективн[ого] сознания.
> [. . .]
> Понятием текущего сознания характеризуется функция связи,
> отличительные ее стороны. (*Lehrjahre* I:276)

This thought is reflected in drafts of *Luvers* in Pasternak's otherwise startling
assertion: "We doubt that an animal develops according to the principles of
the separated living parts" [Мы сомневаемся в том, чтобы животное развивалось по законам разложения животного на части] (*PSS* 3:514).
   Herein lies the crux of an irresolvable paradox. The individual character of
the synthetic processes, imponderable subject-object compound, reflects the
dynamic unity of thought and perception.[51] As Pasternak insists that the sub-

---

51. As Pasternak's notes indicate in numerous entries, Leibniz's monads were for Pasternak

jectivity of impressions is determined not by the materiality of the compound, but by the character and dynamism of the thought processes in consciousness, his position moves beyond the boundaries of psychology.[52] Pointing to Natorp and Rickert in his notes, Pasternak explains the limitation of the discipline: the content, power, and value of intellectual ideas cannot be examined and evaluated by the methodology of psychology. Not only is psychology's approach to the events of the soul (душевные явления) ultimately insufficient, but also *psychology lacks a system of values in its examination of ideas, and for this reason cannot exist without philosophy:*

> The objective nature [of the science of psychology], in its attempt to explain causal connections (rather than discuss their real signification) of world events, finds also that emotional occurrences (events of the soul) constitute an aspect of the data for objective examination. But soon it is evident that the world becomes more and more obscure when examined by means of the objective method. [. . .]
>
> A question arises: how can a subject, as a simple object among objects, have any connection to the values that bring meaning to his/her life? Thus, there emerges the necessity of subjective understanding of the world based upon the pre-existent dilemma of values. [. . .]
>
> The work of objectivizing sciences on reality, if it is to take into consideration pre-existing theoretical values and their meaning—such work can only be the subject of philosophy and value theory [cf. Rickert's article in *Logos*, pp. 20–31].

---

important guiding principles in this regard. In Pasternak's notes, this idea is clearly stated and reintroduced multiple times among the many pages of his philosophical diary. The following is his discussion of Leibniz's monads and the confusion resulting from the nature of the compound in the perceived phenomena: "From this confusion—matter; this phenomenon is well founded. [. . .] As soon as there is a mixture of confused thoughts, there is the meaning, and then there is the matter. But this is not an illusion. For the phenomena are real. But the reality does not lie in matter. It is opened by the mind through the opening of the monads. The matter is an appearance, which is firmly situated in the monad. The monad is the reality in the objects. But the real substance is in opposition to the sensible atoms: it is located in the substantial forms" [Из этой confusion—материя, этот phaenomenon bene fundatum. [. . .] Aussitôt qu'il y a un mélange de pensées confuses, voilà le sens, voilà la matière. Но не иллюзия. Nam et phaenoma sunt realia. Но реальность лежит не в материи. Открывается разумом через открытие монад. Материя—видимость, хорошо обоснованная в монаде. Монада—реальное в вещах. Истинная субстанция в противоположн[ость] чувств[енным] атомам: formes substantielles] (*Lehrjahre* II:61).

52. As observed already, this idea is reflected, in the initial topic of his Marburg dissertation—"the laws of thought as the category of a dynamic material object" [работа о законах мышления как о категории динамического предмета] (Kudriavtseva 66).

Объективизм, стремясь причинно объяснить ([а] не истолковать с
т[очки] зр[ения] смысла) миров[ые] явления, находит *и душевн[ые]
явл[ения]* как объект или к[ак] содержания, доступные объективации. Но в дальнейшем выясняется, что мир становится все непонятнее в объяснении объективн[ого] метода. [. . .]

Вопр[ос]: каким образ[ом] субъект, к[ак] простой объект среди
объектов, может иметь отношение к ценностям, придающим смысл
его жизни. Так потребность в субъективирующ[ем] понимании
мира вырастает из предшествующей ей проблемы ценности. [. . .]

Работа объективирующих наук о действительности с точки зрения лежащих в ее основе теоретических ценностей и присущего ей
теоретического смысла = предмет философии и теории ценностей
[cf. Риккерт, статья в *Логосе*, с. 20–31]. (*Lehrjahre* I: 274–75)

On its own, therefore, psychology deals only with the most partial and mechanistic of experiences. Moreover, this view reflects a deeper seated philosophical conflict—that between the followers of David Hume and Immanuel Kant concerning the role of impressions and ideas in perception.[53] The insistence that the self cannot be discovered purely through its impressions, but that the events of the soul [душевные явления] depend to a great degree on the value and reality of ideas which are integrated within the human self—this view contradicts the position of David Hume that ideas are "pale copies of impressions," for they lose the vitality, "force and liveliness" with which impressions first "strike upon the mind" (*Treatise*, 1.1.1; 2000, 7).

Thus, for all the incompleteness of the archival materials, one begins to sense an emerging picture whose reality is reinforced by Pasternak's philosophical interests prior to 1913. The concomitant strands of documentation suggest that Pasternak's understanding of the constituents of a unified personality is directly related to the individualized, unrepeatable capacity of each human being for synthesizing in a subjective manner both inanimate and animate phenomena, as well as the world of intellectual and spiritual ideas. In this, he accepts Hume's focus on the importance of perception and sensation, but insists, nonetheless, that artistic ideas, in capturing the vitality of sensations, remain dynamic energies fighting against the limitations of a

---

53. The most recent echoes of the debate prove that passions surrounding it are still intense:
"We have seen that on Hume's account, the perception of an event must be a complex impression [. . .]. An act of mind is only required subsequently [. . .]. Nevertheless, I think it is doubtful that the experience of the event can be adequately characterized in this manner. What it leaves out is a dynamic element in such experience, which is emphasized by Kant" (Allison 2008, 110).

particularized time and space. As pointed out earlier (4.1), art for Pasternak goes further than psychology in grasping the individual character of the "synthetic flow," a position of his youth that he acknowledges as late as 1957 in the *Sketch for an Autobiography*. According to his recollection of "Symbolism and Immortality,"[54] the subjectivity of artistic impressions becomes an all-enduring symbol that survives death and destruction:

> My paper was based on the idea that our perceptions are subjective [. . .]. In my paper I argued that this subjectivity was not the attribute of every individual human being, but was a generic and suprapersonal quality [. . .] though the artist was of course mortal like the rest of mankind, the joy of living experienced by him was immortal, and that other people a century later might through his work be able to experience something approaching the personal and vital form of his original sensations. (*Remember* 63–64)

> Доклад основывался на соображении о субъективности наших восприятий [. . .]. В докладе проводилась мысль, что эта субъективность не является свойством отдельного человека, но есть качество родовое, сверхличное, что это субъективность человеческого мира, человеческого рода. [. . .] хотя художник, конечно, смертен, как все, счастье существования, которое он испытал, бессмертно и в некотором приближении к личной и кровной форме его первоначальных ощущений может быть испытано другими спустя века после него по его произведениям. (*PSS* 3:319)

All of this suggests that Pasternak's work in *Luvers* on the perceptions of the little girl, who was expected to become the heroine of a much longer tale, emerged out of a larger vision that had been developing for many years. In preparing for a focused examination of the novella, one can draw at this stage the following conclusions:

1. *The Childhood of Luvers* is directly related to Pasternak's interest in a human self: the story is conceived from within the wider context of his interests in perception and apperception, extending as far back as 1910.

---

54. See here Fleishman's characterization of the paper: "it was semi-literary and semi-philosophical in nature. Thus it was reminiscent of the paper on Natorp that Pasternak had just written" (1990a, 51). See also Livingstone's commentary about the surviving theses of the paper: "Why such difficult concepts? Pasternak was writing for listeners who had spent some three years studying problems of symbolism and to whom his philosophical language would not be daunting" (*MG* 65).

2. It appears more than probable that Pasternak was particularly interested in establishing a paradigm for the development of awareness, as the young girl advances beyond her earlier ability to register impressions toward the act of understanding and absorbing "indelible" ideas. The earlier texts suggest a progression from (a) material inanimate objects confronting consciousness; to (b) the animating work of soul; and finally to (c) the unifying presence of "spirit" and the world of ideas "from the outdoors," the dynamic spiritual centers characterized by power, which enter reality with a force equal to the power of the sun. Further analysis is needed to determine the extent to which this structure is reflected in *Luvers*.

3. This three-layered progression is particularly evident in "Ordering a Drama" with its invitation to the children to "bear this sweet pain: to work; to think for the inanimate objects" [они выносили это сладостное страдание: работать, думать за неодушевленное], an invitation that reflects almost verbatim Pasternak's many philosophical notes.

4. It also seems incontestable that in describing this process of an ever-deepening and expanding apprehension, Pasternak is interested in the synthetic quality of Zhenya's perception as she synchronizes the experiences that are both immediate and very distant or unfocused (туманный). In this, Pasternak echoes some of the major premises of Hume, but as expanded and questioned by Kantianism and Neo-Kantianism. There is a further debt to Hermann Cohen and his insistence that "the finite is not happy to remain finite, but has the courage to overcome the distance from infinity" (*ARG* I:266–67; trans. Poma 1997, 144).

5. There is, thus, an overall impression in Pasternak that consciousness is affected most strongly not only by what is immediate, but also by what is still "outside experience." As Pasternak observes in describing Zhenya's stumbling on the "idea of the third person," the impression is all the more strong because its full reality remains outside of her range of understanding: "the impression that lay behind it all was indelible. [. . .] *It lay beyond the girl's awareness, because it was vitally important and significant*" [Впечатление, скрывавшееся за всем, было неизгладимо. [. . .] *Оно лежало вне ведения девочки, потому что было жизненно важно и значительно*] (*CSP* 178; *PSS* 4:86; trans. altered; emphasis added).

6. Pasternak undoubtedly experiments in this passage with the artistic means of blending categories that both proceed from and precede experience—in short, the Kantian categories of *a posteriori* and

a priori, a pattern which also indicates that Pasternak in *Luvers* may be taking the child in her development toward her first experience of *apperception* whose spiritual and moral context is supplied by the authorial voice and its reference to the commandments.

7. As Pasternak searches for a paradigm for the child's growth that can address the gap existing in the psychology of his day, he is focused on the artistic means that can portray how a developing personality synchronizes the categories of immediate reality and the phenomena of a much wider range, starting from impressions and addressing itself to ideas and questions of morality. In this pursuit he is unrestricted in his artistic work and feels free to select and apply any insight of which he approved before leaving philosophy. Cohen's emphasis on the "other" becomes a powerful moral guide, and the ancient Greek understanding of soul and spirit, augmented by the analytical insight of Hume, is there to be brought into the purview of his own experimentation.

8. In short, he considers the landscape of the developing self as territory only partially explored in philosophy, and his training in this regard presents something of a treasure trove for thematic and technical experimentation.

9. It is also possible then that the last name of the heroine in the *Childhood of Luvers* is a play upon this never-ceasing work of consciousness flowing toward "something" or "someone" to be realigned within itself—*Lu-vers* or *vers le*—a movement of perception that overtakes and synthesizes the ever new data that informs, and is informed by, "the essential self."[55]

10. Thus, in working on *Luvers,* Pasternak pursues an ambitious and comprehensive goal, with many uncertainties and unknowns—all ripe for artistic exploration. The very range of these intentions may, in fact, have been responsible for the puzzling discordance between Pasternak's artistic aims and the critical reaction to his work.

5.4 Beyond the metonymous self:
Moving beyond traditional readings of the novella

In contrast to the reception of Pasternak's earliest prose works, *The Childhood of Luvers* was noted and celebrated, but the focus of the critics (so many of

---

55. This interpretation's sense of ever-expanding journey is supported by a somewhat different etymological route. Fateeva speaks of Luvers (люверс) as a ring in a sail, and by extension with "wind," "sail," "boat" (2003, 225).

whom were Russia's most eminent and perceptive readers) had very little to do with any of the concepts mentioned by Pasternak in the above passages. This situation has hardly changed for the contemporary reader who is often bewildered by Pasternak's theoretical pronouncements, couched in difficult and evasive language. Boris Gasparov, one of the most perceptive contemporary critics, observed that Pasternak's "artistic metaphysics" is a singular blend of Tolstoyan vision and Futurism;[56] yet it appears that it was only the latter aspect—Pasternak's avant-garde or abstract qualities—that was immediately seized upon after the publication of *Luvers*.[57] Sensing the remarkable dynamism of his technical experimentation, critics have focused on Pasternak's ability to present a montage of differentiated details. What fascinated critics was not the writer's search for the pathways of unification of phenomena in an evolving self-consciousness, but rather the break-up of the whole into parts, and eventually—a spectacular series of metonymies and synecdoches. Perhaps reflecting the spirit of the country in upheaval, critics ignored Pasternak's capacity to unify the immediate and infinite, while being drawn to his ability to describe the disunited and broken. In short, critics were fascinated by the disrupted diary of Zhenya Luvers's impressions. The issues of soul and spirit in this regard interested very few.

Thus, while reconnecting Pasternak to Tolstoy's *Detstvo,* Yuri Tynianov sensed the originality of the work and its unprecedented "newness" as he focused his analysis upon the multitude of inanimate objects, broken and reassembled elements, united not by organic life but by artistic montage, reminiscent of abstract or Cubist art:[58]

> Everything is given under the microscope of adolescent transition, which changes phenomena under observation and makes them more brittle, breaks them into a thousand pieces, turns them into living abstractions.
>   An object of everyday life (вещь быта) must be broken into a thousand pieces and glued together again, in order to become a new thing in

---

56. Witt (2000a, 135); B. Gasparov (1992a, 110–11).

57. Kuzmin's reaction to the novella is an exception, rather than the rule: "The interesting aspect of Pasternak's novella lies not so much, perhaps, in the child's psychology, as in the wave of love, warmth, open-heartedness and unusual sincerity of the author's emotional response to the world." [Интерес повести Пастернака не в детской, пожалуй, психологии, а в огромной волне любви, теплоты, прямодушия и какой-то откровенности эмоциональных восприятий автора] (*PSSCom* 3:543).

58. Malmstad, sharing this view, accepted by a greater number of critics, cites Pasternak's conversation with Zoia Maslenikova about poetry of 1917: "At that time I was very caught up with cubism" (1992, 301)

literature. In literature, so it seems, a glued together object is stronger than an unbroken whole one. (1977, 161)

Similarly, Konstantin Loks, praising the story, spoke of "a manner of story-telling, moving forward by means of descriptions of particularized detailed accounts" [так обуславливается особый способ рассказывания, движущегося описанием частностей и деталей] (1925, 286–87). This enthusiastic welcome not only avoided the issue of wholeness of the self, but shared an implicit critical consensus: Pasternak's protagonists, invariably engaged in observation, were simply too passive, and the narrative itself was intrinsically descriptive, with no interest in plot or action. "He is a writer without kith or kin" [без роду и племени], proclaimed Zamyatin, and immediately observed that Pasternak, for all his brilliant innovations in syntax, could not develop a plot: "His own contribution is not in the area of plot (his work is plotless)" [Новое у него не в сюжете. Он бессюжетен] (Zamyatin 1923; [1967, 203]).

Roman Jakobson in 1935 proposed a critical framework[59] that situated these approaches within a wider theoretical view that identified the highly specific quality of Pasternak's artistic gift (see also Chapter 2). In contrast to the metaphoric images of Mayakovsky, Pasternak's hero, in Jakobson's view, blends into the environment. His unification is with the world: he is "concealed in a picture puzzle [. . .] broken down into a series of constituent and subsidiary parts" (1969, 146). Pasternak thus presents cut-up parts of the abstract world:[60] "Show us your environment and I will tell you who you are. We learn what he lives on, this lyric character outlined by metonymies, split up by synecdoches into individual attributes, reactions, and situations" (Jakobson 1969, 147). Jakobson's seemingly incontrovertible assessment of Pasternak as "emphatically lyrical" identified the writer's range as unsuited to an epic theme (or possibly any theme outside his own or his heroes' lyrical feelings[61]) for the simple reason that his "lyricism, both in poetry and prose, is imbued with metonymy; in other words, it is association by contiguity that predominates" (Jakobson 1969, 141).[62] This meant, in turn, that Pasternak's

---

59. In Malmstad's view, Jakobson's position of 1935 became "that overcoat out of which has come most of the commentary on the writer" (1992, 302).

60. Jakobson thereby echoes Tynianov's image of "living abstractions" broken "into a thousand pieces" (Tynianov 161).

61. "This attitude of childhood towards appearances corresponds perfectly to Pasternak's own. An epic attitude to his environment is naturally out of the question for a poet who is convinced that, in the world of prosaic fact, the elements of everyday existence fall dully, stupidly, and with crippling effect upon the soul" (Jakobson 1969, 139).

62. Mikhail Gasparov, as I have noted already, refuted Jakobson's position, having analyzed

characters were happiest when dissolved into the world they observe, and most uninteresting and banal when they had to think or be active:[63] "The hero's activity is outside Pasternak's sphere. When he does deal with action, he is banal and unoriginal, defending in the theoretical digressions his right to triviality. [. . .] Pasternak's stories are similarly empty of action" (Jakobson 1969, 149). Jakobson's judgment—the triumphant acme of Russian theoretical criticism—was a decisive step for Pasternak studies. With the return of interest in Pasternak's work following the Nobel Prize fiasco, *The Childhood of Luvers* was hailed as highly innovative and exceptionally well suited to Pasternak's temperament, a view spearheaded by Jakobson's observation that "this attitude of childhood towards appearances corresponds perfectly to Pasternak's own" (1969, 139). Michel Aucouturier[64] and Angela Livingstone, followed by a generation of critics in the 1970s and 1980s, developed Jakobson's position further by working with the concept of "the receptive hero," a person capable of absorbing and reflecting the world by becoming a metonymous part of his surroundings. The most brilliant discoveries in the construction of Pasternak's world, including Faryno's demonstration of *Luvers*'s "archepoetics" (1993), the quantitative analysis of Mikhail Gasparov (1995), and the postulations of "metatropes" by Fateeva (2003), proved not strong enough to overturn the critical consensus that Pasternak's preoccupations in his early prose were directed by his cubo-futurist experimentations and metonymous relations.[65]

---

quantitatively the use of metaphors and metonymies in the poetry of Mayakovsky and Pasternak (1995).

63. See Glazov-Corrigan (1991, 137). Strictly speaking, Jakobson is not always consistent in this regard. Occasionally he also insists that there is lack of agency, rather than lack of action, in Pasternak's narrative world: "The active voice has been erased from Pasternak's poetic grammar. In his prose ventures he employs precisely that metonymy which substitutes the action for the actor. [. . .] The *agens* is excluded from his thematic material" (1969, 147).

64. In Aucouturier's view, Zhenya Luvers as an artistic self is not yet an individual or a metonymous self—rather she is a receptive generic concept: "Zhenya Luvers unites in herself all the ideal conditions for a receptive attitude towards the world; a child who perceives things directly without the screen of words, solidified concepts, habit; a woman who in her very body is sensitive of the mysteries of life and creation. However, precisely because these are generic and not individual qualities which mark her for the incarnation of the Pasternakian concept of the personality, one cannot consider her as the first metonymous hero of the poet" (1978, 45).

65. As far as the understanding of Pasternak's concept of personality is concerned, Jakobson's influence proved decisive, insofar as it ignored and dismissed a whole range of evidence as ultimately banal. Jakobson acknowledges, for example, Pasternak's "acute awareness of Symbolism" (1969, 137) as well as the writer's emphasis upon the phenomenon of "soul," but he treats both in passing and covertly suggests that metonymy as a principle provides here a sufficient key for the indebtedness in question: one pattern, a grammatical formula of artistic vision, once recognized and named, explains all other constructions. Thus, instead of a concept of personality whose highest idea is to overcome fate (Pasternak's intention for the direction of his work),

Thus, the model of the metonymic or receptive self triumphed, and while it captured some essential features of Pasternak's prose, it cut out a whole range of narrative themes and tropes, as well as the novella's philosophical undertones. It is my position in the present investigation that the critics who accepted the metonymous model for the construction of Pasternak's protagonists made assumptions that mistook the very scope of Pasternak's ambition. In the next two chapters I challenge this prevailing view and argue instead that the fuller picture is far more complex: even if Pasternak's university studies might no longer direct his thought, this earlier training carries the force of initial blueprints for the understanding of reality nourished decisively by the methodology of philosophical inquiry. In short, the goal of the subsequent chapters is to address the rather formidable dislocation between Pasternak's plans "to visit a human self when she is whole" and the picture of Zhenya as a "childlike spontaneity and a feminine receptivity" (Aucouturier 1978, 45) in order to suggest a novel approach to Pasternak's first major prose work.

Jakobson's powerful analysis supplies a picture in which "the genuine agent has no place in Pasternak's poetic mythology" (1969, 148).

6

"The Long Days" in
The Childhood of Luvers
Chronology of a Permeable Self

The analysis of "The Long Days" (Part I of *Detstvo Luvers*) will pursue several interconnected aims. Its principal goal is to emphasize the novella's overall design, which has hitherto escaped critical notice. The Kantian notion of *a posteriori* and *a priori* ranges of perceptions will be approached as fundamental to the organization of the novella: the analysis will explore how the sense of finite and infinite, known and unknown, changes and expands at every major stage of the child's growth, while some key elements of Zhenya's world, reintroduced into this ever renewed context, gain a deepened signification. Thus, the chapter will argue for the presence of meticulously organized narrative layers (reflected in a series of Tables 6a–6d)—the sequential expansion of the phenomenal world as it captures and restructures Zhenya's perception. These layers will be approached as evidence of Pasternak's narrative strategy that goes beyond metonymic paradigms: each major event of the novella, signifying yet another of Zhenya's rites of passage, will be viewed as a familiar, everyday occurrence, disrupted nonetheless by the expanding, startlingly new, and eventually unlimited range of phenomena—a design reminiscent of the three worlds in "Ordering a Drama." While unveiling this narrative pattern, this chapter will emphasize the gradual realignment of metonymic or contiguous series within a taut metaphoric structure that grows ever more elaborate and complex, just as the novella approaches a paradigm shift in Part II, "The Stranger." Table I, entitled "Chronology of a Permeable Self," will conclude the chapter. As it collects the evidence of Tables 6a–6d (and looks forward to completion in Chapter 7), Table I facilitates the demonstration of the philosophical vision underlying the expanding patterns of the child's sensations as they are carefully aligned not only with different seasons of the year, but also with the gradual approach of the as yet unknown external world of Russia at the beginning of the twentieth century.

6.1 Transition from infancy to early childhood:
Zhenya's first awareness of the world beyond

The first scene of the novella, so familiar to all readers of Pasternak—Zhenya Luvers's transition from infancy to early childhood (выход из младенчества)—is often understood by critics as an emblem for much of the writer's early prose.[1] As I argued in Chapter 4, this scene is focused on the impressions of an as yet undeveloped self and, for this reason, its emblematic character must by definition be limited. Nonetheless, the scene presents a series of startling portrayals of the synthetic nature of perception into whose purview enter images that may appear somewhat accidental. The most arresting of these, however, are destined to follow Zhenya throughout her life in the novella and, consequently, to play an important part in the organization of the narrative. The centerpiece of the scene is the contrast between the child's vague understanding of things and images which (for all their baffling appearances) already possess names and her dawning awareness of a reality beyond what is grasped, named, and known.[2] More important still, this unknown world is introduced as more kindred to Zhenya than what is known and familiar. This design is carefully steeped in an overall state of confusion: the child is both drawn to and frightened by everything that has no name and no clear

---

1. See here, for instance, Björling (1982, 141–43) and Faryno: "this whole novella is born if not from its first paragraphs, then at least from its first chapter" (1993, 1–2).

2. In Faryno's reading almost all images of the opening scene have continuous resonances throughout the narrative. For a lack of time "to explore all," he selects certain "key" images or motifs [я остановлюсь лишь на тех мотивах, которые могут рассматриваться как отправные]. Hence, he argues that the mention of Zhenya's childhood toys—ships and dolls [кораблики и куклы]—already contains the notion of the journey and navigation, while dolls indicate motherhood and home, and both of these are the central themes of the narrative (1993, 2). In this context it is all the more important to find the dynamic pathways of the images' realignment—layers of transformation that indicate a direction beyond that of intertextual and intratextual echoes.

delineation,[3] while at the same time everything known that has a name is also characterized by a kind of delirium:

> In those days Zhenya was put early to bed. She could not see the lights of Motovilikha. But once something scared the Angora cat, and it stirred suddenly in its sleep and woke Zhenya up. Then she saw grown-ups on the balcony. The alder overhanging the railings was dense and iridescent as ink. The tea in the glasses was red. [. . .] *It was like a delirium—except that this one had its name, which even Zhenya knew:* They were playing cards.
>
> However, there was no name of determining what was happening far, far away on the other bank. That had no name, and no precise color or definite outlines. *And as it stirred it was familiar and dear,* and was not delirious as was the thing that muttered and swirled in clouds of the tobacco smoke [. . .]. (*CSP* 133; emphasis added)

> Женю в те годы спать укладывали рано. Она не могла видеть огней Мотовилихи. Но однажды ангорская кошка, чем-то испуганная, резко шевельнулась во сне и разбудила Женю. Тогда она увидала взрослых на балконе. Нависавшая над брусьями ольха была густа и переливчата, как чернила. Чай в стаканах был красен. [. . .] *Это было похоже на бред, но у этого бреда было свое название, известное и Жене:* шла игра.
>
> Зато нипочем нельзя было определить того, что творилось на том берегу, далеко-далеко: у того не было названия и не было отчетливого цвета и точных очертаний; *и волнующееся, оно было милым и родным* и не было бредом, как то, что бормотало и ворочалось в клубах табачного дыма [. . .]. (*PSS* 3:34)

The frightening nameless principle that makes Zhenya cry is the dark factory-village, Motovilikha, at night, appearing in the reflected light of either the setting sun, electric lights, or the moon;[4] it is an arresting image of the unknown world surrounded by a halo of light. Equally significant, however, is the fact that the factory produces "cast iron"; metal makes its marginal entry here into an otherwise pastoral home[5] with the "iridescent alder overhanging" its rail-

---

3. Jakobson notes: "For Khlebnikov, as for the little heroine in Pasternak's story, a name possesses the complete and comforting significance it has in childhood" (1969, 139). The emphasis, however, is not so much upon naming, but upon sensing an infinite, as yet unnamed space that retreats behind the name.

4. Gorelik observes that the theme of light always accompanies the description of night in Pasternak (2000, 67).

5. See Faryno: "In the poetic system of Pasternak the motif of the 'factory' becomes one

ings.[6] This emergence of an unfamiliar world[7] (which contains, in the closest of proximities, a great number of details ready to spring into symbols)[8] is dearer to the child than the house, the alder, and the alien but habitual (and already named) card game of the adults. Thus, Motovilikha at night is Zhenya's *first* unnamed presence, introduced pointedly in order to set up a metaphoric place-holder for the new and expanding impressions of the unknown and unreachable[9] that will appear in the narrative each time the child approaches a new stage of growth and traverses a new boundary between what is familiar and what is "beyond" her knowledge or frame of reference.

It should also be noted that the card game, mentioned in the scene as if in passing, is by no means accidental. As Zhenya leaves infancy, Pasternak underscores the importance of the transition by acknowledging and displaying his debt both to the Symbolists and to Rainer Maria Rilke: the playing hands of fate, surrounded by the colors of a masquerade,[10] appear as the child enters the world whose arbitrary and yet significant design will from now on be imprinted on her memory. Moreover, the image of hands will become a recurrent motif throughout *Luvers*, operating as another marker, changing its position and signification every time it denotes the approach of a new stage in Zhenya's growth (see Table 6a below).

---

of the variations of his transformative chains" (1993, 11). In contrast to Faryno's emphasis on the "alchemic" nature of these transformations, the image of metal appears to us as threatening, preparing the image of nature imprisoned and "in chains" [волоча сверкающие цепи ветвей] at the conclusion of the novella (*PSS* 3:84).

6. Faryno's reading of the "iridescent alder" as kindred (in its reflections of light and thickness of color) to the appearance of the Kama River opens up, in our view, a larger theme of the role of nature in the novella (1993, 15). Fateeva, in citing Pasternak's letter of May 1912, suggests that the garden in Pasternak is always linked to a crossing into the world of his "inner infinite garden" (2003, 127).

7. Both Faryno and Fateeva emphasize the etymology and mythological overtones of Motovilikha (*motki* and *motivilo*—the spools of wool and the instrument for their unveiling) (Faryno 1993, 12–13; Fateeva 2003, 128). Faryno observes that Motovilikha's role is broken into two counterparts: "unseen" and "not understood" (1993, 15), while these qualities appear to readers not as opposed, but rather as interconnected. Fateeva notes that the "inanimate"–"animate" world in Pasternak constantly changes its form and calls for an indefiniteness in naming and appearance, so that the text is oversaturated with indefinite neuter pronouns, variations of "some-thing" [что-то, нечто] (2003, 125).

8. Gorelik, following Yuri Lotman and B. A. Uspensky, speaks about post-symbolism as a genre, and of a symbol as a type of a sign that creates "methodological situation" (2000, 6). Fateeva, following Barthes's *Mythologies*, speaks about a creation of a "personal mythology of the author" wherein every detail of the world assumes its own compositional function in the narrative (2003, 137).

9. Gorelik notes about the role of Tsvetkov, "He incarnates an appearance as yet unrevealed [нераскрытое явление] as Motovilikha or the street without a name" (2000, 107).

10. In a somewhat different context Ljunggren observes that the hand was the most "beloved" of Rilke's synecdoches; further, she traces the role of Rilke's hand—"Die hastige Hand"— to the sculptural analogue of Rodin's "hand of God" (1984, 99–100).

TABLE 6A. EARLIEST CHILDHOOD: ZHENYA'S AWAKENING

Boundary: Seasons and stages of growth	Direction of perception and permeable compound	Emotional state	Residue on the margins of the compound	The images of the hands controlling the situation	The character of time and space
1st Boundary: Spring-summer. Awakening from infancy to early childhood.	Toward the unknown Motovilkha, and yet the focus is also on the card game of the parents.	Fear and first realization of the hidden and unknown. Kindredness with the unknown.	The night city, a factory producing cast iron, lit up by an obscured light source.	The card game—red, yellow, green. Hands of destiny, surrounded by the colors of a masquerade.	The first awareness of the distinction/interconnection between inner and outer worlds.

In Pasternak's narrative, then, Zhenya does not simply notice an unknown reality; she internalizes its mystery, and the formation of her character reflects, as in a mirror,[11] the external outlines of this new experience:

> That morning she emerged from the state of infancy she had still been in at night. For the first time in her life she suspected that was something that the phenomena kept to themselves [. . .]. *For the first time, like this new Motovilikha, she did not say everything she thought, but kept to herself what was most essential, vital, and stirring.* (*CSP* 134; emphasis added)

> В это утро она вышла из того младенчества, в котором находилась еще ночью. Она в первый раз за свои годы заподозрила явление в чем-то таком, что явление либо оставляет про себя. [. . .] Она впервые, как и эта новая Мотовилиха, сказала не все, что подумала, и самое существенное, нужное и беспокойное скрыла про себя. (*PSS* 3:35)

Here, then, is Pasternak's first emblem of the child's consciousness in the process of change. While the focus upon new materials entering consciousness is intentionally obscured, the lines of kindredness are most clearly established between the child's inner sense of self and the marginal and *indefinite* content of her experience. The focus of this complex passage, the vague indefiniteness that appears at the boundaries of consciousness, produces in the girl a parallel awareness of a similarly vague and as yet unknown inner world.

Moving further and further away from his studies of philosophy, Pasternak nonetheless signals here his indebtedness to Kant's "synthetic judgment," as the child's awareness of spatial and temporal categories (outer and inner forms of intuition) is introduced as an act of perception that blends and synthesizes both *a priori* (the kindredness with the unknown) and *a posteriori* (impressions already established by experience). This recognition of the unfamiliar and yet kindred as both inner and outer constitutes the first temporal boundary that Zhenya crosses, herself unaware of any dividing line, moved only by an inborn sympathy of the obscure for the obscure, of the hidden for the equally hidden and mysterious.

In this portrayal of emergence from infancy, one finds Pasternak's characteristic and well-analyzed "contiguous series" or "metonymous relations," that is, patterns of narrative that establish ties of kindredness between the girl and

---

11. Fateeva proposes that "mirror" and "reflection" in Pasternak are invariably interconnected with the transformation of the "face" of the lyrical subject (2003, 160).

the external world, obscuring the outlines of personhood. Such descriptions, proposed by Jakobson as comprising Pasternak's essential technique,[12] will, as we shall see, dominate the author's early portrayals of Zhenya's childhood, but they will not characterize her life at the time of her meeting with the mysterious Tsvetkov. At the beginning of the story, however, the contiguous series are a dominant device, for even her passage from childhood is introduced by means of a kindredness between herself and the world, and yet it is just as important to emphasize that while the girl's consciousness synthesizes the surrounding world, her feeling of kindredness is attached not to the familiar, but to the mysterious, unnamed, and unknown.

6.2 Childhood:
Acquaintance with still life and the
quiet plasticity of the northern daylight

> The first: a true story, reality, as a great immobile legend of wood and cloth, objects in need, twilight in need, like a church parish that has grown stale from waiting. [. . .] The first is—reality without movement [. . .].
>
> —"Ordering a Drama" (*MG* 27)

As observed by critics, every major scene in the story's first pages rejects the possibility of agency and draws instead a de-animated human being surrounded by the kindred series of inanimate objects.[13] However, it is equally important to observe that acquaintance with the inanimate world is characteristic only of Zhenya's early childhood, and that a few scenes operate in this regard as emblem-images or emblem-sequences that exemplify the child's earlier state of mind in her instinctual interaction, through perception, with

---

12. Cf. "However rich and refined Pasternak's metaphors may be, they are not what determines and guides his lyric theme. It is metonymical, not the metaphorical passages that lend his work an 'expression far from common.' Pasternak's lyricism, both in poetry and in prose, is imbued with metonymy; in other words, it is association by contiguity that predominates" (Jakobson 1969, 141).

13. See here Jakobson: "The hero is [. . .] replaced by a chain of concretized situations and surrounding objects, both animate and inanimate" (1969, 146–47). Fleishman similarly observes that the focus of the prose is "landscape descriptions, interiors and still lives": "Registration of shifts in the semantics of the world that describes the thing prevails over the conflict of characters, and the movement of the 'word' is more noticeable than the movement of the 'character'" (1979, 48). Rudova echoes: "The reality that Zhenya sees through relationship of things becomes the stream of images" (1997, 55). Wiegers concludes, accepting Jakobson's position that the absence of active agent [отсутствие деятеля] is the result of Pasternak's metonymic prose style (1999, 288).

the material objects around her. Perhaps the most arresting emblem[14] of these earlier sections is another episode involving the movement of hands. The very slow motion of the impersonal hands of the strict English governess as she presides over the dinner table asserts balance between the inner and outer worlds in concentric, ever-widening circles: from the food to the mood of the children, to the pieces of furniture and rooms in the house, and to the quiet and softly lit day. The governess's hands, introduced as a replacement for the parents' card game, reorder the initial memory that Zhenya carries with her upon leaving infancy. Orderly in themselves, the governess's hands no longer play: their focus is a movement from inanimate objects to the world of the growing children, and they belong to a person dehumanized by her proximity to orderly, inanimate reality. Lit by the diffused northern day and herself an emblem of orderly balance, the woman occupies a space next to the "graying" oak sideboard cabinet and a "severe" collection of heavy silver. By contrast with the governess, then, these surrounding objects are almost humanized while the governess, at the center of this design, metes out neither pleasure nor happiness, but a well-ordered, emotionless, tepid universe which promises to last without limit in the narrative section, fittingly entitled "The Long Days":

> The quiet northern daylight streamed through the curtains. It was unsmiling. The oaken sideboard seemed gray. And the silver lay piled there heavy and severe. The lavender washed hands of the governess moved above the tablecloth. She always served everyone his fair portion and had an inexhaustible supply of patience, and a sense of justice was germane to her to the same degree as her room and her books were always clean and neat. The maid who brought the food stood waiting in the dining room and only went to the kitchen to fetch the next course. It was pleasant and comfortable, but dreadfully sad. (*CSP* 134)

> Сквозь гардины струился тихий северный день. Он не улыбался. Дубовый буфет казался седым. Тяжело и сурово грудилось серебро. Над скатертью двигались лавандой умытые руки англичанки, она никого не обделяла и обладала неистощимым запасом терпенья; а чувство справедливости было свойственно ей в той высокой сте-

---

14. According to Wiegers, the infantilism of Luvers is directly linked to the fragmentary nature of the narrative and the fact that her parents are deeply indifferent to her (1999, 232). However, the parents are kept outside of her interests particularly in the first part of the story when her consciousness is developed in relation to objects. This pattern is not general; it will change in other episodes of the novella.

пени, в какой всегда чиста была и опрятна ее комната и ее книги. Горничная, подав кушанье, застаивалась в столовой и в кухню уходила только за следующим блюдом. Было удобно и хорошо, но страшно печально. (*PSS* 3:35)

On the whole, then, this everyday comfortable life of Zhenya's early childhood continues to imitate the movements of the governess's hands. The events move out of the center to the periphery and never back—from the governess's hands to the world outside, but not the other way round, just as the governess's hands only serve, give, measure, but rarely receive.

One should note that there exists—against this balanced, well-measured space—a disorderly and irrational residue that threatens the established order: the electricity of the parents' presence and feelings. However, just like Motovilikha at night at the beginning of the story, the parents' inexplicable irritability remains very much on the outskirts of the children's consciousnesses—experienced on this occasion "within" as a kindred weight of resentment and guilt:[15]

> Totally vulnerable, and somehow unrecognizable and pathetic, *this* father was genuinely terrifying, unlike the merely irritated stranger. He produced more effect on the little girl; his son was left moved.
>
> But their mother bewildered them both. [. . .]
>
> Everything that passed from parents to children came inopportunely and from outside, elicited not by them but by some external cause—and as is always the case, it had a touch of remoteness and mystery, like whimpering outside the city gates at night when everyone is going to bed. (*CSP* 135; emphasis in original)

> Ничем неуязвимый, какой-то неузнаваемый и жалкий,—*этот* отец был—страшен, в противоположность отцу раздраженному,—чужому. Он трогал больше девочку, сына меньше.
>
> Но мать смущала их обоих. [. . .]
>
> Все, что шло от родителей к детям, приходило невпопад, со стороны, вызванное не ими, но какими-то посторонними причи-

---

15. Gorelik observes the correlation between poor relations of parents and children and the narrative focus upon objects and, just like Wiegers, considers these to be characteristic of the world of *Luvers* (2000, 104–5). However, this correlation is characteristic only of the first part of the narrative, of the world characterized by the English governess, when the space, as Gorelik notices, appears comfortable but cold to Zhenya. Parents in this section replace the unknown distant qualities of Motovilikha, awakening in the children not merely the inner concealment of curiosity, but the concealment of resentment.

нами, и отдавало далекостью, как это всегда бывает, и загадкой, как, ночами, нытье по заставам, когда все ложатся спать. (*PSS* 3:36-37)

The parental presences are kept very much at a distance; their actions are literally at the boundary of the children's consciousnesses; the temporal and spatial markers are those of outsiders to the routine of everyday: "like whimpering *outside the city gates* at night *when everyone is going to bed*" [*нытье по заставам, когда все ложатся спать*] (*CSP* 135; *PSS* 3:37; emphasis added). These most "kindred" and immediate people are at this point only strangers who threaten to undermine (but never do) the horizontal symmetry of the children's world while widening and deepening it with a sense of danger—with an unconscious hidden uncertainty of the external and distant, reflected in the unexpected bouts of irritability and guilt, experienced by the children, who otherwise remain surrounded by what is, on the whole, a world of animated objects and de-animated humans (see Table 6b).

As Fleishman aptly observes, this manner of writing destroys the dividing line between subjects and objects (1977, 19–21). Indeed, as noted above, it is not really the governess, but her hands, and more precisely her rooms that continue to inscribe order in the Luverses' house. The subject seems to have no power over objects: objects move in unison with human beings, echoing their thoughts, impulses, and states.[16] The symmetry of subject-object—which slows down time by arresting and even reversing the possibility of incontrovertible action or agency—indicates, however, not merely Pasternak's technical penchant for a weakened agent,[17] but also something of the magical quality of childhood, its wonder and sadness. As human consciousness expands, however, and the subject perceives the world and sees herself reflected in objects,[18] the established balance ensures—at this stage, at least—that no event or action can take place in this world as it continues to hide from the children the reality of their own powerlessness or, what is equally possible, their as yet unknown power.

In the meantime, Zhenya, after lingering for a very long time in the world without clearly defined agents—with its "playing and squabbling, writing and eating in completely empty, solemnly deserted rooms" [Но все чаще и чаще

---

16. See Glazov-Corrigan: "the loneliness and uneventfulness of the children's early years [. . .] is described as an interaction, an acquaintance with the inanimate world around them" (1991, 139). See also Barnes: "Both Pasternak and his heroine thus emerge as enraptured passive observers, rather than demonstrative masculine doers" (1989, 271).

17. See Glazov-Corrigan (1991, 140); Rudova (1997, 55); Wiegers (1999, 288).

18. Glazov-Corrigan (1991, 157 n.11) also emphasizes that in the first part of the "Long Days" Pasternak avoids the question of the interaction between brother and sister by observing that "up till now they had lived as a pair" [до сих пор они жили парой] (*CSP* 146; *PSS* 3:49).

TABLE 6B. THE EARLY CHILDHOOD OF ZHENYA LUVERS

Boundary:

Seasons and stages of growth	Direction of perception and permeable compound	Emotional state	Residue on the margins of the compound	The images of the hands controlling the situation	The character of time and space
2nd Boundary: Winter-like diffused northern light. Early childhood.	Girl's acquaintance with still life.	Orderly existence and sadness. Loneliness. Experience of parental misplaced "electricity."	Weight of hidden hurt and resentment at the erratic behavior of the parents, who act as if they are "outside the city gates at night."	The hands of the English governess smelling of lavender and presiding over the table.	Atemporality of the lonely childhood ("The Long Days"): "playing and squabbling, writing and eating in completely empty, solemnly deserted rooms."

игралось и вздорилось, пилось и елось в совершенно пустых, торжественно безлюдных комнатах] (*CSP* 134; *PSS* 3:35)—will finally transgress
this boundary[19] and turn toward a singular confrontation, this time with the
forces of nature. On this new boundary, however, the new kindredness of patterns will continue to preclude major changes, permitting the state of childhood to last for a while longer, with the deceptive and comfortable promise of
uninterrupted permanence.

6.3 The boundary of spring and the outlines of soul:
New kindredness with nature at the appointed time

It is characteristic for Pasternak that the textual marker for soul is presented
as underlying (rather than coinciding with) expanding consciousness. Soul
in *Luvers* appears initially as an incidental place-holder for misnamed moral
concepts, an inner self of which the growing children are aware very partially, being otherwise guided by superstition and prejudice. It is also noteworthy that "soul" makes its first appearance in the context of the children's
suppressed irritation at their "distant" parents, an irritation, accompanied by
a vague sense of guilt:[20] "the concepts of punishment, retribution, reward,
and justice *had in a childish way already penetrated their souls, while distracting their consciousness*" [понятия кары, воздаяния, награды и справедливости *проникли уже по-детски в их душу и отвлекали в сторону их
сознание*][21] (*CSP* 136; *PSS* 3:37; emphasis added). The children's "souls" in

---

19. Gorelik, in the chapter "The image of a line, frame, boundary in the youthful prose
works" [Образ линии, оправы, границы в юношеских прозаических набросках] (2000,
17–27), suggests the interrelation between boundary and childhood (2000, 17) and notes
(2000, 23) Pasternak's letter to Olga Freidenberg of July 23, 1910, where the writer speaks of
boundary and city outposts [границы и заставы] as an entry into a "spiritual spaciousness"
[духовные пространства] (*PSS* 7:49). In the context of this, the appearance of the phrase
"howling at city gates" [нытье по заставам] in the novella signals a presence of the boundary
and its openness to a "spiritual spaciousness."

20. It is noteworthy that the major change in Zhenya's relationship with her mother, which
coincides with the coming of spring, remains unnoticed in criticism. For Pasternak's critics,
Zhenya's moral development either remains generic, rather than individual (Aucouturier 1978,
45); or it is interconnected exclusively with Tsvetkov (Barnes 1989, 272); or "Pasternak saw
Christianity at that time as only one cultural system among many" (Fleishman 1990a, 104).
Faryno (1993), while emphasizing the connection between Zhenya's early years and the apoc-
ryphal accounts of Mary's childhood, does not note the mother–daughter transformation, while
Björling discounts the reality of the sudden warmth: "Zhenya is in all senses an unenlightened
if not neglected child" (2010, 132).

21. There is a slight alteration of the translation (cf. in *CSP* "had in a childish way already
penetrated their souls, distracting their consciousness"). "While" was placed between "soul" and
"distracting" in order to emphasize that the two concepts are not identical in the narrative.

Luvers, then, enter the narrative as independent principles associated with the concepts of spiritual life, which, initially ill-fitting and misdirected, are blended with unconscious resentment, pain, and misunderstanding, and remain *on the outskirts of the children's consciousness*—a deepening of an inner world by an as yet unnamed, unclear though distant force. Kantian influence is again clearly in evidence here, as the concept of soul is introduced as another example of the synthetic blending of *a posteriori* (diverse threads of poorly understood Christian teachings and dogmas) and *a priori* (a weight or a force for which there is—as yet—no name).

The proximate cause of this inner weight is the children's literally closest kin—their estranged parents—who tend to destroy the orderly symmetry of their lives, otherwise carefully guarded by the English governess. In their disruptive acts and emotions, the parents stand for a painful and unwelcome connection to the external world, as well as to the children's future that still awaits discovery. The emphasis on "soul" is, thus, consistently re-introduced into the context of the direct interrelation between anger at parents and the children's conscience:

> And often, when a calm of rare clarity *came to their souls* and they ceased inwardly to feel they were criminals—when their consciences were relieved of all the mystery that evaded discovery, like fever before a rash, they saw their mother as aloof, remote from them, and irascible without cause. [. . .]
>
> At first they would cry; later, after one especially sharp outburst, they began to take fright; *then, over the years, it turned into a concealed and increasingly deep-rooted antagonism.* (*CSP* 135; emphasis added)

> И часто, когда в их душах наступал на редкость ясный покой, и они не чувствовали преступников в себе, когда от совести их отлегало все таинственное, чурающееся обнаруженья, похожее на жар перед сыпью, они видели мать отчужденной, сторонящейся их и без поводу вспыльчивой. [. . .]
>
> Сначала, случалось, они плакали; потом, после одной особенно резкой вспышки, стали бояться; *затем, с течением лет это перешло у них в затаенную, все глубже укоренявшуюся неприязнь.* (*PSS* 3:36)

Soul as terminology and concept appears first in a world that is almost automaton-like in its orderly balance: the soul's emergence, spearheaded by erratic and inexplicable events, disrupts the world's comfortable but joyless routine. On this occasion the absent-minded animation of the "ensouled" lamps[22] signals the appearance of this new principle, approaching from the outer distances and from the inner, as yet unexamined depth of resentment, hurt, and pain, a principle that psychological terms and religious categories suggest as an ill-fitting, but orderly and symmetrical system of rewards and punishment. Thus, Pasternak compares the children's growing shame with "what in French might be called christianisme (because none of this could be called Christianity)" [что хочется обозначить по-французски "христиа-низмом," за невозможностью назвать все это христианством] (*CSP* 134; *PSS* 3:36). This state of superstition and guilt,[23] as Pasternak emphasizes, has a particularly strong effect on the girl, for it "sometimes seemed to her that things could be no better—nor, indeed, ought they to be so in full view of her perversity and impenitence—and that it all served her right" [то иногда казалось ей, что лучше и не может и не должно быть по ее испорчен-ности и нераскаянности; что это поделом] (*CSP* 134; *PSS* 3:36).

The focus on the girl permits Pasternak to develop a startling psycho-somatic sequence, within which the hidden inner weight of guilt and anger begins to operate as a physical ferment, the hormonal imbalance of a maturing organism: "their whole beings shuttered and fermented, utterly bewildered by their parents' attitude to them" [все их существо содрогалось и бродило, сбитое совершенно с толку отношением родителей к ним] (*CSP* 134; *PSS* 3:37). Moreover, the young girl's guilt for the great number of unnamable sins is no longer supervised by the cold and fair English governess, but by an erratic French woman, obviously the bearer of "le Christianisme." She dis-trusts and torments the young child, already perplexed and burdened by her sense of sinfulness. The French woman has no name, but, in Zhenya's mind, this governess looks like a fly, an instinctual life that has no memorable or intelligible significance. Thus, if the development of the children's conscious-ness is coordinated in the first part of the narrative with the balanced motion of human beings in relation to inanimate objects, then this new stage includes not only inanimate objects, but also emotional, physical, and instinctual forces inside and outside the body of the child.

---

22. The absence of the parents is matched by the absent-mindedness of the lamps whose soul is outside: "The lamps only highlighted the emptiness of the evening air. [. . .] In their souls they were out in the street [. . .]. Here was where the light disappeared for the evening. Their parents were away" [Лампы только оттеняли пустоту вечернего воздуха. [. . .] Душой своей они были на улице. [. . .] Вот где вечерами пропадали лампы. Родители были в отъезде" (*CSP* 137; *PSS* 3:38; trans. altered).

23. Pasternak's opposition between Christianisme and the Russian word for Christian-ity—христианство—is quite a peculiar one. His jab at the French is here a signal of his own attraction to Christianity as a living mystery, rather than as a list of dogmatic rules. In this he never changes. See, e.g., Bodin (1990).

Zhenya's first menstruation, playing a role of purgation on several levels of the narrative, is presented, therefore, as a spectacular series of contiguous relationships, the gathering of an oversaturated synthetic unity that signals the approach of a new and highly meaningful boundary. The initial onset of the blood-flow, just like the French governess, has no name at first and corresponds to a multiplicity of carefully garnered textual layers: Zhenya's fear of the French governess, her growing dislike of her parents, her painful and secretive body (which reflects her own stubborn and instinctual secretiveness), and, finally, the gathering intensity of the Kama River as yet blocked by cold and ice. As in the earlier part of the narrative, all these contiguous motifs appear to possess similar characteristics of inner swelling, sickness, secrecy, concealment, and guilt, evident in the whole spectrum of details, which include:[24]

    a) the description of the lamps in the room:

> They gave no light but swelled up inside like sickly fruits, with a clear and lackluster dropsy that distended their dilated shades. (*CSP* 137)

> Они не давали света, но набухли изнутри, как больные плоды, от той мутной и светлой водянки, которая раздувала их одутловатые колпаки. (*PSS* 3:38)

    b) the psychological state of the child:

> For the girl, these were years of suspicion, solitude, and a sense of sin [. . .]. [I]t therefore sometimes seemed to her that things could be no better—nor, indeed, ought they to be so in full view of her perversity and impenitence. (*CSP* 134)

> А так как для девочки это были годы подозрительности и одиночества, чувства греховности [. . .] то иногда казалось ей, что лучше и не может и не должно быть по ее испорченности и нераскаянности; что это поделом. (*PSS* 3:36)

    c) the girl's behavior during the onset of menstruation:

> She could only deny it and stubbornly disavow the thing that was

---

24. Here, the argument restates the findings of Glazov-Corrigan (1991, 141–42).

most vile of all [. . .]. She could only shudder, grit her teeth, and press herself against the wall, choking with tears. (*CSP* 137)

Приходилось только отрицать, упорно заперевшись в том, что было гаже всего [. . .]. Приходилось вздрагивать, стиснув зубы, и, давясь слезами, жаться к стене. (*PSS* 3:39)

d) the physical, actual state of the body:

Her joints ached and fused in a total hypnotic suggestion. Tormenting and enervating, this suggestion was the work of her organism, which concealed the meaning of everything from the girl, and behaving like a criminal, made her imagine this bleeding was some foul and revolting form of evil. (*CSP* 136)

Суставы, ноя, плыли слитным гипнотическим внушением. Томящее и измождающее, внушение это было делом организма, который таил смысл всего от девочки и, ведя себя преступником, заставлял ее полагать в этом кровотечении какое-то тошнотворное, гнусное зло. (*PSS* 3:40)

e) and the external, natural world—the onset of spring and the initially slow melting of the Kama River:

Sickly and ripening laboriously, spring in the Urals later bursts through broad and vigorous in the course of a single night, and it continues broad and vigorous thereafter. (*CSP* 136–37)

Трудно назревающая и больная, весна на Урале прорывается затем широко и бурно, в срок одной какой-нибудь ночи, и бурно и широко протекает затем. (*PSS* 3:38)

The above juxtaposition of parallel motifs further emphasizes a new symmetrical (or *almost* symmetrical) relationship that expands far beyond the symmetry between subject and object in the earlier section: the text presents the physical growth of the young girl as inseparable from her psychological development, accompanied by yet another parallel, and this time external, natural event—the onset of spring. The contiguous series, in fact, only multiply, as the surrounding world is about to be awakened and animated.[25]

---

25. As Fateeva observes, "the metonymic hero" is a reflection of the creative process, or

Thus, contrary to critical observations about the lack of agency in the early Pasternak, this part of the narrative supplies a surprisingly long list of agents of action, with one important caveat: all of them are, in a strict sense, pseudo-agents.[26] The unshakeable darkness of the night is first pierced by the twinkling of an impatient star, then by Mrs. Luvers's threatening demeanor, and then by the emphatic urgency of gesture—by the hand of the French governess resting on her watch. Whereas the hands of the English governess used to direct the children's lives by exuding order and solemnity, the French governess's gesture propels the world toward an irreversible breakthrough. Through darkness and cold, her hand on the clock shows an urgent pathway from the forms of the *passé* to the *futur antérieur* [среди форм passe и futur anterieur] (*CSP* 136; *PSS* 3:38), and possibly for the first time in the narrative draws Zhenya's attention to the reality and urgency of chronological time, even if the young girl is oblivious to the recognition that the night in question is also the tempestuous beginning of spring:

The ice was moving downstream and, presumably, crackling. A star shimmered. The deserted night showed rough and black and was *malleable, chill, but unchanging.* Zhenya looked away from the window. A note of threatening impatience sounded in her mother's voice. The French girl stood against the wall, all solemnity and concentrated pedagogy. *Her hand was in an adjutant pose, resting on her watch ribbon.* (*CSP* 138; emphasis added)

Шел и, верно, шумел лед. Блистала звезда. *Ковко и студено, но без отлива,* шершаво чернела пустынная ночь. Женя отвела глаза от окна. В голосе матери слышалась угроза нетерпенья. Француженка стояла у стены, вся—серьезность и сосредоточенная педагогичность. *Ее рука по-адъютантски покоилась на часовом шнурке.* (*PSS* 3:40; emphasis added)

---

the relationship of the reflections through the mirror between the poet and the world (2003, 50). This reflective function does characterize Zhenya, but only at a very particular time in her life—in the spring and summer in Perm.

26. See here Fateeva who, summing up the argument of Arutiunova (rpt. 1972) and Kovtunova (1986, 148), sides with Kovtunova's conclusion. Thus, while it may appear that the "lyrical subject" in Pasternak is eliminated, the obverse, in fact, takes place. The predicative relationships of the "subject" become attached to the objects of the external world, and as a result the whole of the text becomes dynamic and filled with predicative action [текст становится "сплошь предикативным"]. In the meantime, the lyrical subject moves to the foreground, reinforced at least twice as a reflection of what was reflected from him into the world (2003, 51).

It must also be emphasized that among a whole series of pseudo-agents, the text clearly points to Zhenya as the ultimate agent of change.[27] Zhenya seems to start a whole chain of events—the flow of the Kama River, the spring in the Urals, and the family's happiness—by her courageous confession, when almost like the ice on the river she decides to move forward, or rather to jump into her words, as if she were jumping into the Kama and moving with the ice:

Zhenya once more glanced at the stars and at the Kama. *She had made up her mind. Despite the cold and the ice floes. And—she plunged. Getting tangled in her words, she gave her mother an unlikely and terror-stricken account of it.* (*CSP* 138; emphasis added)

Женя снова глянула на звезды и на Каму. *Она решилась. Несмотря ни на холод, ни на урывни. И—бросилась. Она, путаясь в словах, непохоже и страшно рассказала матери про это.* (*PSS* 3:40)

Mrs. Luvers's reaction to Zhenya's words points within this section to yet another important agent revealed in the process—the birth-like emergence of Zhenya's soul, recalled into the world out of darkness as if propelled into external reality by her menstrual blood:

Mother let her finish only because she was struck *by how much soul the child put into her story.* To understand—she understood everything from Zhenya's very first word. No, not even from that; from the way the little girl gulped deeply as she started her tale. Mother listened, rejoicing, loving, and consumed with tenderness for this slender little body. She felt like throwing her arms around her daughter's neck and weeping. (*CSP* 138; trans. altered; emphasis added)

---

27. Fateeva poses a direct question regarding the status of the process by means of which the "soul" in Pasternak's works assumes the qualities of its surroundings. Working initially with the poem "The Definition of the Soul" [Определение души], Fateeva gives a three-fold answer. First, she emphasizes the fluidity of referential correspondences: the referential significations of the "soul" are not fixed. Second, the *word* into which the speaker (or the hero in this case) *puts in his/her soul* becomes not merely a vehicle of a trembling soul, but a soul as such. There is therefore a transformation, evident in *Luvers,* from "вложил душу" to "бьешься" and "душа." Third, Pasternak, sensitive to the vegetative meaning of his name, collates natural and spiritual growth. A leaf of the tree becomes a leaf of the page, and both are life and soul. In *The Childhood of Luvers,* one observes an interesting combination of these: Zhenya's "putting of the soul" begins the process wherein the animation of the surrounding world is to spring up as a celebration of awakening nature after winter (2003, 61–62).

Мать дала договорить ей до конца только потому, что ее поразило, *сколько души вложил ребенок в это сообщение.* Понять поняла-то она все по первому слову. Нет, нет: по тому, как глубоко глотнула девочка, приступая к рассказу. Мать слушала, радуясь, любя и изнывая от нежности к этому худенькому тельцу. Ей хотелось броситься на шею к дочери и заплакать. (*PSS* 3:40)

This new qualitative addition[28] to the Luverses' world changes once and for all the mother–daughter relationship, announcing a new animation, a living relatedness, pierced by love, and incomparably preferable to the mechanical symmetry of the previous interactions between human beings. The former weight of resentment against the parents becomes in this context not a fault, but rather a necessary psychosomatic weight defining the reality and outlines of the concealed and as yet unconscious soul. Thus, Zhenya's confession does not merely animate her stilted relationship with her mother; Zhenya redefines the world and all its relations by sharing this newborn energy with the still world around her.[29]

In short, it is not only the spring, or the physical maturation of Zhenya's body, that "sickly and ripening laboriously" has come to fruition: a real triumph occurs as a new vitality pierces the icy cold water, resentment, and shame, and bursts "through broad and vigorous in the course of a single night" to continue flowing "broad and vigorous thereafter" [трудно назревающая и больная, весна на Урале прорывается затем широко и бурно, в срок одной какой-нибудь ночи, и бурно и широко протекает затем] (*CSP* 137; *PSS* 3:39). The text carefully underscores the triumph that follows upon Zhenya's courageous jump, indicating that the event in question is a tangible spiritual victory: as Zhenya finishes her "plunge," the French governess is vanquished and, instead, the mother's voice speaks no longer of winter, but of the coming summer, just as the lamps at home immediately lose their absent-minded indifference. The new warmth of lamps awakens or, more precisely, animates the static object—the mother's sable collar—and all of these, in turn, point to the "blessed" coming of Easter, to Holy Week and the spirit of bless-

---

28. Fateeva suggests that Pasternak's style—its dual reflection—the dynamism of the predication travelling from the hero to the objects and back to the hero—generates a mythological context: the generation of the authorial myths (2003, 51). Cf. Pasternak's own words in the theses of "Symbolism and Immortality" (1913): "The poet submits to the direction of his search, takes them into himself and behaves as the objects around him" [Поэт покоряется направлению поисков, перенимает их и ведет себя, как предметы вокруг] (*PSS* 5:318).

29. In Fateeva, this act of unintentional or intentional self-disclosure of "putting the soul" [вкладывать душу] into nature creates Pasternak's allegorical "code" starting from his earliest works (2003, 62).

edness "blagodat"[30] (according to the words of the telegram that announce Mr. Luvers's return to his family):

> Zhenya could not see the French girl. Only tears, only her mother—filling the whole room. [...]
>
> "Zhenya dear, go to the dining room ... and I'll tell you what a lovely dacha Daddy and I have taken for you ... for us for the summer."
>
> The lamps were again themselves, as in winter, at home with Luvers—warm, zealous, faithful. Mama's sable frisked across the blue wool table-cloth. "Won—remaining Blagodat—Await end Holy Week." (*CSP* 139)

> Женя не видела француженки. Стояли слезы—стояла мать,—во всю комнату. [...]
>
> "Женичка, ступай в столовую, детка, я сейчас тоже туда приду, и расскажу тебе, какую мы чудную дачу на лето вам—нам на лето с папой сняли."
>
> Лампы были опять свои, как зимой, дома, с Люверсами,—горя-чие, усердные, преданные. По синей шерстяной скатерти резвилась мамина куница. "Выиграно задержусь на Благодати жди концу Страстной если." [...] (*PSS* 3:41)

In this victorious state of the girl's deliverance,[31] reflected in the return of her mother's understanding, the family's happiness, and the spring with its promise of the summer, there is a clear indication that the unburdening of the

---

30. Blagodat, etymologically "blessedness" or grace, is a mountain with an adjacent mining settlement in the Eastern part of the Urals (*PSSCom* 3:543).

31. Gorelik observes that the space in the novella is coordinated very precisely. However, uncharacteristically perhaps, the narrative at the end of the "daughter–mother" reconciliation episode moves forward to the occurrence six months later (beyond the forms of the passé to the futur antérieur [*CSP* 136; *PSS* 3:38]) toward another of Zhenya's major spiritual or rather intellectual victories when she passes the entrance exams into the lycée. The compressing of time indicates a capacity to see the future at a glance, akin to the soul in flight: "Zhenya sat down on the end of settee, tired and happy. She sat down modestly and correctly, just as she sat six months later on the end of the cold brown bench in the corridor of the Ekaterinburg lycée, when she gained top marks for her answer in the Russian orals and was told she 'may go'" [Женя села на край дивана, усталая и счастливая. Села скромно и хорошо, точь-в-точь как села полгода спустя, в коридоре Екатеринбургской гимназии на край желтой холодной лавки, когда, ответив на устном экзамене по русскому языку на пятерку, узнала, что "может идти"] (*CSP* 139; *PSS* 3:41).

There is, however, another methodology for formulating the process in question: Pasternak's reaction to both Hume and Kant. For Pasternak, impressions and perceptions are invariably synthetic; they blend the immediate and indefinite, and as the indefinite begins to unveil its hidden qualities, replaced by other aspects of indefiniteness, entering into a purview, the space opens up into a mythopoetic structure.

body is contiguous with the unburdening and purgation of all the previously collected psychological weight underlying the developing consciousness (see Table 6c). It is at this point in the narrative, then, that the contiguous motifs are garnered explicitly within a "natural" all-embracing metaphor that has emerged organically[32] out of the preceding textual strategies. As the woman's body, just like nature in spring, comes into its own and throws away darkness and cold shadows, a deeper ritual of inner cleansing is being effected—delivered and washed not only by the visiting doctor, but by a medicinal light, the new leading agent of change—bright direct sunlight—that is announced to the expanding world:

> And this is how the story of her maidhood's first maturity imprinted herself on her memory: *the resonant echo of the chirruping morning street, which lingered on the stair and freshly penetrated into the house,* the French girl, the maid and the doctor—two criminals and the one initiate, *bathed and disinfected by the daylight, chill, and sonority of shuffling steps.* (CSP 139; emphasis added)

> Так и запечатлелась у ней в памяти история ее первой девичьей зрелости: *полный отзвук щебечущей утренней улицы, медлящей на лестнице, свежо проникающей в дом*; француженка, горничная и доктор, две преступницы и один посвященный, *омытые, обеззараженные светом, прохладой и звучностью шаркавших маршей*. (PSS 3:41)

The pattern of contiguous series surrounding Zhenya's entrance into adolescence is, therefore, more complex than a pattern identified by metonymic constructions. If, in the preceding section, the presence of inanimate objects de-animated humans, then in this part of the narrative, human beings share agency with natural forces, participating themselves in the incontrovertible power of natural events and yet expanding the capacity of human agency. In

---

32. As Pasternak suggests in "The Wassermann Test," only the contiguities can nourish "the intimacy of the individually fostered device" developed in "the lyrical space of the initial conception" [лирик[у] замысла согретого интимностью лично взлилеянного приема] (*PSS* 5:6). Indeed, his series of metonymies in *The Childhood of Luvers* begin to generate his own metaphoric structures, or, as Fateeva would have it, "Pasternak's allegorical code," consistently nourished starting from his earliest works (2003, 62). See here also Gorelik's position that if for the Symbolists the symbol is immaterial, for Pasternak it is developed "on the basis of liberated object" (2000, 140). Fateeva refers to this process as the dynamism of the predication that travels from the hero to the objects and back to the hero, generating in the process a mythological context—the authorial myths (2003, 51).

TABLE 6C. MAIDENHOOD'S FIRST MATURITY

Boundary: Seasons and stages of growth	Direction of perception and permeable compound	Emotional state	Residue on the margins of the compound	The images of the hands controlling the situation	The character of time and space
3rd Boundary: Spring. "Maidenhood's first maturity."	Girl's acquaintance with the forces of nature. Awakening of the inanimate world.	From sickness and confusion to exaltation	The outcast—the French governess banished. For the time being no other outsiders and no shadows.	The hand of the French governess at first with scissors and then "in adjutant pose" resting on her watch.	Opening up of the world in the spring: between "the forms of the passé and the futur antérieur."

creating this almost symmetrical series of contiguous states, Pasternak conceives a narrative where human consciousness, expanded together with the triumphant emergence of soul, can be depicted as not merely linked to objects, physical events, and natural phenomena, but as an animating principle that has just manifested its glorious power within both the child and the external world.[33] Moreover, and only in this part of the narrative, there are no hidden shadows on the margins of consciousness—all, even the French governess who looks like a fly, are temporarily "bathed and disinfected by the daylight" (*CSP* 139; *PSS* 3:41).

As spring comes to Perm, Pasternak's Zhenya is to enjoy a dizzying happiness with the boundaries between inner and outer worlds totally erased; assisted by spring, she will experience an animated world where her mother's sable collar, racing upon the bed cover, will not be the only inanimate object coming to life: even the rooms will rise "clean and transformed"; sighing "sweetly with relief," and echoed by the courtyards, they will announce the "overthrow of night," "reiterating that there would be no more evenings, and that no one would be allowed to sleep" [они объявляли ночь низложенной и твердили, мелко и дробно, день-деньской, с затеканьями, действовавшими как сонный отвар, что вечера никогда больше не будет, и они никому не дадут спать] (*CSP* 140; *PSS* 3:42).

6.4 The boundary of summer:
An infinitely expanding world approaching limits within the unlimited

Apart from Zhenya plunging into the Kama River with her confession, the unexpected happiness that enters the children's lives after that memorable spring night is also given a more realistic explanation. The Luvers family is clearly becoming prosperous: Mr. Luvers's business no longer oppresses him

---

33. In this sense there is definitely room for the debate with the critics' position, summarized best by Gorelik as she argues, on the basis of *The Childhood of Luvers*, that in opposition to the Symbolists, the material and the spiritual in Pasternak's world are from the very beginning inseparably united [материальное и духовное изначально и неразрывно слиты] (2000, 143). For Pasternak, however, the spiritual manifests the dynamism of its landscape in time: there is a periodization and progression of the unveiling in this regard, parallel to a vegetative growth (see here Fateeva 2003, 61–62). In other words, the Kantian vision of a priori and a posteriori is common to Pasternak and the Symbolists, and the synthetic unity of spiritual and material is shared by all these artists. In Pasternak, however, there is a singular periodization of the spiritual unveiling that the critics tend to ignore.

and makes him a stranger to his children; instead, the family's affairs are flourishing, and some of the constant parental anxiety is finally lifted.[34]

This factual explanation, however, remains on the margins of the text—to emerge as a new reality later on—and what is presented centrally instead is the unrestricted passage of joy not only between nature and humans, but also between the Luvers family home, other houses, streets, trees, neighbors, with the piercing light reflected in the relieved air that makes it impossible to distinguish who it is that rushes in, who is hungry, who breathes in, and who speaks out:

> The boring chatter of the courtyards continued around the clock. [. . .] "Feet! Feet!"—but they arrived hotfoot. They came in intoxicated from the open air with ringing in their ears, so they failed to understand properly what was said and rushed in to gulp and chew as fast as possible before . . . running back into that souring daylight that forced its way through suppertime . . . where the blue chirruped piercingly and the earth gleamed greasily like the baked milk. The boundary between house and courtyard was erased. The floor-cloth failed to erase all the footprints. Floors were streaked with dry, light colored daubs and crunched underfoot. (*CSP* 140)

> Круглые сутки стоял скучный говор дворов. [. . .] "Ноги, ноги!"—но им горелось, они приходили пьяные с воли, со звоном в ушах, за которым упускали понять толком сказанное и рвались поживей отхлебать и отжеваться, чтобы, с дерущим шумом сдвинув стулья, бежать снова назад, в этот навылет, за ужин ломящийся день, где просыхающее дерево издавало свой короткий стук, где пронзительно щебетала синева и жирно, как топленая, блестела земля. Граница между домом и двором стиралась. Тряпка не домывала наслеженого. Полы поволакивались сухой и светлой мазней и похрустывали. (*PSS* 3:42)

---

34. One senses this from the parts of the telegram Zhenya sees just before the mother's sable collar comes to life (*CSP* 139: *PSS* 3:41). As Wiegers observes, the fragmented nature of the novella is founded on Zhenya's ignorance of the adult world (1999, 31). In contrast to Wiegers's view (which he shares with Rudova) that the fragmented world is projected onto the same plane as in a cubist painting, it is possible to argue for a formation of several layers in the child's world, which, like the layers in "Ordering a Drama," reflect the worlds of inanimate, animate, and spiritual spheres of existence. In other words, Pasternak controls the disclosure of the fragmented details for the sake of an "organically grown" metaphoric design.

Once again, the overall principle of the narrative construction is no longer pure metonymy or even a phenomenological shift of perception. The agents in the contiguous series—which now include inanimate objects, natural events, forces of light, and feelings of humans for each other—reflect and even replace each other;[35] they cross boundaries and cross-fertilize, intensifying in the process the warmth of spring that started with Zhenya's entry into womanhood.

While Pasternak is cautious not to overuse the concept of the manifested soul during this dizzying spring,[36] he emphasizes nonetheless the process by means of which each newly animated object awakens into life. Thus, in the startling textual emblem, the inanimate stones, the gift of Mr. Luvers to his children, are awakened by this all-reigning call into life. These traditional representatives of the lowest group of inanimate nature announce their appearance as if secreted or borne by the unfolding paper, emerging out of its "frothing" folds. These newborn beings, like blind rabbits (the alliteration suggests that корольки are, in fact, кролики), exude new color and warmth, preparing to breathe and move:

> Moistly rustling, the stones gave warning of their appearance through the gradually coloring tissue paper, which grew more and more transparent as these packets, white and soft as gauze were unwrapped layer by layer. Some of them were like drops of almond milk, others—*like splashes of blue watercolor, while others resembled a solidified tear of cheese. Some were blind, somnolent, or dreamy, while others had a gay sparkle like the frozen juice of blood oranges. One feared to touch them.* They were lovely, displayed on the frothing paper, which exuded them like the dark juice of the plums. (*CSP* 140; emphasis added)

> В доме стало чудно хорошо. Камни с влажным шелестом предупреждали о своем появлении из папиросной, постепенно окрашивавшейся бумаги, которая становилась все более и более прозрачной

---

35. It is precisely this landscape that Fateeva, drawing upon the works of Arutiunova (1972) and Kovtunova (1986, 148), calls a "predicative relationship" of the whole landscape of images and motives [текст становится "сплошь предикативным"] (2003, 51). See also Fateeva's conclusion that the process of blending the motives associated with soul, tree, leaf, branch, and a plant's first growth [душа, дерево, лист, ветка, побег] is used very widely in Pasternak (2003, 64).

36. One must stress that the term "soul" is used very cautiously in "The Long Days" as if in passing through the figures of speech, but always strategically and precisely. Altogether before the Luverses' arrival in Ekaterinburg, the word "soul" is used six times: five times in the context of the pain and joy experienced in the relationship with parents, and once in a train when she observes in their compartment.

по мере того, как слой за слоем разворачивались эти белые, мягкие, как газ, пакеты. Одни походили на капли миндального молока, другие—на брызги голубой акварели, третьи—на затверделую сырную слезу. Те были слепы, сонны и мечтательны, эти—с резвою искрой, как смерзшийся сок корольков. Их не хотелось трогать. Они были хороши на пенившейся бумаге, выделявшей их, как слива свою тусклую глень. (*PSS* 3:42)

This animation of still life can also be sensed in the overflow of mutual support between the parents, an unclouded breakthrough of affection and love, first appearing as sunlight in the eyes of the father, and then reflected through the mother's glance and flowing onto the children:[37]

[W]hen Mother on odd occasions cast a playfully reproachful glance at Father, it seemed as though she drew tranquility from his small and ugly eyes in order then to pour it forth from her own, large and beautiful, upon the children and those around them. (*CSP* 140)

[И] когда мать урывками, с шутливой укоризной взглядывала на отца, то казалось, она черпает этот мир в его глазах, некрупных и некрасивых, и изливает его потом своими, крупными и красивыми на детей и окружающих. (*PSS* 3:42–43)

The intimation of reflected sunlight, which now lives among the Luverses and enters into all aspects of their surroundings, is finally defined as a spirit of the family—the first mention in the text of the word "spirit" or "дух"—a unified family principle, so tangibly real in the parents during those summer months: "Most of all, both were serene in spirit, even-tempered and friendly" [А главное, оба были спокойны, духом ровны и приветливы] (*CSP* 140; *PSS* 3:42). This first mention of "spirit," a force destined to grow in complexity after Zhenya reads *Demon* on an autumn afternoon in Ekaterinburg, is at this point of the narrative just another magnificent gift of the happy spring and summer months.

Initially, then, the family move from Perm to Ekaterinburg also encapsulates the theme of space and time that surpasses all actual temporal and spatial

---

37. The correlation between eyes, reflection, and soul is observed in Fateeva in the context of tree leaves becoming the eyes of the soul (2003, 63). Here, however, the eyes of the parents reflect the sun, and the narrative moves to the new stage—not that of the soul, but that of the spirit—*dukh*. For the correlation of the images of the spirit, air, wind, danger, battle, and inspiration [одухотворение], see again Fateeva (2003, 187ff).

measurements. Within the precise chronology of a one-day train ride, Zhenya discovers "that the day that had all this packed into it—this actual day, now in Ekaterinburg—was still not over yet," and feels in the process "as if she too had assisted in shifting and removing all that weight of beautiful objects and had overstrained herself" [день, вместивший все это—вот этот самый, который сейчас в Екатеринбурге, и тут еще, не весь, не кончился еще. [. . .] Будто и она участвовала в оттискивании и перемещении тех тяжелых красот, и надорвалась] (*CSP* 146; *PSS* 3:46). The lack of clear boundaries between human beings, nature, and still-life is also reflected in the lack of geographical boundaries, a dissipation of the borderline between Europe and Asia (even when a major move from one part of the country into another is being undertaken).

It must be emphasized, nevertheless, that this unlimited vast happiness is itself placed within a precisely defined temporal period: it starts in the early spring with Zhenya's entry into "maidhood" and ends just before her sexual awareness. This temporal space will always be for the later Pasternak something of a signature for understanding the future of the personality,[38] as well as the key to poetic formation. In his poem "So they begin" [Так начинают], the immeasurable space of adolescence equals the unlimited vision of Faust:[39]

> . . . How can a child allow
> A star to exceed his grasp
> If he's Faust? If he's a dreamer?
> This is where Gypsies come from.

> . . . Как он даст
> Звезде превысить досяганье,
> Когда он—Фауст, когда—фантаст?
> Так начинаются цыгане. (*PSS* 1:189)

And in *Safe Conduct*, Pasternak speaks about the "vastness" of adolescence, identifying it as the part that "exceeds the whole," something of a "mathematical paradox." Returning to the fate of Faust, Pasternak insists (contrary to all the evidence) that Faust has gained his understanding of infinity because he has relived his adolescence twice:

---

38. As Lara observes to Zhivago, she lost that essential time of adolescent purity, that is, the time of transition between childhood and youth: "I think that to see it [beauty] your imagination has to be intact, your vision has to be childlike. That is what I was deprived of" [Мне кажется, чтобы ее увидеть, требуется нетронутость воображения, первоначальность восприятия. А это как раз у меня отнято] (*Zhivago* 399; *PSS* 4:396).

39. See here Livingstone (1994).

And everyone knows the vastness of adolescence. [. . .] *In other words, these years in our life constitute a part that exceeds the whole, and Faust, who lived through them twice, lived something utterly unimaginable, to be measured only in terms of the mathematical paradox.* (CSP 24; emphasis added)

А как необозримо отрочество, каждому известно. [. . .] *Другими словами, эти годы в нашей жизни составляют часть, превосходящую целое, и Фауст, переживший их дважды, прожил сущую невообразимость, измеримую только математическим парадоксом.* (PSS 3:151–52)

In *Luvers*, however, during the summer "with its parts that exceed the whole," there pass now and again occasional and fleeting suggestions of danger, as, for example, in the reflected world of a train window, "more serious and gloomy than the one here" [за окном не улица, а тоже комната, только серьезнее и угрюмее] (CSP 145; PSS 3:44), or the expectation of pumas beyond the imagined barrier, suggestions remaining, on the whole, on the outskirts of the text—a new placeholder for a future that is still only an unimportant and very minor detail.

Thus, in this unlimited happy world where parts "exceed the whole," the notions of limit and border emerge in a momentary sense of danger, a "misnomer," in fact, whose fictional unreality is emphasized when in the train the children imagine the borderline between Europe and Asia:[40]

In her enchanted head, the "frontier of Asia" arose in the form of some phantasmagoric barrier, like those iron bars, perhaps, which laid down a strip of terrible, pitch black, stinking danger between the public and the cage with pumas in it. (CSP 144).

В очарованной ее голове "граница Азии" встала в виде фантасмагорического какого-то рубежа, вроде тех, что ли, железных брусьев, которые полагают между публикой и клеткой с пумами полосу грозной, черной, как ночь, и вонючей опасности. (PSS 3:47)

---

40. For Faryno, the "cage with pumas" is the thematic development of the kitten who wakes up Zhenya in the beginning of the novella and the skin of the "white she-bear" in her nursery. This image of the furry animal is developed later into the lioness from Lermontov in "The Stranger" (1993, 9ff.). Faryno also identifies here the transformational series of curtains: the alder handing over the country house in the novella's opening is now replaced by yet another curtain (1993, 20).

Zhenya's fears (and her sense of enchantment) are immediately allayed: there is no barrier and no curtain "rising on the first act of a geographical tragedy" [поднятая занавеса над первым актом географической трагедии] (*CSP* 144; *PSS* 3:48), not even a promised "post on the frontier of Asia and Europe" with "Asia written on it," but instead there is only a renewed animation among the train passengers, an excitement that for a short time manages even to animate the train, but there is simply no corresponding significant or tangible spatial border:[41]

> Zhenya was annoyed by dull and dusty Europe for sluggishly withholding the appearance of the miracle. And how put out was she when, as if in answer to Seriozha's furious shriek, something resembling a small tombstone flashed past the window, turned sideways to them, then rushed away [. . .]. At that instant, as if by arrangement, several heads leaned out of the windows of all classes, *and the train came alive as it traced down the slope in the cloud of dust* [. . .]. *On and on they flew past the same dusty alders, which recently had been European, and were for some time now already Asian.* (*CSP* 144; emphasis added)

> Женя досадовала на скучную, пыльную Европу, мешкотно отдалявшую наступление чуда. Как же опешила она, когда, словно на Сережин неистовый крик, мимо окна мелькнуло и стало боком к ним и побежало прочь что-то вроде могильного памятника [. . .]. В это мгновение множество голов, как по уговору, сунулось из окон всех классов *и тучей пыли несшийся под уклон поезд ожився. [. . .] и летели все, в облаках крутившегося песку, летели и летели мимо все той же пыльной, еще недавно европейской, уже давно азиатской ольхи.* (*PSS* 3:47)

In Pasternak's rendering of the move, the boundary is both suggested and erased, for as far as the experience of the children's happiness is concerned, there is no tangible difference between the original locale and the new destination.

Similarly, no demarcation lines between past and present can as yet be

---

41. See here Glazov-Corrigan (1991). See also Faryno, who views the boundary in the context of a death resurrection motif (further supported by the image of a gravestone as a marker on the border). Faryno also suggests that the image of the train accelerating and flying together with the landscape invokes the image of the serpent with many heads, traveling together with the miraculous nature and the cloud of alders that had awakened Zhenya in the beginning of the story (1993, 18).

found. Upon arrival, the actual changes in the new locality become blended with old memories in an immediate acceptance of the already well-known world of Ekaterinburg; instead of a real difference, the children simply register a sense of cleanliness and renewed spaciousness, as if the old world is only being repaired and cleaned, so that it can now store both the old and the new, expanding Europe into Asia:

> Everything was fine and spacious. [. . .] [Father] unbuttoned his waistcoat, and his shirt front curved outward, fresh and vigorous. He said this was a splendid European-style town, and he rang for them to clear away and serve the next course [. . .]. (*CSP* 145)

> Было хорошо и просторно. [. . .] Он расстегнул жилет, и его манишка выгнулась свежо и мощно. Он говорил, что это прекрасный европейский город и звонил, когда надо было убрать и подать еще что-то, и звонил и рассказывал. (*PSS* 3:48)

In coordination with this theme, Zhenya's new maid quickly becomes an old acquaintance, and the new kitchen imagined as dark turns out to be full of light, just as Zhenya believes she has known all along:

> And down unknown passages from rooms still unknown there came a silent maid in white, all starched and pleated, with neat black hair; she was addressed in a formal manner, and though new, she smiled at the mistress and children as though they were already friends. She was given some instruction regarding Ulyasha, who was out there in the unknown and exceedingly dark kitchen [. . .].
>
> [. . .] The kitchen turned out to be fresh and bright, exactly, it seemed to the little girl a minute later—exactly as she had guessed and imagined in the dining room. (*CSP* 145)

> И по неизвестным ходам из еще неизвестных комнат входила бесшумная белая горничная, вся крахмально-сборчатая и черненькая, ей говорилось "вы" и, новая,—она, как знакомым, улыбалась барыне и детям. И ей отдавались какие-то приказания насчет Ульяши, которая находилась там, в неизвестной и, вероятно, очень-очень темной кухне [. . .].
>
> [. . .] Кухня оказалась свежая, светлая, точь-в-точь такая,—уже через минуту казалось девочке,—какую она наперед загадала в столовой и представила. (*PSS* 3:48)

The infinitely expandable space and the erasure of chronological borders between past and future reflect the spirit of the summer: a sense of the all-penetrating sunlit season visiting the world with no borderlines observed between Europe and Asia, between old and new, or between expectation and reality. However, within this space, with its quickly fleeting shadows of darkness, Pasternak's readers are served yet another image of hands—a metamorphosis of a recurrent self-transforming emblem. This time it reflects and summarizes the atmosphere of the summer trip, its boundless overflowing expansion and yet hidden, unknown potentiality of the approaching fall.

If the hands of the English governess had served food, moving outwards in a precise punctual gesture, and those of her French successor had pointed directly and urgently to the watch on that memorable spring night, there appears during the summer journey another singular human presence, a seemingly kind, overweight co-traveler in the train, whose hands are drawn as a wave-like expanding surface, directly reflecting the swaying rays of the sun and yet holding something back, as if hiding a foreign element. This portly man offers an indiscernible presence next to which Zhenya and her brother also become unknown and indiscernible, losing their sense of the earth that bears the world:

> He was a very portly man. He read his newspaper and swayed about. One glance on him was sufficient to reveal the swaying, which flooded the whole compartment like the sunshine. [. . .] She surveyed him and wondered where he had come from to sit in their compartment, and when he had managed to wash his dress. She had no idea of the real time of the day. [. . .] He could not see her because occasionally he too glanced up from the news or aslant, or sideways, and when he looked up at her bunk, their eyes never met. [. . .] But Seryozha is not down there either. "So where is he?" [. . .] "But where is the earth?"—the question gaped inside her soul. (*CSP* 142)

> Это был очень полный человек. Он читал газету и колыхался. При взгляде на него становилось явным то колыханье, которым, как и солнцем, было пропитано и залито все в купэ. Женя [. . .] разглядывала его и думала, откуда он взялся к ним в купэ, и когда это успел он одеться и умыться? Она понятия не имела об истинном часе дня. [. . .] Она его разглядывала, а он не мог видеть ее; полати шли наклоном вглубь к стене. [. . .] и когда он подымал глаза на ее койку, их взгляды не встречались. [. . .] "А Сережи нет и внизу. Так, где же он?" [. . .] "А где же земля?" ахнуло у ней в душе. (*PSS* 3:45)

TABLE 6D. YOUNG ZHENYA'S ENTRY INTO AN ANIMATED WORLD

Boundary: Seasons and stages of growth	Direction of perception and permeable compound	Emotional state	Residue on the margins of the compound	The images of the hands controlling the situation	The character of time and space
4th Boundary: Summer. Entering animated world.	Animation of the surrounding world and its overflow.	Spirit, "serene, even-tempered and friendly." Happiness. Move to Ekaterinburg.	A first apprehension of the presences of other people; a stranger in the train compartment.	The hands of the stranger on the train, who "took things with the gesture of actually giving."	Parts that exceed the whole: unlimited expansion of space and time during the summer months.

This passenger, unbeknownst to himself, represents a reality that for the first time in the narrative breaks the parallelisms of the earlier series—Zhenya observes him while remaining unobserved herself, as she loses, with a sudden yet still fleeting anxiety, the sense of time and space.

This stranger, then, who carefully explains the boundary between Europe and Asia to Zhenya (even if this border proves to be no real border at all) absorbs into himself the qualities of the limit, border, boundary. This near-sighted, overweight, wave-like man brings out a pocket watch and raises it to his face as if he is about to swallow whatever he is holding, and yet he does not swallow, but instead repeats the gesture back and forth, moving like a pendulum, forwards and backwards,[42] or like a rubber ball, himself not quite Chronos or a Nutcracker, but fully equipped with sighing, giving, and taking fingers. He brings a sense of disorientation to the children, as he moves his hands to check the time with a gesture, highly suggestive and yet mysterious and unclear, becoming himself the measure and signpost, which as yet has no real content, but rather remains a point of punctuation—in this case, a question mark:

> He was amusing and probably a kind man, and as he talked, he constantly lifted a plump hand to his mouth. His speech would often swell up and then break off, suddenly constricted. It turned out that he himself was from Ekaterinburg, had traveled the length and breadth of the Urals and knew them well, and when he took a gold watch from his waistcoat pocket and lifted it right up to his nose before popping it back, Zhenya noticed what kindly fingers he had. As is the nature of the stout people, he took things with the gesture of actually giving, and all the time his hand kept sighing as if proffered for someone to kiss, and bobbing gently as though bouncing a ball on the floor. (*CSP* 144)

> Он был смешной и, вероятно, добрый и, разговаривая, поминутно подносил пухлую руку ко рту. Его речь пучилась и, вдруг спираемая, часто прерывалась. Оказалось, он сам из Екатеринбурга, изъездил Урал вкривь и вкось и прекрасно знает, а когда, вынув золотые часы из жилетного кармана, он поднес их к самому носу и стал совать обратно, Женя заметила, какие у него добродушные пальцы. Как это в натуре полных, он брал движением дающего, и рука у него все время вздыхала, словно поданная для целования, и мягко прыгала, будто била мячом об пол. (*PSS* 3:46)

---

42. The movement of the pendulum is suggested rather than clearly stated.

This almost[43] august stranger, whose hands are offered as if for a kiss, becomes an emblem of the as yet unknown future—of a summer that gave joy and merriment, and yet took away its gifts, bringing the children to another threshold which, once passed, changes them once and for all. This threshold is the reality of other wills, and it is here that Pasternak's narrative acquires a new, and as yet unobserved, complexity.

---

43. Everything appears either seeming or *almost* exact.

6.5 TABLE I: CHRONOLOGY OF A PERMEABLE SELF: "THE LONG DAYS" OF *DETSTVO LUVERS*

Boundary: Seasons and stages of growth	Direction of perception and permeable compound	Emotional state	Residue on the margins of the compound	The images of the hands controlling the situation	The character of time and space
1st Boundary: Spring-summer. Awakening from infancy to early childhood.	Toward the unknown Motovilkha, and yet the focus is also on the card game of the parents.	Fear and first realization of the hidden and unknown. Kindredness with the unknown.	The night city, a factory producing cast iron, lit up by an obscured light source.	The card game—red, yellow, green. Hands of destiny, surrounded by the colors of a masquerade.	The first awareness of the distinction /interconnection between inner and outer worlds.
2nd Boundary: Winter-like diffused northern light. Early childhood.	Girl's acquaintance with still life.	Orderly existence and sadness. Loneliness. Experience of parental misplaced "electricity."	Weight of hidden hurt and resentment at the erratic behavior of the parents, who act as if they are "outside the city gates at night."	The hands of the English governess smelling of lavender and presiding over the table.	Atemporality of the lonely childhood ("The Long Days"): "playing and squabbling, writing and eating in completely empty, solemnly deserted rooms."
3rd Boundary: Spring. "Maidenhood's first maturity."	Girl's acquaintance with the forces of nature. Awakening of the inanimate world.	From sickness and confusion to exaltation	The outcast—the French governess banished. For the time being no other outsiders and no shadows.	The hand of the French governess at first with scissors and then "in adjutant pose" resting on her watch.	Opening up of the world in the spring: between "the forms of the passé and the futur antérieur."
4th Boundary: Summer. Entering animated world.	Animation of the surrounding world and its overflow.	Spirit, "serene, even-tempered and friendly." Happiness. Move to Ekaterinburg.	A first apprehension of the presences of other people; a stranger in the train compartment.	The hands of the stranger on the train, who "took things with the gesture of actually giving."	Parts that exceed the whole: unlimited expansion of space and time during the summer months.

7

"The Stranger" in
The Childhood of Luvers

Disruptions in Chronology and the Collision with Other Worlds

Although *The Childhood of Luvers* is by far the best-known prose work of Pasternak's early period, critics (with some notable exceptions) concentrate on the overriding importance of the metonymic series in the earlier parts of the narrative, approaching these as prototypical of Pasternak's early style.[1] However, in his letter to Sergei Bobrov of 16 July, 1918[2] (the only surviving letter of this period that discusses *Luvers* directly), Pasternak, while sending the manuscript, directs Bobrov's attention to the "second and third notebooks" [вторая и третья скрепленные порции (тетради)] (*PSS* 7:348),

---

1. See, for example, the findings of Wiegers (1999): "Only fragments are given in the text, for they stand in metonymic (or causal) relationship to the hidden occurrences. The fragmentary nature is a result of a metonymic shift, which is explained in turn by the ignorance of the heroine and her childish innocence" (233). Similarly Junggren finds no significant distinction between the behavior of Zhenya in Perm and in Ekaterinburg (1991, 489–500). See also Rudova's view that "the style of his early fiction was marked by metonymy and gravitated towards the abstract" (1997, 166). Alongside these views Fateeva introduces "metatropes": intertextual (or rather autotextual) units within the texts of Pasternak that integrate his mythopoetic images (2003, 17–21).

2. A larger question can be posed as to what Pasternak might have meant by this "abstract moment" in a cultural context where, quite apart from his own philosophical training, the notion of abstraction already included a wide range of different representations in philosophy, literature, Russian symbolism, constructivism, abstract art, cubism, and futurism. This chapter will attempt to answer this question.

parts that were collected under the title "The Stranger" [Посторонний].[3] In the same letter, Pasternak characterizes these parts as an attempt to unveil an important shift in the child's developing personality—her confrontation with an "abstract moment"[4] that he chose, as he states, to be represented through "the *idea* of a third person" (*PSS* 7:348).[5] The exact meaning of Pasternak's formulation remains something of a mystery, and yet it exposes the living nerve of Pasternak's youthful interest in human psychology—his belief (supported by his studies in Neo-Kantianism) that the formation of selfhood, or the emergence of a unified self, is inexorably tied to intellectual interests that move the developing personality ever more decisively away from self-preoccupation.

In my earlier work on the novella (Glazov-Corrigan 1991), I argued for the importance of the figure of Lermontov in the overall construction of the story, for in Ekaterinburg, as the weather turns cold and the leaves turn yellow, Zhenya reads Lermontov's long poem *Demon* in the yard, an event that is linked in her mind to several traumatic events that are soon to follow. The importance of the Demon-Lermontov theme has now been accepted by several critics (Faryno 1993; Fateeva 2003, 120), but the larger framework that calls for Demon-Lermontov's presence in the narrative still remains a mystery, especially when Pasternak claimed in the drafts of the novella that his aim in writing was to embrace "truly artistic materialism" [истинный художественный материализм] (*PSS* 3:515). The popularity of the Demon theme in the Silver Age, or the "Lermontov-Vrubel-Blok complex" (Kurganov 2001, 86), equally does not explain Pasternak's adoption of the theme,[6] even though its nuanced and skillful employment presents him as an able and rather crafty practitioner of Symbolism. Most problematic in all of this is the figure of Tsvetkov, whom Zhenya sees while reading *Demon*. Tsvetkov (a person one never meets, a friend of a friend just beyond one's grasp, always appearing at a distance) carries major weight in the novella—he is simultaneously the instrument of "demonic" powers, an innocent sufferer, and a "third person," whom

---

3. For the account of the difficulties associated with the identification of the "three parts" of *The Childhood of Luvers* and the loss of the manuscript of a larger novel, see Barnes (1989, 270–72). See also Fleishman (1975, 119), and finally *PSSCom* 3:542–43.

4. For Wiegers (1999), for example, the abstraction of the novella's fragmentary nature is directly linked to cubism and the development of abstract art, and these are determined by the young age of the heroine. There is no indication in his analysis that the narrative strategy changes as the heroine grows.

5. See Junggren's suggestion that the third, the "other" or the stranger, is, in fact, the female heroine, drawn by the male writer (1991, 489ff).

6. Fateeva suggests that Pasternak's leg injury, received in his youth, made him feel this connection with "the living spirit" of Lermontov [объединяет его с живым духом Лермонтова] (2003, 120). However, as I shall argue in this chapter, there was an earlier and more "living" precursor to this image in Pasternak's work—the composer Shestikrylov in "Ordering a Drama," a figure connected directly to Alexander Scriabin and his effect on the young Boris.

"the commandments have in mind" (*CSP* 178; *PSS* 3:85). The conception that could have led to the construction of such a personality is, again, by no means transparent.

In responding to these riddles, the present chapter argues that the narrative of Zhenya's growth in "The Long Days" (characterized by the heroine's metonymous relationship with objects, natural forces, and other human beings) is altered drastically in "The Stranger." A highly innovative narrative pattern is woven into an earlier, already complex web of relations, and this new pattern reflects the formation of Zhenya's intellectual and moral understanding that coincides with the beginning of the processes that will lead to the catastrophic realignment of Russian history.[7] In this context, Pasternak's employment of ghostly images of a Lermontov-Demon entering reality from the pages of Zhenya's book must be understood not as demonic possession as such (Faryno 1993; Fateeva 2003, 225–45), but as a much more assured and far-ranging development of the role of the composer Shestikrylov, who used to pierce through the children's lives in "Ordering a Drama," albeit with the following significant difference: references to Pushkin (and his "shestikrylyj serafim") and Scriabin in "Ordering a Drama" are replaced in *Luvers* by Lermontov's poetry. The intrusion of the writer and his spirit can also be approached as a continuation of the themes connected to Heinrich Heine's appearance in modern Italy during the spectacular sunset of "The Mark of Apelles," or again to Tolstoy's role "as a lever to set the whole revolving stage in motion" for the disoriented young poet during one very dark night in "Letters from Tula." In contrast to the dramatic settings of these earlier works, Lermontov's entry into the narrative is quiet (and for this reason unnoticed by critics for many decades)—after all, could anything untoward actually happen when a well-protected child reads a book before the onslaught of winter and sees in the far distance a lame man whose name, as she eventually finds out, is Tsvetkov?[8]

---

7. See in *Zhivago:* "In this third year of the war the people have become convinced that the difference between those on the front line and those at the rear will sooner or later vanish. The sea of blood will rise and submerge all who stayed out of the war. The revolution is this flood" [На третий год войны в народе сложилось убеждение, что рано или поздно граница между фронтом и тылом сотрется, море крови подступит к каждому и зальет отсиживающихся и окопавшихся. Революция и есть это наводнение] (*Zhivago* 182; *PSS* 4:180). The image of the unhappy Demon who brings disaster is, therefore, an introduction to what is soon to unveil. Thus, in contrast to Fateeva's brilliant comparison of the narratives of Pasternak's *Luvers* and Nabokov's *Lolita*, I will argue against the image of "deflowering" connected to Tsvetkov-Demon (see 2003, 329–30). It is precisely Pasternak's view in this story that the maturation of the personality can be examined outside of the issues of sex; reading for a child may have a prophetic connotation, pointing to events larger than the life of the girl.

8. There is an ironic parallel here between Zhenya's reading and that of Tatiana Larina, an obedient and quiet girl, initiating a series of most traumatic events, totally unnoticed by her

The call to a child by the intellectual world, its opening into the world of the unknown that will form her future character and destiny, comes in "The Stranger" at a point when Zhenya, during the unsparing progress of autumn, wonders at the facelessness of the people around her (7.1). The intimation that only the birth of thought overcomes a generic human "facelessness"[9] is articulated by Pasternak in a startling instance of "synthetic blending of impressions," a masterful fusion of Symbolism and Realism (7.2–7.4), of his personal biography and his love of Scriabin (7.5), and, of course, his philosophical studies (7.6). In *Luvers* a complex literary intertext redirects the themes of sexual longing, associated with *Demon*'s Tamara (7.3), to what will remain from then on the principal impulse in Pasternak's search for new forms of prose writing: the need to find artistic means commensurate with the theme of an unsparing historical reality both destroying and honing a genuine artistic self that is fused with the wounded organic life of his/her land (7.7–7.8). In addressing the emerging metaphoric or symbolic patterns of the narrative, Chapter 7 expands and re-aligns the themes of Chapter 6. In order to clarify the changing narrative strategies of the story and to elucidate further these altogether new levels or boundaries that Zhenya crosses in her growth, Table I (6.5) is modified and expanded throughout Chapter 7, and a revised Table II is provided at the chapter's conclusion (7.9).

7.1 The boundary of fall:
Erased faces of others and turpentine sun

It is curious that while critics observe Pasternak's *penchant* for "receptive" heroes and his inability to create a strong decisive personality,[10] they tend to overlook Zhenya's horror during her first autumn in Ekaterinburg as she

family. At Tatiana's very young age, as Pushkin notes with mild irony, her father never wondered what "secret volume slept under the pillow of his daughter" [Он, не читая никогда, / Их почитал пустой игрушкой / И не заботился о том, / Какой у дочки тайный том / Дремал до утра под подушкой] (*Evgenii Onegin,* Ch. II, st. XXIX; Pushkin 1994, 6:44). The reorientation from Lermontov to Pushkin is actually suggested in the text, just before the tragedy strikes (somewhat too late to avert it since the mother is already in the theater): "She glanced out in the yard and began to think of Pushkin. She decided to ask the tutor to assign her an essay on Onegin" (*CSP* 168; *PSS* 3:73). Fateeva argues, for example, that Lara in *Zhivago* is actually an abbreviation of Larina (2003, 226).

9. It is significant that in the excised passages, describing Zhenya's life in Ekaterinburg, Pasternak emphasizes the emergence of Zhenya's already recognizable and distinct personality: "She loved that city because it noticed her, Zhenya" [Она полюбила его за то, что он ее, Женю, заметил] (*PSS* 3:545).

10. I refer here to the critical tradition that follows upon Aucouturier's postulation of the "metonymous hero" (1978).

watches how other people blend into each other, lose their faces, and, when unchecked, slide out of themselves into another self without ever noticing their own disintegration.[11] After the triumphant openness of the "outflowing" of nature during the summer months, this realization does not please the child; in fact, it comes as a shock. In the meantime, the "soul" of the child has not only emerged, it has now "budded" (завязывавшаяся душа), and "the elements of everyday existence entered the budding soul" [попадали элементы будничного существования в завязывавшуюся душу] (*CSP* 147; *PSS* 3:50). The first sober experience of this maturation is the growing girl's awareness at the end of the summer that she is severely limited by the presence of other people and the external forces they appear to command. Signs of implicit danger are initially oblique: in Pasternak's words, these new facts and realities, as opposed to the "poetic trifles" of early childhood, enter as "metallic presences" into Zhenya's "budding soul."[12] It is also true that these metallic objects do not necessarily stay unchanged. At the end of "The Long Days," the "metal" at the depth of the soul begins to melt as if in a chemical reaction, transforming itself into "phantasmagoric ideas"—thus providing the first mention of "ideas" in the text and initiating a confusing and disorienting process that eventually "burns" through the fabric of nature.[13]

---

11. On the whole, it has been accepted by Pasternak critics and theoreticians that there exists an unmistakable transformability and transferability between Pasternak's images: "The interrelationship of mutual transferability brings about a neutralization of similarity-contiguity [. . .] which was studied in detail in the works of Roman Jakobson about the prose of Pasternak" (Fateeva 2003, 31). The question of how this affects the process of individuation, however, remains open.

12. This image was particularly disliked by Roman Jakobson, who used it as conclusive proof of Pasternak's disinterest in factual reality and, thus, as a sign of the writer's ineptitude for writing an epic: "An epic attitude to his environment is naturally out of question for a poet who is convinced that, in the world of the prosaic fact, 'the elements of everyday existence fall dully, stupidly and with crippling effect upon the soul and sink to the bottom, real, hardened and cold, like drowsy tin spoons,' and that only the passion of the elect can transform this 'depressingly conscientious truth' into poetry. Only feeling proves to be obviously and absolutely authentic. [. . .] Pasternak bases his poetics on the personal, emotional experience—indeed even approbation—of reality" (1969, 139). Faryno, on the other hand, argues most persuasively about the growing importance of the metal in the story, a theme that starts with the factory called Motovilikha (1993, 12ff.).

13. It is noteworthy that the novella's "programmatic passages," later excised from the final text, followed immediately after this chapter—that is, after the first mention of the "ideas." See Fleishman (1975, 119) and the fuller text of the excised passages in *PSS* 3:514 and in the commentaries of E. B. and E. V. Pasternak in *PSSCom* 3:544–45. Moreover, in the final text, Zhenya's painful awareness of reality after the move to Ekaterinburg is very gradual, but in the drafts this transition is more abrupt, and after the image of the "pewter spoons" one reads: "Ekaterinburg in her memories became a place occupied by the heart in the thoughts of the heart patient" [Екатеринбург занял в ее воспоминаниях место сердца у сердечно больного] (*PSS* 3:544).

This difficult process begins in the late summer (at the very end of Part I of the novella) when Zhenya has to study with a tutor, pointedly named Dikikh (the Wild One), as she prepares for the *lycée*.[14] It is on these occasions, mildly reminiscent of Ida Vysotskaya studying with young Boris Pasternak,[15] that Zhenya finds herself highly irritated at so many potentially nightmarish forces and faceless people controlling her life:[16]

It began while it was still summer. It was announced to her that she would be going to the *lycée*. This was entirely pleasant. But it was announced to her. She had not invited the teacher into the classroom. [. . .] She had not given him the ridiculous surname Dikikh. And was it by her wish that from now on the soldiers always drilled at midday [. . .]? Of course, not everything settled so heavily on her soul. There was much that was pleasant, like her forthcoming start at the *lycée*. *But this too was announced to her. Ceasing to be a poetical trifle, life began to ferment like a stern, black fairytale, because it had become prose and turned into fact. Dull, painful, and somber, as though in an eternal state of sobering up, the elements of everyday existence entered the budding soul. They sank deep into it, real, solidified, and cold, like sleepy pewter spoons. There at the bottom, this pewter began to melt, congealing into lumps, forming into droplets, falling down as obsessive ideas.* (*CSP* 147; emphasis added)

Это началось еще летом. Ей объявили, что она поступит в гимназию. Это было только приятно. Но это объявили ей. Она не звала репетитора в классную [. . .]. Она не позвала его, когда, в сопровождении мамы, он зашел сюда знакомиться "со своей будущей ученицей." Она не назначала ему нелепой фамилии Диких. И разве это она того хотела, чтобы отныне всегда солдаты учились в полдень [. . .]. Не все, разумеется, ложилось на душу так тяжело. Многое, как ее близкое поступление в гимназию, бывало приятно. *Но, как*

---

14. In the excised drafts, the boundary that Dikikh and his very name signify is explicit and is compared to the dreamlike boundary experienced by Zhenya when she waited on the train to enter Asia. The words "his name was reminiscent of that very thing she was expecting from the signpost on the pillar put on the boundary between two countries" [похожей на фамилию того, чего ждала она от столба на границе двух стран]. See commentaries of E. B. Pasternak and E. V. Pasternak in *PSSCom* 3:544.

15. Pasternak started to tutor Ida when both were finishing the gymnasium in the winter of 1908 (E. B. Pasternak 1997, 88).

16. Björling comments, "Intimately connected with the concept of 'other people's words' is the idea of 'other people's ideas,' second-hand initiation into the facts of life when [. . .] she has no part in forging her own destiny" (2010, 131).

*и оно, все это объявлялось ей. Перестав быть поэтическим пустяч-
ком, жизнь забродила крутой черной сказкой постольку, поскольку
стала прозой и превратилась в факт. Тупо, ломотно и тускло, как
бы в состоянии вечного протрезвления, попадали элементы будничного существования в завязывавшуюся душу. Они опускались на ее
дно, реальные, затверделые и холодные, как сонные оловянные ложки.
Там, на дне, это олово начинало плыть, сливаясь в комки, капая
навязчивыми идеями.* (*PSS* 3:50)

Very shortly, "obsessive ideas," all signaling the instability of personal identities around the young girl, are projected onto her mother: at the beginning
of autumn, Mrs. Luvers (pregnant like her maid Aksinya, a fact not really
understood by Zhenya) appears to her daughter to be transforming into her
illiterate maid:[17]

Suddenly something strange occurred to her [. . .]. It occurred to her that
recently there had been a certain elusive similarity between Mama and the
janitor's wife. Something quite indefinable. She stopped. [. . .] Nevertheless, it was Aksinya who set the tone of this compelling comparison. The
association was weighed in her favor. The peasant woman gained nothing
from it, but the mistress lost. (*CSP* 152)

Вдруг ей пришло в голову что-то странное. [. . .] Ей пришло в
голову, что с недавнего времени между мамой и дворничихой заве-
лось какое-то неуследимое сходство. В чем-то совсем неуловимом.
Она остановилась. [. . .] А между тем именно Аксинья задавала
тон этому навязывавшемуся сравнению. Она брала перевес в этом
сближенье. От него не выигрывала баба, а проигрывала барыня.
(*PSS* 3:56)

---

17. In late autumn, just before the fateful snowstorm, Zhenya asks her mother to repeat
certain phrases (significantly not only about the loss of face, but of the whole head, as in the
case of St. John the Baptist). The girl is almost certain that her mother will start speaking like an
uneducated Aksinya, a thought piercing to her and bewildering for Mrs. Luvers: "She repeated
it, puzzled. She did not say 'Babtist'. That was how Aksinya said it. [. . .] But Mama just stood
there. She could not believe her ears. She looked at it with eyes wide open. This sudden caprice
had nonplussed her. The question sounded like some mockery; yet her daughter had tears
in her eyes." [Мать повторила, недоумевая. Она не сказала: "Предтеича". Так говорила
Аксинья. [. . .] А мать все стояла. Она ушам не верила. Она глядела на нее широко
раскрытыми глазами. Эта выходка поставила ее втупик. Вопрос походил на издевку;
между тем в глазах у дочки стояли слезы] (*CSP* 164; *PSS* 3:70).

In Zhenya's responses, Pasternak's knowledge of philosophy is central to the depiction of the girl's discomfort. Zhenya, in fact, is pondering the essential dilemma of Post-Kantianism (and Paul Natorp's work in psychology); the girl searches for the tangible outlines of selfhood or the basis of a distinct unified personality.[18] Unable to find firm individual outlines, Zhenya at the beginning of autumn is haunted by the fear of obliteration of all personal identities,[19] an experience particularly painful in the case of Seryozha's friendship with his classmates, the Akhmedyanovs, whose father just happens to trade in iron.[20]

As Zhenya watches, her brother Seryozha's features become defaced[21] just as the first cold begins to strip the lusciousness of nature:

The most true to type fourth-formers in the fourth form were the brothers Akhmedyanovs [. . .]. Seryozha made friends with them in August. By the end of September the boy had lost all personality [lit. had no face]. (*CSP* 155)

Самыми заправскими четвероклассниками в четвертом классе были братья Ахмедьяновы. [. . .] Сережа сдружился с ними в августе. К концу сентября у мальчика не стало лица. (*PSS* 3:59)

In other words, what critics see as a fundamental principle of Pasternak's world—its parallel contiguous or metonymous series that both presuppose and facilitate the absorption of the hero into his/her surrounding world—is

---

18. In his philosophical diaries, while preparing to travel to Marburg, Pasternak muses at Natorp's view that without a critical intellectual self-examination, without an *episteme*, there is no foundation for the unified personality, no real "I" or selfhood: "Even then the idea is not unconditional and presupposes the thinking of the idea and presupposes [. . .] one's own consciousness and "I" as a direction of this self-consciousness" [Но и тогда идея—не безусловна и предполагает мышление идеи и предполагает, поскольку он мыслим,—свою сознанность и я как направление этой сознанности] (*Lehrjahre* I:275 ff.).

19. See Pasternak's notations on Natorp's work about the paradox that exists between monological self-consciousness and the understanding of the personality of the other (*Lehrjahre* I:275 ff).

20. A mechanical, rather than natural, force directs the image of the Akhmedyanovs: "The Akhmedyanovs' father traded in iron. [. . .] The children were a splendid success insofar as they followed the prescribed pattern, and they retained the speed and sweep of their father's will, noisy and destructive as a pair of flywheels set whirling and left to spin by inertia" [Отец Ахмедьяновых торговал железом. [. . .] Дети удались на славу, то есть пошли во взятый образчик, и шибкий размах отцовой воли остался в них, шумный и крушительный, как в паре закруженных и отданных на милость инерции маховиков] (*CSP* 156; *PSS* 3:59).

21. See here the incisive observation of Fateeva, albeit appearing in a somewhat different context: "The conflict of the 'living' and 'death-bearing,' formulated by Bely and Briusov, [. . .] became most significant for Pasternak" (Fateeva 2003, 194).

experienced by Zhenya during her autumn in Ekaterinburg as a nightmarish pattern, at first only troubling, but eventually terrifying. This pattern also signals great danger to the identity and power of the "soul," which lives at this point only instinctively, answering the pulse of seasons. Thus, as the children's "budding" selves proceed to blend not only with the world outside, but also with other human beings, the awareness of others enters into the girl's consciousness as an increasingly threatening force, disarming and disabling.[22] Moreover, these "other" presences, with all their capacity for obliteration, do not preserve their own identities—they too blend and lose their singularity, presenting the typical or generic, rather than personal, face.[23]

22. The presence of others in Pasternak is always an invitation into battle, which will end in a protagonist's eventual (and often only apparent) defeat (but not after a lifetime of effort and even some accomplishment in the process). A sense of danger, for example, overwhelms both Heine in "The Mark of Apelles"—"Signora Camilla, you would not have listened to half my words if we had not bumped into each other in such a dangerous place" (*CSP* 110)—and the distraught poet of "Letters from Tula" who exclaims to his beloved, "Oh, my dear, they are all strangers around me" (*CSP* 120). Even the adoration of Scriabin in *Safe Conduct* is described as a profoundly devastating, "ravaging" experience, from which young Pasternak is protected only by love: "This adoration attacked me more cruelly and undisguisedly than any fever. [. . .] [A]nd the fiercer it was, the more surely it protected me from the ravaging effect of his indescribable music" [Обожанье это бьет меня жесточе и неприкрашеннее лихорадки. [. . .] Только оно, и чем оно горячее, тем больше ограждает меня от опустошений, производимых его непередаваемой музыкой] (*CSP* 23; *PSS* 3:150). This theme is articulated most powerfully, perhaps, in Pasternak's well-known poem "Mature Hunter" [Рослый стрелок], where the outflow of the poet's soul discloses a presence of a hunter, who will eventually shoot the speaker—the question is not that of finding safety, but rather of gaining time for self-realization in the permitted duration of a lifetime:

Mature archer, careful hunter
The ghost with a rifle at the boundaries of the soul's overflow
Do not collect me as a hundredth victim to make a clean hundred . . .

Рослый стрелок, осторожный охотник,
Призрак с ружьем на разливе души! Не добирай меня сотым до сотни . . .
(*PSS* 1:221)

23. The faces of the Akhmedyanovs, for example, are slowly erased by cold: "snubbed nose self-assurance that peeled away in frost" [они состояли из . . . шелушившейся в морозы, краснощекой и курносой самоуверенности] (*CSP* 156; *PSS* 3:59). This view of faces and the forces that erase their personhood will stay with Pasternak throughout his career and only deepen with lifelong exposure to the impersonal ideology of the Revolution. Lara, for example, speaks of Strelnikov's face and her suspicion that it has been marked by depersonalization, which signifies the approach of death: "It was as if something abstract had crept into his face and made it colorless. As if a living human person had become an embodiment of a principle, the image of an idea. My heart sank when I noticed it. [. . .] It seemed to me that he was a marked man and this was the seal of his doom" [Точно что-то отвлеченное вошло в этот облик и обесцветило его. Живое человеческое лицо стало олицетворением, принципом, изображением идеи. У меня сердце сжалось при этом наблюдении. [. . .] Мне показалось, что он отмеченный, и что это перст обречения] (*Zhivago* 401–2; *PSS* 4:399).

The emphasis on the deeper awareness of others and their will, initially so confusing to a child, echoes Hermann Cohen's insistence on the role of the *other* in the ethical development of the individual [*Der Anderer, der Alter Ego*] (*Ethik* 201).[24] Cohen's belief that the external freedom of the individual "is broken down in relation to an *other* person" (Gibbs 2005, 206) is transformed in Pasternak's rendering into a new boundary with the "unknown,"[25] which appears in this text as initially indeterminate and phantasmagoric.[26] At the beginning of autumn, however, the awareness of other individuals and their wills stimulates not so much the expansion of perception as a confused intellectual growth while the same synthetic blending that characterized the previous themes of the story is now attached to the effect of ideas threatening the identity of the growing self.

The experience is further deepened by the endangered power of the sun,[27] even though the intimation of the approaching bloody battle does not break the bounds of the realistic narrative; Pasternak's "artistic materialism"[28] is maintained as he presents an unusual but still rather faithful rendition of the reddening sunsets of the last summer days. Just as Pasternak's young heroine finds herself restricted in her freedom, the sun holds to the walls of the house with what seems to be a crimson effort of will:

24. See here Fleishman's summary of Cohen's view of "the other" (*Lehrjahre* I:97).

25. Fateeva points out the long-term importance of this theme, which she connects with the image of Adam's rib, that is, a boundary. Many years later, for example, Pasternak in the poem "Eve" speaks of Eve's creation as a line from the *other* cycle [Ты создана как бы вчерне, / Как строчка из другого цикла] (Fateeva 2003, 340).

26. Transitions and boundaries in *Luvers* seem to receive the epithets of wildness, phantasmagoria, delirium, named and unnamed reality, and the call of the kindred, and it is not always clear at what side of the boundary these epithets fall. The image of Motovilikha, which starts this pattern, is described as breaking through the delirium of reality that has a name—the parents' card game—and then appearing as a mixture of fantastic, kindred, and frightening, and the same images were excised from the text that follows upon the passage of the "pewter spoons" at the depth of the soul, that is, the passage that speaks of Zhenya's first awareness of the external and controlling reality of others: "And the force, capable of foregrounding this mute fever, this hidden fairy tale and delirium, was against the same force: the force of daily prose; the force of repressive, fantastic ache of existence" [А силой, способной выделить этот особенный глухой жар, эту скрытую сказочность и бред, оказалась все та же сила: сила прозы: сила гнетущей, фантастической тоски существования] (*PSSCom* 3:544).

27. Fateeva comments on the role of the colors associated with the sunset (закатное солнце) in Pasternak's poetry of this period: "Turning retrospectively to the description of this historical process in his poetry, we note the predominance of 'bloody-maroon' [кроваво-кумачевый] 'frozen' color, symbolizing the spread of ice and the 'breaking apart' of the time into 'pieces'" (2003, 288). See also Fateeva's observation that the image of the young girl appears in both Pasternak and Nabokov in the rays of the sun "between home and garden" [между солнцем и садом] (2003, 342).

28. Pasternak is careful not to undermine the realistic account of the child's impressions. See his definition of the artistic style at which he aims as "artistic materialism" [художественный материализм] in the excised pages of the novella (*PSS* 3:515).

It was not she who invited the teacher into the classroom where sunlight hues stuck so firmly to the walls with their glue paint wash that only by drawing blood was the evening able to rip away the clinging daylight. (*CSP* 147)

Она не звала репетитора в классную, где солнечные колера так плотно прилипали к выкрашенным клеевою краской стенам, что вечеру только с кровью удавалось отодрать пристававший день. (*PSS* 4:51)

This new sense of danger and conflict is then shared with the season, and the suggestion of a battle with the sun indicates for readers familiar with the opening scene of "The Mark of Apelles" that a phantasmagoria of powerful presences is about to begin[29]—a pattern foregrounded to some degree by the title of the story's second part, "The Stranger" [Посторонний].[30]

The theme of others entering into the family home gains gravity almost imperceptibly. At first, at the very end of "The Long Days," the Belgians, strangers from afar, replacing the somewhat threatening "wave-like" stranger on the train, appear in the house together with the first change of weather. The visitors strike the family as both eccentric and almost banal until their appearance is placed in the emerging context of the continuing obliteration of personal characteristics. The Belgians, who begin visiting the Luvers family at the end of August, are indistinguishable from each other, with the mild exception of one—Negaraat, a figure closely associated with rain.[31] The group on the whole is so washed clean that their faces remind the children of soap, an image that covertly signals defacement or the emergence of forces that, while being defaced themselves, may eventually whitewash and obliterate their interlocutors:[32]

---

29. The August–September transition operates, therefore, as an important textual marker, appearing first in "The Mark of Apelles" where, as Barnes observes, the importance of the season's change is emphasized by the intentional chronological error: "On one of those September evenings [. . .] why I remember the exact day perfectly well, it was the evening of August 23" (*CSP* 101; *PSS* 3:6). See here Barnes (1989, 194).

30. For the formation of the opposition kindred vs. alien [формирование системы противопоставлений 'свой—чужой'] as the central "metatropos" of the function of the lyrical subject, see Chapter 2 of Fateeva (2003, 110–219).

31. See, for example: "he always chose nasty, rainy weather" [Иногда он приходил один, ненароком, в будни, выбрав какое-нибудь нехорошее, дождливое время] (*CSP* 147; *PSS* 3:50–51). Fateeva observes, following Frank: "In Pasternak water [. . .] is signified as two hypostases: as 'living water' and as 'dead water'—snow and ice. Snow indicates the freezing of life, water—its bloom" (Fateeva 2003, 127; Frank 1962, 245ff.).

32. Björling proposes a somewhat different reading: "The general tenor of the similes is of something new, fresh and satisfying to the needs of children [. . .]. The narrator has threaded

Belgians often began to appear at the house for tea. That was what they
were called. That was what father called them. "Today the Belgians would
be here," he would say. There were four of them. The clean-shaven one came
only seldom and was not talkative. Sometimes he would pay a chance visit
on a weekday, and he always chose nasty, rainy weather. The other three
were inseparable. Their faces resembled cakes of fresh soap, unstarted,
straight from the wrapper, fragrant and cold. One of them had a beard,
thick and fluffy, and downy chestnut hair. (*CSP* 147–48)

У них часто стали бывать за чаем бельгийцы. Так они назывались.
Так называл их отец, говоря: сегодня будут бельгийцы. Их было чет-
веро. Безусый бывал редко и был неразговорчив. Иногда он приходил один, ненароком, в будни, выбрав какое-нибудь нехорошее,
дождливое время. Прочие трое были неразлучны. Лица их были
похожи на куски свежего мыла, непочатого, из обертки, душистые
и холодные. У одного была борода, густая и пушистая и пушистые
каштановые волосы. (*PSS* 4:52)

Whether or not the four guests are meant to remind readers of the four
remaining months of the year, with September-Negaraat already on the way
out and the fourth Belgian, denoting December, ritualistically equipped with
a beard (and thus explaining an earlier reference to reality appearing as a stark
black fairy tale[33]); and whether or not the inner group of the three carries a
deeper echo of the three visitors to Sarah and Abraham, suggesting an unexpected pregnancy that on this winter occasion will end in miscarriage—all
this ultimately amounts in the text only to a fleeting sensation, along with
many other *phantasmagoriae* of the fall.

Within any reading, however, the visitors remain linked to running or
pouring cold water, to fresh "outdoor" water brought inside the house:

Everyone in the house liked them. They talked like spilling water on the
tablecloth—noisily, freshly, and all at once, away to one side where no one

these sensations together by means of the comparison of faces to new pieces of soap, and speech
to spilled water" (2010, 137).

33. Faryno tends to see in the Belgians the Trinity from the Old Testament and the fact
of their learning Russian as the transformation of the immediate reality into the country of
the miraculous (1993, 55). The textual opposition between a poetic trifle and a stark fairy tale
is once again noteworthy in this context: "Ceasing to be a poetical trifle, life began to ferment
like a stern, black fairytale, because it had become prose and turned into fact" [Перестав быть
поэтическим пустячком, жизнь забродила крутой черной сказкой постольку, поскольку стала прозой и превратилась в факт] (*CSP* 147; *PSS* 3:50). For an opposing view of the
Belgians, see Björling (2010, 137).

expected, and their jokes and stories, which were always understood by the children, always thirst-quenching and clean, left trails behind, which took a long time to dry out. (*CSP* 148)

В доме все их любили. Они говорили, будто проливали воду на скатерть: шумно, свежо и сразу, куда-то вбок, куда никто не ждал, с долго досыхавшими следами от своих шуток и анекдотов, всегда понятных детям, всегда утолявших жажду и чистых. (*PSS* 4:52)

The emphasis on washing out, coming from the outside—whether it is water pouring onto the tablecloth or the visitors' clean-shaven, washed-out faces—is one of *Luvers*'s signature themes of autumn.[34] In this construction one approaches the crux, even the cause, of the absence of events or actions in Part I of the novella.[35] In any interactions in the text up to this point, the recipient of the others' actions, presences, or addresses cannot act as an independent agent. And in the months of autumn when the outlines of the personality become more distinct, all personal features are explicitly portrayed as overpowered and subjectless, reflecting the quality of the season that itself is unable to resist the onslaught of the cold.

The threat of depersonalization is thus constructed with great care. "The Stranger" opens with a depiction of Zhenya in the yard—possibly wrapped in a shawl because of the cold weather, yet it is altogether unclear whether it is Zhenya or a little Tatar girl or even a small boy, Kolka, who walks up and down in the yard:

The little girl's head and body were wrapped in a thick woolen shawl, which reached down to her knees, and she strutted up and down the yard like a small hen. Zhenya wanted to go up and talk to the little Tatar girl. At that moment the two sides of a small window flew open with a bang. "Kolka" called Aksinya. Looking like a peasant's bundle with felt boots hastily stuck into the bottom, the child toddled quickly to the janitor's lodge. (*CSP* 149)

---

34. As Frank observes, rain (and, by extension, autumn) signifies in Pasternak "the operation of mysterious, unearthly force upon nature" (1962, 240). Equally suggestive is Fateeva's observation that the rain is a "demonic" "first-born of creation" [первенец творенья] (2003, 331).

35. It is in this context that Aucouturier observes that the characterization of Zhenya is that of an emphatically "generic" hero: "However, precisely because these are generic and not individual qualities which mark her for the incarnation of the Pasternakian concept of the personality, one cannot consider her as the first metonymous hero of the poet" (Aucouturier 1978, 45). However, one of the goals of such a narrative is to indicate the boundary where individualization becomes possible. This boundary has not as yet been reached. See also Glazov-Corrigan (1991).

Девочка была с головой увязана в толстый шерстяной платок, доходивший ей до коленок, и курочкой похаживала по двору. Жене хотелось подойти к татарочке и заговорить с ней. В это время стукнули створки разлетевшегося оконца. "Колька,"—кликнула Аксинья. Ребенок, походивший на крестьянский узел с наспех воткнутыми валенками, быстро просеменил в дворницкую. (*PSS* 4:54)

This description at the outset of Part II, therefore, introduces a motif that dominates a significant layer in "The Stranger": the disappearance of the face in a material world, alongside other disappearing faces. Not only do Mr. Luvers, Seryozha, and the visiting Belgians possess no personal features, but every personal relationship experiences self-erasure, a process reinforced by the fact that Mr. Luvers's incurable sickness is announced at a point where the text is saturated with impersonal pronouns, whose antecedents are intentionally vague (the end of Chapter III and the beginning of Chapter IV in Part II). Thus, Pasternak's intimation of Luvers's sickness appears in the narrative at a break between chapters and paragraphs—a technique that foregrounds the facelessness and anonymity of personal pronouns with their obscure references:

By the end of September the boy lost all personality. [. . .]

Luvers did not try to hinder his son's friendship. He saw no change in him, and even if he did, he ascribed it to the effect of adolescence. Besides his head was filled with other cares. Sometime ago he had begun to suspect that he was ill and that his illness was incurable.

IV

She was not sorry for him, though everyone around could only say how really awkward and incredibly annoying it was. Negaraat was too complicated even for their parents, and all that the parents felt about others also dimly conveyed itself to the children, like spoiled household pets. (*CSP* 153–54)

К концу сентября у мальчика не стало лица. [. . .]

Люверс не препятствовал дружбе сына. Он не видел перемены в нем, а если что и замечал, то приписывал это действию переходного возраста. К тому же голова у него была занята другими заботами. С некоторых пор он стал догадываться, что болен и что его болезнь неизлечима.

IV.

Ей было жаль не его, хотя все вокруг только и говорили, что как это в самом деле до невероятности некстати и досадно. Негарат был слишком мудрен и для родителей, а все, что чувствовалось родителями в отношении чужих, смутно передавалось и детям, как домашним избалованным животным. (*PSS* 3:59–60)

A sensation of pity is thus evoked by a series of obliterated agents: Mr. Luvers's incurable sickness (again experienced during August and September), Seryozha's loss of face, followed by Zhenya's compassion for another, "he" this time—Negaraat, who is conscripted to war and will leave Ekaterinburg (just as September draws to a close).

Even more startling in this regard is Zhenya's attempt to understand Negaraat's predicament, an incident narrated again as an act of depersonalization. As she grasps the objective facts of military conscription, the narrative, quite emphatically—in a telling and difficult passage—presents Zhenya's very act of comprehending others as a demystification and a stripping of color from the subjects/objects of her inquiry. In understanding the fate of the conscripts, Zhenya depersonalizes not only Negaraat, but all the soldiers she sees in Ekaterinburg, just as—paradoxically—she shares in and "animates" [одушевила] their state. The steps of comprehension take place as follows: having understood the conscripts' experience, she inhabits the soldiers' circumstances and, in the process, erases the boundary that has kept them at bay in their initially colorful and mysterious aloofness.

> The man explained everything so clearly to the girl. Nobody had explained things like that before. The veil of soullessness, an amazing veil of obviousness, was removed from the picture of white tents; companies of men faded and became a collection of individuals in soldier's dress, and she began to pity them at the very moment when they were animated and elevated, brought close and drained of color by their newly acquired significance. (*CSP* 157)

> Так хорошо разъяснил девочке все этот человек. Так не растолковывал ей еще никто. Налет бездушья, потрясающий налет наглядности сошел с картины белых палаток; роты потускнели и стали собранием отдельных людей в солдатском платье, которых стало жалко в ту самую минуту, как введенный в них смысл одушевил их, возвысил, сделал близкими и обесцветил. (*PSS* 3:61)

The process of the soul's expansion toward the other, represented as an act of understanding, is portrayed emphatically as a loss of color [налет бездушья

[. . .] сошел [. . .] в ту самую минуту, как введенный в них смысл оду-
шевил их [. . .] и обесцветил] (*PSS* 3:61).

The textual paradox can be presented as follows: the expansion of self that
animates the inanimate world depersonalizes the other selves. And to rein-
force this unconditional process of defacement set against the background of
the fall, Zhenya's friendship with Liza Defendova (a relationship instinctual
and, because of this, generic) is presented explicitly as a self-extinction moved
by the instinct of the person in love, a process Pasternak is careful to distinguish from any deeper personal influence:

> She fell in love with her; that is, she played the passive role in their relation-
> ship, became its pressure gauge, watchful and excitedly anxious [. . .]. Her
> feeling was as random in its choice of an object as its origins were dictated
> by the powerful demands of instinct, which knows no self-love and can
> only suffer and consume itself in honor of some fetish as it experiences
> feelings for the first time.
>
> Neither Zhenya, nor Liza had the slightest influence on the other, and
> they met and parted—Zhenya as Zhenya, Liza as Liza—the one with deep
> feelings, the other without any. (*CSP* 155)

> Она влюбилась в Дефендову, то есть стала страдательным лицом в
> отношениях, их манометром, бдительным и разгоряченно-тревож-
> ным. [. . .] Ее чувство было настолько же случайно в выборе пред-
> мета, насколько в своем источнике отвечало властной потребности
> инстинкта, который не знает самолюбия и только и умеет, что стра-
> дать и жечь себя во славу фетиша, пока он чувствует впервые.
>
> Ни Женя, ни Лиза ничем решительно друг на друга не влияли,
> и Женя Женей, Лиза Лизой, они встречались и расставались, та—с
> сильным чувством, эта—безо всякого. (3:59)

In Hermann Cohen's view of the other, "[n]o one can be regarded as expanded
by the other. Both must remain standing isolated" (*Ethik* 212–13; 10a–b; trans.
Gibbs 2005, 206–7). In this context, it is clear that Pasternak's contiguous
series of the narrative organization of the fall presents a dilemma for a personality that knows as yet nothing of individualization. In the fall, the individuals that Zhenya meets display patterns of personal relationships that go in the
opposite direction from Cohen's thought; they do not present their personalities as "isolated," but show instead depersonalized faceless subjects merging into each other or consuming themselves, all overtaken at the same time
by the unconditional power of leaden facts. Thus, as the text approaches the

limits of the power of the animated soul, reinforced by the loss of fertility and warmth in nature, it is altogether unclear whether the self-effacing process can ever be arrested or reversed.

7.2 Metaphoric narrative and spirits meeting at the threshold:
Reading Lermontov's Demon *at sunset*

It is clear, nonetheless, that this erasure of human identities, often viewed as a leading characteristic of Pasternak's prose, cannot dominate the entire length of the novella. The landscape of the fall as a psycho-physical reality is explicitly portrayed as limited in time[36]—with the full realization on the part of the reader that an important boundary has been reached. Thus, as the narrative approaches the conflict in human relationships and human destinies, contiguous parallel series reach an impasse. For this reason, the opening passages of "The Stranger," directly following upon the image of the featureless child, "wrapped in thick woolen shawl," point to the threshold of the Luvers's house and to mysterious presences facing each other, the most recognizable of which is "the house spirit" that seems to the child eternally safe and guarded by the house furniture.[37] In the very next paragraph of the opening of "The Stranger," however, Pasternak informs his readers of an approach of a very different spirit in opposition to the house guardian—"this time it was Lermontov" (*PSS* 3:53). The passage, like all the previous descriptions of the thresholds and boundaries, is intentionally confusing, presenting an intermingling of views and perspectival angles, but this time, perhaps, the text is most disorienting, and it is altogether unclear which spirit belongs indoors and which comes "out of doors," and how precisely Lermontov, taken out of doors, is connected to this chaotic narrative.

> The rooms inside seized one at the doorstep with their peculiar semi-gloom and chill, and with that peculiar, always unexpected peculiarity of furniture that has taken up an allotted position once and for all and remained there.

---

36. About the importance of seasons for the themes of the child's maturation in Pasternak, see Glazov-Corrigan (1991) and Fateeva (2003, 118).

37. This confusing description is by no means accidental. There is a clear parallel between the house spirit supervising the "unexpected peculiarity" of the house furniture and the life of the children in "Ordering a Drama" (1910) that takes place inside "the dear, perhaps, dearest of *all,* inanimate world" [дорогой, может быть, самый дорогой неодушевленный мир] (*MG* 28; *PSS* 3:461).

[. . .] One could not foretell the future, but it could be seen entering the house from outside. Here its scheme is already in evidence—a distribution to which it would be subject despite its recalcitrance in all else. *And there was no dream induced by the moving outdoor air that could not be shaken off quickly by the fatal and alert spirit of the house, which struck one of a sudden from the threshold of the hall.*

This time it was Lermontov. (CSP 149–50; emphasis added)

Они разом, с порога прохватывали особым полумраком и прохладой, особой, всегда неожиданной знакомостью, с какою мебель, заняв раз-на-всегда предписанные места, на них оставалась. [. . .] Будущего нельзя предсказать. Но его можно увидеть, войдя с воли в дом. Здесь на-лицо уже его план, то размещенье, которому, непокорное во всем прочем, оно подчинится. *И не было такого сна, навеянного движеньем воздуха на улице, которого бы живо не стряхнул бодрый и роковой дух дома, ударявший вдруг, с порога прихожей. На этот раз это был Лермонтов.* (PSS 3:53)

The text introduces—with a jolt—the world of spirit, the in-door and out-of-door confrontation, which points to an altogether new layer of textual organization, a layer described by Pasternak to Bobrov as the story's most significant "abstract moment," "taking shape in consciousness" to be "reflected in the character of the personality" (PSS 5:542). This transition is introduced by Pasternak as a series of startling metaphoric images that undermine the established patterns of the contiguous relationships, and, what is equally important, appear in the narrative when the sphere of the "spirit" begins to expand (or even subsume) the power of the soul.

Reminiscent of the indoor-outdoor layering of "Ordering a Drama" with the composer Shestikrylov "eternally" sewing together the layers of the children's world,[38] the text of *Luvers* places a carefully concealed emphasis on the long-term effects of the introspective quietness of reading.[39] This seemingly imperceptible moment of inner expansion also reflects Pasternak's belief, reinforced by his study of psychology with Natorp, that the development of

---

38. Ljunggren is one of the few who observes the correlation between the youthful "Ordering a Drama" and "The Stranger" (1984, 101–2).

39. The notion that the real personal face emerges only in response to the intellectual or artistic tradition is emphasized in *Safe Conduct* when Pasternak speaks of his own adolescent love for Scriabin and muses on the contrast between face and facelessness: "To personality they preferred nonentity, afraid of the sacrifices tradition demands from childhood" [Оно лицу предпочло безличье, испугавшись жертв, которых традиция требует от детства] (CSP 24; PSS 3:151).

the individual is singly dependent on ideas and values he or she is about to adopt (*Lehrjahre* I:274–75).[40] Thus, having forgotten the featureless Tatar girl, Zhenya "creases up the book with its binding folded inward," entering yet another a new space, characterized by a careful synthetic blending of multiple contradictory impressions.[41] Too lazy to read Lermontov's *Demon,* she observes nonetheless how the river Terek, "springing like a lioness with shaggy mane on the back" (*CSP* 150; *PSS* 3:53),[42] is accompanied by (or accompanies) "the *devilish,* blustering bark of the general's little hairless dogs" [клубящийся дьявольский лай голеньких генеральских собачек] in the yard next door (*CSP* 150; *PSS* 3:53; emphasis added). This new instance of the blending of impressions is very carefully nuanced: the child, struck by an image in the book, gazes at the soldier and the dogs next door while the dogs' "devilish, blustering bark" signals something more than an autumn day.[43] Two realities begin to co-exist and merge in such a manner that "the golden clouds from the southern lands afar" hardly have time to accompany the river Terek "northward,"[44] but manage to bring with them an unexpected guest, another "he" (unless the pronoun refers to the river Terek, which has simultaneously turned into water in the bucket carried by the soldier, Prokhor, in the general's yard next door). Within this syntactical confusion, which suggests the presence of a new indefinable male figure who has traveled with the clouds and now upsets the dogs, there is also a new complex interaction of two sets of hands confronting each other, one set washing out the colors and the other holding up the book and changing everyday reality.

The soldier Prokhor's hands (or, perhaps, syntactically even the hands of the traveling clouds) clean, wash, and whitewash, armed with a bucket of water and bast scrubber, assisted by the "turpentine" sun that bleaches Prokhor's

---

40. Fateeva, in an altogether different context, comments on "the girl with a book" as a step toward maturity [растение-растление] (2003, 329).

41. See Pasternak's student notes developing his view that the life of self-identical and unified consciousness consists of a constantly renewed series of changing impressions: "A knot of impressions. Unity and self-identity of selfhood—abstract equivalency of changing contents, does not have absolute character" [Пучок пр<е>дст<а>влений. [Единство и] Тождество личности подрывают его абсолютный характер] (*Lehrjahre* I:174). Hume, as Pasternak is careful to point out in the same passage, did not accept the unity and self-identity of consciousness.

42. This passage, a citation from Lermontov's *Demon,* happens to be Lermontov's famous error, as any zoologist would be happy to point out. Only lions, not lionesses, have manes. Pasternak obviously uses this passage to point to a longevity and reality of a fictional construction.

43. Fateeva points here to Kurganov's treatment of the theme of the Demon and the "Lermontov-Vrubel-Blok complex" in the literature of Silver Age (Kurganov 2001, 86; Fateeva 2003, 329).

44. On the unstable identity of Lermontov, Demon, Terek, the house, and the garden, see Fateeva (2003, 329).

uniform. As the images of washing, whitewashing and bleaching echo the processes Zhenya confronts everywhere during the fall, her own hands crease the poems of Lermontov, exposing its contents to the adjacent world:

> This time it was Lermontov. *Zhenya creased up the book with its binding inward.* Had Seryozha done it indoors, she herself would have been up in arms about this "disgraceful habit." Outside it was quite another matter. [. . .]
>
> Meanwhile the river Terek, "springing like a lioness with shaggy mane on the back," continued to roar [. . .]. She was too lazy to follow the book, and "golden clouds from the southern lands afar" had hardly had time to "accompany the Terek northward" when there they were to meet *him*[45] at the general kitchen's doorstep holding a bucket and *a bast scrubber in [their / Prokhor's?] hands.*
>
> The batman set down the bucket, bent over, and after taking apart the freezer, proceeded to wash it. The August sunlight burst through the tree foliage and came to rest on the soldier's hindquarters. It settled, red, in the faded clothes of his uniform and greedily impregnated it, like turpentine. (*CSP* 150; trans. altered; emphasis added)

> На этот раз это был Лермонтов. Женя мяла книжку, сложив ее переплетом внутрь. В комнатах она, сделай это Сережа, сама бы восстала на 'безобразную привычку.' Другое дело—на дворе. [. . .]
>
> Между тем, Терек, прыгая как львица, с косматой гривой на спине, продолжал реветь[. . .]. Справиться с книгой было лень, и золотые облака, из южных стран, издалека, едва успев проводить его на север, уже встречали у порога генеральской кухни *с ведром и мочалкой в руке.*
>
> Денщик поставил ведро, нагнулся и, разобрав мороженицу, принялся ее мыть. Августовское солнце, прорвав древесную листву, засело в крестце у солдата. Оно внедрилось, красное, в жухлое мундирное сукно и как скипидаром жадно его собой пропитало. (*PSS* 3:53–54)

A few minutes later, the young heroine meets a new man, perhaps the very male presence, identified by the personal pronoun "he" that was delivered into

---

45. The pronoun in question without an antecedent points to yet another unaccounted presence.

the story by "the golden clouds from southern lands afar."[46] One of the stranger's textual names is Tsvetkov (color and flower),[47] and even in this naming he already sends a clear challenge to the general loss of color and natural growth in Ekaterinburg—a rebellion against more than the northern weather of the fall.

The presence of Tsvetkov, the stranger, who comes from across the boundary (по-сторонний), suggests a major thematic shift: Zhenya meets this lame man as she reads a specific Lermontov text that will have a bizarre link to the house spirit of the Luvers family, ably protected until now, at least in the eyes of the little girl, by the house furniture. The Demon of Lermontov's poem— "the sad demon, the exiled spirit" [печальный демон, дух изгнанья]—was invisible to mere mortals, but very much active in the unhappy destinies of their households. And as Zhenya hears the roar of the Terek River intermingling with the bark of the dogs next door, Pasternak initiates a whole chain of remarkable passages (within which the symbolic presences, characteristically muffled, are nonetheless worthy of a virtuoso Symbolist writer, and certainly not expected from an author who has been regarded primarily as a virtuoso of the metonymic series). As the imaginative and real worlds of the girl begin to superimpose and clash, she observes at first only a commonality of rhythm and visual echoes in these separate spheres, just as Pasternak warns in *Safe Conduct*: "And when, after taking it, a person entered with gigantic strides into a gigantic reality, both his strides and the world round him were accounted ordinary" [И когда по ее приеме человек гигантскими шагами вступал в гигантскую действительность, поступь и обстановка считались обычными] (*CSP* 28–29; *PSS* 3:156).

How then do Lermontov and his *Demon* appear in this barely perceptible manner in the world of Zhenya Luvers? Just as Zhenya, while reading the book, begins to occupy herself with the animal roar of the river Terek and finds herself distracted by the similarly noisy "devilish, blustering bark of the general's little hairless dogs" (*CSP* 150; *PSS* 3:53), Pasternak carefully unveils

---

46. See here Faryno's nuanced treatment of the scene, suggesting Zhenya eventually sees the Demon (1993, 30ff.).

47. Here, one may also solve the enigma of "The Three Names," the title considered by Pasternak for these parts of the narrative: the lame Tsvekov, who enters Zhenya's life from the cautiously lit stage of a street hidden behind the Luvers's house, is not alone. He travels with Lermontov, and very possibly with Lermontov's Demon—and in a manner not dissimilar from Pasternak's Henrich Heine, who appeared in modern Italy during the spectacular sunset of "The Mark of Apelles," or from Tolstoy acting "as a lever to set the whole revolving stage in motion" for the disoriented young poet during one very dark night in "Letters from Tula." Lermontov's complex entry is enacted in the context of one of the most elaborate settings of Pasternak's early prose, constructed as carefully as Pisa's sunset or the dance of compass needles in Tula.

the uncanny events underscored by the sun's rays spreading from Lermontov's *Demon* to Zhenya's actual world. With open book in hand, Zhenya travels around the garden and finds a rarely visited corner between "the janitor's
lodge and the coach house," "overgrown with short curly grass, which in the
afternoon emitted the sort of bitter medicinal smell that hangs around hospital in hot weather" (*CSP* 150; *PSS* 3:54).[48] Inundated by piercing hypnotic
smells, she finds the woodpile, leaves the book, slides down to an uncomfort-
able but interesting perch "on the middle rung," and then discovers, "open-
mouthed and entranced," an entry—if not onto a theatrical stage, then into
what appears to be a totally separate reality, a separate world, not so very different, one may add, from the pathway once indicated by the Golden Bough,
but now introduced by the "yellow acacia, drying, curling up and shredding":

> There were no bushes in the other garden, and as the age-old trees raised
> their lower branches up into the foliage as though into a night sky, *they laid
> the garden bare below, even though it stood there and never emerged from
> its permanent state of solemn, airy semi-gloom.* Fork-trunked, mauve as a
> thunderstorm, and covered with gray lichen, *they provided a good view of
> the little-used deserted alleyway that the other garden gave on to on the far
> side. There was yellow acacia growing there. Now the shrubbery was drying,
> curling up and shredding.*
>
> *Borne through the gloomy garden from this world to the other, the far-
> away alley glowed with the light that illuminates events in a dream—very
> brightly, very minutely and noiselessly, as if the sun over there had put on
> spectacles and was fumbling among the buttercups.*
>
> But what was Zhenya gaping at so?—She was gazing at her discovery,
> which intrigued her much more than those who had helped her to make it.
> (*CSP* 150–51; emphasis added)

> Кустов в чужом саду не было, и вековые деревья, унеся в высоту, к
> листве, как в какую-то ночь, свои нижние сучья, снизу *оголяли сад,
> хоть он и стоял в постоянном полумраке, воздушном и торжествен-
> ном, и никогда из него не выходил.* Сохатые, лиловые в грозу, покры-
> тые седым лишаем, они позволяли хорошо видеть *ту пустынную,
> малоезжую улочку, на которую выходил чужой сад тою стороной.*

---

48. Pasternak is careful to suggest the smell of ether coming from the grass—the boundary
to the world of the dead [булыжник густо порос плоской кудрявой травкой, издававшей
в послеобеденные часы кислый лекарственный запах, какой бывает в зной возле боль-
ниц] (*PSS* 3:54).

*Там росла желтая акация. Теперь кустарник сох, скрючивался и осы-
пался.*

*Вынесенная мрачным садом с этого света на тот, глухая улочка
светилась так, как освещаются происшествия во сне; то-есть очень
ярко, очень кропотливо и очень бесшумно, будто солнце там, надев
очки, шарило в курослепе.*

*На что ж так зазевалась Женя? На свое открытие, которое зани-
мало ее больше, чем люди, помогшие ей его сделать.* (*PSS* 3:54)

Drawing with great precision Zhenya's movements in the garden, Pasternak
presents the already well-practiced scene of the bridge or crossing between the
two worlds—the carefully lit stage which in "The Mark of Apelles" appeared
in the middle of a city with its spotlights directed upon the intruder.[49] On this
occasion, surrounded by a bucolic world, Zhenya too discovers a separate and
separated world, with sharp spotlights focused upon a constructed stage in the
middle of its semi-gloom.

In this emphatically natural setting behind a dark garden that opens onto
"another world" [вынесенная мрачным садом с этого света на тот] (*PSS*
3:54), Zhenya meets four figures. At first, it is only a group of three women, at
which Zhenya "gazes" because "her discovery [. . .] intrigued her much more
than those who had helped her to make it" [свое открытие, которое зани-
мало ее больше, чем люди, помогшие ей его сделать]. The three women,
black hermits or anchorites, Pasternak tells us, move in unison, and at this
particular moment seem to be united by a kind of "filial dozing" [состояние
дружной сонливости] until, once again, all together they turn their heads
toward something still outside Zhenya's vision:[50]

"Happy people!" she envied those unknown girls. There were three of them.
They showed up black, like the word "anchorite" in the song. The three
even necks with hair combed up under three round hats leaned as if the
one at the end, half hidden by a bush, was sleeping propped on her elbow,
while the other two also slept, huddling against her. The hats were a dark
gray-blue and kept flashing in the sun, then fading, like insects. They were

---

49. cf. Heine's protestation: "Yes, it is a stage again. But why not let me stay a little in this
pool of bright light? [. . .] Everything else is sunk in gloom. On such a bridge, let us say a stage,
a man flares up in the light of the flickering rays as if he had been put on show, surrounded by
a railing against the backdrop of the town, of chasms and signal lights in the river bank" (*CSP*
109–10; *PSS* 3:15–16).

50. Here, as in several other aspects of this chapter, I draw on my earlier work (Glazov-
Corrigan 1991).

tied about with black crepe. At the moment the three strangers all turned their heads the other way. Something had, no doubt, attracted their attention at the far end of the street. (*CSP* 151)

"Счастливые," позавидовала она незнакомкам. Их было три.

Они чернелись, как слово "затворница" в песне. Три ровных затылка, зачесанных под круглые шляпы, склонились так, будто крайняя, наполовину скрытая кустом, спит обо что-то облокотясь, а две другие тоже спят, прижавшись к ней. Шляпы были черно-сизые, и гасли и сверкали на солнце, как насекомые. Они были обтянуты черным крепом. В это время незнакомки повернули головы в другую сторону. Верно, что-то в том конце улицы привлекло их внимание. (*PSS* 3:54–55)

The women's position on the enchanted street strikes a familiar note: "Lucky people" [*счастливые*], thinks Zhenya, that is, blessed, *makarioi* or *beati*, classical epithets for Gods, Immortals, or Fates, while the women's glance, unperturbed by the sun, slightly expands the frames of both time and space, reintroducing a summer note into the autumnal air:

For a minute they looked toward the far end—just as people look in summer when an instant is dissolved in light and extended, and you have to screw up your eyes and shield them with the palm of your hand—for just a minute they looked; then they relapsed into their former state of filial dosing. (*CSP* 151; trans. altered)

Они поглядели с минуту на тот конец так, как глядят летом, когда мгновение растворено светом и удлинено, когда приходится щуриться и защищать глаза ладонью—с такую-то минуту поглядели они, и впали опять в прежнее состояние дружной сонливости. (*PSS* 3:55)

Like the three Graces (à la Canova, only in black), the three women gaze, and their momentary contemplation brings out another enchanted figure—a lame man:

One by one in turn they came through the gate. A short man followed after them, walking with a strange crippled gait. Under his arm he carried an enormous album or atlas. (*CSP* 151)

Они поодиночке, друг за дружкой прошли в калитку. За ними странною, увечной походкой следовал невысокий человек. Он нес под мышкой большущий альбом или атлас. (*PSS* 3:55)

The three women in black usher a lame man onto this rural stage and into Zhenya's life, a stranger who carries not only with his hands, but with his whole torso "an enormous album or an atlas"—that is, a mysterious object, representing either the world or art or both (an ambiguous object, indicating, among a multiplicity of other meanings, the merging layers of Zhenya's present vision).[51]

Struck forcibly by this annunciation, Zhenya considers the situation: "So that was what they had been doing, peering over each other's shoulders. And she had thought they were asleep" [Так вот чем занимались они, заглядывая через плечо друг дружке, а она думала—спят] (*CSP* 151; *PSS* 3:55). The overdetermination of this last remark also permits several readings; the unknown women are either dreaming the lame man into existence, or watching him emerge, or helping this apparition emerge in their contemplation, or, finally, dressed in black, they are grieving over his fate and his fateful presence in the world of other people. In the meantime, however, the mysterious lame man attracts the attention not only of the three female companions who, after this occasion, depart from the story. His first brief appearance indicates his connection to the elemental forces of nature, while his entry into Zhenya's life signals the passing of day into night, a change of setting accompanied by a mysterious music in the air. He also appears to give Zhenya temporary power over the garden, for bending to pick up the Lermontov volume she had earlier forgotten, she too commands the beginning of the dusk, and, as the evening

51. Analyzing this scene, Faryno concentrates on the opposition between sexual love that the Demon brings to Tamara and the education in pre-fallen love in the text of Pasternak: "Since the direct exchange between Zhenya and the Demon leads to the fact that from her 'log' Zhenya can see the Demon (and actually does see him), the movement to the 'pre-text' leads to the 'genesis' of the Demon [. . .]. This has a sanction in Lermontov's text: Lermontov's Demon is 'sinful lover-tempter.' Pasternak, inheriting the 'eroticism' of the Demon reconstructs, so to speak, its pre-fallen invariant" (1993, 30–31). This reading overlooks altogether the role of the three Graces who usher the mysterious man, carrying "an enormous album or an atlas" onto the scene. A parallel reading of the scene would suggest Pasternak's announcement of his debt to the Symbolists and his own rendition of the programmatic image of Briusov's "pantheon, temple of all Gods" [Пантеон, храм всех богов] and particularly the three gifts or counsels that a young poet receives in "To the Young Poet" [Юному поэту]. The last admonition, "Safeguard the third: worship art, / Art alone, without thought or goal" [Третий храни: поклоняйся искусству, / Только ему, безраздумно, бесцельно], is, perhaps, the central theme of *Luvers,* and the power of art is viewed as equivalent to the highest, all-embracing and life-changing gift.

descends, its enchantment is deepened by the rising and falling melody, imitating even in this detail the movements of the lame man.

Thus, "the stranger" appears as night falls, welcomed by the strumming of a balalaika as its sounds move up and down, in a pattern reminiscent of "a strange crippled gait," repeated by the swarming movement of the midges:[52]

The sun was already sinking. As she retrieved her book, Zhenya disturbed the stack of logs. The whole pile awoke and stirred as though alive. A few logs rolled down and fell onto the turf with a gentle thump. *This served as a signal, like the night watchman's rattle. Evening was born, and with it a multitude of noises, soft and misty. The air began to whistle some old-time melody* from across the river.

Low down, just above the grass, here spread the melancholy twang and strumming of a soldier's balalaika. Above her a fine swarm of quiet midges weaved and danced, *plunged and fell, hanging in the air, fell and hung again, then without touching the ground rose up once more.* But *the strumming of the balalaika* was finer and quieter still. *It sank earthward lower than the swarm of midges, and without getting dusty soared aloft again more easily and airily than they, shimmering and breaking off, dipping and rising unhurriedly.* (*CSP* 151–52; emphasis added)

Уже низилось солнце. Доставая книжку, Женя потревожила поленницу. Сажень пробудилась и задвигалась, как живая. Несколько поленьев съехало вниз и упало на дерн с легким стуком. *Это послужило знаком, как сторожев удар в колотушку. Родился вечер. Родилось множество звуков, тихих, туманных. Воздух принялся насвистывать что-то старинное, заречное.*

Двор был пуст. Прохор отработал. Он вышел за ворота. Там, низко-низко над самой травой стручато и грустно сталось бренчанье солдатской балалайки. Над ней вился и плясал, *обрывался и падал, замирая в воздухе, и падал, и замирал, и потом, не достигнув земли, подымался ввысь тонкий рой тихой мошкары.* Но *бренчанье балалайки было еще тоньше и тише. Оно опускалось ниже мошек к земле, и не запылясь, лучше и воздушней, чем рой, пускалось назад в высоту, мерцая и обрываясь, с припаданьями, неспеша.* (*PSS* 4:56–57)

---

52. The last stanza of John Keats's "To Autumn" is another suggestive Romantic intertext for this scene: "Where are the songs of Spring? Ay, where are they? / Think not of them, thou hast thy music too,— / While barred clouds bloom the soft-dying day, / And touch the stubble plains with rosy hue; / Then in a wailful choir the small gnats mourn" (434–35).

The man who enters the narrative in this bucolic setting later receives the name of Tsvetkov, and the importance of his appearance is summarized by Pasternak at the end of the story as an ethical lesson, an education in learning how to act alongside indefinable and uncontrollable reality, just as "the Commandments have in mind":

> "As a living individual human," they say, "you must not do to this *feature-less generalized* man what you would not wish for yourself as a living individual." (*CSP* 178; emphasis in original)

> Не делай ты, особенный и живой,—говорят они—*этому, туманному и общему*, того, чего себе, особенному и живому, не желаешь. (*PSS* 3:85)

Fated to vanish under the hooves of Mrs. Luvers's horse and depart several nights later from the house across from the Defendovs, Tsvetkov (*tsvetok*, a flower[53] destined to die in winter and, thus, already mourned by the Graces) manages, however, like the three women dozing in unison, to extend and even break the duration of temporal measurements within the chronology of the story. The indefinable object he carries under his arm—"an enormous album or an atlas"—indicates that his art, the work of his hands, is indistinguishable from the events in the world at large. Thus, displaying physical characteristics that connect him directly to the author of *Demon*,[54] his very appearance and posture strongly suggest that he has stepped out of the book folded inside out and that he promises, at this moment only indirectly, that his future effect on the Luverses' house will be that of the master of shadows and storms sweeping over the world at large.

---

53. Fateeva links the vegetative aspects of the name both to *My Sister Life* and to the vegetative meaning of Pasternak's last name, suggesting (see here also the next note) that Tsvetkov is linked not merely to Lermontov or his Demon, but to Pasternak as well: "To remind the reader, the name 'Zhenya' is paronomasically linked to *zhizn'* (life) and *zhenschina* (woman), and if in *My Sister Life* the concept of 'sister-life' is connected to Lermontov, then in *The Childhood of Luvers* this coordination in embodied in the compositional line—Girl-Tsvetkov-Dikikh (the Wild One)-Lermontov, where Tsvetkov becomes an analogue of the 'vegetative' name and a replacement of Pasternak's 'I'" (2003, 330).

54. Lermontov's lameness in his mind linked him to Byron, and was in Lermontov's mind a sign of his chosenness. In Pasternak's mind, however, his accident with the broken leg must have, in time, become a connection to Lermontov. See Faryno (1993).

7.3 What does Tsvetkov do?
The world of the indefinable other

For all the ambiguity surrounding Tsvetkov's identity, both in itself and as it is enhanced by Lermontov's poem, the stranger's every appearance turns out to be significant, and even his name magnetizes the most trivial events with a sense of an impenetrable mystery. It is possible, then, that in conceiving this "postoronnyj" (or stranger) who brings excitement to the fading reality of the natural world, Pasternak constructs a mildly ironic pun on Victor Shklovsky's "ostranenenie"—a quality of "estrangement" or defamilarization proposed by the theoretician in his 1916 essay "Art as Technique":[55]

> Habitualization devours works, clothes, furniture, one's wife, and the fear of war. 'If the whole complex lives of many people go on unconsciously, then such lives are as if they had never been.' And art exists that one may recover the sensation of life; it exists to make one feel things, to make the stone stony. [. . .] The technique of art is to make objects 'unfamiliar,' to make forms difficult, to increase the difficulty and length of perception because the process of perception is an aesthetic end in itself and must be prolonged. (1988, 19–20)

Pasternak would never agree, of course, that any specific artistic method or technique can return animation and vitality to what has been "habitualized" and discolored. Thus, the covert reference may equally indicate an implicit debate with Shklovsky and not only by means of an alliteration that implies at the very least an apposition of terms: estrangement versus the appearance of a stranger (остранение vs. посторонний). What defamiliarizes reality in *Luvers* is not a specific technique, but rather a suggestion of the immaterial mystery that Tsvetkov exudes during the very season when the process of nature's fading is all-embracing.

It is noteworthy, then, that Tsvetkov's name is mentioned for the first time just as Zhenya, in her understanding, discolors Negaraat, and yet the young Belgian regains his previous mysterious indefinability when he promises, on leaving Ekaterinburg, to leave "some books with Tsvetkov" (a friend, about whom apparently he has before told "so much" to everyone). The name Tsvetkov, appearing for the first time directly after the girl's act of understanding, "de-glamorizes" and "decolors" her interlocutor and calls the reader's atten-

---

55. "Art as Technique," published in 1917, "remains the most important statement made of early Formalist method" (Leon and Reis 1965, 4)

tion to the multiple meanings of Tsvetkov's name, which points etymologically not only to a flower (цветок), but also to color (цвет).[56] Thus, Tsvetkov reestablishes a connection to the infinite and immeasurable; literally his role is to return mystery and color to a discolored world,[57] and this means that Zhenya's expanding understanding, accompanied by her action of turning the book inside out, reaches toward a new stage in the apprehension of her surrounding—beyond both the inanimate landscape and nature's animation, all embracing, but limited in time—toward the "infinity" of art and the very world it represents—the very object, in fact, carried by the stranger, the "enormous album or atlas" [большущий альбом или атлас] (*CSP* 151; *PSS* 3:55).

The change in the construction of the narrative when compared with "The Long Days" (see Table I in 6.5) is considerable, particularly since several narrative worlds (rather than one, albeit ever-expanding) appear to blend together in "The Stranger." The images of hands, presented with crisp precision in "The Long Days," still remain significant, but they lose clarity of depiction in the highly condensed text. The shifts of narrative paradigms are presented in Table 7A.

The interplay with the *Demon*, therefore, plays a very specific role. In contrast to the Tamara of Lermontov's poem, the extraordinarily beautiful young woman on the threshold of marriage, seduced by her immortal visitor, thirteen-year old Zhenya does not long for a sexual embrace.[58] What is of principal

---

56. It is curious that Fateeva, who dedicates a whole chapter of her book to "The Colors of Boris Pasternak's World" (2003, 282–93), emphasizes mostly the etymological significance of the flower in Tsvetkov's name, viewing it as "an analogue of the 'vegetative' last name" (2003, 330). See Zholkovsky (1999) addressing the dialogue between Tsvetaeva and Pasternak within the context of their vegetative last names. For a potential interconnection between the last name of Tsvetkov and the "flowers" of St. Francis, see Gardzonio (1999).

57. Witt, in a chapter entitled "Creation as Zhivopis," examines the question of color in *Zhivago* and suggests that the loss of personality, observed by Yuri during his pre-revolutionary work in the hospital, a phenomenon he names "igra v ljudej," is counteracted only by the themes of color painting, connected to iconography and the Book of Revelation (2000a, 30–47).

58. Pasternak, as already noted (see Chapter 5.1), objects in the drafts of *Luvers* to psychologists and novelists who concentrate upon the sign of maturity of characters only in terms of sexual maturation: "We permit ourselves to think that absolutely the entire psychological inventory, totally without exception, was maturing and had matured in the human soul with the very same painful full-blooded materiality that (with the help of physicians) was focused by the naturalist-practitioners of the novel on a very limited piece of novelistic meat—on matters of sexuality" [мы позволяем себе думать, что весь решительно душевный инвентарь, весь без изъятия, назревал и назрел в человеческой душе с той же тягостной, кровавой матерьяльностью, какую, с легкой руки врача, натуралистам в романе угодно было сосредоточить в небольшом куске романического мяса—в поле] (*PSS* 3:514–15). Fateeva, in fact, develops Faryno's insistence that Zhenya's fascination with the Demon is pre-sexual into a more complex comparison of young girls' "demons" in Pasternak and Nabokov (Faryno 1993; Fateeva 2003, 323–45).

TABLE 7A. FALL: LOSS OF FACE AND THE BOOK IN THE GARDEN.

Seasons. Stages of growth	Direction of perception and permeable compound	Emotional state	Residue on the margins of the compound	The images of the hands controlling the situation	The character of time and space
Early Fall.	1. Relations with Others. 2. Reading Lermontov. 3. "Happy people!" Three Muses or Fates in black— or neighbors next door?	1. Alarm at one's own subservience and at the facelessness of others. 2. Interest in the street from the "other world" and the "stranger."	"Metallic facts." Mr. Luvers's sickness. A short man with a crippled gait on the street behind the garden.	3 sets of hands: 1. A bast scrubber in the soldier Prokhor's [?] hands (or in the hands of the clouds[?]). 2. The book, turned outward, in Zhenya's hands. 3. The stranger with a gait, carrying under his arm "an enormous album or atlas."	Space and time transfixed by atemporal presences: "Borne through the gloomy garden from this world to the other, the faraway alley glowed with the light that illuminates events in a dream."

significance, however, is a comparison rather than a contrast: the fact that Tamara's awareness of the Demon, for all its erotic overtones, figures a longing[59] for the infinite and eternal:

A familiar image sometimes
Moved without sound and trace
In the light mist of incense
It was shining quietly, like a star:
It was inviting and calling, but where?

. . . Знакомый образ иногда
Скользил без звука и следа
В тумане легком фимиама:
Сиял он тихо, как звезда:
Манил и звал он, но куда? (Lermontov 2:363)

Thus, given the differences in the texts, the emphasis on the presence of mystery unifies the sensibilities of both heroines, and Zhenya, like Tamara, cannot really define this new presence in her life, but watches for it and guards it. In the meantime, Tsvetkov, an indefinite stranger, does not simply enhance the mystery of Ekaterinburg's streets. Promising the beginning of something new and unknown, Tsvetkov also indicates the passing of an occasion, an ending either of the day or of good weather or health, or, again, of the transformation of autumn into winter, and, finally, of the passing of Zhenya's childhood.

The language of longing, confusion, ecstasy, sinfulness, fatality, demonic visitation, satanic jubilation, and tragic denouement travel from Lermontov's *Demon* to *The Childhood of Luvers,* but it denotes in these texts expressly different meanings. Only the drama of the Demon's feelings—the longing of the immortal, suffering, and conflicted loner—is kept in *Luvers* quite faithfully, although this gamut of feelings is suggested, rather than fully articulated. Without sustaining the virtuosity of the scene where Tsvetkov appears in the yard for the first time, Pasternak is nonetheless consistent in developing a significant inner division in the nature of the mysterious stranger, characterized by a serious philosophical tension at the heart of the figure (see 7.5 and 7.6). To sketch a chronology, a dramatic crescendo of sorts, associated with Tsvetkov's appearances is to trace an intensification of meanings that pull simultaneously in opposed directions. On the one hand, as someone remaining outside Zhenya's comprehension and control, Tsvetkov represents an impulse

---

59. The philosophical resonances of this longing for the infinite will be discussed in 7.6.

of mysterious energy, a gathering snowstorm falling upon the earth and subduing it. On the other hand, as a flower in the winter months, he is bound by the forces he initiates and brings with him, and in this Tsvetkov becomes a prophetic and suffering figure.

In contrast to all the previous boundaries in *Luvers* that appear initially confusing but that were eventually clarified and resolved in the earlier parts of the novella, the role of Tsvetkov is to deepen confusion until it is conflated with (and swept away by) the elemental chaos of the winter blizzard. The first indication of Tsvetkov's disorienting influence is signaled when Zhenya and Seryozha see him walking behind Dikikh, while the tutor seems to be arguing, proving something emphatically "with all ten fingers" (*CSP* 159; *PSS* 3:64). The spirit of argumentation and intangible conflict spreads across the straightforward journey of Zhenya and Seryozha—the children's walk begins to exhibit one complication after another, even though all these first instances of approaching chaos are merely trifles. First, the shopkeeper thinks that Tsvetkov, and not Dikikh, is their tutor (*CSP* 159; *PSS* 3:63–64); then the children's outing, connected to their meeting with Dikikh and Tsvetkov, ends in their total loss of orientation: they leave the store literally with nothing (пошли ни с чем), although Zhenya at this point finally—and not without Seryozha's reference to a light in the window (пьют, свет в окне)—links Tsvetkov to the man she saw on the hidden street. It is also at this moment that the mysterious street proves not to be hidden at all, but to be located, according to Seryozha's explanation, at the center of all their walks, right next to the smithy, that is, side by side with the world of metal:[60] "Why, we've been past it today already. [. . .] And we'll be going by it again soon. [. . .] You know the coppersmith's [. . .] on the corner" (*CSP* 160; *PSS* 3:63–64). On the way back, the street is missed yet again, and only the smell of "brass knobs and candlesticks" indicates the presence of the coppersmith's shop, adjacent to the street in question, which makes Zhenya somehow understand "that [the] Tsvetkov mentioned by the bookseller was the same man with the limp" [что тот Цветков, о котором говорил книгопродавец, и есть этот самый хромой] (*CSP* 160; *PSS* 3:65).

A sense of disruption is intensified in the rather disquieting chapter VI of "The Stranger," which presents a bewildering description of a man moving with all his belongings, undermining Zhenya's earlier sense that the inner spirit of the house is solid and inviolate, with its furniture settled in "its allotted position once and for all" (*CSP* 149; *PSS* 3:53). While it is altogether unclear whether it is Tsvetkov who moves into Negaraat's quarters or Nega-

---

60. Cf. the room in Moscow where Zhivago lives before his death.

raat's own belongings that are now being moved, the emphasis of the passage is upon the contents of the house being emptied into the outside world in a chaotic and disorderly manner: "the meager equipment of the study was not loaded but simply placed on the dray just as it stood in the room" (*CSP* 161; *PSS* 3:66). Nonetheless, as Zhenya visualizes the lame man's movements in his new home, the emphasis on color returns. In contrast, then, to all the earlier passages that describe Zhenya's interaction with other people, emphasizing the inevitable fading of the glamorous novelty of the world, the processes associated with the presence of Tsvetkov present the opposite, obverse condition. Coldness, nastiness, and rain, so forcefully emphasized in this passage, cannot dilute the piercing whiteness of the cart:

> [A]t every jolt of the cart the armchair casters peeping from beneath their white covers trundled around the dray as if on a parquet floor. *Despite the fact that they were sodden through and through, the covers were white as snow. So sharply did they catch the eye that when one looked at them everything else became the same color:* cobblestones gnawed by the foul weather, shivering water beneath the fences, birds flying from stable yards and trees flying after, chunks of lead, and even that ficus in its tub, which swayed and bowed awkwardly from the cart to everybody as it flew past.
>
> It was a crazy cartload. It could not help but draw attention. (*CSP* 161; emphasis added)

> [К]олесца кресел, глядевшие из-под белых чехлов, ездили по полку, как по паркету при всяком сотрясении воза. *Чехлы были белоснежны, несмотря на то, что были промочены до последней нитки. Они так резко бросались в глаза, что при взгляде на них одного цвета становились:* обглоданный непогодой булыжник, продрогглая подзаборная вода, птицы, летевшие с конных дворов, летевшие за ними деревья, обрывки свинца и даже тот фикус в кадушке, который колыхался, нескладно кланяясь с телеги всем пролетавшим.
>
> Воз был дик. Он невольно останавливал на себе внимание. (*PSS* 3:66)

The duality of the image, however, is startling. While the whiteness is preserved in any constitution, the lame man (introduced yet again as "unknown" to Zhenya) will not, according to Zhenya's expectations, be well and healthy. Threatened by the elements he resists but to which he also belongs, he will eventually become ill:

"When he unpacks his things he will catch a chill," she reflected, thinking of an unknown owner. And she imagined the man—*any man, in fact, with a shaky and uneven gait*—setting his belongings out in different corners. She vividly pictured his mannerisms and movements, and especially how he would take a rag and hobble around the tub as he started wiping down the drizzle-clouded leaves of the ficus. Then he would catch a cold, a chill and fever. (*CSP* 161; emphasis added)

"Он простудится, только разложит вещи,"—подумала она про неизвестного владельца. И она представила себе человека,—человека вообще, валкой, на шаги разрозненной походкой расставляющего свои пожитки по углам. Она живо представила себе его ухватки и движения, в особенности то, как он возьмет тряпку и, ковыляя вокруг кадки, станет обтирать затуманенные изморосью листья фикуса. А потом схватит насморк, озноб и жар. (*PSS* 3:66–67)

The scene of the house turned upside down no longer seems banal or trifling; it presages approaching sickness and disaster, even though, at first, it will be Zhenya, and not the lame man, who will become seriously ill, "lying in fever for two weeks," as if stung by a serpent (*CSP* 162; *PSS* 3:67–68).

As the snowstorm replaces the rain and fog in the next section, Tsvetkov is no longer named, and Seryozha's insistence that they have seen the stranger during their outing to observe the gathering snowstorm provokes Zhenya's outburst:

"When we went out, we saw Negaraat's friend. Do you know him?"

"Evans?" Father inquired distractedly.

"We don't know that man!" blurted Zhenya hotly. (*CSP* 166)

'Как выезжать, мы видели Негаратова знакомого. Знаешь?'— 'Эванса?' рассеянно уронил отец. 'Мы не знаем этого человека,' горячо выпалила Женя. (*PSS* 3:72)

Tsvetkov becomes, therefore, the unnamable spirit of the snow blizzard, for the narrative of the outing, while painstakingly concentrating on the children's impressions during the short coach journey, never mentions their seeing anyone at all. Instead, their perceptions are totally arrested by their premonition of the gathering storm: "Her vague premonitions came true [. . .]. But they had not had time to reach beyond the bridge when separate snowflakes ceased to be and a solid, fused coagulum came heaving down" [Смутные ее предчувствия сбылись. [. . .] Но не успели они выехать за мост, как отдельных снежинок не стало и повалил сплошной, сплывшийся лепень] (*CSP* 165; *PSS* 3:70). Zhenya's protection of Tsvetkov's strangeness, then, indicates that while powerful elemental forces are now reaching their crescendo, Zhenya is somehow implicated in the process by welcoming and guarding the spirits of the approaching whirlwind, the visitors from worlds that have nothing to do with the earth:

> *The heavens quivered, and down from them tumbled whole white kingdoms and countries. They were countless, and they were mysterious and dreadful.* It was clear that these lands falling from goodness knows where had never heard of life and earth: coming blind from the northern darkness, they covered them over without ever seeing or knowing of them.
>
> *They were ravishingly dreadful, those kingdoms—quite satanically entrancing. Zhenya was breathless as she looked at them* [. . .]. Everything was confused. The night rushed at them, infuriated by the low swept gray hair that flogged and blinded it. Everything was scattered, shrieking, and unable to discern the road. (*CSP* 165; emphasis added)

> *Небо тряслось и с него валились белые царства и края, им не было счета, и они были таинственны и ужасны.* Было ясно, что эти неведомо откуда падавшие страны никогда не слышали про жизнь и про землю, и полуночные, слепые, засыпали ее, ее не видя и не зная.
>
> *Они были упоительно ужасны, эти царства; совершенно сатанински восхитительны. Женя захлебывалась, глядя на них.* [. . .] Все смешалось. Ночь ринулась на них, свирепея от низко сбившегося седого волоса, засекавшего и слепившего ее. Все поехало врозь, с визгом, не разбирая дороги. (*PSS* 3:71)

And just like Lermontov's heroine, Zhenya becomes a magnet for a disaster brought about by expectations of meetings with her extraordinary visitor in a world that can be schematized as in Table 7b.

In Tamara's case a fiery horse brings its dead master, Tamara's unfortunate bridegroom, home from battle, while, in *Luvers,* the frightened horse tramples the stranger (Tsvetkov), and the horrific scene leads to Mrs Luvers's miscarriage. And just like Tamara, Zhenya cannot shake off the burden of responsibility as she weeps over her own reckless persistence in seeing Tsvetkov everywhere and thus bringing him, together with all the presences associated with him, into the family:

> And Zhenya wept because she considered herself to blame for everything. For it was *she* who had brought him into the life of the family that day

when she noticed him on the far side of someone else's garden. And, having noticed him quite needlessly, without sense or purpose, she had then started meeting him at every step, constantly, directly, or indirectly, and even, as on the last occasion, quite contrary to all possibility. (*CSP* 178)

А плакала Женя оттого, что считала себя во всем виноватой. Ведь ввела его в жизнь семьи она в тот день, когда, заметив его за чужим садом, и заметив без нужды, без пользы, без смысла, стала затем встречать его на каждом шагу, постоянно, прямо и косвенно и даже, как это случилось в последний раз, наперекор возможности. (*PSS* 3:85)

The decisive difference between the female protagonists of Lermontov and Pasternak is located, nonetheless, not only in Pasternak's rejection of sexual maturation as the threshold upon which personality becomes unified. If Lermontov's emphasis is upon the suffering of the supernatural Demon and his power over the life of mortals whom he despises and for whom he longs, Pasternak works with those layers in human perception that take his heroine seemingly naturally and realistically outside material, measured, and ultimately discolored impressions. Her longing for the infinite and distant (evident already when as a little child she cried for the unknown Motovilikha, dearer to her than her known and named surroundings) is at the center of Pasternak's interest. However, the fact that Tsvetkov is both the spirit and the victim of the forces he brings with him indicates something of a conceptual contradiction between an all-powerful master of the shades and a suffering servant (for further clarification of this hidden contradiction, see also 7.5–7.6 below). And while some critics believe that Pasternak in both *My Sister Life* and *The Childhood of Luvers* says good-bye to the "demonism" of his childhood years (Fateeva 2003, 330), the longing for the infinite sets the compass of his artistic inquiry, for it is only with this longing and the quest for the unknown, he suggests, that one can defamiliarize the surrounding discolored world.

7.4 In the sanctuary of the sacristan Defendov

With all their differences in conception, Lermontov's *Demon*, as a tale about the Spirit who brings disaster to those he visits, emerges as the clearest counterpoint for the structure of both the plot and narrative in "The Stranger." In an event parallel to Tamara's entering the convent, Zhenya, after the tragedy

TABLE 7B. THE BLIZZARD: THE ERASURE OF BRIDGES AND BOUNDARIES.

Seasons. Stages of growth	Direction of perception and permeable compound	Emotional state	Residue on the margins of the compound	The images of the hands controlling the situation	The character of time and space
Late Fall and Arrival of winter	Multiple worlds coming into collision. Zhenya's witnessing "ravishingly dreadful [. . .] kingdoms—quite satanically entrancing."	1. Excitement at the storm and the pleasure of the quiet home. 2. Pain.	Facts still unknown to Zhenya: Mrs. Luvers's miscarriage as she steps out of the theater during the storm, her sickness, and the death of Tsvetkov under the hoofs of the horse.	Hands indicating irresolvable contradiction: "Dikikh [walking with Tsvetkov] frequently raising his hands with fingers splayed. He would not agree, and he tried to prove with all fingers that his companion . . . ."	The shaking of time and space. The overwhelmed earth: "The heavens quivered, and down from them tumbled whole white kingdoms and countries."

wrought by the storm, is taken from her home to the house of the sacristan Defendov who, just as his name and occupation indicate, is chosen to protect the girl from the outside world and from its demonic realities. Defendov is by no means the holy angel who finally reclaims the soul of Zhenya, cleanses it of her former memories, and offers a heavenly sanctuary from the hellish spirit. Nonetheless, the sacristan clearly, if unsuccessfully, wants to bring joy into Zhenya's life, and it is in his home that Pasternak portrays his heroine as finally reaching the "line" that serves as a basis for her integral selfhood.

As one might have expected, while portraying this major change in his heroine's awakening, Pasternak takes time to establish Zhenya's absolute ignorance of sexual matters, thus refusing to equate sexual and emotional maturity. When Zhenya discusses the process of birth pangs with Liza Defendov, the power of the "sanctuary" ensures that Liza "spared her [Zhenya's] ignorance because she never suspected that one could tell her about it without using expressions that could not be spoken here at home" [ее неведение она пощадила потому, что и не подозревала, чтобы об этом можно было рассказать иначе, чем в тех выражениях, которые тут, дома, перед знакомой, не ходившей в школу, были не произносимы] (*CSP* 174; *PSS* 3:80). The change in Zhenya is spearheaded not by sexual knowledge, but rather by a decisive inner transformation. In Pasternak's description, Defendov *searches for Zhenya's soul,* attempting to find that singular, "unmistakable" and tangible "trait" (or actual line—черта, as in "Апеллесова черта") that might be a beginning or turning. Moreover, this explicit awareness of the soul's "outlines" is no longer masked or hidden in the text by colloquial or habitual turns of phrase. Instead, the whole episode of Defendov's actions appears surprisingly out of place, drawing the reader's attention by their unquestionable awkwardness:

Defendov realized what was the matter. He tried to amuse her. [. . .] In the darkness he was groping the soul of his daughter's friend, as if he were asking her heart how old it was. When once he had caught one of Zhenya's traits unmistakably, it was his intention to work on this observation and help the child to forget about home—but by his probings he had reminded her that she was in a strange home. (*CSP* 171)

Дефендов понимал, что с ней. Он старался развлечь ее. [. . .] Это он ощупывал впотьмах душу дочкиной подруги, словно спрашивал у ее сердца, сколько ему лет. Он вознамерился, уловив безошибочно одну какую-нибудь Женину черту, сыграть на подмеченном и помочь ребенку забыть о доме, и своими поисками напоминал ей, что она у чужих. (*PSS* 3:78)

Even if Defendov's attempts to find her single essential feature are unsuccessful, it is in the sacristan's home that Zhenya begins to enter a new stage of her life; and it is equally meaningful that it is in the house of the Defendovs, where the vocabulary of the soul is reintroduced, that Tsvetkov—or rather a ghost (призрак), or the Demon associated with him—finally departs.

To emphasize the deeper significance of Zhenya's transition, three new sets of hands are introduced into the narrative, and their movements play out, as if within a cameo frame, the significance of these seemingly insignificant occurrences whose every detail constitutes, nonetheless, a symbolic gesture. First, Defendov's hands, old and shaking, attempt to adjust the light inside a room pervaded by remnants of organic life, beauty and horror, house plants and cockroaches. The movements of the hands, turning on the light, appear to raise the overfilled but invisible wine glass—a sacramental gesture, successful in its aim, and yet attracting every kind of insect:

> They were sitting down for supper at the Defendovs. Their grandmother crossed herself and flopped into an armchair. The lamp burned dimly and kept smoking. At one moment it was turned down too far, and the next they let it out too much. Mr. Defendov's dry hand would often reach out for the screw and when he slowly settled in his seat, his hand quivered minutely, not like an old man's hand, but as though he were lifting a glass filled to the brim. His fingernails and fingertips trembled. [. . .]
>
> The bulbous neck of the lamp flared, edged about by the tendrils of geranium and heliotrope. (*CSP* 171)

> У Дефендовых садились ужинать. Бабушка, крестясь, колтыхнулась в кресло. Лампа горела мутно и покачивала; ее то перекручивали, то чересчур отпускали. Сухая рука Дефендова часто тянулась к винту, и, когда медленно отымая ее от лампы, он медленно опускался на место, рука у него тряслась, маленько и не по-старчески, будто он подымал налитую через рюмку. Дрожали концы пальцев, к ногтям. [. . .]
>
> Припухлое горлышко лампы пылало, обложенное усиками герани и гелиотропа. (*PSS* 3:77)

The complex syntax of the narrative minimizes the successful completion of the action, but implies, nonetheless, that Defendov—in a sacred gesture—reclaims both space and time from their external, cold and evil-smelling duration, exposing in the process a new ripeness: the swelling of time ready to be lanced—as if an infectious boil is finally ready to burst. And just as Defendov's hands touch the lamp,

Cockroaches ran to congregate by the glowing glass, and the hands of the clock stretched out carefully. Time moved at a hibernal crawl. Here it was swelling, festering. Out in the yard it was numb and malodorous. Outside the window it scuttled and scurried, doubling and trebling in the gleaming lights. (*CSP* 171)

К жару стекла сбегались тараканы и осторожно тянулись часовые стрелки. Время ползло по-зимнему. Здесь оно нарывало. На дворе— коченело, зловонное. За окном—сновало, семенило, двоясь и троясь в огоньках. (*PSS* 3:77)

At this very moment, looking over Defendov's books on the shelves (a forbidding set of *North* magazines and the dingy gold of Karamzin's complete works suggest the significations of space and time, geographical directions, and historical narratives), Zhenya finds that she can regain inner balance only by recollecting her mother; and here she experiences the first real barrier of differentiation and separation in her life—a rebirth through which she reclaims her separation and identity.

As cockroaches run toward the light and away from Zhenya's space, she, in her mind, returns to the train station, which in summer, during the animation of the surrounding world, admitted no boundaries and farewells. However, this time Zhenya sees her mother as a figure left behind on the platform, a departing memory separated temporally and spatially:

And something in her turned over, releasing tears at the very same moment when mama emerged in her memories: suffering and left standing in the chain of yesterday's events like one of a crowd who were seeing her off, and now set spinning back there by the train of time, which was bearing Zhenya away. (*CSP* 172)

И что-то в ней перевернулось, дав волю слезам в тот самый миг, как мать вышла у ней в воспоминаниях: страдающей, оставшейся стоять в веренице вчерашних фактов, как в толпе провожающих и крутимой там, позади, поездом времени, уносящим Женю. (*PSS* 3:78)

Precisely at this moment, however, Zhenya is pierced by her recollection of her mother's glance, a moment when Zhenya's empty hands—in the second highly significant motif of hands in these passages—receive an invisible heavy weight. This time, however, Zhenya's hands are in control of the situation. The text meanwhile is saturated with multiple reconstructions of (and departures from) the Kantian experience of apperception: the mother's glance from a recent mother-daughter conversation reaches Zhenya's inner vision. Two instances of inner eyesight meet at this crossing, awakening Zhenya's inner self and its personal, genetic (rather than generic) outlines.[61] Thus, Pasternak finally draws Zhenya's entry into maturity as a moment when she actually carries, in her empty hands, a past that henceforth lives in her, full of separated spatial and temporal measurements, invisible and intangible, yet offering in her a new intelligible life. It is here that she is finally able to re-enact another as herself.[62] Her mother's tears, held back on that memorable night in Perm when the spring was breaking through and the Kama River was ready to burst, are now Zhenya's tears, and mother begins to live in daughter, in a significant metaphoric replacement, intended, it would seem, to be a moment of textual maturity that accompanies the maturation of the protagonist:

> But utterly, utterly unbearable was the penetrating glance that *Madame* Luvers had fixed on her yesterday in the classroom. It was carved deep in her memory and would not go. Everything that Zhenya now felt was bound up with it. As though it were something that should have been taken and treasured, but which was forgotten and neglected.
>
> This feeling could have made her lose her wits. Its drunken, crazy bitterness and inescapability spun her so giddily. *Zhenya stood by the window and wept silently; tears flowed and she did not wipe them away: Her hands and arms were occupied, though she was holding nothing in them. Something caused them vehemently, impulsively, and obstinately to strengthen.*
>
> A sudden thought dawned on her. She suddenly felt that she was *terribly* like Mama. *This feeling was combined with a sense of vivid certainty, capable of turning conjecture into fact (if the latter were not established), and of making her like her mother by the mere strength of the striking, sweet condition she was in. This sensation was piercing, sharp enough to make her groan. It was a sensation of woman perceiving from within, or inwardly, her outward appearance and her charm.* Zhenya was incapable of realizing what it was. She was experiencing it for the first time. In one thing she was not mistaken. This was just how *Madame* Luvers had once been as she had stood by the window, turning away from her daughter and the governess in agitation, biting her lips and tapping her lorgnette against a kid-gloved palm. (*CSP* 172–73; emphasis added)

---

61. See Aucouturier's analysis of Zhenya's "generic and not individual qualities" (1978, 45).

62. Cf. the description of the old man in "Letters from Tula": "He was the only one in the story [who] made another to speak through his own lips" [В рассказе только он [. . .] застави[л] своими устами говорить постороннего] (*CSP* 126; *PSS* 3:32).

Но совершенно, совершенно несносен был тот проникновенный взгляд, который остановила на ней госпожа Люверс вчера в классной. Он врезался в память и из нее не шел. С ним соединялось все, что теперь испытывала Женя. Будто это была вещь, которую следовало взять, дорожа ей, и которую забыли, ею пренебрегнув.

Можно было голову потерять от этого чувства, до такой степени кружила пьяная шалая его горечь и безысходность. *Женя стояла у окна и плакала беззвучно; слезы текли, и она их не утирала: руки у ней были заняты, хотя она ничего в них не держала. Они были у ней выпрямлены, энергически, порывисто и упрямо.*

Внезапная мысль осенила ее. Она вдруг почувствовала, что страшно похожа на маму. *Это чувство соединилось с ощущением живой безошибочности, властной сделать домысел фактом, если этого нет еще на-лицо, уподобить ее матери одною силой потрясающе-сладкого состояния. Чувство это было пронизывающее, острое до стона. Это было ощущение женщины, изнутри или внутренне видящей свою внешность и прелесть.* Женя не могла отдать себе в нем отчета. Она его испытывала впервые. В одном она не ошиблась. Так, взволнованная, отвернувшись от дочери и гувернантки, стояла однажды у окна госпожа Люверс и кусала губы, ударяя лорнеткою по лайковой ладони. (*PSS* 3:79)

True to his conception, Pasternak immediately establishes Zhenya's innocence in sexual matters in the conversation "about it" with Liza Defendov. Then Pasternak moves to another farewell and yet another significant instance of this symbolic gesture of hands.

Across from the Defendovs' house, Zhenya, ignorant of Tsvetkov's death, observes his departure; or rather the hands of the departing Ghost at midnight carry a lamp, except that these are not real hands, but the empty sleeves of a light-bearing or Luciferic Demon who finally moves on, partially because this new Zhenya is no longer fascinated by him, and lets go of the apparition, of the lighted window, the shadows, the snow, and even the horse:

In a small window across the way a lamp was burning. Two bright stripes fell beneath the horse and settled on its shaggy pasterns. *Shadows moved across the snow; the sleeves of a phantom moved, wrapping a fur coat around itself; the light moved in a curtained window. But the little horse stood motionless and dreaming.*

Then she saw him. She recognized him immediately by his silhouette. The lame man lifted the lamp and began to walk away with it. The two bright stripes moved after him, distending and elongating, and behind the stripes—a sleigh, which quickly flashed into view and plunged back into the gloom even faster as it slowly went around the house to the porch.

It was strange that Tsvetkov should still appear before her gaze even here in the suburbs. But it did not surprise Zhenya. She was hardly concerned with him. Soon the lamp appeared again. It passed steadily across the curtains and was at the point of retreating again when suddenly it turned up once more behind the same curtain on the windowsill from which it had been taken. (*CSP* 175; emphasis added)

В окошке через дорогу горела лампа. Две яркие полосы, упав под лошадь, ложились на мохнатые бабки. *Двигались тени по снегу, двигались рукава призрака, запахивавшего шубу, двигался свет в занавешенном окне. Лошадка же стояла неподвижно и дремала.*

Тогда она увидала его. Она сразу его узнала по силуэту. Хромой поднял лампу и стал удаляться с ней. За ним двинулись, перекашиваясь и удлиняясь, обе яркие полосы, а за полосами и сани, которые быстро вспыхнули и еще быстрее метнулись во мрак, медленно заезжая за дом к крыльцу.

Было странно, что Цветков продолжает попадаться ей на глаза и здесь, в слободе. Но Женю это не удивило. Он ее мало занимал. Вскоре лампа опять показалась и, плавно пройдясь по всем занавескам, стала-было снова пятиться назад, как вдруг очутилась за самой занавеской, на подоконнике, откуда ее взяли. (*PSS* 3:82)

The return of the lamp to its proper place and the end of the play of shadows do not constitute a romantic interlude equal in splendor to the description, in *Demon*, of the secret life of shadows at night in an abandoned castle,[63] but this scene in *Luvers* does imply a finality, even closure, as dark superhuman presences depart and a young girl enters upon a new stage of maturity that promises further upheavals, since Zhenya's world (see Table 7c) has been already punctured, from childhood, by fatality and impending danger.

---

63. See *Demon*: "There are no imprints of the former years: the hand of centuries was clearing them for a long time" [нет нигде следов / Минувших лет: рука веков / Прилежно, долго их сметала] (Lermontov 2:382).

TABLE 7C. WINTER: IN THE PROTECTIVE SANCTUARY OF THE DEFENDOVS.

Seasons. Stages of growth	Direction of perception and permeable compound	Emotional state	Residue on the margins of the compound	The images of the hands controlling the situation	The character of time and space
Deep winter	In the house of the sacristan Defendov before returning home. External and internal gaze.	Loss of the familiar. Regaining mother inside. Wonder at the departing shadows.	Sexual knowledge.	3 sets of hands: 1. Defendov's "dry hand would often reach out for [. . .] the lamp as though "he were lifting a glass filled to the brim. " 2. "Madame Luvers's glance [. . .] would not go. [. . .]. Zhenya's hands and arms were occupied, though she was holding nothing in them." 3. "the sleeves of a phantom moved [. . .] the light moved in a curtained window. [. . .]Zhenya was hardly concerned with him."	The porous nature of the new space and time.

7.5 "Three Names" and the construction of the "Demonic" or spirit-bearing protagonist

In his letter to Bobrov of July 16, 1918, Pasternak mentions his plans for the title of the novel—*Three Names*. This provisional title, which on the surface has very little to do with the text of *The Childhood of Luvers,* suggested to critics that the title is connected to the rest of the work, lost in subsequent years.[64] However, since this is the only title that Pasternak mentions to Bobrov while sending him the earlier part of his future novel, it is very probable that *Three Names* and the text published later as *The Childhood of Luvers* were more directly linked than hitherto thought, and that the conception responsible for the title was to reflect the multifaceted role of Tsvetkov (and, perhaps, any other protagonist constructed along similar lines at future points of the novel).[65]

Several considerations support this view. In more recent studies, Russian scholars have begun to approach Pasternak's construction of lyrical subjects as a reflection of the wide spectrum of "that natural and cultural universe, in which he or she is initially reflected, as in the part of the whole" (Han 1988, 99). The lyrical subject, then, "possesses, on the one hand, a multiplicity of expressions, and, on the other, indefiniteness as a textual category" (Fateeva 2003, 87). The transformation of Pasternak's poetic subject into the protagonist of a prose narrative remains a highly disputed question, and the multifaceted figure of the indefinable Tsvetkov helps to disclose Pasternak's aims in this regard. In the personality of Tsvetkov, Pasternak hones his earlier technique of constructing the protagonist by bringing together and superimposing several themes and presences, and it is highly important that these presences are not drawn from the immediate surrounding world, from the proximities to which critics tend to point in their characterization of Pasternak's "metonymous heroes."[66] Rather, in a manner similar to the formation of Heinrich

---

64. Pasternak's letter is somewhat elusive in this regard, for sending to Bobrov only a part of the future novel, he still lets him know only one title—that of *Three Names* (and then in his characteristic manner insists that this is hardly important: "The novel will be called *Three Names* or something of the kind. At this point it's unimportant" [Роман будет называться "Три имени" или что-то в этом роде. Пока что это неважно] (*PSS* 7:348). Still he gives no other title to the work (Barnes 1989, 269ff).

65. Fateeva's summary of Tsvetkov's role in the text is apt (though in this chapter I tend to disagree with her stress on the "synthesis" and "naturalness" of Zhenya's growth in "The Stranger" and view the process instead as contradictory and counterpointed): "The synthesis of the idea of spiritual and organic growth as a reflection of the 'naturalness' of the individual development can be seen in the name 'Tsvetkov'" (2003, 225).

66. According to Michel Aucouturier, the character based on the metaphoric relations, "by analogy or opposition, connects the entire universe to the 'I' of the poet, while the art of

Heine in "The Mark of Apelles," where Heine is simultaneously a traveling stranger, a poet, a character in a manuscript, an ahistorical figure appearing at sunset, a power able to pierce darkness, and finally a great German poet, Tsvetkov becomes shaped not merely by his last name, or by the fact that he is associated with the approach of winter blizzards, but also by Lermontov and Lermontov's supernatural Demon (see Glazov-Corrigan 1991; Fateeva 2003, 225). In other words, Tsvetkov becomes the focus of multiple lines of relationship during the fall, as well as by their indefinite residue, and his trio of personalities—Lermontov, his Demon, and Tsvetkov—surely must bear some relation to the mysterious title planned for the larger novel.

Tsvetkov, it should be noted, belongs to a group of characters in Pasternak's world that simply do not fit the profile of the metonymic hero (who tends to dissolve into the surrounding world);[67] the outlines of selfhood in Tsvetkov's case present him as a receptacle of presences from "lands afar," that is, from very distant worlds. And even though the existence of the triadic relationship Tsvetkov-Lermontov-Demon has begun to be accepted in criticism,[68] the implications of this artistic technique are far from straightforward. The indefinite Tsvetkov has an everyday life that ultimately does not interest his author, apart from the fact that Tsvetkov, like Lermontov, is a lame artist; what interests Pasternak instead is how to construct a narrative subject who is, in effect, a *psychopompos*—a spirit or soul carrier.[69] The choice of the title *Demon* is itself an indicator of this aim, and because of the multilayered nature of this narrative construction, Tsvetkov's entry into the text opens an altogether new world in front of Zhenya's eyes. To emphasize the new layer of vision, a vocabulary of spirits gathering at the threshold of the Luvers's house is introduced at the very beginning of "The Stranger," but with all the Symbolist echoes that such a construction may suggest, the originality of Pasternak's

---

Pasternak, founded upon metonymy, on the contrary *dissolves the 'I,' and generally any kind of conscious or self-willed agent, in the image of a world where the "subject" is nothing but a grammatical fiction* because there exists only one single real subject, life, whose essence is supra-individual" (1969, 222; emphasis added). The relationship of Tsvetkov is, in fact, created by oppositions—to Lermontov, the Demon, storms, winter, discoloration—and if the protagonist is dissolved, it is definitely not in the surrounding world, but in other literary and intellectual universes of discourse.

67. See previous note.

68. Faryno (1993, 30ff) and Fateeva (2003, 329ff).

69. Pasternak actually indicates as much in "Some propositions" through his unusual emphasis on the relationship between the spirituality of prose [одухотворенность] and the emergence of the individual in the narrative: "By its feeling, through its spirituality, prose seeks and finds man in the category of speech. And when the man is found lacking in an age, then it recreates him from memory [. . .]" [Чутьем, по своей одухотворенности, проза ищет и находит человека в категории речи, а если век его лишен, то на память воссоздает его] (*CSP* 261–62; *PSS* 5:23–24).

narrative lies in his ability to fold the narrative world of spirits that crosses time and space into the framework of his earlier metonymous constructions. These layers are fused, and yet they are also distinct and bear different artistic attributes. Thus, the "strange little street," never to be visited or found by Zhenya again,[70] is a simple street crossed by others every day, and the three grieving women in black—Graces, Muses, or Fates, who suggest the presence of a Romantic poet destined to die young—might for other spectators simply be strange next-door neighbors. Seryozha's innocent reference to the lame man's "light in the window, late gatherings, and all night celebration" [Помнишь, я рассказывал—собирает людей, всю ночь пьют, свет в окне] (*CSP* 159, *PSS* 3:64) suggests to the Russian ear an unmistakable echo of Lermontov's "Tamara" and her illumined window's invitation to nightly visitors [И там сквозь туман полуночный / Блистал огонек золотой / Кидался он путникам в очи], as well as the feast in the darkness of night [шипели два кубка вина], to which she welcomes her visitors before destroying them with her caresses. And yet Seryozha can be (and is) totally unaware of the implication of these words. If Zhenya's life and character are to be changed by this "abstract moment," it is important to note that its narrative design pursues at least two interrelated goals. First, it suggests an altogether distinct world of symbolic presences and forces; and, second, it ensures that this other world remains masked and barely perceptible in the everyday reality of Ekaterinburg's life. To say that Pasternak simply tries to reconstruct the universe of the book in the child's mind is to trivialize a much more complex vision. For him such a narrative reflects a philosophical understanding of reality which has also become an artistic program that he is free to explore with all the artistic means within his power.

In a letter to Eugene Kayden (August 22, 1958) after the success of *Zhivago* awakened in the West interest in his early work, Pasternak carefully reconstructs the nature of Lermontov's presence in his own life of 1917. He writes to Kayden not of Lermontov's influence or of his memory, but of Lermontov's reality as a living person and (what is equally important) as an active living *spirit,* who had entered contemporary life and art, in order to assert the poetic freedom of everyday reality:

---

70. In the earlier draft of the scene of Tsvetkov's first appearance, Pasternak crosses out a passage with Seryozha and the Akhmedyanovs appearing on this hidden street as they return from "unknown destinations" [они прошли той дорогой, и, значит, не из дому, а неведомо откуда] (*PSS* 3:545–46). Zhenya's surprise at the boys' appearance is followed by the authorial voice observing that Zhenya was never able to find a way to that street (*PSS* 3:546). In the final text of *Luvers,* Pasternak emphasizes the "unfindability" of the street when the children return from a bookstore and meet Dikikh with the stranger (*CSP* 160; 3:64–65).

I dedicated *My Sister Life* not to the memory of Lermontov *but to the poet himself as though he was living in our midst*—to this spirit still effectual in our literature. What was he to me, you ask, in the summer of 1917?—*The personification of creative adventure and discovery, the principle of free poetical statement.* (Kayden 1959, ix; emphasis added)

Я посвятил "Сестру мою жизнь" не памяти Лермонтова, *но самому поэту, точно он сам жил среди нас*—его духу, все еще действенному в нашей литературе. Вы спрашиваете, чем он был для меня летом 1917 года. *Олицетворением творческой смелости и открытий, началом свободного поэтического утверждения повседневности.* (*PSS* 10:380)

In the same letter, Pasternak asserts that every historical period possesses "two time sequences": "the one known to all and the other that has not as yet taken place, infinite and concealed, for the future is always part of this ungraspable and unknown infinity [два времени —известное и еще не наставшее, бесконечное и неведомое, поскольку будущее всегда—часть этой неизведанной и незвестной бесконечности] (*PSS* 10:379). In the world of Pasternak in 1957 it is, perhaps, no longer appropriate to seek echoes of Kantian *a posteriori* and *a priori* time, and yet it is also clear that this philosophical manner of approaching reality never left the writer. His rendition of Lermontov's influence is to be understood in that context—the Romantic poet was for Pasternak in 1917 a necessary writer, a compatriot in acquiring a poetic voice and yet also a reminder of an "immeasurable" larger force of spirit, unfolding an otherwise impenetrable future.[71]

According to Pasternak's curious admission, Lermontov's entry into his own world in 1917 was tantamount to a huge biographical and artistic event. By contrast, however, Tsvetkov's entry into the life of Zhenya is of a somewhat different nature, for the child is only forming, and one cannot speak in her case about the discovery of a new poetic voice. This difference[72] may

---

71. See in *Luvers* at the beginning of "The Stranger," prior to the introduction of Lermontov: "One could not foretell the future, but it could be seen entering the house from outside. Here its scheme is already in evidence—a distribution to which it would be subject despite its recalcitrance in all else" [Будущего нельзя предсказать. Но его можно увидеть, войдя с воли в дом] (*CSP* 149; *PSS* 3:53).

72. Neither Faryno nor Fateeva comments on Lermontov's very different roles in Pasternak's poetry and prose of the period, an emphatic versus covert appearance (Faryno 1993). In fact, Fateeva believes that, in their textual references to Lermontov, both *My Sister Life* and *Luvers* express a similar position, namely, the author's farewell to the demonic sense of life, characteristic of childhood: "Pasternak says farewell to this child-like "demonic" sense of life in *My Sister Life* when he opens the poetic cycle with the poem "In the Demon's memory" [Памяти

explain why the subtlety of the correlation between Tsvetkov and Lermontov has no parallel in Pasternak's poetry of this period. In contrast to the evocative and indefinite resonances in the novella, Pasternak's *My Sister Life* is not only dedicated to Lermontov but opens with a clear celebration of Lermontov's storms[73]—a poem entitled "To the Memory of the Demon" [Памяти Демона] that depicts the Demon's elemental power in the ensuing chaos of nature after his nightly visits to Tamara:

> He came at night,
> With blue ice, from Tamara,
> With two wings he marked
> Where the nightmare would begin and end.

> Приходил по ночам
> В синеве ледника от Тамары
> Парой крыл намечал,
> Где гудеть, где кончаться кошмару. (*PSS* 1:114)

In poetry, Pasternak accepts unconditionally Lermontov's spirit and his longing for the storm, as in the poem "The sail" [А он мятежный ищет бури / Как будто в буре есть покой] as a new guide in the eventful summer of 1917. In the case of Pasternak's young fictional protagonist, however, there is a covert link to Lermontov, and the girl's momentary embrace of the elemental power of the winter blizzard is followed almost immediately by death and devastation in her family (see 7.6 below). In other words, the biographical intrusion of Lermontov into Pasternak's life and art is of a very different character than that visited on his heroine, and it is very possible that in this highly nuanced difference one finds a further key to Pasternak's manner of constructing his prose. The writer's own childhood may also provide an important textual clue.

7.6 Alexander Scriabin and "the freshness of his spirit"

Lermontov or his Demon enters Zhenya's life as both a living person and a spirit, emerging during the sunset from the enchanted street behind her house.

демона] while *The Childhood of Luvers* ends with "And without another word Lermontov was returned by the same hand and pushed back into the little slanting row of classics" (2003, 330).

73. After the dedication to Lermontov in *My Sister Life,* there follows the epigraph from Nicolaus Lenau within which the face of the beloved is intertwined with storms and clouds.

These presences will be superimposed on Tsvetkov and will have a profound effect upon the girl, while bringing her no happiness and signaling instead the approach of turmoil and disaster. As observed above (5.2), the composer Shestikrylov, whose very name suggests the image of a spiritual messenger, a Six-Winged Seraphim, is the closest textual prototype in this regard, for, just like Lermontov, Shestikrylov enters the inanimate world of the children's lives in "Ordering a Drama" with a storm of snowflakes and makes the children unrecognizable by awakening their self-consciousness and preparing them for the oncoming drama of life (and their future in art):

> Here is the scenario: twilight in the composer's apartment—and either there is no meaning in it or else it is to be followed by a drama. This is how it was in life too—there stood the inanimate principles, demanding to be set in motion, and people would start off here at a run, and some of them, the ones who always thought further than others, and more quickly became unrecognizable, they endured this delicious suffering: to work, to think upon the inanimate. And grew conscious of it. [. . .]
>
> Later, they became artists. (*MG* 29)

> Вот тут сценарий: сумерки в квартире композитора, и они или не имеют смысла, или за ними должна следовать драма; так и было в жизни,—стояли неодушевленные начала и требовали разбега; люди разбегались здесь, и некоторые из них, те, которые думали всегда дальше других и скорее становились неузнаваемыми для своих знакомых, они выносили это сладостное страдание работать, думать за неодушевленное. И сознавали его. [. . .]
>
> Впоследствии они стали художниками. (*PSS* 3:462)

The authorial insistence that the future speed of thought was initially found at this juncture [люди разбегались здесь], and the phrase "this was how it was in life" [так и было в жизни], constitute a valuable signal, simultaneously textual and autobiographical.

There was, in fact, only one artistic figure who influenced Pasternak's character in his adolescence with such force—the composer Alexander Scriabin.[74]

---

74. Barnes notes the interconnection between the role of Scriabin in Pasternak's life and his unpublished "Story of Counter-Octave," but omits altogether the references to the composer in "Ordering a Drama." He insists, nonetheless, that "Pasternak's early fascination with music, as well as the influence of Scriabin's personality and artistry, was not easily—nor was it ever completely—eradicated" (Barnes, 1977, 14).

"Ordering a Drama," then, can be viewed as Pasternak's first quasi-autobiographical sketch, as well as his first articulation of a three-layered universe, the creation of the necessary frame to explain Scriabin's power. Similarly to Scriabin's role, described in both of Pasternak's published autobiographies, Shestikrylov uncovers for his young pupils a layer of reality that was mute and invisible until his appearance, or rather until the entry of his music, which he always carries with him and by means of which he starts all the motion and commotion. Scriabin's link to Tsvetkov appears unlikely until one recollects that the very meaning of the name Tsvetkov must have a direct link to Scriabin's so-called "synesthetism," the composer's famous ability to hear musical notes as colors, and to his well known experiments with light-color-music synthesis.[75] Even the lameness of Tsvetkov, this clear reference to Lermontov, may yet refer to Scriabin, since, according to some critics, it was Scriabin's effect on the Pasternaks and their household in 1903 that resulted in Boris's fall from the horse[76] and his subsequent handicap: one of his legs considerably shorter than the other.

There is further biographical evidence to consider. In contrast to "Ordering a Drama," there is no mention of music in *Luvers,* but there is a poet and a spirit of his poetry. The enchanted street, opening a pathway "from this world to the other" is actually a reconstruction in fiction of the childhood event that both Pasternak and his brother Alexander narrated in their memoirs—namely their roaming in the park-like forest in the late spring of 1903 at the dacha at Obolenskoe and hearing the sound of a piano—their first introduction to what would prove later to be piano pieces from the *Divine Poem* (the Third Symphony), composed by their as yet unknown neighbor, Alexander Scriabin. Alexander Pasternak's recollection of the event is straightforward and factual:

> Unexpectedly, amidst the surrounding silence, which was deepened further by the singing of birds and the crackling sounds of the squirrels, we heard, very much from the distance, constantly breaking separated pieces of piano music. [. . .] We began to find our way towards the sounds. [. . .] In the forest's meadow, where we finally arrived, there were the thick impenetrable bushes. On the meadow in the sun's rays, there appeared a country house (dacha), the same as ours.

---

75. For documentary material on Scriabin's "color hearing," see Galeev and Vanechkina (2001).

76. See here Boris Gasparov's 1995 article in which he links Pasternak's fall from a horse on August 6, 1903, to Scriabin's "polyrhythmia" [полиритмия]. Gasparov views the rhythm of gallop ending in a fall as the imagery emblematic of Pasternak's prose, embodying an arrival of catastrophe intermixed with a "secret voice"—a call to transcendence.

It was from that house that the music was coming; it sounded as though someone were deciphering a new piece, but for that it sounded strange, unusual, without uncertain pauses at the more difficult parts. [. . .] My brother, who understood music more than I did, said, that without a doubt someone was composing there, and not memorizing or studying a new work. (*PSS* 11:11)

In Boris Pasternak's own recollection of the event in the *Sketch for an Autobiography* (May-June 1956), the setting of the mysterious street in *Luvers* is anticipated by the portrayal of an opening among the trees and the alteration of "the light and shade [that] followed each other in the forest" (*Remember* 36; *PSS* 3:302). There is once again an emphasis on the *spirit* of the artist's art—an elemental force, a fallen angel, not unlike Lermontov's Demon, but more playful and mischievous, and there emerges also the theme of eventual destruction, "the tragic force of the composition," corresponding to the character of the time:

Lord, what music it was! The symphony was continually crumbling and tumbling like a city under artillery fire, and was all the time growing and being built up out of debris and wreckage. It was brimful of ideas worked out to the point that was indistinguishable from frenzy, and at the same time as new as a forest, breathing life and freshness and, indeed, arrayed, surely, in the morning of a spring foliage of 1903 and not of 1803. [. . .] [T]he tragic force of the composition in the process of creation put out its tongue triumphantly at everything that was decrepit and generally accepted and majestically obtuse, and was bold to the point of frenzy, to a point of mischievousness, playfully elemental. And free like a fallen angel. (*Remember* 36–37)

Боже, что это была за музыка! Симфония беспрерывно рушилась и обваливалась, как город под артиллерийским огнем, и вся строилась и росла из обломков и разрушений. Ее всю переполняло содержание, до безумия разработанное и новое, как нов был жизнью и свежестью дышавший лес, одетый в то утро, не правда ли, весенней листвой 1903-го, а не 1803 года. [. . .] [Т]рагическая сила сочиняемого торжественно показывала язык всему одряхлело признанному и величественно тупому и была смела до сумасшествия, до мальчишества, шаловливо стихийная и свободная, как падший ангел. (*PSS* 3:302–3)

The spring setting in the memoirs of both brothers contrasts with the fall-winter world of "Ordering a Drama" and "The Stranger," but the portrait of Scriabin in *Safe Conduct* emphasizes both the winter blizzard and the evocation of the rebellious and destructive spirits in his art. Pasternak's adoration of Scriabin is animated through the description of the little demon who jumps from music posters onto young Pasternak's back as the boy walks through Moscow streets, while the power of adoration is not only "fierce" and "cruel," but "feverish" and "ravaging":

> So it was winter out of doors. The street was chopped a third shorter by dusk and full of errand running all day long. A whirl of streetlamps chased along after the street, lagging behind in the whirl of snowflakes. On my way home from school, the name Scriabin, covered with snow, *skipped from a poster onto my back*. [. . .] This adoration attacked me more cruelly and undisguisedly than any fever. [. . .], and the fiercer it was, the more surely it protected me from the ravaging effect of his indescribable music. (*CSP* 23; emphasis added)

> Итак, на дворе зима, улица на треть подрублена сумерками и весь день на побегушках. За ней, отставая в вихре снежинок, гонятся вихрем фонари. Обожанье это бьет меня жесточе и неприкрашеннее лихорадки. Дорогой из гимназии имя Скрябина, все в снегу, *соскакивает с афиши мне на закорки*. [. . .] [Э]то именно то безответное, неразделенное чувство, которого я и жажду. Только оно, и чем оно горячее, тем больше ограждает меня от опустошений, производимых его непередаваемой музыкой. (*PSS* 3:150)

In fact, in *The Childhood of Luvers,* as in both of his memoirs, Pasternak's meditation on the demonic aspect of these artistic intruders and on the spiritual reality they unfold is ultimately ambiguous. If in *Safe Conduct* Pasternak is still in awe of his "idol" and his compositions' "lyrical dwelling [. . .] materially equal to the whole universe, which had been ground down to make its bricks" [вымышленное лирическое жилище, материально равное всей ему на кирпич перемолотой вселенной] (*CSP* 25; *PSS* 3:152), then in the *Sketch for an Autobiography* his assessment of Scriabin's developing "superman" influence is very carefully nuanced.

Given that Scriabin had won him over "by the freshness of his spirit" [Скрябин покорял меня свежестью своего духа] (*Remember* 38; *PSS* 3:303), there is a distancing on Pasternak's part from the spiritual reality sought by the composer. The Pasternak of *Sketch for an Autobiography* clearly resists the Nietzschean direction of Scriabin's world view,[77] but the very manner in which Pasternak describes Scriabin's "superman" influence resonates with the depiction of Tsvetkov, particularly the belonging of both the fictional protagonist and the composer to a heroic "other world" that brings sorrow, and both figures' ability in their otherworldliness to define the situations they touch:

> That was the negative side of Scriabin's influence, which in everything else became decisive for me. His egocentric nature was appropriate and justified only in his case. The seeds of his views, childishly misinterpreted, fell on favorable ground.
>
> [. . .] *Almost since the night described by Rodionov, I had believed in the existence of a higher heroic world, which must be served rapturously, it might bring suffering.* [. . .]
>
> Actually not only must music be supermusic to mean anything, *but everything in the world must excel itself to be itself. Man, man's activity must include an element of infinity which lends form and character to everything.* (*Remember* 40–42; trans altered; emphasis added)

> Это была оборотная сторона скрябинского влияния, в остальном ставшего для меня решающим. Его эгоцентризм был уместен и оправдан только в его случае. Семена его воззрений, по-детски превратно понятых, упали на благодарную почву.
>
> [. . .] *Чуть ли не с родионовской ночи я верил в существование высшего героического мира, которому надо служить восхищенно, хотя он приносит страдания.* [. . .]
>
> Действительно, не только надо быть сверхмузыкой, чтобы что-то значить, но и все на свете должно превосходить себя, чтобы быть собою. *Человек, деятельность человека должны заключать элемент бесконечности, придающий явлению определенность,* характер. (*PSS* 3:305–6)

Thus, a most singular blend of Pasternak's autobiographical and intertextual resonances defines Tsvetkov's featureless presence, his "fog and mist" [туманное и общее],[78] while the superman motif of Scriabin's vision clearly

---

77. See here Barnes (1977, 15ff); Levi (1990, 21–23; 42–43).

78. See *Demon*: "This was not a horrifying spirit of Hell, / a sinful sufferer – oh, no. / He looked like a bright evening/ neither day, nor night / —neither darkness, nor light!" [То не был ада дух ужасный, / Порочный мученик—о нет! / Он был похож на вечер ясный: / Ни

had a conduit to Lermontov's *Demon,* "a speechless stranger of the fog" [при-
шлец туманный и немой] (Lermontov 2:361). In all of this, Pasternak's
conception of the human being resonates with the *a priori* of infinity and
indefiniteness that underlies sensation, in *Luvers* brought into the open and
given reality by the world of poetry and art that emerges when Zhenya reads
Lermontov.

7.7 Philosophical overtones of the indefinable Tsvetkov

In *Sketch for an Autobiography,* Pasternak describes Marina Tsvetaeva in a
somewhat puzzling manner, but one that is not exactly irrelevant to the issue
at hand: "in her work she rushed impetuously, eagerly, and almost rapaciously
toward the achievement of finality and definiteness" [В жизни и творчестве
она стремительно, жадно и почти хищно рвалась к окончательности и
определенности] (*Remember* 110; *PSS* 3:340). It is very probable that in this
oblique fashion Pasternak establishes his difference from Tsvetaeva, for ever
since his student notes the question of indefiniteness in art and in sensations
was a concept he tended to emphasize. The question of the indefinable residue
associated with human destiny is evident, for example, in Pasternak's student
notes on Kant, Cohen, and Natorp, particularly when he speaks about psychology and the need to "break" through the limits of materiality to introduce
the human self whose teleological "end" is antagonistic to the material "thing-
ness" in the sphere of experience:

> The more clear is our organism as an object of study, the more mysterious
> it is as a unity of life; and then considering its living principle, we break its
> material thingness, its sphere of experience. And separating it, on the one
> side, from its belonging to the laws which constitute material thingness, we
> grant to it, on the other side, its own empirical law, as we return it to the
> unity of the subject, which as an object, in its own idea, is not constituted,
> but regulated and teleological. In other words, its teleological principle is
> antagonistic to the material thingness.

> Чем яснее нам организм, как предмет познания, тем он непонятнее,
> как единство жизни; и тогда мысля его жизненность, мы прорываем
> сферу предметности, сферу опыта. И лишая его, с одн[ой] стороны,
> причастности всеобщему закону, конституирующему предметность,

день, ни ночь,—ни мрак, ни свет!] (Lermontov 2:362).

с друг[ой] стороны наделяя его собств[енным] эмпирич[еским] законом, возвращаем его единству субъекта, кот[орый] как предмет, в своем мыслимом происхождении не конститутивен, а регулятивен и телеологичен. Т.е. телеологический принцип антагоничен принципу предметности. (*Lehrjahre* II:141)

The question of the indefiniteness and incompleteness in a human being is reflected most strongly in Cohen's "ethical ideal," which the founder of the Marburg school described in the following terms: "The ethical ideal contains three moments: completeness, fulfillment, the incompleteness of fulfillment" (*ERW* 424; trans. Poma, 2006, 151). From within this context one can approach the ethical education of Zhenya, which emphasizes the power of commandments toward "a third person, totally indifferent, with no name, or only a fortuitous one, neither arousing hatred nor inspiring love" (*CSP* 176; *PSS* 3:84). This manner of defining an ethical pathway in otherwise indefinable territory reflects Cohen's insistence that the foundational principle of selfhood is the "yearning of the self" for the subject beyond material experience, the yearning for the indefinable "other" which—and this is highly important—possesses no clear outlines and remains a receding, teleological goal that is invariably incomplete:

> Yearning (*Sehnsucht*) is above all an expansive feeling of the Ego; it spreads the Ego beyond the limits within which it must move and feel itself. [. . .]
> Thus the monologue of yearning becomes a dialogue, a duel between lovers, or even that of a single partner in the various phases of his love or under the different connected effect of other feelings. (*ARG* 2, Bd. 1, pp 26ff; trans. Poma 2006, 377–78)

The importance of the indefinite range within the human self (both in Zhenya's growth and in the human subject who becomes the indefinable focus of her interest), which can be thus only regulated by laws and commandments, both corresponds to and reflects Cohen's emphasis on the overlap of ethical and religious frameworks.

There is more than an accidental overlap between Pasternak's introduction of the Commandments concluding his portrayal of the "featureless man" and Cohen's philosophical postulation of laws. While Cohen insists: "Better a man who acts because he received a commandment than a man who has not received a commandment and acts" (*RV* 381; trans. Kajon 114), Pasternak concludes with respect to the theme of Tsvetkov:

[T]he impression [. . .] lay beyond the girl's control, because it was vitally important and significant, and its significance consisted in the fact that was the first time another human being had entered her life—a third person, totally indifferent, with no name, or only a fortuitous one, neither arousing hatred, not inspiring love, but the *person whom Commandments have in mind,* addressing men with names and consciousness, when they say: "Thou shall not kill." "Thou shalt not steal." et cetera. . . . (*CSP* 176; emphasis added)

То впечатление [. . .] заключалось в том, что в ее жизнь впервые вошел другой человек, третье лицо, совершенно безразличное, без имени или со случайным, не вызывающее ненависти и не вселяющее любви, но *то, которое имеют в виду заповеди,* обращаясь к именам и сознаниям, когда говорят: не убий, не крадь и все прочее. (*PSS* 3:84)

Pasternak's concluding insistence that there is "no name for such an impression" corresponds to Cohen's argument that the preservation of the inexhaustible potential in every human activity must be preserved in perception, knowledge, and art:

The concept is a question and remains a question, nothing but a question. The answer which it contains must also be a new question, it must raise a new question. This is precisely the intimate methodological relation which exists between question and answer: that every question must itself be an answer; therefore every answer also can and must be a question. It is a new type of reciprocal conditioning, of reciprocal action, which is question and answer. No solution can be regarded as definitive. The concept is not an absolute totality. (*LRE* 378; trans. Poma 2006, 151)

There is, however, a further theme in common between Cohen and Pasternak: this "infinite" or "incomplete" principle of selfhood is connected in Cohen with the notion of suffering as a characteristic of the human subject, a theme reflected in Pasternak in the death of Tsvetkov. Readers of Cohen identify this emphasis on suffering with his "anti-eudaimonism" or with Cohen's radical opposition to Nietzsche's Superman.[79] As Cohen writes in *Die Messiasidee,*

---

79. For Cohen's dislike of Nietzsche, see Renz (2005, 308) and Poma (1997, 242).

[. . .] the entire cult of heroes must be destroyed. This gives birth to the moving image of the servant of God, who, like a miserable, afflicted, despised man of pain and suffering, with neither appearance nor beauty, is led, like a lamb, to the slaughter, and, like a sheep, falls dumb before its shearers. (*Die Messiasidee,* J1:114; trans. Poma 2006, 243–44)

In opposition to the triumph of power in Nietzsche, Cohen—who, one should add, would never shake the hand of a Jew who had accepted Christianity— viewed this overlapping emphasis on the suffering man in both the Jewish and Christian religious traditions as history's deepest puzzle:

It is truly an unparalleled irony of history that the story of Jesus Christ's life, sealed by his death, should have become the source of the main difference between Christianity and Judaism. The history of this passion is an imita- tion of the messianic imagination of the Deutero-Israel, while the latter, as is now commonly agreed, anticipated the history of 'the remnant of Israel.' And hence, according to this poetic image, the history of Christ is actually the history of Israel. The philosophy of history of future generations will have to consider and fathom the riddle of the most intimate history of the spirit, as far as it has unfolded up to this time. (RoR, 439–40)

This philosophical context underlies the principle of the indefinite "other" in human life, introduced in Pasternak in his seemingly vague sketch of the lame stranger.

7.8 Sensing transition:
Temporal and spatial complexities of the conclusion

When Zhenya returns home after her mother's miscarriage and subsequent sickness, she suddenly notices that the spirit of her house no longer guards its inhabitants against the enclosing threat of external darkness. This darkness is now ominous; the sounds of mangling linen echo like the rumbling of a vio- lent attack,[80] and the dark forest outside the windows is slowly surrounding her family and moving step by step toward her hitherto protected world:

---

80. Faryno approaches the sound of the mangling of clothes as an important part of the burial rite for Tsvetkov (1993, 37). It is more probable, however, that the rhythms attached to this repetitive washing are linked with the upcoming endangerment of the house. The house spirit, inviolable at the beginning of the fall, is now clearly under attack.

The curtains reached down to the floor, and down to the floor the starry night also hung through the window, and low down, waist deep in the snow-drifts, two thick, dark trees rambled into the clear light of the window, trailing the glittering chains of their branches through deep snow. And somewhere through the wall the firm rumble of the mangling went up and down, tightly constricted by the sheets. (*CSP* 177)

Гардины опускались до полу и до полу свешивалась зимняя звездная ночь за окном, и низко, по пояс в сугробах, волоча сверкающие цепи ветвей по глубокому снегу, брели дремучие деревья на ясный огонек в окне. И где-то за стеной, туго стянутый простынями, взадвперед ходил твердый грохот раскатки. (*PSS* 3:84)

With great care, Pasternak sets the final scene of the story in such a way that both temporal and spatial descriptions appear to become porous, pervaded by invisible presences. The temporal chronology has already been twisted by the appearance of Tsvetkov after his death at Defendov's house and by all of Zhenya's experiences with him "at every step, constantly, directly or indirectly, and even, as on the last occasion, quite contrary to all possibility" [на каждом шагу, постоянно, прямо и косвенно и даже, как это случилось в последний раз, наперекор возможности] (*CSP* 178; *PSS* 3:85). Time as a single unit, like the death of Tsvetkov, contains a hidden multiplicity of presences, and this new elasticity of time is perhaps Zhenya's last lesson from Tsvetkov. It also marks the stranger's last appearance in the story, when Zhenya realizes as she talks with Dikikh that her quantitative count of deaths was faulty:

> "Do you have some sorrow too? So many deaths—and all of a sudden!" she sighed.
>   But he was about to tell her his story when something quite inexplicable occurred. The young girl suddenly changed her ideas about this quantity, and clearly forgetting the evidence provided by the lamp she had seen that morning, she said anxiously, "Wait. One time you were at the tobacconist's—Negaraat was leaving—I saw you with someone. Was it he?"—She was afraid to say "Tsvetkov." (*CSP* 177)

> —И у вас тоже горе? Сколько смертей—и все вдруг,—вздохнула она.
>   Но только собрался он рассказывать, что имел, как произошло что-то необ'яснимое. Девочка внезапно стала других мыслей об их количестве, и видно забыв, какою опорой располагала в виденной в то утро лампе, сказала взволнованно: "Погодите. Раз как-то вы

были у табачника, уезжал Негарат; я вас видала еще с кем-то. Этот?"
Она боялась сказать: "Цветков?" (*PSS* 3:85)

The room where Zhenya meets Dikikh offers an equally porous firmament.
The floor has become a receptacle for multiple worlds, so much so that Dikikh
has to step very gingerly across the dark room, and Zhenya warns him of the
corner chest that might as well be a mountain because of the linguistic double-
entendre (горка-гора):

> Dikikh [. . .] stood up and looked like a stork. He stretched his neck
> and raised one foot, ready to fly to her aid. He rushed to look for the girl,
> deciding there was nobody at home and that she had fainted. And all the
> time he bumped in the dark in the puzzles made of wool, wood, and metal,
> Zhenya was sitting in the corner weeping. But he continued to rummage
> and grope, and in thought he was already raising her from the carpet in a
> dead faint. He shuddered when a voice sounded loudly at his elbow, amid
> whimpers: "I am here. Be careful, there is the cabinet [mountain] there.
> Wait for me in a classroom. I'll come in a moment." (*CSP* 177)

> Диких [. . .] встал, похожий на аиста. Вытянул шею и припод-
> нял ногу, готовый броситься на помощь. Он кинулся отыскивать
> девочку, решив, что никого нет дома, а она лишилась чувств. А тем
> временем, как он тыкался впотьмах на загадки из дерева, шерсти
> и металла, Женя сидела в уголочке и плакала. Он же продолжал
> шарить и ощупывать, в мыслях уже подымая ее замертво с ковра.
> Он вздрогнул, когда за его локтями раздалось громко, сквозь всхли-
> пывание: "Я тут. Осторожней, там горка. Подождите меня в клас-
> сной. Я сейчас приду." (*PSS* 3:84)

These temporal and spatial layers, gathered in a single unit and a single person, are reflected in the theme of the commandments addressed to the living
self and yet concerned with the "featureless generalized man." This theme
appears on the last page of the story, and is completed by the indefinable
hand of the author shaking the row of classics, as Dikikh and Zhenya prepare
for a new lesson and she abruptly refuses to read the book pointed out by her
tutor.

> When she saw which book Dikikh was taking from the shelf, she frowned
> and said, "No, I can't answer on that today. Put it back in its place. Excuse
> me, please . . . ."

And without another word Lermontov was returned by the same hand and pushed back into the little slanting row of classics. (*CSP* 178)

Когда она увидела, какую книгу берет Диких с полки, она нахмурилась и заявила: "Нет. Этого я сегодня отвечать не стану. Положите на место. Виновата: пожалуйста."

И без дальних слов, Лермонтов был тою же рукой втиснут назад в покосившийся рядок классиков. (*PSS* 3:85)

The fact that the row of classics is shaken at the story's conclusion intimates Pasternak's indirect celebration of his own artistic achievement, emphasizing the final movement of a hand that has completed the story—a hand whose textual identity is unknown since its syntactical antecedent cannot be located within the narrative. As a result, the image points indirectly to the hand of the story's author while it also recapitulates all the "hands" that signal transitions in Zhenya's growth (see 7.8).

Zhenya Luvers's story ends surrounded by darkness—Pasternak's only direct reference to the immediate historical reality of 1917–18. This theme is stated in *Safe Conduct* with more emphasis, as Pasternak points to a world in need of color and remembers his tutoring of Inna Vysotskaya on the eve of unparalleled and fateful changes. Reconstructing this once peaceful setting, he speaks of white space in need of color, of a blackboard with traces of instruction, and of time impregnated by its as yet invisible content, collecting twelve years later so many themes that appeared first in *The Childhood of Luvers*:

It was the time of year when people dissolve paint in pots of boiling water, and gardens, left to their own devices, warm themselves idly in the sunshine, all cluttered with snow shovelled down from everywhere. [. . .]

I do not know why all this impressed itself on me in the image of a school blackboard with the chalk not quite rubbed off. Oh, if we had been made to stop then, and the blackboard wiped to a gleaming wetness, and if instead of theorems about isometric pyramids, they had expounded to us in fine copperplate, with carefully thickened strokes of the pen, just what lay ahead of us both. Oh, how dumbfounded we should have been. (*CSP* 46)

Это было то время года, когда в горшочках с кипятком распускают краску, а на солнце, предоставленные себе самим, праздно греются сады, загроможденные сваленным отовсюду снегом. Они до краев налиты тихою, яркою водой. [. . .]

Не знаю, отчего все это запечатлелось у меня в образе классной доски, недочиста оттертой от мела. О, если бы остановили нас тогда и, отмыв доску от влажного блеска, вместо теорем о равновеликих пирамидах, каллиграфически, с нажимами изложили то, что нам предстояло обоим. О, как бы мы обомлели! (*PSS* 3:176)

Boundary: Seasons and stages of growth	Direction of perception and permeable compound	Emotional state	Residue on the margins of the compound	The images of the hands controlling the situation	The character of time and space
5th Boundary Early Fall	1. Relations with Others. 2. Reading Lermontov. 3. "Happy people!" Three Muses or Fates in black—or neighbors next door?	1. Alarm at one's own subservience and at the facelessness of others. 2. Interest in the street from the "other world" and the "stranger."	"Metallic facts." Mr. Luvers's Sickness. A short man with a crippled gait on the street behind the garden	3 sets of hands: 1. A bast scrubber in the soldier Prokhor's [?] hands (or in the hands of the clouds [?]). 2. The book, turned outward, in Zhenya's hands. 3. The stranger with a gait, carrying under his arm "an enormous album or atlas."	Space and time transfixed by atemporal presences: "Borne through the gloomy garden from this world to the other, the faraway alley glowed with the light that illuminates events in a dream."
6th Boundary Late Fall and Arrival of winter	Multiple worlds coming into a collision. Zhenya's witnessing "ravishingly dreadful [...] kingdoms—quite satanically entrancing."	1. Excitement at the storm and the pleasure of the quiet home. 2. Pain.	Facts still unknown to Zhenya: Mrs. Luvers's miscarriage as she steps out of the theater during the storm, her sickness, and the death of Tsvetkov under the hoofs of the horse.	Hands indicating irresolvable contradiction: "Dikikh [walking with Tsvetkov] frequently raising his hands with fingers splayed. He would not agree, and he tried to prove with all fingers that his companion . . ."	The shaking of time and space. The overwhelmed earth: "The heavens quivered, and down from them tumbled whole white kingdoms and countries."
7th Boundary Deep winter	In the house of the sacristan Defendov before returning home. External and internal gaze.	Loss of the familiar. Regaining mother inside. Wonder at the departing shadows.	Sexual knowledge.	3 sets of hands: 1. Defendov's "dry hand reach out for [...] the lamp as though "he were lifting a glass filled to the brim." 2. "Zhenya's hands and arms were occupied, though she was holding nothing in them." 3. "the sleeves of a phantom moved [...] the light moved in a curtained window."	The porous nature of the new space and time.
8th Boundary The hoarfrost had gone from the frames. Winter entering the house.	Multiple worlds unified in the new state of Zhenya's grasp of the situation.	Approaching the world of the Commandments.	The outer world of "thick dark trees" in chains approaching the "clear light of the window."	"And without another word Lermontov was returned by the same hand and pushed back into the little slanting row of classics."	"The puzzles made of wool, wood, and metal."

8

Conclusion

Pasternak's Symbolic World: Prose and Philosophy

Pasternak did not like his early style and rarely spoke about the influence of philosophy upon his thought. For the last three years of his life, he was openly distressed when his publishers in the West, in order to capture the interest of the market after the success of *Doctor Zhivago,* proceeded to seek out, translate, and publish his early prose. These prose works generated very little critical debate even when they were read by Russia's expert readers, and they could promise their author no change in this regard, especially after the critical exegeses of *Zhivago* that he so often found disappointing. Thus, he expected nothing good from unearthing works that he assessed not merely as immature, but as aesthetically and morally opposed to what he tried to do in his later art. This was altogether a harsh judgment. As far as this study is concerned, it also presents a formidable problem. In the process of analysis, it has been established (not without an element of surprise) that many of Pasternak's later ideas, metaphors, and symbols were already present in their essential and even intricately developed form in these earlier stories. How then can one explain Pasternak's explicit negativity, and how does this affect the status of the underlying philosophical themes that pervade so many of Pasternak's earlier images and symbols? In drawing conclusions and evaluating our findings and premises in a focused manner, we must re-evaluate not only the metaphor–metonymy opposition so central to the issue of Pasternak's symbolic language; we must also discuss, where appropriate, the unexpected longevity of these earlier images and paradigms within his later style known for its simplicity of expression. However, as we draw conclusions, it is equally important to determine, as far as possible, the deeper reasons for his rejection of these earlier stories.

8.1 Assessing Pasternak's later view of his early prose

In his letter to the German musicologist Renata Schweitzer (December 1958),[1] Pasternak insists that the very intensity of the spirit of *Zhivago* was undermined by the republication of his earlier prose, which had participated, or so he claims, in the overall "destruction of form," characteristic of the beginning of the twentieth century:

> It is all tarred with the brush of the expressionist era, of the disintegration of form, of half-baked content, abandoned to the mercies of the manner that was adventitious, poorly understood, weak, and empty. The reason *Zhivago* rises above all this is because it is a spiritual act—a spiritual achievement. (Ivinskaya 1978a, 308; trans. altered)

> Все это носит на себе клеймо . . . эпохи экспрессионизма, распада формы, невыдержанного содержания, отданного на произвол случайности неполного понимания, слабого и пустого. Именно потому поднимается Ж. над всем этим, что в нем есть сгущение духа, что он является духовным подвигом. (quoted from Ivinskaya 1978b, 329)

He finds it ironic, he writes to Natalya Sologub in June 1959, that his efforts to address the madness of the century and his earlier acquiescent role of follower have resulted in new interest in the very works he wants most to forget. Participation in the "destruction of forms" is mentioned again:

> In the years of turmoil which we all went through together, I managed, through the lack of seriousness, to commit very many errors and sins. How

---

1. Pasternak's letters to Renate Schweitzer were published by her in German in 1963. The Russian original has not survived, and scholars question on occasion the authenticity of some of the letters published by Schweitzer (see *PSSCom* 10:486). Ivinskaya, however, kept copies of some of Pasternak's letters, so several letters to Schweitzer (both originals and English translations) are cited from Ivinskaya's memoirs.

terrible and inexpressibly sad that not only Russia, but the whole "civilized world" was afflicted by this disintegration of forms and concepts during several decades. [. . .]

The success of the novel, with its evidence of my wish to contribute to the belated work of bringing our age to its senses, has meant that everywhere people are rushing to translate and publish all the stuff put out by me in those years when we lapsed into folly and barbarism [. . .] (quoted from Ivinskaya 1978a, 308)

В годы основных общих нам всем потрясений я успел, по несерьезности, очень много напутать и нагрешить. Как страшно и непоправимо грустно, что не одну Россию, а весь "Просвещенный мир" постиг этот распад форм и понятий в течение нескольких десятилетий. [. . .]

Успех романа и знаки моей готовности принять участие в позднем образумлении века повели к тому, что везде бросились переводить и издавать все, что я успел пролепетать и нацарапать именно в эти годы дурацкого одичания. (*PSS* 10:509)

However, while writing to George Reavey (December 10, 1959), he not only admits his own "inexpressibly painful" reaction to the publication of his earlier prose, but he explicitly isolates the causes of his weariness: the immaturity of the prose and its schematic, deadening execution:

My inexpressible pain and grief are caused by the fact that again and again I am reminded about those rare grains of life and truth that are intermixed with great quantities of deadening schematic nonsense and unreal and raw material. I am surprised at the reason that makes you and Kayden attempt to save works clearly destined to perish.

Мое невыразимое горе и боль в том, что мне вновь и вновь напоминают, что эти редкие зерна жизни и правды перемешаны с огромным количеством мертвой, схематичной бессмыслицы и несуществующего сырья. Я удивляюсь, зачем Вы и Кайден пытаетесь спасти вещи, заведомо обреченные на гибель. (*PSS* 10:550)

For the purposes of analysis, epithets like "schematic nonsense" and "unreal and raw material" present the clearest point of departure: for even a cursory comparison between what he expected from art as a young man and his expressed aims during the composition of *Zhivago* indicate a major contrast. In "The Black Goblet" (1914), Pasternak argues that an artistic text is a tightly packaged parcel, made up of symbols placed in intense proximity to each other and exhibiting a controlled multi-layered space—a craft for which he thanked the Impressionists. The artistic narrative becomes in this rendition a *"coffre volant,"* filled with carefully selected goods, ready to travel through the centuries:

> You [impressionists] have brought up the whole generation of skillful packaging experts. You began by inviting from abroad the most experienced teachers—symbolists—to wrap up with symbols the whole oversaturated globe in the blue valleys. And you opened your own school.
>
> You, impressionists, have taught us how to roll the paintings, roll the evenings, to lower into the cotton of twilight the fragile objects of fancy.

> Вы воспитали поколение упаковщиков. Вы стали выписывать из-за границы опытных учителей: *des symbolistes pour emballer la globe comblée dans les vallées bleues des symboles.* И открыли собственную школу.
>
> Вы, импрессионисты, научили нас сверстывать версты, сверстывать вечера, в хлопок сумерек погружать хрупкие продукты причуд. (*PSS* 5:12)

Already in *Safe Conduct* he denigrates this earlier form of expression as a handicap that "forces a person into performing acrobatics" [как иное увечье обрекает на акробатику] (*CSP* 31; *PSS* 3:159). And in *Sketch for an Autobiography* he expresses dislike for his style prior to 1940 and proceeded to inform his readers that, as a young artist, he had been far too attached to the fashionable mannerisms of artistic expression. The "break up of forms" appears again:

> The general disintegration of forms in those days, the impoverishment of thought, the uneven and impure style are foreign to me. (*Remember* 81) Everything spoken in a normal way rebounded from me. I forgot that words by themselves can mean and contain something apart from the cheap toys with which they are strung. [. . .] It was not the essential I looked for in everything, but some additional spice. (*Remember* 105)

> Мне чужд общий тогдашний распад форм, оскудение мысли, засоренный и неровный слог. (*PSS* 3:327)
> Все нормально сказанное отскакивало от меня. Я забывал, что слова сами по себе могут что-то заключать и значить, помимо побряку-

шек, которыми их увешивали. [. . .] Я во всем искал не сущности, а посторонней остроты. (*PSS* 3:338)

The Pasternak of *Doctor Zhivago,* of course, would never speak of the narrative text as a carefully packaged parcel; nor would he seek additional "spice." As he tells Gladkov in June of 1948, he is dreaming about a covert, thoroughly "camouflaged" originality; he conceives of a prose where images contain clear thought with no need for further translation, schematization, or explanation:

No—I am not by any means saying I am for giving up originality of expression, but I aim at a kind of originality unobtrusive, concealed in a simple and familiar form, restrained and unassuming—so that the subject matter is absorbed by the reader without noticing. I dream of a form by virtue of which the reader becomes, so to speak, one's co-author—an inconspicuous style in which nothing intervenes between the idea of a thing and its depiction. (Gladkov 1977, 133)

A similar goal is pursued by his protagonist Yuri Zhivago:

It had been a dream of his life to write with originality so discreet, so well concealed, as to be unnoticeable in its disguise of current and customary forms; all his life he had struggled for a style so restrained, so unpretentious that the reader of the hearer would fully understand the meaning without realizing how he assimilated it. He had striven constantly for unostentatious style, and he was dismayed to find how far he still remained from this ideal. (*Zhivago* 440)

Всю жизнь мечтал он об оригинальности сглаженной и приглушенной, внешне неузнаваемой и скрытой под покровом общеупотребительной и привычной формы, всю жизнь стремился к выработке того сдержанного, непритязательного слога, при котором читатель и слушатель овладевают содержанием, сами не замечая, каким способом они его усваивают. Всю жизнь он заботился о незаметном стиле, не привлекающем ничьего внимания, и приходил в ужас от того, как он еще далек от этого идеала. (*PSS* 4:438)

These passages are as famous as they are elusive (for all their insistence on simplicity). The apparent unpretentiousness of his hoped-for narratives expects from writing an organic transformation and natural growth, free life, and air—hence Pasternak appears to reject his early prose for being too much governed by abstract and schematic intellectual constructions. Yuri Zhivago, for example, attributes to the works of Pasternak's favorite writer, Chekhov, a natural ability to ripen with time as if they were apples, getting ready for harvest and acquiring ever more sweetness and sense [подобно снятым с дерева дозревающим яблокам сама доходит в преемственности, наливаясь все большею сладостью и смыслом] (*PSS* 4:284). The natural metaphor thus employed is not accidental; the emphasis on living narrative is everywhere, including the very name of his protagonist, Zhivago. "I would landscape my poems as a garden, with all the tremor of my veins" [Я б разбивал стихи как сад /Всей дрожью жилок], says Pasternak in 1956 (*PSS* 2:149). His own earlier works, he truthfully thought, did not possess this quality—they were, just as he had announced in "The Black Goblet," highly complex, intensely layered and carefully controlled texts.

And yet it is also true that the leopard never really changes its spots. If in *Zhivago* Pasternak is trying to camouflage originality by writing a love story full of events and collisions, Pasternak's earlier prose camouflages its tightly packaged thought, the precision of its construction, and its philosophical intensity by a certain eccentricity of expression. The intensity of his earlier writing is startling, but it puzzles rather than illuminates, tending on the whole, as Pasternak admitted to V. P. Polonsky in 1921 (*PSS* 7:370–72), to keep "the technical effects outside the reader's field of vision and serve them up to him in a ready form, hypnotically" (quoted from Barnes 1989, 270). Pasternak's later writing exhibits, by contrast, a simplicity of narrative style and an engrossing speed, but again it leaves the reader perplexed about the apparent obliqueness of its symbolic vision and its "concealed originality"; over time critics have found it easier to assess these experimentations as evidence of political and historical, rather than artistic value. Thus, both periods (earlier and later) employ a covert strategy with different aims, but, perhaps, with similar results—the symbolic language of his narratives throughout his life brought their author much disappointment, as far as their critical reception was concerned. Whether in 1918 or in the 1950s, Pasternak misjudged his readers and critics: all too frequently in both periods he met with the incomprehension of his contemporaries.

Moreover, philosophy played a definitive role in both periods, even though Pasternak was very reluctant to elucidate or clarify this. The late 1950s were no different. Only when thoroughly downhearted about the reception of *Zhivago* did Pasternak start to admit to his Western correspondents that the key to his symbolism was "a philosophical rendition of reality." In a letter to Jacqueline de Proyart of May 20, 1959, frequently cited by critics, Pasternak states unequivocally that the essence of *Zhivago*'s symbolism consists in presenting "reality as a philosophical category" [реальность как явление или как философскую категорию] (*PSS* 10:489). In clarifying his aims, he stresses that his prose argues for the existence of "a particular kind of reality," unified as a single movement, an inner impulse. Such reality, he insists, has been known to philosophers of different ages under different names and different approaches:

> One should not think that it is something totally new, that earlier no one had such a goal. On the contrary, "larger art" always attempted to communicate the unified picture of life, life in its wholeness, but it was done and commented upon always in a different way, in accordance with the philosophy of the époque and because of this by different methods. [...]

> Не надо думать, что это что-то совсем новое, что раньше не задавались подобными целями. Наоборот, великое искусство всегда стремилось зарисовать общее восприятие жизни в целом, но это делалось (толковалось ее неделимое единство) каждый раз по-разному, в согласии с философией своего времени. [...] (*PSS* 10:489–90)

The conclusion to the present study must offer, then, some clarification of this statement, for if Pasternak's symbolism reflects reality as a category of philosophy, it must also echo—even as a point of contrast—the philosophical concerns of his younger self. For the earlier period we have the testimony of his student philosophical notes; no such archival data can be marshaled for his later work, and the dialectical materialism practiced *en masse* in his country was certainly not a philosophical school to which such a reality could testify. Thus, one has to start at the beginning and assess whether or not his earlier philosophical interests may have still served as a guide, however partial, to Pasternak's later corpus in a manner reminiscent of their effect on his earlier work.

8.2 Metaphor and metonymy:
Pasternak's philosophical studies and their role in his early prose

In "The Wassermann Test," Pasternak distinguishes, as we remember, between association by similarity and association by contiguity, an opposition developed under the influence of David Hume and proposed as part of his literary credo in his negative review of Vadim Shershenevich. According to Pasternak's argument, metaphors can be developed both by contiguity and similarity, and he finds "association by contiguity" an essential principle in the development of metaphoric language. His criticism of Shershenevich is simple: Shershenevich's metaphors rely only on "the fact of similarity," not even "association by similarity," and for this reason these metaphors possess no integral character; the necessary inner poetic work required for synthesis and integration is lacking:

> A lyrical agent, call him by any name or term, is, first of all, a principle of integration. The elements which are submitted to such integration or, better still, receive their life from it, are less significant than the process itself. [. . .]
>
> The fact of similarity, rarer the association through similarity and never through contiguity—this is the genesis of Shershenevich's metaphors.

> Лирический деятель, называйте его как хотите,—начало интегрирующее прежде всего. Элементы, которые подвергаются такой интеграции или, лучше, от нее только получают свою жизнь, глубоко в сравнению с нею несущественны. [. . .]
>
> Факт сходства, реже ассоциативная связь по сходству и никогда не по смежности—вот происхождение метафор Шершеневича. (*PSS* 5:9; 10)

In Roman Jakobson's rendition, the similarity–contiguity opposition becomes the famous contrast between metaphor and metonymy: metaphor is an association by similarity between images that belong to different realities; metonymy is an association by contiguity between elements in adjacent series. This terminology has since become the language of linguistics and poetics, its straightforward simplicity catapulting an unknowing David Hume into the enigmatic world of literary symbolism in general, and Pasternak's symbolism in particular.

In contrast to Jakobson's view of Pasternak as a virtuoso of metonymy, this study has argued for the metaphoric depth and complexity of his early prose, while demonstrating that these qualities emerge most powerfully when his artistic narratives are placed alongside his philosophical interests. This study has shown that metaphoric relationships—association by similarity—emerge when Pasternak's texts are examined not within their generic classifications, but rather when they are assessed across genres and disciplines, and understood as infused by a philosophical understanding of selfhood. Pasternak's image of the book fern in *Safe Conduct* (see Chapter 1) offers in this regard a significant direction for inquiry, all the more so because the writer himself uses this image ostensibly to explain the reasons for his farewell to a professional career in philosophy, and draws instead a picture of intense philosophical involvement, albeit with specific emphasis—in bridging the transitions between philosophical themes and literary exempla:

> [W]hen [. . .] I turned to books, I was drawn to them not from interest and knowledge but by the wish to find literary references in support for my idea. And despite the fact that my work was being accomplished by means of logic, imagination, paper and ink, I loved it most for the way in which in the course of the writing it became overgrown with a thicker and thicker ornamentation of comparisons and quotations from books. (*CSP* 51)

> [К]огда я [. . .] обращался к книгам, я тянулся к ним не из бескорыстного интереса к знанью, а за литературными ссылками в его пользу. Несмотря на то, что работа моя осуществлялась с помощью логики, воображенья, бумаги и чернил, больше всего я любил ее за то, что по мере писанья она обрастала все сгущавшимся убором книжных цитат и сопоставлений. (*PSS* 3:183)

Resonating similarities and internal echoes between philosophical themes and literary images became, in turn, a major characteristic of the metaphoric patterns of his early prose. Jakobson's view that the early metaphoric Pasternak is too preoccupied with emotions to try out an epic genre (1969, 139) is based upon an implicit indifference to Pasternak's engagement with philosophy. For this reason his approach to Pasternak's craft—together with his assessment of its stylistic technique primarily as a mastery of metonymy—cuts out the whole scope of the paradigms that consolidate the reality of Pasternak's metaphors, namely, his highly significant evocations of major philosophical themes and his frequent disagreement with them. For this reason the juxtaposition of Pasternak's student diaries and his early fictional narratives proves to be both puzzling and illuminating, and it demonstrates that philosophical themes are never superimposed as foreign objects upon a literary narrative; neither are they concealed in Pasternak's prose. They are an intrinsic part of his early symbolic language, and the resulting tension signals a need for further exploration and comparison. If we rephrase Pasternak's words in "The Wassermann Test," philosophical paradigms offer "a key to the ornamental lock" [метафору хочется сравнить с тем узорчатым замком] (*PSS* 5:10) that clarifies the principles of his metaphoric vision.

This approach proves singularly fruitful for the analysis of his earliest published story, "The Mark of Apelles," written in 1914 (Chapter 3). The interplay between Plato and Kant in Pasternak's diaries and the habitual comparison of the two philosophers in the works of Hermann Cohen offer a new heuristic pathway into the story: in this context the story's protagonist Heinrich Heine assumes, and does so gracefully, the otherwise unlikely role of an atemporal, lyrical force. "The Black Goblet," also written in 1914 and saturated with philosophical resonance, confirms such a reading; in the essay's context, Heine acquires a further identity to augment his personality—in its light he becomes the "apriorist of lyricism," who has stepped out of the "*coffre volant*" (see *PSS* 5:14–16) of cultural wealth into the autumn night of Pisa. The "association by similarity" also suggests in this context an implicit reference to Plato's power of ideas and the Platonic *topos* of the sun as the physical image of the highest good. Since Heine appears exclusively in darkness, his own awareness of the danger of such "crossings" invokes Plato's allegory of the cave with its emphasis on the perils associated with the deceptiveness of its shadows and its pervasive parade of reflections, all promising death to the lonely visionary returning into the darkness. This philosophical allusion is further strengthened by Pasternak's sketches of 1910, where his hero Pourvit Reliquimini dies in darkness, in a street car near a child "poisoned by electric lights" (*PSS* 3:487). As he dies, Pourvit wonders at the reflections of his childhood that appear in his memory as if they were "negatives of a film, archiving all the white past as a black line" [жизнь [. . .] как негатив, запечатлела белое прошлое черной чертой] (*PSS* 3:488)—in other words, as copies reflected in quasi-cinematographic fashion on the cave-wall, echoing implicitly the principles of Platonic mimesis.

The juxtaposition of fictional and philosophical texts suggests, as shown in Chapter 3, the presence of a design that is both stunning and original, one that closely fits Pasternak's interests prior to World War I. What is particularly significant is that the discovery of this philosophical substratum in "The Mark of Apelles" is intrinsic to the story's success—it is, in fact, a key to its metaphoric design. Without the involvement of philosophical parallels the story remains eccentric and puzzling, with its abrupt finale reinforcing the overall challenge of the narrative. In other words, the story calls for genuine inquiry: the emerging philosophical subtext, signaled by the narrative's intentional obscurities, is Pasternak's principal technique of establishing metaphoric relationships. Pasternak tries to say as much, albeit in his usual enigmatic manner, in "The Wassermann Test" when he insists that the need for metaphor must be created from within the text—from within the dramatic intensity of its contiguous series:

> [T]he presence of metaphor justifies the inner tensions of the contiguous series in the text. An independent need for association through similar-

ity is simply unthinkable. However, such and only such association can be necessitated from within.

[Т]олько явлениям смежности и присуща та черта принудительности и душевного драматизма, которая может быть оправдана метафорически. Самостоятельная потребность в сближении по сходству просто немыслима. Зато такое и только такое сближение может быть затребовано извне. (*PSS* 5:11)

The need for a metaphorical solution (necessarily accompanied by philosophical parallels) emerges, therefore, from the tension created by the narrative elements of "Apelles." The philosophical level, or the world of ideas that deepen and enrich the story, enters into the narrative to ease the quandary created by its puzzling surface, and the need to find this other relationship—to find the "association by similarity" that explains the puzzle—is necessitated by the story's disquieting dynamism.

These philosophical strands constituting the story's metaphoric level are, one should add, by no means banal: Pasternak creates a vibrant symbolic interconnection with one of the major texts of world culture, proposing an innovative rendering of Plato's cave allegory, as well as offering to philosophy his own *apologia* for choosing poetry as his future path. The metaphoric image also speaks in this context with the formidable power of a chilling foresight, as the poet, rather than the philosopher, is threatened by the darkness in Pasternak's tale. Many years later, with great sadness and without any hidden allusions, Pasternak will describe exactly this role, mourning his own destiny and the destinies of so many of his contemporary artists:

It is unfortunate that in the days of the Great Soviet,
Where spaces are given to higher powers,
The vacancy of the poet is not cancelled out.
That position is dangerous when taken up.

Напрасно в дни великого совета,
Где высшей власти отданы места,
Оставлена вакансия поэта.
Она опасна, если не пуста. (*PSS* 2:212)

This pattern of indicating metaphoric design—or association by similarity—represented by a philosophical theme is by no means unique to the works written in 1914. A similar reliance on metaphoric relationships grounded in philosophical questions underlies the extraordinary rich context of "Letters from Tula," which develops, in fact, the patterns already suggested by "The Mark of Apelles." The earlier story's emphasis upon its protagonists' "vitality of vision" in discerning reality and apprehending shadows already indicates an interest in different angles of perception; awareness of this theme and its resonance in "Letters from Tula" prove productive from the first paragraphs of the story (see Chapter 4), which centrally employ Plato's parable of the poor eyesight of the philosopher who returns to the cave. However, the confusion of the story's poet between the immediate and the distant, deepened by the opposition between the moral and artistic questions raised by the narrative, points not merely to Plato, but also to Pasternak's dialogue with Kantian "apperception," the *a posteriori* and *a priori* experiences of time and space, synthesized in "transcendental consciousness" (whose reality the story both investigates and problematizes). Pasternak's student notes offer striking support for such a reading; there is no need to search far and wide for Pasternak's interest in the synthetic unity of consciousness, a transcendental ego unifying all subjective experience, the *a priori* and *a posteriori* of all impressions, or the notion of open-ended and ongoing synthetic flow—these topics are simply everywhere in his *Lehrjahre,* Kantian apperception remaining the diary's major theme.

His later writings confirm his essential adaptation of the Kantian and Neo-Kantian view that personality emerges through the work of integration, a synthetic unity, however problematic, of all subjective experiences, realigned each time a new element enters the series. As late as 1956, in *Sketch for an Autobiography,* Pasternak gives one of his most powerful renditions of this philosophical view of selfhood when he depicts the obverse condition—the cessation of the synthetic work of consciousness, which necessarily results, in his view, in self-annihilation. The examples he gives are painful testimony to a century that constitutes the historical foil to his maturing art; the Kantian notion of the synthetic unity of subjective experience is tested for its applicability against the state of consciousness during torture and preparation for suicide:

> We have no idea of the mental agony that precedes suicide. [. . .] Subjected to torture by a hangman, a man is not yet utterly destroyed; [. . .] his past belongs to him, his memories are with him, and, if he so desires, he can make use of them and they may be of some use to him before he dies.
>
> Having arrived at the thought of suicide, one abandons all hope, one turns away from one's past, one declares oneself a bankrupt and his memories non-existent. These memories are no longer capable of reaching the

would-be suicide to save him, to sustain him. The continuity of one's inner experience is destroyed, the personality has ceased to exist. In the end, perhaps, one kills oneself not out of loyalty to the decision one has made, but because one can no longer endure the agony that does not seem to belong to anyone in particular, suffering in the absence of a sufferer, the empty suspense which is not filled up by a life that still goes on. (*Remember* 89)

Мы не имеем понятие о сердечном терзании, предшествующем самоубийству. [. . .] [Ч]еловек, подвергнутый палаческой расправой, еще не уничтожен [. . .] его прошлое принадлежит ему, его воспоминания при нем, и если он захочет, может воспользоваться ими, перед смертью они могут помочь ему.

Приходя к мысли о самоубийстве, ставят крест на себе, отворачиваются от прошлого, объявляют себя банкротом, а свои воспоминания недействительными. Эти воспоминания уже не могут дотянуться до человека, спасти и поддержать его. Непрерывность внутреннего существования нарушена, личность кончилась. Может быть, в заключение убивают себя не из верности принятому решению, а из нестерпимости этой тоски, неведомо кому принадлежащей, этого страдания в отсутствие страдающего, этого пустого, не заполненного продолжающейся жизнью ожидания. (*PSS* 3:331)

Thus, as he describes the days leading to the eventual suicides of Vladimir Mayakovsky, Marina Tsvetaeva, Paolo Yashvili, and Alexander Fadeeev, Pasternak views their torment as deeper and more unbearable even than that of a tortured person because the ongoing work of synthesis has stopped. They reject part of their experience, and, thus, arrest the work of consciousness, destroying in the process any possibility of an integral self, leaving in its place an empty gap.

The synthetic unity of experience, an inalienable part of Pasternak's approach to the human self, finds in "Letters from Tula" its first artistic rendering that will in time shape some of his most distinctive and intricate artistic traits. If in Kant the synthetic unity of experience is gathered within the inner self—within a transcendental autonomous "spiritual substance underlying the fleeting succession of conscious experience [inaccessible] to direct introspection, but rather inferred from introspective evidence" (Runes 88)—Pasternak, by contrast, never accepts the autonomous isolation of this integral process. His insistence on the "animation" spreading from a thinking self to the surrounding material world (and vice versa) is already present in the prose pieces of 1910, including "Ordering a Drama," with its emphasis upon "this sweet pain: to work; to think for inanimate objects" [сладостное страдание: работать, думать за неодушевленное] (*PSS* 3:462). Similarly, neither in his *Lehrjahre* nor in "Letters from Tula" does Pasternak regard the transcendental ego as an autonomous and self-dependent receptacle. I argued in Chapters 4 and 5 that Pasternak was indebted to Hermann Cohen for the latter's emphasis on the role of the "other" in the development of the self: Cohen, in fact, held the striking view that moral growth began when the external freedom of the individual was "broken down in relation to an *other* person" (Gibbs 2005, 206). However, Pasternak's own development of this vulnerable process is highly original. The experimentation with perception in "Letters from Tula" does not at any level point to the possibility of the unified isolated consciousness of either the story's young poet or its elderly artist. What emerges instead is an insistence that artistic consciousness is renewed and integrated not within itself, but in its impulse towards, from, and in others. For the poet and the actor of the story, this means an ongoing quest for creative endeavor, a quest concerned not so much with self-expression and self-unification, as with "making the other speak through one's lips" (*CSP* 126; *PSS* 3:32). One may plausibly suggest that for Pasternak it also meant that the work of art—the expression of selfhood—equally cannot be integrated within itself as an independent autonomous construction. From its first moments of inception, art is the gift from the *other*. In its development it progresses into its reception, into its being grasped by the reader, which means that the author under no conditions holds the key to the final meaning of the text.

In *Safe Conduct*, Pasternak plays most openly with this conception, even somewhat teasing his readers by suggesting that the poet's biography can be found only in the biography of others. His own memoirs, he claims in 1930, are not merely dedicated to Rilke. Since Rilke's power over Pasternak is all pervasive, Rilke, more than Pasternak, is the memoir's genuine, motive cause:

> *The poet deliberately gives the whole of his life such a steep incline that it cannot exist in the vertical line of biography, where we expect to meet it. It cannot be found under its own name and has to be sought under those of others, in the biographical columns of those who follow him.* The more the productive individuality is closed upon itself, the more collective—and this is no allegory—is his story. The realm of the subconscious is a genius that does not submit to measurement. It consists of everything that happens to his readers and that he does not know. I am not presenting my reminiscences in memory of Rilke. On the contrary, I myself received it from him as a gift. (*CSP* 30; emphasis added)

Всей своей жизни поэт придает такой добровольно крутой наклон, что ее не может быть в биографической вертикали, где мы ждем ее встретить. Ее нельзя найти под его именем и надо искать под чужим, в биографическом столбце его последователей. Чем замкнутее производящая индивидуальность, тем коллективнее, без всякого иносказания, ее повесть. Область подсознательного у гения не поддается обмеру. Ее составляет все, что творится с его читателями и чего он не знает. Я не дарю своих воспоминаний памяти Рильке. Наоборот, я сам получил их от него в подарок. (*PSS* 3:158)

Just as Pasternak insists that the poet's biography "cannot be found under his own name," he also suggests—and this theme is to play an ever-expanding role in his art—that the poet's power is always in process of transference, if not simply to the reader, then to the poet's "image," while so-called "autonomous" expression is necessarily shut off: "In art man falls silent and the image begins to speak. And it turns out that *only* the image can keep pace with the progress of nature" [В искусстве человек смолкает и заговаривает образ. И оказывается: только образ поспевает за успехами природы] (*CSP* 47; *PSS* 3:178). The image, then, has an infinite capacity for self-renewal and expansion, not because the poet has some autonomous transcendental self, but because the image, having received the integrating power of the poet's sight, continues to live, synthesizing into itself an ever-growing series of approaches and perceptions. As we have also seen, this thought, namely, the transference of the synthesizing power of vitality to the "other," underlies the development of Pasternak's symbolic expression, in both its metaphoric and contiguous series, although the need for these categories is altogether minimized in his later work.

There is, nonetheless, no more important theme in Pasternak's *oeuvre* than that of ongoing, open-ended and living, synthetic understanding. This philosophical theme takes a slight adjustment of vision before one recognizes a similar principle operating in *Safe Conduct,* when Pasternak describes his trip to Italy immediately following his Marburg experience. Even then, however, Pasternak's mixture of evasiveness and transparency mutes the fact that his accounts of Italian museums (he leaves Marburg for Italy in August 1912 [Barnes 1989, 143]) present an opportunity to demonstrate—as if in passing—a period of "crossing" from philosophical aesthetics (and his apprenticeship in Neo-Kantianism) to art, for as he points out in *Safe Conduct,* "This is what interested me at the time, this is what I then understood and loved" [Вот чем я тогда интересовался, вот что тогда понимал и любил] (*CSP* 72; *PSS* 3:207). Thus, he describes his trips to Italian museums as crystallizing his understanding that the "other," apart from the "image" or the reader, may also be the work's subject matter in the moment of its being perceived. In the activity of being observed, the object of the artist's perception in a poem or a painting begins to unfold, continuing its new integral or "synthetic" life that expands by accepting the glance of the "other." Artistic perception unveils, then, not so much the autonomous life of the observer, as the awakened life of the observed:

> I saw what is the first observation to strike the painter's instinct. How one suddenly understands what it is like for the visible object, when it begins to be seen. Once noticed, nature moves aside with the obedient spaciousness of a story, and in this condition, like one asleep, is quietly transferred into the canvas. (*CSP* 70)

> Я увидел, какое наблюдение первым поражает живописный инстинкт. Как вдруг постигается, каково становится видимому, когда его начинают видеть. Будучи запримечена, природа расступается послушным простором повести, и в этом состоянии ее, как сонную, тихо вносят на полотно. (*PSS* 3:205)

The synthetic unity of consciousness is, therefore, transferred to an ever self-renewing synthetic artifact, animating what initially appeared only as a material object.

And in what seems to be a triumphant *tour de force* in *Safe Conduct*, Pasternak applies the image of the synthetic unity of consciousness in apperception to cultural artifacts and to culture in general, which he visualizes as living and animated—as an open-ended synthetic chain of never-ending data, renewing itself with every genuine new insight and work of art, synchronizing what is distant, "everlasting" [вековечное], and immediate:

> I understood that the Bible, for instance, is not so much a book with a definitive text as the notebook of humankind, and that everything everlasting is like this. That it is vital not when it is enforced but when it is receptive to all the analogies by means of which the subsequent ages, issuing from it, look back at it. I understood that the history of culture is a chain of equations in images which link in pairs the next unknown thing with something already known, whereby the known, constant for the whole series, is legend, set at the base of the tradition, and the unknown, new each time, is the actual moment in the flow of culture. (*CSP* 71)

Я понял, что, к примеру, Библия есть не столько книга с твердым текстом, сколько записная тетрадь человечества, и что таково все вековечное. Что оно жизненно не тогда, когда оно обязательно, а когда оно восприимчиво ко всем уподоблениям, которыми на него озираются исходящие века. Я понял, что история культуры есть цепь уравнений в образах, попарно связывающих очередное неизвестное с известным, причем этим известным, постоянным для всего ряда, является легенда, заложенная в основание традиции, неизвестным же, каждый раз новым—актуальный момент текущей культуры. (*PSS* 3:207)

As one looks at these series of images one can begin to sympathize with Pasternak's disheartened attitude to his earlier style. "Letters from Tula," a text implicitly containing all these observations, but in a somewhat oblique and "hermetic" form, emerges as one of the most carefully conceived and intellectually stimulating texts of the Russian avant-garde, and yet it remains a concealed puzzle, resisting interpreters and interpretations (unless the story is read alongside Pasternak's philosophical notes). This is equally true of many passages from *Safe Conduct*.

These far-reaching themes of "Letters from Tula" tend to elude the reader, of course, and it is ironic that Pasternak should appear almost banal and self-indulgent in a work where he passionately espouses the need for the other in the creative act. There is then, as we have shown, a considerable dislocation between the story's taut, ingenious design and the depth of its philosophical involvement, on the one hand, and the surface appearance of an eventless enigmatic narrative, on the other. However, once the inner vitality of the philosophical context is grasped, it becomes indisputable that "Letters from Tula" marks a major threshold in Pasternak's development as an artist: the story rejects the autobiographical pose of the poet and announces the resolve of a prose writer who searches to expand his understanding. The narrative also invokes Lev Tolstoy's example and, thus, points to Pasternak's reorientation to an epic style and to the creation of other selves. It also contains some of Pasternak's most characteristic and deeply held themes, including the opposition between the self, who in his/her search for inner alignment reaches (or hopes to reach) unparalleled moral and artistic stature, and the altogether opposed figure—the imitator or circulator of the most fashionable symbols, capable (by virtue of an imitation that bypasses the work of any deeper integration within the self) of a violent crudeness and cruelty.

The story also emphasizes the "dramatic" vitality of the world that surrounds artistic vision even after the writer's death: the dance of the "magnetic" needles of Tula still remembers Lev Tolstoy, many years after his death. Thus, "Letters from Tula" does not so much employ contiguous series as grapple with the depiction of the vitality of a world caught by dynamic creative perception and represented within a seemingly straightforward narrative pattern. The metonymic series alone do not explain this complex organization. Rather, the text presents a metaphoric structure that already contains the principal outlines of a new genre—the design of an open-ended tale-within-a-tale, where the first frame and its first protagonist operate as a generating principle of the story's second half ("Letters from Tula" echoes in this the structure of Rilke's *Malte Laurids Brigge,* and predates Jorge Luis Borges's circular "ficciones" by many a decade). This emphasis on the transference of poetic intensity to the *other*—the passing of living energy from the story's poet to the old actor, a fictional protagonist, who comes to life alongside the poet by overhearing the poet's words—this structure encapsulates best what is known as Pasternak's famous ability to evoke animation in the world surrounding his protagonists.

Equally important, however, is that the design in question goes far beyond the principal characteristic of the "metonymy" that Jakobson sees as the main organizing principle of Pasternak's world: "Instead of a hero it is, as often as not, the surrounding objects that are thrown in turmoil; the immovable outlines of the roofs grow inquisitive, a door swings shut with a silent reproach, the joy of family reconciliation is expressed by a growing warmth, zeal and devotion on the part of lamps" (1969, 141). My argument throughout is that Jakobson's assessment is both precise and yet too severely restricted as far as Pasternak's early prose is concerned. Indeed, material objects, occasional plants and trees get animated, but they are not the only elements in the series chosen for the process of animation. Pasternak's experimentation in animation, proceeding from a person involved in a vital creative work, includes temporal sequences, nature, relationships with other individuals and works of art, and the creative impulse of living protagonists. In other words, Pasternak's understanding of the animated world strives to be more comprehensive and expansive, and precisely this goal will both propel his later work in prose and eventually demand from him a search for an altogether new style. And while the design—its narrative *mise-en-abyme,* with one character generating another—will not become an essential part of his fiction, Pasternak's focus on the energy of the creative glance turned toward the other or others will remain a major characteristic of his symbolic world.

For Pasternak, then, the creative work of perception will never stay isolated within the individual: it will always flow into the world since the energy it generates enhances the vitality of life. Furthermore, for the rest of his life,

Pasternak will be convinced that creative work for the artist is the only way he or she can continue to integrate the catastrophically disassembled realities of the twentieth century. One hears this insistence in *Sketch for an Autobiography*: in his tribute to Marina Tsvetaeva, Pasternak notes that her suicide was all but assured when she stopped working; the surrounding chaos became then too horrific and finally overwhelming. There was no poet's insight to keep chaos at bay, to synthesize the impossible, to dispel the immovable heaps of stagnation:

> Marina Tsvetaeva all her life shielded herself by her work against the humdrum affairs of everyday existence. When it seemed to her that it was an inadmissible luxury and that for the sake of her son she must for a time sacrifice her all-absorbing passion, she cast a sober look around her and she saw the chaos that had not been filtered through her creative work, immovable, stagnant, monstrous, and recoiled in panic. Not knowing how to protect herself from that horror, she hurriedly hid herself in death, putting her head into a noose as under a pillow. (*Remember* 90)

> Марина Цветаева всю жизнь заслонялась от повседневности работой, и, когда ей показалось, что это непозволительная роскошь и ради сына она должна временно пожертвовать увлекательной страстью и взглянуть кругом трезво, она увидела хаос, непропущенный сквозь творчество, неподвижный, непривычно косный, и в испуге отшатнулась и, не зная, куда деться от ужаса, впопыхах спряталась в смерть, сунув голову в петлю, как под подушку. (*PSS* 3:331)

The same conviction can be discerned in one of Pasternak's letters to Renate Schweitzer written in 1958, where he observes that even Rainer Maria Rilke could not find the reality worthy of the power of his insight while the tragedy of Russia—with its overwhelming heaps of cold, deadening, and heart-rending material—waits to be noticed and transformed by its artists:

> [I] have simply relit the candle of Malte Laurids which had been standing extinguished and unused, and gone out with this light of Rilke's into the darkness of the streets, into the midst of the ruins. To think that when he wrote his novel (like Proust) he had nothing to apply his brilliant insight to, but now look at the mountain of the subject matter around us . . . the terrifying pretext for art begging to be used. How grimly in earnest it is, this reality, how tragic and stern—but it is nevertheless the reality of our earth, a defined poetic entity. And so we want to weep from joy and awe. (quoted from Ivinskaya 1978a, 221)

[. . .] как будто зажег я свечу Мальте, стоявшую холодной, неиспользованной, и вышел со светом Рильке в руке из дома в темноту, во двор, на улицу, в гущу развалин. Подумай только, в своем романе он (как и Пруст) не находил применения для своего гениального проникновения,—и теперь, посмотри,—горы причин . . . жуткие, умоляющие предлоги творчества. Как действительность не для шуток, как трагична и строга она, и все же это—земная действительность, поэтическая определенность. И вот мы хотим плакать от счастья и трепета. (quoted from Ivinskaya 1978b, 242)

Forty years have passed since the poet in "Letters from Tula" observed the putrefying smell of the earth pervading the whole territory of conscience (*CSP* 123; *PSS* 3:30) and acknowledged that he was unable as yet to lift or dispel this raw decay. The power of Tolstoy's presence, vital even after the great writer's death, explained on that occasion the nuances and responsibilities of this raw call of the environment. The perception of the artist, then, was understood as testifying only partially to the laws of Kantian apperception. The artist for Pasternak does not merely sift through these disparate forms of chaos in order to synthesize them within his or her self; the artist pierces through immobile, inanimate existence, and his or her power of perception grants even static monstrosity the vitality of life and movement. Tolstoy's figure in this regard (echoing the example of Rilke's Malte Laurids Brigge) is a brilliant development of Pasternak's implicit argument with the Kantian insistence upon the autonomy of individual consciousness: in Pasternak's rendition, the writer's search for inner alignment results not in self-understanding and inner harmony, but in the creation of multiple narrative worlds inhabited by many protagonists and shared with an ever-growing multitude of readers.

While this formidable philosophical subtext of the "Letters from Tula" lacks the active power of projection (it operates in the story as a theme, rather than as a medium of delivery with actual communicative force), it signals, nonetheless, the range of Pasternak's ambition. Thus, the poet promises to his beloved that he intends to stand utterly alone and not turn into a decadent actor when *The Time of Troubles* (that is, his own historical time) appears on the screen. This promise indicates both a moral conviction and an artistic program, even though the power of this pledge is lost somewhat in the carefully constructed evasiveness of the story's political overtones. In *Sketch for an Autobiography*, Pasternak points to a similar theme in Mayakovsky. He first quotes the latter's poem:

Time, I beseech you; though you be
A lame icon painter, my image paint

In the shrine of this century's misshapen selves!
I am alone, as the last eye
Of the man going to the blind. (*Remember* 93; trans. altered)

Время! Хоть ты, хромой богомаз,
Лик намалюй мой в божницу уродца века.
Я одинок, как последний глаз
у идущего к слепым человека (*PSS* 3:333)

He then comments on its plea: "Time obliged and did what he asked. His image is written in the shrine of the century" [Время послушалось и сделало, о чем он просил. Лик его вписан в божницу века] (*Remember* 93; *PSS* 3:333). This was also Pasternak's ambition, and it was first articulated somewhat covertly in "Letters from Tula." Sensing his eventual appearance on a screen (as a future protagonist of a historical account), Pasternak's lyrical poet (as well as his author), however, does not long merely for fame or for survival in cultural memory; he longs not to lose his moral orientation among "the smells of putrefaction and of clay" [несло гнилостью и глиной] (*CSP* 123; *PSS* 3:30).

The Childhood of Luvers, written the same year as "Letters," demonstrates ever more pointedly the strength of Pasternak's artistic ambition and his determined experimentation with metaphoric design. It was not without reason that for a long time Pasternak considered this story his central work (see the *Questionnaire of Profsoyuz* of 1919 [*PSSCom* 3:542]): the overall philosophical conception of the story is realized with confident, even grand strokes. As the development of personality is presented as a widening and deepening series of perceptions reintegrated within a maturing self, the transition from contiguous to metaphoric series is no longer left for the reader to discern: this transition is presented as moral and intellectual growth, so that the emergence of the overall metaphoric pattern confirms and expands Zhenya's artistic sensibility and her awakening gift of clairvoyance (or her acute apprehension of the future, brewing all around the disquieting Urals). In contrast to previous stories where "association by similarity" was directed toward a philosophical text and grounded in philosophical themes, Zhenya's encounter with "the abstract moment" is represented by Lermontov's *Demon,* read by the child on an autumn afternoon when the leaves are already shriveled by cold. This metaphoric design—an approaching future emerging both from a literary text, the first cold days of the fall season, and out of an unknown stranger appearing on a back street[2]—does not diminish the philosophical context of the story.

---

2. See Pasternak's letter to D. E. Maksimov (October 25, 1957), explaining that the "dedication to Lermontov" of *My Sister Life* rather than to "the memory of Lermontov" was an indi-

In portraying the development of the child, struck in her early adolescence by the energy of the departed poet, Pasternak creates a paradigmatic progression from the first moments of awakened consciousness to the invigoration of the life of soul, and then to the next stage—awareness of "spirit" and a spiritual world—literally the daimonic world whose boundary is first signaled by Lermontov's *Demon*. And if the first two levels of this expansion of personality, those of consciousness and soul, are described to some extent by means of association by contiguity, the clairvoyant awakening of the spiritual level is conceived as a metaphoric or symbolic relationship that integrates the metonymic series and points through them to the outlines of the child's future, so that the Demon, the herald of pain and suffering, can appear only when the natural cycle of nature's flourishing and growth is arrested and for a time reversed.

As far as the structure of *Luvers* is concerned, it is not easy or desirable to indicate any single philosophical framework that Pasternak might have followed while working on the story—indeed, Pasternak brings together a great number of approaches. The Kantian (and Neo-Kantian) tradition is clearly present in the portrayal of Zhenya's growth as a process of synthetic perception that blends the finite and the immeasurable and integrates the phenomenal world with things named together with phenomena still unnamed and out of focus. Pasternak's choice of the idea of the "third person" echoes Hermann Cohen's "other," while *Luvers's* portrayal of the "animation" of the surrounding world, so central to Pasternak's future writing, expands in startling fashion the "second state"—"movement without reality" [движение без действительности] (*PSS* 3:460)—or animation transfixing inanimate objects in "Ordering a Drama" (1910). It also clearly echoes Plato's idea of the soul as "incessant" movement, conspicuously noted in his philosophical diaries:

Ψ[υχή] = the beginning of self-directing motion (The inanimate is distinct from the animate precisely because it contains the source of its motion. *Ψ[υχή]* (a self-generating motion) moves always, cannot arrest itself; its life is without cessation.

---

cation "not so much that Lermontov was alive, but that he was there in accidental passers-by, still unknown and not as yet sufficiently immortalized by their sucess and fame, as if in that summer it was still possible to meet him, [. . .] to express the feeling of something as yet very immediate, for instance, the remaining wetness of the night rain or the quieting echoes of a disappearing sound—[. . .] this secretive grandeur of Lermontov's essence" [не то что в живых, но в рядах случайных прохожих, еще неведомых или недостаточно увековеченных абстрактностью признания, точно его тем летом где-нибудь еще можно было встретить, [. . .] выразить это чувство чего-то совсем недавнего, непросохших следов ночного дождя или затихающих, неотзвучавших отголосков только что прокатившегося звука, —[. . .] это таинственное могущество Лермонтовской сущности] (*PSS* 10:270).

$\Psi[v\chi\acute{\eta}]$ = начало самоопределяемого движения. (Одушевл[енное] отлич[ается] от неодушевл[енного] тем, что носит в себе источник своих движений). $\Psi[v\chi\acute{\eta}]$ (как самостоятельное движущееся) движется вегда, не может сама себя остановить ее жизнь неистребима. (*Lehrjahre* I:361)

On the whole, this philosophical subtext—the progression of awakened consciousness from ensouledness to spirit—indicates here a carefully worked out and highly original narrative design that reflects to a considerable degree the ideas of Plato, Kant, Cohen, Solovyev, and, to some extent, Mikhail Gershenson (see 5.2).

However, when placed in the context of Pasternak's later writing it is precisely the carefully worked out systematic organization of the story that marks the beginnings of Pasternak's dissatisfaction. If "Letters from Tula" contains philosophical principles that are destined to play a major part in Pasternak's later work, the stylistic innovations in the organization of *Luvers* will be later reconsidered and altered in a radical manner. In *Doctor Zhivago,* for instance, it is no longer the spirit of Lermontov (or any poet for that matter) or his daimonic protagonist that will awaken young Yuri into his first understanding of the incommensurable forces of the approaching future: it will be his mother's death and then the winter storm, knocking on the window, reminding him of the necessity of remembering and articulating something for which he, as a child, as yet has no language. This change of setting is just a detail upon a much larger canvas, but it signals a major reorientation.

The power of the call that accesses the future creative potential of the child's consciousness remains an overall theme of the novel's opening, but compared to *The Childhood of Luvers,* the metaphoric structure of *Doctor Zhivago* appears radically simplified: realistic events, rather than complex schematic "abstractions," awaken the child's self, and it is in this context, I suggest, that one can begin to see the artistic principles that made Pasternak reconsider his earlier narrative patterns. The "schematic" organization that informed his early style is gone, written off in the letter to George Reavey (December 1959) as "those rare grains of life and truth that are intermixed with great quantities of deadening schematic nonsense and unreal and raw material" [редкие зерна жизни и правды перемешаны с огромным количеством мертвой, схематичной бессмыслицы и несуществующего сырья] (*PSS* 10:550). What could have been the cause of this change? The lack of critical response to his carefully executed narrative designs must have indicated the necessity for a new path (especially when the writer is so intent on reaching the *other*), but the change was also demanded by the new reality and challenges of the post-revolutionary experience. Thus the novel, of which *The Childhood of Luvers* was to have been just a beginning, was never finished. With the exception of "Aerial Ways" in 1924, Pasternak's future style was altered drastically, and the very principles and their philosophical underpinnings that gave Pasternak his first themes in narrative fiction appear to have become something of an obstacle to the vitality of his future fiction. Or was their earlier execution viewed as still insufficiently open-ended, too abstract to be thoroughly integrated into the narrative? As I conclude this study, this question needs a more careful analysis.

8.3 New symbolism:
Toward "the soul" of the later prose

In *Doctor Zhivago*, Pasternak depicts the visit of Nikolay Nikolayevich Vedenyapin to Moscow during post-Revolutionary chaos and hunger. Yuri, of course, is overwhelmingly happy to see his philosopher-uncle who had so strongly influenced his art, but he senses that his uncle's brilliance, as well as his carefully coiffed image, does not live up to the weight and scale of events in Russia:

> He was seeing the idol of his childhood, the teacher who dominated his youthful thoughts—alive, in the flesh, was standing in front of him.
>
> His gray hair was becoming to him, and his loose foreign suit fitted him well. He was very young and handsome by his years.
>
> Admittedly, he was overshadowed by the grandeur of the events; seen beside them, he lost in stature. But it never occurred to Yuri to measure him by such a yardstick.
>
> He was surprised at Nikolay Nikolayevich's calm, at his light and detached tone in speaking of politics. He was more self-possessed than most Russians could be at that time. (*Zhivago* 178)

> Кумир его детства, властитель его юношеских дум, живой во плоти опять стоял перед ним.
>
> Николаю Николаевичу очень шла седина. Заграничный широкий костюм хорошо сидел на нем. Для своих лет он был еще очень моложав и смотрел красавцем. Конечно, он сильно терял в соседстве с громадностью совершавшегося. События заслоняли его. Но Юрию Андреевичу и не приходило в голову мерить его таким мерилом.

Его удивило спокойствие Николая Николаевича, хладнокровно шутливый тон, которым он говорил на политические темы. Его умение держать себя превышало нынешние русские возможности. (*PSS* 4:176)

This minor scene captures something of Pasternak's quandary after 1918: the narrative style he had developed with such care and intellectual precision was the fruit of his youthful thought, but it was simply not commensurate with the overwhelming catastrophe enveloping his country. Just as he had done during his other re-envisionings of himself, Pasternak moved forward by reworking the intellectual insight of the past. This new reorientation, however, may not have been as abrupt and dramatic as his earlier abandonment of music and then philosophy, but it was a considerable personal quest—and the main artistic challenge of his life.

By 1958, during both the signs of triumph and the political scandals associated with *Doctor Zhivago,* Pasternak felt oppressed by at least two painful realizations. First, there was the clear and painful awareness that he might not be able to get any closer to his readers than the narrow window of correspondence with his foreign admirers, an activity permitted, but barely tolerated, by the State. Second, he understood vividly (and with considerable alarm) that the lack of readers' comprehension had not been alleviated by the simplified narrative style of his later prose. Thus, Pasternak put aside his earlier proclamation of a reticence he shared with his reader ("I cannot conceive of any correspondence with him" [1928 essay published in *Chitatel' i pisatel'* (*CSP* 267–68; *PSS* 5:220)]) and began to clarify the artistic goals of his new prose through his letters. In the letter to Jacqueline de Proyart cited above (dated May 20, 1959), he notes that while conceiving reality as a philosophical category, he was also addressing a specific historical setting: "It portrayed a particular reality—a reality that also reflected a particular period of time. And more specifically—Russian reality of the last fifty years" [русская реальность последних пятидесяти лет] (*PSS* 10:489). This statement does not merely signify a dual goal, which implies a contrast between locality and general philosophical truth found in symbolic language. Rather, Pasternak also speaks about the symbolic expression of a *particular* reality, noting that the depiction of this reality as a historical phenomenon eschewed the symbolism he practiced in his youth. He also insists that his adherence to "reality as a philosophical category" demanded from him a strong objection to narrative style conceived as an intellectual puzzle and that this new artistic code also entailed a categorical rejection of partial and autonomous symbols, as well as the presence of ideas to be fitted into some crossword problem. Moreover, in order to explain the style of his novel, he refers to the example of the Impressionists, echoing his 1914 entry into artistic debates in "The Black Goblet." In 1958, however, he demonstrably replaces the experience of packing and packaging symbols with images of the soul and open, unrestricted air. The word "soul," in fact, appears in opposition to "self-identical symbols" and to "ideas" as solutions to "crossword puzzles":

I wanted to write to Hélène about false interpretations of my style which are becoming highly popular. [. . .] Critics are searching for a secret meaning in every syllable of the novel, decode words, the names of the streets and protagonists as if these are allegories and cryptoquotes. There is nothing of this in [Zhivago]. I reject even the possibility of existence of complete, partial or self-identical symbols for anyone who is an artist. If the work of art is not fully exhausted by what is said and printed in it, if it contains something else—this can only be that common quality, breathing, movement, infinite urge forward that transfixes the whole work and makes it to be a particular work, not because it hides an idea, equal to the solved puzzle—this other is the likeness of soul, because soul, in our view, fills the body, and cannot be extracted from it.

In other words, if the soul of the art of French impressionists—is air and light, then what is the soul of the new prose of *Doctor Zhivago*? In its appearance, its execution and its goals it was a realistic work. It portrayed a particular reality—a reality that also reflected a particular period of time. And more specifically—Russian reality of the last fifty years. When this was accomplished, there remained a certain residue, which deserves to be characterized and described. What is this residue? Reality as such, reality itself as a phenomenon or a philosophical category—the very fact of existence of a particular reality.

Я хотел написать Элен о получившем распространение ложном толковании моего стиля. [. . .] Ищут тайный смысл в каждом слоге романа, расшифровывают слова, названия улиц и имена героев как аллегории и криптограммы. Ничего этого у меня нет. Даже возможность существования отдельных, изолированных символов я отрицаю у кого бы то ни было, если он художник. Если произведение не исчерпывается тем, что в нем сказано, если есть еще что-то сверх того, это может быть только его общее качество, дыхание, движение или бесконечное устремление, пронизывающее произведение все целиком и делающее его тем или другим. Это не идея, которая в нем скрыта, как решение загадки, но подобие души, заключенной в теле и его наполняющей, которую нельзя из него извлечь.

Итак, если душой живописи французской импрессионистической живописи были воздух и свет, то какая душа у этой новой прозы , которую представляет собой "Д<октор> Ж<иваго>"? По замыслу, задаче и исполнению это были реалистическое произведение. Потому что в нем была точная реальность определенного периода,—русская реальность последних пятидесяти лет. Когда эта работа была выполнена, осталось еще одно, что надо было также охарактеризовать и описать. Что именно? Реальность как таковую, реальность как явление или философскую категорию—самый факт бытия какой-то действительности. (*PSS* 10:488–89)

Thus, the concept of soul is not merely introduced: it is presented as a key to his philosophical view of reality (at the very same time as Pasternak restates his adherence to realism) and an implicit rejection of his early intellectualized style of prose; the philosophical rendition of reality is its breath, movement, impetus, unifying sweep, and new dynamic direction, which enter into all aspects of life, so that the artistic text becomes the ground and spectacle of this incarnated impulse.

However, the echoes of Kantian and Neo-Kantian synthesis, of apperception not as personal autonomy, but as a principle in the world at large, are still evident as a mark of the reality he wants to capture in his novel—recreating something of the figure of a world soul animating all at every point. This, indeed, is precisely what he had written to Jacqueline de Proyart when he observed that great art always "attempted to communicate the unified picture of the life, life in its wholeness, but it was done and commented upon always in a different way, in accordance with the philosophy of the époque and because of this by different methods" [великое искусство всегда стремилось зарисовать общее восприятие жизни в целом, но это делалось (толковалось ее неделимое единство) кажды раз по-разному, в согласии с философией своего времени] (*PSS* 10:489–90). In short, all the impetus of his early prose is contained in this "philosophical rendering of reality," but the canvas of the narrative is much larger, so that it is no longer even possible to identify philosophical echoes and to fit them into a puzzle in order to explain philosophical precursors of the reality in question. The tableau is both more unapologetic and yet more tragic, for this world and the reality that Pasternak aims to capture are not permanent and secure—they are wounded and endangered by incarnated ideas of "iron causality" that enter the dynamism of animation and arrest its freedom and flow. Having written *Doctor Zhivago*, he may, perhaps, feel that as the artist of such awakened, animated surroundings he has escaped the laws of iron causality at least for the time being. He clarifies this position to de Proyart:

> I described the characters, situations, details and particulars with the single goal: to question the idea of iron causality and absolute necessity; to show reality as I always saw it and felt it: as an inspired spectacle of as yet unrealized, as a reality engendered into movement by free choice, as a potential among potentials, as free path.
>
> [. . .] From this springs the optimism of my manner. The understanding of existence not as enslaving and disappointing, but as surprising and freeing mystery.

> Я описывал характеры, положения, подробности и частности с единственною целью: поколебать идею железной причинности и абсолютной обязательности; представить реальность такой как я всегда ее видел и переживал; как вдохновенное зрелище невоплощенного; как явление, приводимое в движение свободным выбором; как возможность среди возможностей; как произвольность.
>
> [. . .] Отсюда некоторый оптимизм этой манеры. Понимания бытия не как чего-то порабощающего и разочаровывающего, а как удивительной и освобождающей тайны. (*PSS* 10:488–89)

In short, if Pasternak in *The Childhood of Luvers* sees the moral maturation of personality as the progression from "soul" to "spirit" and to the world of "abstract ideas," then the Pasternak of *Zhivago* reclaims the concept of the soul as his primary and most comprehensive focus, which helps to integrate on a much broader tableau the stylistic findings of his early narrative. Nonetheless, he also aims to name the conflict of his age—the carriers of the "spirit of the age," or individuals sacrificing the vitality of self-renewing reality, the agents of ideas that bring about the eventual extirpation of life.

The artistic realization of this tableau and its philosophical underpinnings needs a more sustained analysis that goes beyond the parameters of this study, yet it is possible to summarize at least some signposts of this artistic re-orientation. Pasternak's style no longer reflects any progression of the awakened consciousness from the world of soul to that of spirit. Instead, he sees the spirited agents of ideas attacking and destroying the dynamic spaciousness of soul. At the turning points of *Doctor Zhivago*, Pasternak seeks to clarify some significant elements of this opposition. Zhivago, for instance, tries to explain to Liberius, who "chairs" the "forest brotherhood," that their "ideas of social betterment" are not only paid by "a sea of blood," but that they are based on the crudest dismissal of any animating principle. On this occasion the words "soul" and "spirit of life" are interchangeable:

> Reshaping life! People who can say that have never understood a thing about life—they have never felt its breath, its heartbeat—however much they have seen or done. They look on it as a lump of raw material that needs to be processed by them, to be ennobled by their touch. But life is never a material, a substance to be molded. If you want to know, life is a principle of self-renewal, it is constantly renewing and remaking and changing and transfiguring itself, it is infinitely beyond your or my obtuse theories about it. (*Zhivago* 338)

> Переделка жизни! Так могут рассуждать люди, хотя может быть и видавшие виды, но ни разу не узнавшие жизни, не почувствовавшие ее духа, души ее. Для них существование это комок грубого, не облагороженного их прикосновением материала, нуждающегося в их обработке. А материалом, веществом, жизнь никогда не бывает. Она сама, если хотите знать, непрерывно себя обновляющее, вечно себя перерабатывающее начало, она сама вечно себя переделывает и претворяет, она сама куда выше наших с вами тупоумных теорий. (*PSS* 4:336)

Or, again, in comparing his own thought to that of Lev Tolstoy in the concluding chapters of *Zhivago*, Pasternak pushes Tolstoy's organic philosophy further than even Tolstoy had done, setting up an opposition between organic life and the self-appointed carriers of ideas, the self-limiting agents of doom and idolatry:

> History cannot be seen, just as one cannot see grass growing. Wars and revolutions, kings and Robespierres, are history's organic agents, its yeast. Revolutions are made by fanatical men of action with one-track minds, geniuses in their ability to confine themselves to a limited field. They overturn the old order in a few hours or days, the whole upheaval takes a few weeks or at most years, but the fanatical spirit that inspired the upheavals is worshipped for decades thereafter, for centuries. (*Zhivago* 454)

> Истории никто не делает, ее не видно, как нельзя увидать, как трава растет. Войны, революции, цари, Робеспьеры это ее органические

возбудители, ее бродильные дрожжи. Революции производят люди действенные, односторонние фанатики, гении самоограничения. Они в несколько часов или дней опрокидывают старый порядок. Перевороты длятся недели, много годы, а потом десятилетиями, веками поклоняются духу ограниченности, приведшей к перевороту, как святыне. (*PSS* 4:452)

These passages begin to clarify what Pasternak means by "the destruction of forms," mentioned so often in those letters concerning his earlier artistic "participation in the sins of the age." He is least concerned with the formal appearance of order, or with cultural history where, as he mockingly observes in *Safe Conduct,* "a knot of old men in chlamys and sandals, or periwigs and camisoles, fib up some impenetrable mumbo jumbo" [некоторая богодельня, где кучка стариков в хламидах и сандалиях или парках и камзолах врет непроглядную отсебятину] (*CSP* 39; *PSS* 3:169). He does, however, speak of "form [as] the key to organic life, since no living thing can exist without it" [форма же есть органический ключ существования, формой должно обладать все живое, чтобы существовать] (*Zhivago* 454; *PSS* 4:452). The schematic organization of his earlier prose, he suggests, was part of the overall dismissal of the organic power of renewal and animation that can be discerned as invigorating reality, releasing its still sleeping potential. At the same time, it is also clear that Pasternak's early prose work (while lacking the broader historical tableau and the depth of the ongoing conflict depicted in the later work) has already experimented with many of these artistic ideas.

It is also noteworthy that Pasternak's early stories examined in this book are all centered on the spirited carriers of "ideas": Heine, whose power competed with that of the sun; Tolstoy, the force of conscience in Tula, who directed the dance of the compass needles [тут начинают плясать магнитные стрелки] (*CSP* 122; *PSS* 3:29); Lermontov, the "spirit of living adventure" who presages suffering and storms. Even Pasternak's understanding of the roles of Scriabin, Cohen, and Mayakovsky (agent of the spirit of the age) should be understood in this context—the admired faces of his youth and the re-makers of his life. The striking opposition of his mature years emerges centrally as an opposition between the ideas that destroy the world and the soul of life itself [ее дух, душа ее] (*Zhivago* 338; *PSS* 4:336). In finishing his *Sketch for an Autobiography,* Pasternak thematizes his life's work by drawing the portraits of two Georgian poets, Titian Tabidze and Paolo Yashvili, whose fate, together with that of Marina Tsvetaeva, became his "greatest sorrow." The portrayal of these poets exterminated in the unequal conflicts of the century is centered on the centripetal and centrifugal directions of soul's agency, the poets' inexhaustible clairvoyant potential projected into their surroundings and their art:

> If Yashvili was turned outwards, all in a centrifugal direction, Titian Tabidze was turned inwards and every line he wrote and every step he took called you into the depths of his rich *soul,* so full of intuitions and forebodings. [. . .] This presence of the untouched store of *spiritual* reserves creates the background and lends depth to his poems and imparts that special mood with which they are imbued. [. . .] There is *as much soul in his poems* as there was in himself, *a complex, esoteric soul, directed wholly toward good, capable of clairvoyance and self-sacrifice. (Remember* 116; emphasis added)

> Если Яшвили весь был во внешнем, центробежном проявлении, Тициан Табидзе был устремлен внутрь и каждою своей строкой и каждым шагом звал в глубину своей богатой, полной догадок и предчувствий *души.* [. . .] Это присутствие незатронутых душевных запасов создает фон и второй план его стихов и придает им то особое настроение, которым они пронизаны и которое составляет их главную и горькую прелесть. *Души в его стихах столько же, сколько ее было в нем самом, души сложной, затаенной, целиком направленной к добру и способной к ясновидению и самопожертвованию. (PSS* 3:343)

This other tableau, then, of "years, circumstances, people, and destinies within the framework of the Russian revolution" [о годах, обстоятельствах, людях и судьбах, охваченных рамою революции] (*Remember* 122; *PSS* 3:345) was, Pasternak claims, the work of his life—and it was to be a realistic narrative, which sought for new forms in order not to cheapen this living memory with unnecessary artistic mystification. For this reason, only the most careful analysis, and another study altogether, can do justice to the later stages of Pasternak's continuing artistic work.

Bibliography

Primary Texts

Cahn, Stephen M., ed. 2002. *Classics of Western Philosophy.* Indianapolis: Hackett.

Davydov, Danila. 2009. "Eto bylo goryacho i talantlivo. Pis'ma S. P. Bobrova k A. P. Kviatkovskomu: Publikatsia Yaroslava Kvyantkovskogo." *Novyi mir* 8 (2009): 8ff.

Deleuze, Gilles, and Félix Guattari. 1987. *A Thousand Plateaus: Capitalism and Schizophrenia.* Minneapolis: University of Minnesota Press.

Derrida, Jacques. 1976. *Of Grammatology.* Trans. Gayatri Chakrovorty Spivak. Baltimore: Johns Hopkins University Press.

Elam, Keir. 1980. *The Semiotics of Theatre and Drama.* New York: Routledge. Reprint, 2002.

Fleishman, Lazar, Hans-Bernd Harder, Sergey Dorzweiler, and Boris L. Pasternak. 1996. *Boris Pasternaks Lehrjahre. Neopublikovannye konspekty i zametki Borisa Pasternaka.* 2 vols. Stanford, CA: Stanford University Press.

Guénon, René. 2003. *The Metaphysical Principles of the Infinitesimal Calculus.* Hillsdale, NY: Sophia Perennis.

Hume, David. 2000. *A Treatise of Human Nature.* Ed. David F. Norton and Mary J. Norton. Oxford: Oxford University Press.

———. 2007. *An Enquiry Concerning Human Understanding and Other Writings.* Ed. Stephen Buckle. Cambridge: Cambridge University Press.

Kant, Immanuel. 1996. *Critique of Pure Reason.* Trans. Werner S. Pluhar and Patricia Kitcher. Indianapolis: Hackett.

Keats, John. 1973. *The Complete Poems.* New York: Viking Penguin.

Levinas, Emmanuel. 1961. *Totalité et infini: Essai sur l'extériorité.* Paris: Kluver Academic, le Livre de Poche.

Lermontov, M. Iu. 1910–13. *Polnoe sobranie sochinenii v piati tomakh.* Ed. D. I. Abramovich. St. Petersburg: Akademiia nauk.

Mandelstam, Osip E. 1993. *Sobranie sochinenii v chetyrekh tomakh.* Ed. Pavel M. Nerler and Aleksandr Nikitaev. Moscow: Art-Biznes-Centr.

Pasternak, Boris. 1959. *Poems.* Introd. and trans. Eugene M. Kayden. Ann Arbor: University of Michigan Press.

———. 1977. *Collected Short Prose.* Ed. and trans. Christopher Barnes. New York: Praeger.

———. 1981. *Perepiska s Olgoi Freidenberg.* Ed. Elliott Mossman. New York and London: Harcourt Brace Jovanovich. Trans. Elliott Mossman and Margaret Wettlin as *The Correspondence of Boris Pasternak and Olga Freidenberg, 1910–1954.* New York: Harcourt Brace Jovanovich, 1982.

———. 1986. Ed. and trans. Christopher J. Barnes. *The Voice of Prose: 1.* Edinburgh: Polygon.

———. 1988. *Pis'ma k roditeliam i sestram.* Ed. E. B. and E. V. Pasternak. Stanford, CA: Stanford University and Berkeley Slavic Specialities.

———. 1989–92. *Sobranie sochinenii v piati tomakh.* Ed. A. A. Voznesensky, D. S. Likhachev, D. F. Mamleev, A. A. Mikhailov, and E. B. Pasternak. Commentaries by E. V. Pasternak and K. M. Polivanov. Introd. by D. S. Likhachev. Moscow: Khudozhestvennaia literatura.

———. 1990. Ed. and trans. Christopher J. Barnes. *The Voice of Prose: 2.* Edinburgh: Polygon.

———. 1994. *Lettres à mes amies françaises 1956–60.* Introd. and notes by Jacqueline de Proyart. Paris: Gallimard.

———. 1997. *Doctor Zhivago.* Trans. Max Hayward and Manya Harari. Introd. John Bayley. "The Poems of Yurii Zhivago" trans. Bernard Guilbert Guerney. New York: Pantheon.

———. 2003–5. *Polnoe sobranie sochinenii s prilozheniiami, v odinnadtsati tomakh* [Complete Collected Works with Appendices, in Eleven Volumes]. Ed. D. V. Tevekelian. Compiled and provided with commentaries by E. B. Pasternak and E. V. Pasternak. Introd. Lazar Fleishman. Moscow: Slovo.

———, and David Magarshack. 1959. *I Remember: Sketch for an Autobiography.* New York: Pantheon.

Pasternak, E. B., E. V. Pasternak, and K. M. Azadovsky, eds. 1986. *Letters Summer 1926. Pasternak. Tsvetaeva. Rilke.* Trans. Margaret Wettlin and Walter Arndt. London: Jonathan Cape.

Pasternak, E. B., and Konstantin Polivanov. 1990. "Pis'ma Borisa Pasternaka iz Marburga." In *Pamiatniki kul'tury. Novye otkrytiia. Pis'mennost.' Iskusstvo. Arkheologiia. Ezhegodnik 1989,* 51–75. Moscow: Nauka.

Plato. 2005. *The Collected Works of Plato.* Ed. Edith Hamilton and Huntington Cairns. New York: Pantheon.

Plato.1969. *Plato: In Twelve Volumes.* Trans. Paul Shorey, Vols. 5 & 6 . Cambridge, MA: Harvard University Press, (orig. vers. 1935).

Plotinus. 1966–88. *Enneads. In Seven Volumes.* Ed. and trans. A. H. Armstrong. Cambridge, MA: Harvard University Press.

Pushkin, Aleksandr S. 1994. *Polnoe Sobranie Sochinenii, v deviatnadtsati tomakh* [Complete Collected Works, in Nineteen Volumes]. Ed. Maksim Gorky, V. D. Bonch-Bruevich, and Ivan Zhukov. Moscow: Voskresen'e.

Rilke, Rainer Maria. 1990. *The Notebooks of Malte Laurids Brigge.* Trans. Stephen Mitchell. New York: Vintage.

———. 2008. *Poems, 1906 to 1926.* Trans. and introd. J. B. Leishman. New York: Ballou Press.

Solovyov, Vladimir Sergeyevich. 2000. *Politics, Law, and Morality: Essays.* Ed. and trans. Vladimir Wozniuk. Foreword by Gary Saul Morson. New Haven, CT: Yale University Press.

Tsvetaeva, Marina. 1979. *Izbrannaia proza v dvukh tomakh: 1917–1937.* New York: Russica Publishers.

———. 1980. *A Captive Spirit: Selected Prose.* Trans. J. M. King. Ann Arbor: Ardis.

——— and Boris Pasternak. 2004. *Dushi nachinaiut videt'. Pis'ma 1922–1936 godov.* Eds. E. B. Korkina and I. D. Shevelenko. Moscow: Vagrius.

Secondary Texts

Abashev, V. V. 1990. "Pis'ma 'Nachal'noi pory' kak proekt poetiki Pasternaka." In *Pasternakovskie chteniia: materialy mezhvuzovskii konferentsii, oktiabr,' 1990 g. Perm,'* ed. R. V. Komina, V V. Abashev, and B. V. Kondakov, 3–9. Perm: Permskii gosudarstvennyi universitet.

Al'fonsov, V. 1990. *Poeziia Borisa Pasternaka.* Leningrad: Sovetskii pisatel'.

Allen, Elizabeth Cheresh, and Gary Saul Morson, eds. 1995. *Freedom and Responsibility in Russian Literature: Essays in Honor of Robert Louis Jackson.* Evanston, IL: Northwestern University Press.

Allison, Henry E. 2008. *Custom and Reason in Hume: A Kantian Reading of the First Book of the Treatise.* Oxford: Oxford University Press.

Anderson, Roger B. 1987. "The Railroad in *Doctor Zhivago.*" *Slavic & East European Journal* 31 (4): 503–19.

Anderson-Gold, Sharon. 2008. "The Purposiveness of Nature: Kant and Environmental Ethics." In *Recht und Frieden in der Philosophie Kants: Akten des X. Internationalen Kant-Kongresses,* ed. International Kant Congress and Valério Rohden, 3–12. Berlin: De Gruyter.

Arutiunova, N. D. 1972. "O sintaksicheskikh tipakh khudozhestvennoi prozy." In *Obshchee i romanskoe iazykoznanie,*189–99. Moscow: Nauka.

Aucouturier, Michel. 1963. *Pasternak par lui-même.* Paris: Editions du Seuil.

———. 1969. "The Legend of the Poet and the Image of the Actor in the Short Stories of Pasternak." In *Pasternak: Modern Judgments,* ed. Donald Davie and Angela Livingstone, 220–30. London: Macmillan.

———. 1978. "The Metonymous Hero or the Beginnings of Pasternak the Novelist." In *Pasternak. A Collection of Critical Essays,* ed. Victor Erlich, 43–50. Englewood Cliffs, NJ: Prentice Hall.

———. 1979. "Ob odnom kliuche k 'Okhrannoi gramote.'" In *Boris Pasternak, 1890–1960 (Colloque de Cerisy-la-Salle,* 11–14 septembre 1975), ed. Michel Aucouturier, 337–48. Paris: Institut d'Etudes slaves.

———, ed. 1979. *Boris Pasternak, 1890–1960 (Colloque de Cerisy-la-Salle,* 11–14 septembre 1975). Paris: Institut d'Etudes slaves.

———. 1998. "Pol i 'poshlost": tema pola u Pasternaka." In *Pasternakovskie chteniia 2,* eds. M. L. Gasparov, I. Iu. Podgaetskaia, and Konstantin Polivanov, 71–81. Moscow: Nasledie.

———. 2004. "Poet i filosofiia (Boris Pasternak)." In *Literaturovedenie kak literatura. Sbornik v chest' S.G. Bocharova,* 255–73. Moscow: Iazyki slavianskoi kul'tury.

Avins, Carol J. 1995. "Yuri Zhivago's Readers: Literary Reception in Pasternak's Novel and in His Time." In *Freedom and Responsibility in Russian Literature: Essays in Honor of Robert Louis Jackson,* eds. Elizabeth Cheresh Allen and Gary Saul Morson, 213–20. Evanston, IL: Northwestern University Press.

Azadovsky, Konstantin. 1993. "Boris Pasternak i Rainer Mariia Ril'ke." In *Beiträge zum Internationalen Pasternak-Kongress 1991 in Marburg,* eds. Sergey Dorzweiler and Hans-Bernd Harder, 1–12. Munich: Verlag Otto Sagner.

Baker, James M. 1986. *The Music of Alexander Scriabin.* New Haven, CT: Yale University Press.

Barnes, Christopher. 1972. "Boris Pasternak and Rainer Maria *Rilke*: Some Missing Links." *Forum for Modern Language Studies* 8:61–78.

———. 1977. "Pasternak As Composer and Scriabin-Disciple." *Tempo* n.s. 121: 13–25.

———. 1989. *Boris Pasternak: A Literary Biography. Volume I: 1890—1928.* Cambridge: Cambridge University Press.

———. 1998. *Boris Pasternak: A Literary Biography. Volume II: 1928–1960.* Cambridge: Cambridge University Press.

———. 2006. "The Image of Chopin (à propos of Pasternak's article on Fryderyk Chopin)." In *A Century's Perspective: Essays on Russian Literature in Honor of Olga Raevsky Hughes and Robert P. Hughes,* eds. Lazar Fleishman and Hugh McLean, 307–22. Stanford, CA: Stanford University Press.

Baróthy, Judit. 1996. "The Androgynous Mind: A Contrastive Analysis of Virginia Woolf's *To the Lighthouse* and Boris Pasternak's *Zhenya Luvers's Childhood.*" *AnaChronisT*: 79–97.

Beiser, Frederick C. 2004. *The Romantic Imperative: the Concept of Early German Romanticism.* Cambridge, MA: Harvard University Press.

Berlin, Isaiah. 1980. *Meetings with Russian Writers in 1945 and 1956.* London: Hogarth Press.

———. 2004. *The Soviet Mind: Russian Culture under Communism.* Ed. Henry Hardy. Washington, DC: Brookings Institution Press.

Bethea, David M. 1989. "Doctor Zhivago: The Revolution and the Red Crosse Knight." In *The Shape of Apocalypse in Modern Russian Fiction,* 230–68. Princeton, NJ: Princeton University Press.

Birnbaum, Henrik. 1989. "Further Reflections on the Poetics of Doktor Živago: Structure, Technique and Symbolism." In *Boris Pasternak and His Times: Selected Papers from the Second International Symposium on Pasternak,* ed. Lazar Fleishman, 284–314. Berkeley, CA: Berkeley Slavic Specialties.

Björling, Fiona. 1976. "Aspects of Poetic Syntax: Analysis of the Poem 'Sestra moia zhizn' i segodnia v razlive' by Boris Pasternak." In *Boris Pasternak. Essays,* ed. Nils Ake Nilsson, 162–79. Stockholm: Almquist and Wiksell International.

———. 1982. "Child Perspective: Tradition and Experiment. An Analysis of 'The Childhood of Lovers' by Boris Pasternak." In *Studies in 20th Century Russian Prose.* (Stockholm Studies in Russian Literature), ed. Neils Ake Nilsson, 130–55. Stockholm: Almquiest & Wiksell International.

———. 2000. "The Complicated Mix of the Private and the Public. Pasternak's Obituary for Mayakovsky in *Safe Conduct* Part Three." In *Severnyi sbornik, Proceedings of the NorFa Network in Russian Literature 1995–2000,* eds. Peter Alberg Jensen and Ingunn Lunde, 255–66. Stockholm: Almquist and Wiksell International.

———. 2001. "Blind Leaps of Passion and Other Strategies to Outwit Inevitability. On Pasternak and the Legacy from the Turn of the 19th to the 20th Century." In *On the Verge. Russian Thought between the 19th and the 20th Centuries,* ed. Fiona Björling, 131–50. Lund: Lund University.

———. 2006. "Speeding in Time: Philosophy and Metaphor in a Presentation of *Okhrannaia gramota.*" In *Eternity's Hostage: Selected Papers from the Stanford International Conference on Boris Pasternak, May 2004. In honor of Evgeny Pasternak and Elena Pasternak,* ed. Lazar Fleishman, 285–303. Stanford, CA: Stanford University Press.

———. 2010. "Child Perspective: Tradition and Experiment. An Analysis of *Detstvo Luvers* by Boris Pasternak." In *The Russian Twentieth-Century Short-Story: A Critical Companion,* ed. Lyudmila Parts, 117–142. Brighton, MA: Academic Studies Press.

Bodin, Per-Arne. 1976a. *Nine Poems from Doctor Zhivago. A Study of Christian Motifs in Boris Pasternak's Poetry.* Stockholm: Almqvist and Wiksell International.

———. 1976b. "Pasternak and Christian Art." In *Boris Pasternak. Essays,* ed. Nils Ake Nilsson, 203–14. Stockholm: Almquist and Wiksell International.

———. 1986. "God, Tsar, and Man: Boris Pasternak's Poem 'Artillerist.'" *Scottish Slavonic Review* 6:69–80.

———. 1990. "Boris Pasternak and the Christian Tradition." *Modern Language Studies* XXVI: 382–401.

Borisov, Vadim. 1992. "Imia v romane Borisa Pasternaka 'Doktor Zhivago.'" In *"Byt' znamenitym nekrasivo,"* ed. I. Iu. Podgaetskaia, 101–9. Moscow: Nasledie.

———, and Evgeny Pasternak. 1988. "Materialy k tvorcheskoi istorii romana B. Pasternaka 'Doktor Zhivago.'" *Novyi mir* 6:205–48.

Bortnes, Jostein. 1994. "Christianskaia tema v romane Pasternaka 'Doktor Zhivago.'" In *Evangel'skii tekst v russkoi literature XVIII-XX vekov. Citata, reminiscenciia, motv, siuzhet, zhanr: Sbornik nauchnykh trudov,* ed. V.N. Zakharov, 361–77. Petrozavodsk: Izd-vo Petrozavodskogo universiteta.

Bykov, Dmitry. 2006. *Boris Pasternak.* Moscow: Molodaya Gvardiya.

Carlisle, Olga Andreyev. 1963. *Voices in the Snow; Encounters with Russian Writers.* New York: Random House.

———. 1970. *Poets on Street Corners. Portraits of Fifteen Russian Poets.* New York: Random House.

Chiaromonte, Nicola. 1969. "Pasternak's Message." In *Pasternak: Modern Judgments,* ed. Donald Davie and Angela Livingstone, 231–39. London: Macmillan.

Ciepiela, Catherine. 2006. *The Same Solitude: Boris Pasternak and Marina Tsvetaeva.* Ithaca, NY: Cornell University Press.

Clowes, Edith W., ed. 1995. *Doctor Zhivago: A Critical Companion.* Evanston, IL: Northwestern University Press.

———. 2002. "Pasternak's 'Safe Passage' and the Question of Philosophy." Festschrift in honour of Arnold McMillin. *New Zealand Slavonic Journal* 36: 39–48.

Conquest, Robert. 1962. *The Pasternak Affair: Courage of Genius; a Documentary Report.* Philadelphia: Lippincott.

Cornwell, Neil. 1986. *Pasternak's Novel: Perspectives on "Doctor Zhivago."* Keele, England: Keele University Press.

Danow, D. K. 1981. "Epiphany in 'Doctor Zhivago.'" *The Modern Language Review* 76:889–903.

Davidson, John. 1906. *A New Interpretation of Herbart's Psychology and Educational Theory through the Philosophy of Leibniz.* Edinburgh: Blackwood.

Davidson, Pamela. 1989. *The Poetic Imagination of Vyacheslav Ivanov: A Russian Symbolist's Perception of Dante.* Cambridge: Cambridge University Press.

Davie, Donald, and Angela Livingstone, eds. 1969. *Pasternak: Modern Judgments.* London: Macmillan.

Demkova, N. S. 1997. "Iz istorikoy-liternaturnogo kommentariia k romanu B. Pasternaka 'Doktor Zhivago': Drevnerusskie temy i paralleli." In *Ars philologiae. Sbornik statei,* 329–49. St. Petersburg: St. Petersburg University.

Döring, J. R. 1973. *Die Lyrik Pasternaks in den Jahren 1928–1934.* Munich: Verlag Otto Sagner.

Dorzweiler, Sergey. 1993. "Boris Pasternak und Gottfried Wilhelm Leibniz." In *Beitrage zum Internationalen Pasternak-Kongress 1991 in Marburg,* ed. Sergey Dorzweiler and Hans-Bernd Harder, 25–31. Munich: Verlag Otto Sagner.

———, and Hans-Bernd Harder, eds. 1993. *Beitrage zum Internationalen Pasternak-Kongress 1991 in Marburg.* Munich: Verlag Otto Sagner.

Durylin, S. N. 1991. *V svoem uglu: iz starykh tetradei,* ed. G. E. Pomerantseva and E. I. Liubushkina. Moscow: Moskovskii rabochii.

Duvakin V. D., S. G. Bocharov, V. V. Radzishevskii, and V. V. Kozhinov. 1996. *Besedy V. D. Duvakina S M. M. Bachtinym.* Moscow: Izd. Progress.

Erlewine, Robert. 2010. *Monotheism and Tolerance: Recovering a Religion of Reason.* Bloomington: Indiana University Press.

Erlich, Victor. 1979. "'Strasti razriady': Zametki o 'Marburge.'" In *Boris Pasternak 1890–1960: Colloque de Cerisy-al-Salle (11–14 septembre 1975),* ed. Michel Aucouturier, 281–88. Paris: Institut d'Etudes slaves.

———, ed. 1978. *Pasternak. A Collection of Critical Essays.* Englewood Cliffs, NJ: Prentice Hall.

Evans-Romaine, Karen. 1997. *Boris Pasternak and the Tradition of German Romanticism.* Munich: Verlag Otto Sagner.

Faryno, Jerzy. 1993. *Belaja Medvedica, Ol'cha, Motovilicha i Chromoj Iz Gospod: Archeopoetika Detstva Ljuvers Borisa Pasternaka.* Stockholm: Inst. för slaviska och baltiska språk, Stockholms universitet.

Fateeva, Natal'ia. 2003. *Poet i proza: Kniga o Pasternake.* Moscow: Novoe literaturnoe obozrenie.

———. 2004. "Ot 'slozhnogo' k 'prostomy' i obratno: ob evoliutsii khudozhestvennoi sistemy B. Pasternaka." In *Lotmanovskii sbornik 3,* ed. L. N. Kiseleva, R. G. Leibov, and T. N. Fraiman, 696–707. Moscow: OGI.

————. 2008. "O tom kak zhivet i rabotaet pasternakovskaia lestnitsa: k voprosu o femibizatsii prostranstva v khudozhestvennom mire." In *Liubov' prostranstva: poetika mesta v tvorchestve Borisa Pasternaka*, ed. V. V. Abashev and Viacheslav V. Ivanov, 159–69. Moscow: Iazyki slavianskoi kul'tury.

Fleishman, Lazar. 1971. "Neizvestnyi avtograf Borisa Pasternaka." In *Materialy XXVI nauchnoi studencheskoi konferentsii*. Tartu: Tartu State University.

————. 1975. "K kharakteristike rannego Pasternaka." *Russian Literature* 12: 79–129.

————. 1977. *Stat'i o Pasternake*. Bremen: K-Presse.

————. 1979. "Problems in the Poetics of Pasternak." Trans. Ann Shukman. *PTL: A Journal for Descriptive Poetics and Theory* 4: 43–61.

————. 1980. *Boris Pasternak v dvadtsatye gody*. Munich: Wilhelm Fink Verlag.

————. 1984. *Boris Pasternak v tridtsatye gody*. Jerusalem: Magnes Press, The Hebrew University.

————, ed. 1989. *Boris Pasternak and His Times: Selected Papers from the Second International Symposium on Pasternak*. Berkeley: Berkeley Slavic Specialties.

————. 1990a. *Boris Pasternak: The Poet and his Politics*. Cambridge, MA, and London: Harvard University Press.

————. 1990b. "In Search of the Word: an Analysis of Pasternak's poem 'Tak nachinaiut . . .'" *Zeszyty naukowe Wyzszej szkoly pedagogicznej v Bydgoszczy. Studia Filologiczne; Filologia rosyjska. Poetika Pasternaka* 31 (12): 65–90.

————. 1991. "Ot 'Zapisok Patrika' k 'Doktoru Zhivago.'" In *Izvestiia Akademii nauk SSSR. Serija literatury i iazyka* 50 (2): 114–23.

————. 1993. "Nakanune poezii: Marburg v zhizni i v 'Okhrannoi gramote' Pasternaka." In *Beiträge zum Internationalen Pasternak-Kongress 1991 in Marburg*, ed. Sergey Dorzweiler and Hans-Bernd Harder, 59–74. Munich: Verlag Otto Sagner.

————. 1998. "Pasternak i predrevoliutsionnyi futurism." In *Pasternakovskie chteniia 2*, ed. M. L. Gasparov, I. Iu. Podgaetskaia, and Konstantin Polivanov, 244–58. Moscow: Nasledie.

————. 2005. *Boris Pasternak i literaturnoe dvizhenie 1930-kh godov*. St. Petersburg: Akademicheskii proekt.

————, ed. 2006. *Eternity's Hostage: Selected Papers from the Stanford International Conference on Boris Pasternak, May 2004. In honor of Evgeny Pasternak and Elena Pasternak*. Stanford, CA: Stanford University Press.

————, and Hugh McLean, eds. 2006. *A Century's Perspective: Essays on Russian Literature in Honor of Olga Raevsky Hughes and Robert P. Hughes*. Stanford, CA: Stanford University Press.

Frank, V. S. 1962. "Vodianoi znak (Poeticheskoe mirovozrenie Pasternaka)." In *Sbornik statei, posviashcsennykh tvorchestvu Borisa Leonidovicha Pasternaka*, ed. Boris Ivanov, 240–52. Munich: Institut po izucheniiu SSSR.

Galeev, B. M., and I. L. Vanechkina. 2001. "Was Scriabin a Synesthete?" *Leonardo* 34(4): 357–61.

Gardzonio, S. 1999. "'Sestra moia zhizn'' B. Pasternaka i nasledie sv. Frantsiska Assizskogo." In *Poetry and Revolution. Boris Pasternak's "My Sister Life,"* ed. Lazar Fleishman, 66–75. Stanford: Stanford University Press.

Gasparov, Boris. 1989. "Vremennoi kontrapunkt kak formoobrazuiushchii printsip romana Pasternaka 'Doktor Zhivago.'" In *Boris Pasternak and His Times: Selected Papers from the Second International Symposium on Pasternak*, ed. Lazar Fleishman, 315–58. Berkeley, CA: Berkeley Slavic Specialties.

————. 1992a. "Gradus ad Parnassum. (Samosovershenstvovanie kak kategoriia tvorcheskogo mira Pasternaka)." In *"Byt' znamenitym nekrasivo,"* ed. I. Iu. Podgaetskaia, 110–35. Moscow: Nasledie.

————. 1992b. "Poetika Pasternaka v kul'turno-istoricheskom izmerenii (B. L. Pasternak i O. M. Freidenberg)." In *Sbornik statei k 70-letiiu prof. Iu. M. Lotmana*, ed. A. Malts, 366–84. Tartu: Tartuskii universitet, Kafedra russkoi literatury.

———. 1995. "Ob odnom ritmiko-muzykal'nom motive v proze Pasternaka. (Istoriia odnoi trilo-gii)." In *Studies in Poetics: Commemorative Volume: Krystyna Pomorska (1928–1986)*, ed. Elena Semeka-Pankratov, 233–59. Columbus, OH: Slavica.

Gasparov, Mikhail L. 1990. "Rifma i zhanr v stikhakh Borisa Pasternaka." *Russkaia rech'* 1:17–22.

———. 1995. "Vladimir Maiakovskii." In *Ocherki istorii iazyka russkoi poezii XX veka: Opyty opisaniia idiostilei*, ed. V. P. Grigoriev and V. V. Vinogradova, 363–95. Moscow: Nasledie.

———, and I. Iu. Podgaetskaia. 1999. "Chetyre stikhotvoreniia iz *Sestry moei-zhizni*: sverka poni-maniia." In *Poetry and Revolution. Boris Pasternak's "My Sister Life,"* ed. Lazar Fleishman, 150–66. Stanford, CA: Stanford University Press.

———, I. Iu. Podgaetskaia, and Konstantin Polivanov, eds. 1998. *Pasternakovskie chteniia 2*. Moscow: Nasledie.

———, and Konstantin M. Polivanov. 2005. *"Bliznets v tuchakh" Borisa Pasternaka: Opyt kommentariia*. Moscow: Rossiiskii gosudarstvennii gumanitarnii universitet, inst. vysshich gumanitarnykh issledovanii.

Gibian, George. 1983. "Doctor Zhivago, Russia, and Leonid Pasternak's *Rembrandt*." In *The Russian Novel from Pushkin to Pasternak*, ed. John Garrard, 203–24. New Haven and London: Yale University Press.

Gershenzon, Mikhail. 1918. "Dukh i dusha." In *Slovo o kul'ture: Sbornik kriticheskikh i filosofskikh statei*, 3–20. Moscow: Izd. M. Gordon-Konstantinovoi.

Gibbs, Robert. 2005. "Jurisprudence is the Organon of Ethics: Kant and Cohen on Ethics, Law and Religion." In *Hermann Cohen's Critical Idealism*, ed. Reinier Munk, 193–230. Dordrecht: Springer.

Gifford, Henry. 1977. *Pasternak: A Critical Study*. Cambridge: Cambridge University Press.

———. 1990. "Pasternak and European Modernism." In *Forum for Modern Language Studies* 26 (4): 301–14.

Gladkov, Aleksandr. 1973. *Vstrechi s Pasternakom*. Paris: YMCA Press.

———. 1977. *Meetings with Pasternak: A Memoir*. Trans., ed., notes and introd. Max Hayward. London: Collins & Harvill.

Glazov-Corrigan, Elena. 1991. "The Status of the Concepts of 'Event' and 'Action' in Pasternak's *Detstvo Luvers*." *Wiener Slawistischer Almanach* 27: 137–58.

———. 1994. "A Reappraisal of Shakespeare's Hamlet: In Defense of Pasternak's *Doctor Zhivago*." *Forum for Modern Language Studies* 30 (3): 219–38.

Golubeva, O. D., D. B. Aziattsev, and N. G. Zakharenko. 1995. *Russkie Pisateli Poety: Sovetskii Period : Biobibliograficheskii Ukazatel'. 18, B. Pasternak*. St. Petersburg: Rossiiskaia Natsional'naia biblioteka.

Goodchild, Philip. 1996. *Deleuze and Guattari: an Introduction to the Politics of Desire*. London: SAGE.

Gordin, Ia. A., ed. 1993. 1993. *Osip Mandel'shtam*. St. Petersburg: Lenizdat.

Gorelik, L. L. 1994. "Pushkinskii mif o meteli v povesti Pasternaka 'Detstvo Liuvers.'" In *Russkaia filologiia: uchenye zapiski. Tom 1*, 256–78. Smolensk: Smolenskii gos. pedagog. universiteit.

———. 2000. *Rannaia proza Pasternaka: mif o tvorenii*. Smolensk: Smolenskii gos. pedagog. universitet.

———. 2011. *"Mif o tvorchestve" v proze i stixax Borisa Pasternaka*. Moscow: RGGU.

Greber, Erika. 1988. "Pasternak's 'Detstvo Lyuvers' and Dostoevsky's 'Netochka Nezvanova': An Intertextual Approach." *Irish Slavonic Studies* 9: 62–79.

———. 1989. *Intertextualität Und Interpretierbarkeit Des Texts Zur Frühen Prosa Boris Pasternaks*. Munich: W. Fink.

———. 1992. "Das Erinnern des Erinnerns. Die mnemonische Aesthetik Boris Pasternaks." *Poetica* 24 (3–4): 356–93.

———. 1997. "The Art of Memory in Pasternak's Aesthetics." *Russian Literature* 42: 25–46.

Grene, Marjorie and David J. Depew. 2004. *The Philosophy of Biology: An Episodic History.* Cambridge: Cambridge University Press.

Han, Anna. 1988. "Osnovnye predposylki filosofii tvorchestva B. Pasternaka v svete ego rannego esteticheskogo samoopredeleniia." *Acta Universitatis Szegediensis de Attila Jozsef Nominatae, Dissertationes slavicae, Sectio Historiae Literarum* 19: 39–135. Szeged: University of Szeged.

Hasty, Olga. 2006. "Representing Ephemerality: Pasternak's 'Groza momental'naia navek.'" In *Eternity's Hostage: Selected Papers from the Stanford International Conference on Boris Pasternak, May 2004. In honor of Evgeny Pasternak and Elena Pasternak,* ed. Lazar Fleishman, 116–32. Stanford, CA: Stanford University Press.

Helle, Lilian J. 1988. "Between Poetry and Painting. Pasternak's 'Christmas Star.'" *Scando-Slavica* 44: 57–74.

Hingley, Ronald. 1983. *Pasternak: A Biography.* New York: Knopf.

Holzhey, Helmut. 2005. "Cohen and the Marburg School in Context." In *Hermann Cohen's Critical Idealism,* ed. Reinier Munk, 3–37. Dordrecht: Springer.

Hughes, Olga. 1974. *The Poetic World of Boris Pasternak.* Princeton, NJ: Princeton University Press.

———. 1989. "O samoubiistve Maiakovskogo v 'Okhrannoi gramote.'" In *Boris Pasternak and His Times: Selected Papers from the Second International Symposium on Pasternak,* ed. Lazar Fleishman, 141–52. Berkeley, CA: Berkeley Slavic Specialties.

Hutcheon, Linda. 1984. *Narcissistic Narrative: The Metafictional Paradox.* New York: Methuen.

Ivanov, Boris, ed. 1962. *Sbornik statei, posviashcsennykh tvorchestvu Borisa Leonidovicha Pasternaka.* Munich: Institut po izucheniiu SSSR.

Ivanov, Vyacheslav Vsevolodovich. 1988. "Pasternak i OPOIAZ." In *Tynianovskii sbornik: Tret'i Tynianovskie chteniia,* 70–82. Riga-Moscow: Zinatne.

———. 1992. "Soliarnye Mify." In *Mify narodov mira. Tom 2,* ed. S. A. Tokarev, 461–62. Moscow: Sovetskaia Entsiklopediia.

Ivinskaya, Olga. 1978a. *A Captive of Time.* Trans. Max Hayward. New York: Doubleday.

———. 1978b. *V plenu vremeni: gody s Pasternakom.* Paris: Fayard.

Jackson, Robert Louis. 1978. "Doctor Zhivago: Liebestod of the Russian Intelligentsia." In *Pasternak. A Collection of Critical Essays,* ed. Victor Erlich, 137–50. Englewood Cliffs, NJ: Prentice Hall.

Jakobson, Roman. 1956. "Two Aspects of Language and Two Types of Aphasic Disturbances." In *Fundamentals of Language,* ed. Roman Jakobson and Morris Halle, 55–82. The Hague: Mouton.

———. 1960. "Closing Statement: Linguistics and Poetics." In *Style in Language,* ed. Thomas A. Sebeok, 350–77. Cambridge, MA: Technology Press of Massachusetts Institute of Technology.

———. 1969. "Marginal Notes on the Prose of the Poet Pasternak." In *Pasternak: Modern Judgments,* ed. Donald Davie and Angela Livingstone, 131–51. London: Macmillan.

———. 1979. "Randbemerkungen zur Prosa des Dichters Pasternak." In *Selected Writings V: On Verse, Its Masters and Explorers,* ed. Stephen Rudy and Martha Taylor, 416–32. The Hague, Paris, New York: Mouton.

Jensen, Peter Alberg. 1987. "Boris Pasternak's 'Opredelenie poezii.'" In *Text and Context. Essays to Honor Nils Ake Nilsson,* ed. Peter Alberg Jensen, 96–110. Stockholm: Almquist and Wiksell International.

———, ed. 1987. *Text and Context: Essays to Honor Nils Ake Nilsson.* Stockholm: Almqvist and Wiksell International.

———. 1995a. "Boris Pasternak kak khudozhnik esteticheskogo sklada (v k'erkegorovskom smysle)." *Put'. Mezhdunarodnii filosofskii zhurnal* 8: 181–217.

———. 1995b. "Nil's Ljune i Yuri Zhivago: Forma i preemstvennost.'" In *Christianity and the Eastern Slavs: Vol. III,* ed. Boris Gasparov, 244–87. Berkeley: University of California Press.

———. 1997. "Strel'nikov i Kaj: 'Snezhnaia koroleva' v 'Doktore Zhivago.'" *Scando-Slavica* 43: 68–107.

———. 2006. "Ot liriki k istorii: Poiavlenie "tret'ego litsa" v *Detstve Liuvers.*" In *A Century's Perspective: Essays on Russian Literature in Honor of Olga Raevsky Hughes and Robert P. Hughes,* ed. Lazar Fleishman and Hugh McLean, 279–306. Stanford, CA: Stanford University Press.

———, and Ingunn Lunde, eds. 2000. *Severnyi sbornik: Proceedings of the NorFa Network in Russian Literature 1995–1999.* Stockholm: Almqvist and Wiksell International.

Junggren, Anna. 1991. "Ural v 'Detstve ljuvers' B. Pasternaka." *Russian Literature* 29 (4): 489–99.

Kagan, Iu. M. 1996. "Ob 'Apellesovoi cherte' Borisa Pasternaka. Popytka postizheniia." *Literaturnoe obozrenia* 4:43–50.

Kajon, Irene. 2005. "Critical idealism in Hermann Cohen's writings on Judaism." In *Hermann Cohen's Critical Idealism.* Ed. Reinier Munk. Dordrecht: Springer: 371–94.

Kayden, Eugene, ed. and trans. 1959. *Boris Pasternak: Poems.* Ann Arbor, MI: Ardis.

Kling, Oleg. 1999. "Evoliutsiia i 'latentnoe' sushchestvovanie simvolizma posle Oktiabria." *Voprosy literatury* 4: 37–64.

———. 2002. "Boris Pasternak i simvolizm." *Voprosy literatury* 2: 25–59.

Kluback, William. 1989. *The Legacy of Hermann Cohen.* Atlanta: Scholars Press.

Knobloch, Eberhard. 2002. "Leibniz's Rigorous Foundation of Infinitesimal Geometry by Means of Riemannian Sums." *Synthese* 133 (1–2): 59–73.

Kompridis, Nikolas. 2006. *Philosophical Romanticism.* New York: Routledge.

Koretskaia, I. V. 1978. "O 'solnechnom' tsikle Viacheslava Ivanova." *Izvestiia Akademii nayk SSSR. Seriia literatury i iazyka.* 37 (1): 54–60.

Kornblatt, Judith. 1992. "The Transfiguration of Plato in the Erotic Philosophy of Vladimir Solov'ev." *Religion and Literature* 24 (2): 35–50.

Kovtunova, Irina I. 1986. *Poeticheskii Sintaksis.* Moscow: Nauka.

Krotkov, Yuri. 1960. "Pasternaks." *Grani* 60(1960): 36–74.

Kudriavtseva, E. L. 2001. *Marburg Borisa Pasternaka.* Moscow: Russkii put'.

Kurganov, Efim. 2001. *Lolita i Ada.* St. Petersburg: Izd-vo zhurnala "Zvezda."

Kuzmin, Mikhail. 1923. *Uslovnosti: stat'i ob iskusstve.* Petrograd: Poliarnaia zvezda.

Lamont, Rosette. 1977. "Yuri Zhivago's 'Fairy Tale': A Dream Poem." *World Literature Today* 51 (4): 517–21.

Layton, Susan. 1978. "Poetic Vision in Pasternak's *The Childhood of Luvers.*" *Slavic & East European Journal* 22 (2): 163–74.

Lekic, Maria. 1983. "The Genesis of the Novel 'Doctor Zhivago': Four Modes of Literary Borrowing." Ph.D. diss., University of Pennsylvania.

———. 1988. "Pasternak's 'Doctor Zhivago': The Novel and its Title." *Russian Language Journal* 42 (141–143): 177–91.

Leon, Lee T., and Marion J. Reis, eds. 1965. *Russian Formalist Criticism: Four Essays.* Lincoln: University of Nebraska Press.

Lepachin, V. 1988. "Ikonopis' i zhivopis', vechnost' i vremia v 'Rozhdestvenskoi zvezde' B. Pasternaka." In *Acta Universitatis Szegediensis de Attila Jozsef Nominatae, Dissertationes slavicae, Sectio Historiae Literarum* 19: 255–78. Szeged: University of Szeged.

Levi, Peter. 1990. *Boris Pasternak.* London: Hutchinson.

Levy, Ze'ev. 1997. "Hermann Cohen and Emmanuel Levinas." In *Hermann Cohen's Philosophy of Religion: International Conference in Jerusalem, 1996,* ed. Stephane Moses and Hartwig Wiedebach, 133–44. Hildesheim: Georg Olms Verlag.

Likhachev, D. S. 1988. "Razmyshleniia nad romanom Borisa Pasternaka Doktor Zhivago." *Novyi mir* 1: 5–10.

Livingstone, Angela. 1963. "'The Childhood of Luvers': An Early Story of Pasternak's." *Southern Review* 1: 74–84.

———. 1971. "Allegory and Christianity in *Doctor Zhivago.*" *Melbourne Slavonic Studies* 5–6: 24–33.

——. 1978. "Pasternak's Last Poetry." In *Pasternak. A Collection of Critical Essays*, ed. Victor Erlich, 166–75. Englewood Cliffs, NJ: Prentice Hall.

——. 1979. "At Home in History: Pasternak and Popper." *Slavica Hierosolymitana* 4: 131–45.

——. 1983. "Affinities in the Prose of the Poets Rilke and Pasternak." *Forum for Modern Language Studies* 29 (3): 274–84.

——. 1985. *Pasternak on Art and Creativity* (Cambridge Studies in Russian Literature). Cambridge: Cambridge University Press.

——. 1988. "'Integral Errors': remarks on the writing of *Doctor Zhivago*." *Essays in Poetics* 13 (2): 83–94.

——. 1989. *Boris Pasternak. Doctor Zhivago*. Cambridge: Cambridge University Press.

——. 1994. "A Transformation of Goethe's *Faust*." In *Themes and Variations: In Honor of Lazar Fleishman*, eds. Konstantin Polivanov, Irina Shevelenko and Andrey Ustinov, 81–92. Stanford, CA: Dept. of Slavic Languages and Literatures, Stanford University.

——. 1998. Review of *Boris Pasternaks Lehrjahre: neopublikovannye filosofskie konspekty i zametki Borisa Pasternaka*. *Slavic Review* 57 (4): 945–46.

——. 2006a. "Two Notes: How to Translate the Title '*Okhrannaia gramota*'; Footnote to an Epigraph." In *Eternity's Hostage: Selected Papers from the Stanford International Conference on Boris Pasternak, May 2004. In honor of Evgeny Pasternak and Elena Pasternak*, ed. Lazar Fleishman, 80–93. Stanford, CA: Stanford University Press.

——. 2006b. "Re-reading *Okhrannaia gramota*: Pasternak's Use of Visuality and His Conception of Inspiration." In *Eternity's Hostage: Selected Papers from the Stanford International Conference on Boris Pasternak, May 2004. In honor of Evgeny Pasternak and Elena Pasternak*, ed. Lazar Fleishman, 262–84. Stanford, CA: Stanford University Press.

——. 2008. *The Marsh of Gold: Pasternak's Writings on Inspiration and Creation*. Brighton, MA: Academic Studies Press.

Ljunggren, Anna. 1984. *Juvenilia Pasternaka. Shest' fragmentov o Relikvimini*. Stockholm: Almqvist and Wiksell International.

Lock, Charles. 1997. "Debts and Displacements: On Metaphor and Metonymy." *Acta Linguistica Hafniensia* 29: 321–37.

——. 1998. "Roman Jakobson." In *Encyclopedia of Semiotics*, ed. Paul Bouissac, 327–30. New York: Oxford University Press.

Loewen, Donald. 2008. *The Most Dangerous Art: Poetry, Politics and Autobiography after the Russian Revolution*. Lanham, MD: Lexington Books.

Loks, Konstantin. 1925. "*Detstvo Luvers*. Retsenziia." *Krasnaya Nov'* 8: 286–87.

——. 1993. "Povest' ob odnom desiatiletii: 1907–1917 gg." In *Minuvshee: Istoricheskii almanakh* 15: 7–162. Moscow and St. Petersburg: Atheneum: Feniks.

Lonnqvist, Barbara. 1993. "From Dewdrops to Poetry: the Presence of Egorii Khrabrii in *Doctor Zhivago*." *Russian Literature* 34 (2): 161–85.

Lotman, Yuri. 1969. "Stikhotvoreniia rannego Pasternaka." *Trudy po znakovym sistemam* 4: 470–77.

——. 1978. "Language and Reality in the Early Pasternak." In *Pasternak. A Collection of Critical Essays*, ed. Victor Erlich, 21–31. Englewood Cliffs, NJ: Prentice Hall.

MacKinnon, John Edward. 1988. "From Cold Axles to Hot: Boris Pasternak's Theory of Art." *British Journal of Aesthetics* 28: 145–61.

Mallac, Guy de. 1979. "Pasternak and Marburg." *Russian Review* 38 (4): 421–33.

——. 1981. *Boris Pasternak: His Life and Art*. Norman: University of Oklahoma Press.

Malmstad, John. 1992. "Boris Pasternak—The Painter's Eye." *The Russian Review: An American Quarterly Devoted to Russia Past and Present* 51 (3): 301–18.

Marvin, Miranda. 2008. *The Language of the Muses: The Dialogue between Roman and Greek Sculpture*. Los Angeles: J. Paul Getty Museum.

Mandelstam, Osip. 1969. "Notes on Poetry." In *Pasternak: Modern Judgments*, ed. Donald Davie and Angela Livingstone, 67–72. London: Macmillan.

Masing-Delic, Irene. 1977. "Some Alternating Opposites in the Zhivago Poems." *The Russian Review* 36 (4): 438–62.

———. 1981. "Zhivago as Fedorovian Soldier." *The Russian Review* 40 (3): 300–316.

———. 1982. "Bergsons 'Schopferische Entwicklung' und Pasternaks 'Doktor Shiwago.'" In *Literatur- Und Sprachentwicklung in Osteuropa Im 20. Jahrhundert: Ausgewahlte Beitrage Zum Zweiten Weltkongress Fur Sowjet Und Osteuropastudien,* ed. Eberhard Reissner, 112–30. Berlin: Berlin Verlag.

———. 1991. "Pasternaks naturfilosofiska vandringsdikter fran Peredlkinocykeln." In *Boris Pasternak och hans tid. Foredrag vid symposium i Vitterhetsakademien 28–30 maj 1990,* ed. Peter Alberg Jensen, Per-Arne Bodin, and Nils Ake Nilsson, 27–38. Stockholm: Almqvist and Wiksell International.

———. 1992. *Abolishing Death: a Salvation Myth of Russian 20th Century Literature.* Stanford, CA: Stanford University Press.

Matlaw, Ralph. 1959. "A Visit with Pasternak." *The Nation* 189.12 (Sept. 1959): 134–35.

Milosz, Czeslaw. 1970. "On Pasternak Soberly." *Books Abroad* 44 (2): 200–209.

Moeller, Peter Ulf. 1979. "Doktor Zhivago—en lyrikers verdensbillede." In *Mennesker og temaer i sovjetlitteraturen: En artikkelsamling,* eds. Erik Egeberg, Sigurd Fasting, and Geir Kjetsaa, 147–73. Oslo: Universitetsforl.

Mossman, Elliot. 1972. "Pasternak's Short Fiction." *Russian Literature Triquarterly* 2: 279–302.

———. 1989. "Towards a Poetics of the Novel Doctor Zhivago: The Fourth Typhus." In *Boris Pasternak and His Times: Selected Papers from the Second International Symposium on Pasternak,* ed. Lazar Fleishman, 386–97. Berkeley, CA: Berkeley Slavic Specialities.

Muchnic, Helen. 1961. *From Gorky to Pasternak: Six Writers in Soviet Russia.* New York: Random House.

Munk, Reinier, ed. 2005. *Hermann Cohen's Critical Idealism.* Dordrecht: Springer.

Nerler, P. M. 2010. *Slovo i "delo" Osipa Mandel'shtama: Kniga Donosov, Doprosov i Obvinitel'nykh Zakliuchenii.* Moscow: Petrovskii park.

Nilsson, Nils Ake., ed. 1976. *Boris Pasternak: Essays.* Stockholm: Almqvist and Wiksell International.

———. 1978. "Life as Ecstasy and Sacrifice: Two Poems by Boris Pasternak." In *Pasternak. A Collection of Critical Essays,* ed. Victor Erlich, 51–67. Englewood Cliffs, NJ: Prentice Hall. Rev. version [first published in *Scando-Slavica* 5 (1959)].

———. 1995. "Pasternak's My Sister—Life: The Faustian Connection." In *Freedom and Responsibility in Russian Literature: Essays in Honor of Robert Louis Jackson,* ed. Elizabeth Cheresh Allen and Gary Saul Morson, 199–212. Evanston, IL: Northwestern University Press.

Obolensky, Dmitry. 1978. "The Poems of Doctor Zhivago." In *Pasternak. A Collection of Critical Essays,* ed. Victor Erlich, 151–65. Englewood Cliffs, NJ: Prentice Hall.

O'Connor, Katherine Tiernan. 1988. *Boris Pasternak's My Sister—Life. The Illusion of Narrative.* Ann Arbor, MI: Ardis.

Pasternak, E. B. 1989. *Materialy dlia biografii.* Moscow: Sovetskii pisatel'.

———. 1990. *Boris Pasternak: The Tragic Years 1930–60.* Trans. Michael Duncan. Poetry trans. Ann Pasternak Slater and Craig Raine. London: Collins Harvill.

———. 1994. "Pamiat' i zabvenie kak osnova 'Vtoroi vselennoi' v tvorcheskoi filosofii Borisa Pasternaka." In *Themes and Variations: In Honor of Lazar Fleishman,* ed. Konstantin Polivanov, Irina Shevelenko, and Andrey Ustinov, 26–39. Stanford, CA: Dept. of Slavic Languages and Literatures, Stanford University.

———. 1997. *Boris Pasternak. Biografiia.* Moscow: Tsitadel'.

Pasternak, E. V. 1977. "Iz rannikh prozaicheskikh opytov Borisa Pasternaka." In *Pamiatniki kul'tury,* 106–18. Moskva: Nauka.

———. 1990. "Leto 1917 goda: 'Sestra moja—zhizn' i 'Doktor Zhivago.'" *Zvezda* 2: 158–65.

———. 1992. "'Ty tsar'—zhivi odin . . . ' (Boris Pasternak i Vladimir Maiakovskii)." *Scando-Slavica* 38: 64–76.

———, and M. Fejnberg, eds. 1993. *Vospominaniia o Borise Pasternake*. Moscow: Izd-vo Slovo.

———, and E. B. Pasternak, eds. 1990. *Boris Pasternak ob isskustve*. Moscow: Iskusstvo.

Pasternak, Zhozefina. 1990. "Patior." *Znamia* 2:183–93.

Payne, Robert. 1961. *The Three Worlds of Boris Pasternak*. Bloomington: Indiana University Press.

Podgaetskaia, Irina. 1993. "Pasternak i Verlen." In *Beiträge zum Internationalen Pasternak-Kongress 1991 in Marburg*, eds. Sergey Dorzweiler and Hans-Bernd Harder, 107–21. Munich: Verlag Otto Sagner.

———, ed. 1992. "*Byt' znamenitym nekrasivo*." Moscow: Nasledie.

Polivanov, Konstantin. 2006. "Otprysk luchshego russkogo proshlogo." In *Eternity's Hostage: Selected Papers from the Stanford International Conference on Boris Pasternak, May 2004. In honor of Evgeny Pasternak and Elena Pasternak*, ed. Lazar Fleishman, 450–66. Stanford, CA: Stanford University Press.

———, Irina Shevelenko and Andrey Ustinov, eds. 1994. *Themes and Variations: In Honor of Lazar Fleishman*. Stanford, CA: Dept. of Slavic Languages and Literatures, Stanford University.

Polivanov, Mikhail. 1993. "'Vtoraia vselennaia' u Pasternaka." In *Beiträge zum Internationalen Pasternak-Kongress 1991 in Marburg*, eds. Sergey Dorzweiler and Hans-Bernd Harder., 135–45. Munich: Verlag Otto Sagner.

Pollack, Nancy. 2006. "Pasternak's Botanical Parsings." In *Eternity's Hostage: Selected Papers from the Stanford International Conference on Boris Pasternak, May 2004. In honor of Evgeny Pasternak and Elena Pasternak*, ed. Lazar Fleishman, 94–115. Stanford, CA: Stanford University Press.

Poma, Andrea. 1997. *The Critical Philosophy of Hermann Cohen: La Filosofia Critica Di Hermann Cohen*. Trans. John Denton. Albany: State University of New York Press.

———. 2006. *Yearning for Form and Other Essays on Hermann Cohen's Thought*. Dordrecht: Springer.

Pomerantsev, Il'ia. 1999. "Detstvo Liuvers': Povest' o vzroslenii." *Russian, Croatian and Serbian, Czech and Slovak, Polish Literature*. 45 (2): 197–208.

Pomorska, Krystina. 1973. "Music as theme and constituent of Pasternak's poems." In *Slavic Poetics. Essays in Honor of Kiril Taranovsky*, ed. Roman Jakobson, C. H. van Schooneveld, and Dean S. Worth, 333–49. The Hague, Paris: Mouton.

———. 1975. *Themes and Variations in Pasternak's Poetics*. Lisse: Peter de Ridder Press.

Proskurina, Vera. 2001. "'Cor Ardens': smysl zaglaviia i ezotericheskaia traditsiia." *Novoe literaturnoe obozrenie* 51: 196–213.

Rashkovskaia, M. A. 1988a. "Boris Pasternak v poslevoennye gody (Novye dokumenty)." *Literaturnaia ucheba* 6: 108–16.

———. 1988b. "Pasternak o Maiakovskom." In *Pasternakovskie chteniia 2*, ed. M. L. Gasparov, I. Iu. Podgaetskaia, and Konstantin Polivanov, 355–61. Moscow: Nasledie.

———. 1992. "Dve sud'by (Pasternak i Durylin. K istorii vzaimootnoshenii." In "*Byt' znamenitym nekrasivo*," ed. I. Iu. Podgaetskaia, 235–44. Moscow: Nasledie.

Renz, Ursula. 2005. "Critical idealism and concept of culture: philosophy of culture in Hermann Cohen and Ernst Cassirer." In *Hermann Cohen's Critical Idealism*, ed. Reinier Munk, 327–53. Dordrecht: Springer.

Rowland, Mary, and Paul Rowland. 1967. *Pasternak's "Doctor Zhivago."* Carbondale: Southern Illinois University Press.

Rudova, Larissa. 1994. *Pasternak's Short Fiction and the Cultural Vanguard*. New York: Peter Lang.

———. 1997. *Understanding Boris Pasternak*. Columbia: University of South Carolina Press.

Runes, Dagobert D. 1984. *Dictionary of Philosophy, Revised and Enlarged*. Totowa, NJ: Rowman & Allenheld.

Schäfer, Jörg. 1997. "Tod und Trauer. Rilke's 'Requiem.'" In *Grenzgänger: Haben als hätten wir nicht in Literatur und Religion. Essays*, 193–208. New York: Peter Lang.

Segal, Dmitrii. 1981. "Literatura kak ochrannaia gramota." *Slavica Hierosolymitana* 5–6: 186–93.

Sendelbach, Donnie. 2001. Review of *Boris Pasternaks Lehrjahre: neopublikovannye filosofskie konspekty i zametki Borisa Pasternaka. Slavic & East European Journal* 45 (4): 764–65.

Senderovich, Savelii. 1991. "K geneticheskoi eidologii 'Doktora Zhivago.' 1. Doktor Zhivago i poet Chekhov." *Russian Language Journal* 45 (150): 3–16.

Sendich, Munir. 1991a. "Boris Pasternak in Literary Criticism (1914–1990): An Analysis." *Russian Language Journal* 45 (151–152): 129–83.

———. 1991b. "Boris Pasternak: A Selected Annotated Bibliography of Literary Criticism (1914–1990)." *Russian Language Journal* 45 (150): 41–259.

———. 1994. *Boris Pasternak: A Reference Guide.* New York: G. K. Hall.

———, and Erika Greber. 1990. *Pasternak's Doctor Zhivago: An International Bibliography of Criticism (1957–1985).* East Lansing, MI: Published by the Russian Language Journal.

Sergay, Timothy D. 2008. "Boris Pasternak's 'Christmas Myth': Fedorov, Berdiaev, Dickens, Blok." Ph.D. Diss, Yale University.

Shatin, Iu. V. 2002. "*Detstvo Liuvers:* B. Pasternaka-povest' XX v." In *Russkaia povest' kak forma vremeni,* ed. and introd. A. S. Ianushkevich, 274–80. Tomsk: Izdatel'stvo Tomskogo universiteta.

Shcheglov, Yuri. 1991. "O nekotorykh spornykh chertakh poetiki pozdnego Pasternaka. Avantiurno-melodramaticheskaia tekhnika v 'Doktore Zhivago.'" In *Boris Pasternak 1890–1990: Centennial Symposium: Papers,* ed. Lev Losev, 190–216. Northfield, VT: Russian School of Norwich University.

Shklovsky, Victor. 1965. "Art as Technique." In *Russian Formalist Criticism: Four Essays,* ed. Lee T. Leon and Marion J. Reis, 3–24. Lincoln: University of Nebraska Press.

———. 1988. "Art as Technique." In *Modern Criticism and Theory: A Reader,* ed. David Lodge, trans. Lee T. Leon and Marion J. Reis, 16–30. London: Longmans.

Shore, Rima. 1979. "A Note on the Literary Genesis of Doctor Zhivago." *Ulbandus Review* 2 (1): 186–93.

Sil'man, Tamara. 1977. *Zametki o lirike.* Leningrad: Sov. Pisatel'.

Simmons, Cynthia. 1988. "An Autobiography for the Twentieth Century: Pasternak's Okhrannaia gramota." *Russian Language Journal* 42 (141–143): 169–75.

Simplichio, Dasha di. 1989. "B. Pasternak i zhivopis.'" In *Boris Pasternak and His Times: Selected Papers from the Second International Symposium on Pasternak,* ed. Lazar Fleishman, 195–211. Berkeley, CA: Berkeley Slavic Specialties.

Siniavskii, Andrei. 1964. "Poeziia Pasternaka." In *Stikhotvoreniia i poemy* by Boris Pasternak, 9–62. Moscow/Leningrad: Sovietskii Pisatel'.

———. 1989. "Nekotoryie aspekty pozdnei prozy Pasternaka." In *Boris Pasternak and His Times: Selected Papers from the Second International Symposium on Pasternak,* ed. Lazar Fleishman, 359–71. Berkeley, CA: Berkeley Slavic Specialties.

Smirnov, Igor'. 1985. *Porozhdenie interteksta. Elementy intertekstual'nogo analiza s primerami iz tvorchestva B. L. Pasternaka.* Vienna: Inst. fur Slawistik der Univ. Wien.

———. 1991. "Dvoinoi roman (o *Doktore Zhivago*)." *Wiener Slawistischer Almanach* 27: 119–36.

———. 1993. "Rafael' i Yuri Zhivago." In *Beiträge zum Internationalen Pasternak-Kongress 1991 in Marburg,* ed. Sergey Dorzweiler and Hans-Bernd Harder, 154–71. Munich: Verlag Otto Sagner.

———. 1996. *Roman tain, Doktor Zhivago.* Moscow: Novoe literaturnoe obozrenie.

Solomon, Norman. 2005. "Cohen on Antonement, Purification and Repentance." In *Hermann Cohen's Critical Idealism,* ed. Reinier Munk, 395–411. Dordrecht: Springer.

Stepun, Fedor. 1959. "B. L. Pasternak." *Novyi zhurnal* 56: 187–206.

———. 1962. "B. L. Pasternak." In *Sbornik statei, posviashcsennykh tvorchestvu Borisa Leonidovicha Pasternaka,* ed. Boris Ivanov, 45–59. Munich: Institut po izucheniiu SSSR.

———. 1978. "Boris Pasternak." In *Pasternak. A Collection of Critical Essays*, ed. Victor Erlich, 110–25. Englewood Cliffs, NJ: Prentice Hall.

Struve, Gleb. 1970. "The Hippodrome of Life: The Problem of Coincidences in *Doctor Zhivago*." *Books Abroad* 44 (2): 231–36.

Taranovsky, Kiril. 1981. "On the Poetics of Boris Pasternak." *Russian Literature* 10 (4): 339–57.

Timenchik, Roman. 1975. "Avtometaopisanie u Akhmatovoi." *Russian Literature* 10/11: 213–26.

Traiger, Saul. 2006. *The Blackwell Guide to Hume's Treatise*. Oxford: Blackwell.

Tropp, E. A. 1996. "Leibnits na granitse sovremennogo i ne sovremennogo." In *Filosophskii Vek: Al'manakh. G. V. Leibnitz i Rossiia. Materialy Mezhdunarodnoi konferentsii. Sankt-Peterburg, 26–27 iiunia, 1996 g*, ed. T. V. Artem'eva and M. I. Mikeshin, 145–62. St. Petersburg: SPB NTs.

Tsvetaeva, Marina. 1969. "A Downpour of Light." In *Pasternak: Modern Judgments*, ed. Donald Davie and Angela Livingstone, 42–66. London: Macmillan.

Tynianov, Yuri. 1977. *Poetika, Istoriia Literatury, Kino*. Moscow: Nauka.

Vigilianskaya, A. 2007. "Vtoroe rozhdenie. Ob odnom filosofskom istochnike tvorchestva Borisa Pasternaka." *Voprosy literatury* 6: 131–45.

Vil'mont, Nikolai. 1989. *O Borise Pasternake: Vospominaniia i mysli*. Moscow: Sov. pisatel'.

Vuletić, I. 2004. "Marginal notes on Boris Pasternak's *Detstvo Ljuvers*." *Russian Literature* 56 (4): 483–98.

Weststeijn, Willem G. 1982. "Metaphor and Simile in *Doktor Živago*." *Essays in Poetics* 10 (2): 41–57.

———. 1983. "Poets are not Aphasics. Some Notes on Roman Jakobson's Concept of the Metaphoric and Metonymic Poles of Language." In *Dutch Contributions to the Ninth International Congress of Slavists, Kiev, September 6–14, 1983*, ed. International Congress of Slavists and A. G. F. van Holk, 125–46. Amsterdam: Rodopi.

———. 1997. "*Doktor Zhivago*—poeticheskii tekst." *Russian, Croatian and Serbian, Czech and Slovak, Polish Literature* 42 (3–4): 477–90.

Wiegers, Ben. 1999. "O fragmentarnosti v *Detstve Liuvers* Pasternaka." In *Dutch Contributions to the Twelfth International Congress of Slavists, Krakow, August 26–September 3, 1998*, ed. Willem G. Weststeijn, 225–39. Amsterdam: Rodopi.

Witt, Susanna. 1994. "Doktor Zhivopis': O 'romanakh' Borisa Pasternaka 'Doktor Zhivago.'" In *Klassitsizm i modernizm: Sbornik statei*, 140–67. Tartu: Tartu Ulikooli Kirjastus.

———. 2000a. *Creating Creation: Readings of Pasternak's Doktor Živago*. Stockholm: Almqvist and Wiksell International.

———. 2000b. "Gastronomicheskaia metafizika Pasternaka." In *Severnyi sbornik: Proceedings of the NorFa Network in Russian Literature 1995–1999*, ed. Peter Alberg Jensen and Ingunn Lunde, 267–76. Stockholm: Almqvist and Wiksell International.

———. 2000c. "Mimikriia v Doktore Zhivago." In *V krugu Zhivago: Pasternakovskii sbornik*, ed. Lazar Fleishman, 87–122. Stanford, CA: Stanford University, Dept. of Slavic Languages and Literatures.

Zamyatin, Evgeny. 1923. "Novaia russkaia proza." *Russkoe iskusstvo* 2–3 (1923): 56–57. [Reprinted in Zamyatin (1967), *Litsa* (New York: Mezhdunar. literaturnoe sodruzhestvo: 191–210).]

———. 1970. "The New Russian Prose." In *A Soviet Heretic: Essays by Evgeny Zamyatin*, ed. and trans. Mirra Ginsburg, 92–106. Chicago: University of Chicago Press.

Zelinsky, Bodo. 1975. "Selbstdefinitionen der Poesie bei Pasternak." *Zeitschrift fur Slavische Philologie* 38: 268–78.

Zholkovsky, Aleksandr. 1978. "Mesto okna v poeticheskom mire Pasternaka." *Russian Literature* 6 (1): 1–38.

———. 1984a. "The 'sinister' in the poetic world of Pasternak." *International Journal of Slavic Linguistics and Poetics* 29: 109–31.

———. 1984b. *Themes and Texts: Toward a Poetics of Expressiveness*. Ithaca, NY: Cornell University Press.

———. 1985a. "Iz zapisok po poezii grammatiki: On Pasternak's figurative voices." *Russian Linguistics* 9 (2): 375–86.

———. 1985b. "Mekhanizmy vtorogo rozhdeniia: O stikhotvorenii Pasternaka 'Mne khochetsia domoi, v ogromnost.'" *Sintaksis* 14: 77–97.

———. 1992. "O trekh grammaticheskikh motivakh Pasternaka." In *"Byt' znamenitym nekrasivo,"* ed. I. Iu. Podgaetskaia, 55–66. Moscow: Nasledie.

———. 1994. "Ekstaticheskie motivy Pasternaka v svete ego lichnoi mifologii." In *Bluzhdaiushchie sny i drugie raboty,* 283–95. Moscow: Nauka.

———. 1999. "O zaglavnom trope knigi 'Sestra moia zhizn.'" In *Poetry and Revolution. Boris Pasternak's "My Sister Life,"* ed. Lazar Fleishman, 26–65. Stanford, CA: Stanford University Press.

———. 2004. "Iz zapisok po poezii grammatiki: o perenosnykh zalogakh Pasternaka." *Kritika i semiotika* 7: 203–16.

Index of Works by Boris Pasternak

General Index

345